Evaluating Project Decisions

Evaluating Project Decisions

Case Studies in Software Engineering

Carol L. Hoover
Mel Rosso-Llopart
Gil Taran

Addison-Wesley

Upper Saddle River, NJ • Boston • Indianapolis • San Francisco
New York • Toronto • Montreal • London • Munich • Paris • Madrid
Capetown • Sydney • Tokyo • Singapore • Mexico City

Library of Congress Cataloging-in-Publication Data
Hoover, Carol L., 1955-
Evaluating project decisions : case studies in software engineering / Carol L. Hoover, Mel Rosso-Llopart, Gil Taran.
p. cm.
Includes bibliographical references and index.
ISBN 978-0-321-54456-8 (pbk. : alk. paper)
1. Software engineering. 2. Software engineering—Case studies. 3. Project management—Case studies. I. Rosso-Llopart, Mel, 1956- II. Taran, Gil, 1972- III. Title.
QA76.758.H66 2010
005.1—dc22

2009030151

ISBN-13: 978-0-321-54456-8
ISBN-10: 0-321-54456-0
Text printed in the United States on recycled paper at Courier in Stoughton, Massachusetts.
First printing, October 2009

To my dad, who shared his interest in science with me.
—Carol L. Hoover

To my mom and my brother, who thought I wouldn't read let alone write a book.
—Mel Rosso-Llopart

To my beloved three girls and my family across the ocean,
for their everlasting support.
—Gil Taran

Contents

Preface

Software engineering professionals and students all over the world make decisions every day that impact the outcome of their software projects. Although some people are very successful, others unfortunately do not take the steps necessary to ensure that their decisions are likely to lead to success. For instance, not asking the right questions generally leads to solutions that do not adequately solve the problems being considered. Likewise, the formulation of faulty assumptions is often the root cause of poor decisions. A common challenge for software professionals is the identification and correction of poor decisions before they can cause even bigger problems. This may be because it is much easier to judge software engineering decisions after the fact than to monitor and evaluate them before their full impact is known.

Through our own professional experiences as software engineers and project managers, we observed firsthand the need for systematic approaches to evaluating and making decisions for software engineering. We observed that, in general, decision making for software projects lacks an analytical approach that can be applied systematically and consistently to increase the likelihood of making decisions that lead to successful projects. As educators of graduate students in the Carnegie Mellon University Master of Software Engineering (MSE) Program, we use textbooks in software engineering that discuss issues involving decisions to be made but do not specifically talk about how to evaluate and make these decisions. We found numerous publications on decision making in the fields of general business and project management. Unfortunately, these works do not address the specific decisions that must be made for software development projects or the nuances of the issues related to these decisions.

We have searched for case studies to help students learn about software engineering issues in the context of real-world scenarios. Though the use of simulated case studies is recognized to be an effective teaching tool for computer science and engineering, we found few published cases that address the specific problems faced by software project managers or software developers and discuss the decision-making aspects of software engineering. To help fill the gap between theory and practice, we decided to write a book that would address the need of both practitioners and students of software engineering to understand decision making in the context of real software projects.

The purpose of this book is to help practitioners, managers, students, and educators acquire the knowledge and skills needed to evaluate and make good decisions as well as to recognize bad decisions for software project management and software development. The book focuses on case studies constructed to help readers comprehend and apply concepts important to forming, implementing, monitoring, and evaluating critical decisions in real software projects. The case studies are based upon real project scenarios in organizations that differ in industry, size, and budget, but the names of the organizations and stakeholders have been changed to keep the real entities confidential. The book does not exhaustively cover every possible software engineering event that might occur. Rather, the case studies focus on issues and decisions that typically make or break today's software projects.

Readers who have hands-on development or management experience with the full life cycle of a software project will benefit the most from this book. We intend for the book to serve as a handbook of professional guidance for managing the decisions that can lead to software project success. Upper-level undergraduate or graduate students who have some undergraduate-level coursework in software engineering or professional software engineering experience will also find the case materials to be a stimulating way to explore decision making in real-world software projects.

Readers of this book can acquire **knowledge** of issues and problems that notoriously contribute to software project failure. Readers will learn about issues and problems that occur frequently, have a high impact on today's software projects, or are of emerging and growing importance. The case studies illustrate important decisions in the mapping between the user's expectations and the provider's software solution. The case study analyses highlight effective questions to ask to better analyze software engineering issues or problems and to determine the best decisions or solutions to make. The book also discusses indicators to assess whether a decision or solution for a particular software project issue or problem is working.

By reading and analyzing the software engineering case studies, you can develop **skills** needed to identify key factors that characterize software project problems. You can learn how to analyze the issues and problems that relate to a specific software project scenario. The case analysis activities will guide you through the study of alternative decisions that could be made to address the case issues. They will help you develop ideas about how to apply the case concepts to real software projects. We hope that you will find the case studies to be an interesting way to learn about critical issues in software engineering and about how to apply decision-making techniques to real-world software engineering projects.

Synopses of Book Chapters

Following is a synopsis of the topics and case studies for each chapter. You will notice that all of the chapter titles include the word *managing*. We use *managing* to emphasize the need for project managers and software engineers proactively to identify issues or problems in a particular management area, to analyze and evaluate their nature and importance, to decide upon actions that need to be taken, to implement decisions by taking action, and to monitor results. We would like to promote the idea that all software professionals, not just managers, need to manage the decisions that they make on the job. The case studies illustrate decisions made or that need to be made by various software project stakeholders. In some cases, the stakeholders manage the decisions in a way that leads to project success. In other cases, the stakeholders do not manage the decisions they make very well and thereby encounter project problems and sometimes failure.

Chapter 1: Managing Decisions

Chapter 1 discusses decision making in software engineering, presents a model for evaluating decisions, and shows how the model can be applied to the decisions made by stakeholders in the case studies. The chapter illustrates the application of the model through several decision scenarios that involve technical issues.

Chapter 2: Managing Requirements

Chapter 2 overviews the following activities involved in managing requirements: eliciting and stating requirements, verifying and validating requirements, negotiating and contracting requirements, managing requirements change and scope, and validating software deliverables with respect to requirements. The chapter provides an in-depth discussion of issues and decisions for each requirements activity. The chapter emphasizes the idea that managing requirements does not end until the software is retired.

Case studies:

- **The New Account Project at HBC:** This case study highlights the activities and decisions involved in establishing the requirements. In particular, the case illustrates problems that can occur regarding decisions about the selection and involvement of stakeholders.
- **On Time, Within Budget, but Wrong:** This case study illustrates how decisions made when establishing and managing requirements can result in software project deliverables that do not satisfy the user stakeholder's expectations even though the project appears to be going well. In particular, the case scenario covers both functional and nonfunctional requirements including statements about required quality attributes.

Chapter 3: Managing Estimates

Chapter 3 illuminates the importance of estimation in planning and managing software projects and other software engineering efforts. The chapter discusses the following activities involved in managing estimates: understanding requirements, conceptually designing a solution, performing element-wise decomposition (divide), allocating resources from the bottom up (conquer), allocating overhead, estimating construction, and estimating change management. The chapter presents ways to factor considerations of scope, time, quality, and cost into decisions about project estimates.

Case studies:

- **Estimation as a Tool:** This case study examines process improvement in managing estimates via collecting, studying, and applying historical data. In the case, a software project manager must determine the appropriate inputs to make a good decision regarding an estimate for a job.
- **When a Team Runs a Race:** This case study examines factors that influence estimation and how these factors can lead to poor decisions about estimates. The case also looks at issues related to the concurrent execution of multiple projects with interdependent resources, personnel, and developments.

Chapter 4: Managing Plans

Chapter 4 examines the role of decision making in planning software projects. The chapter overviews planning activities such as the following: defining project objectives, policies, and scope; planning tasks and milestones; planning schedules; planning budgets; staffing and other resource planning; tracking and controlling the budget and schedule; managing midstream changes to project plans; managing processes with respect to project objectives, policies, and other project plans; and managing software development with respect to project objectives, policies, schedule, and budget.

Case studies:

- **To Replan or Not to Replan?:** This case study discusses the evaluation and decision of when, why, and how to adjust the budget, schedule, or staffing plans.
- **Managing Plans Is in the Details:** This case study looks at problems and decisions that a software development organization faces in planning and tracking software projects, especially those that share resources with other projects or engineering groups.

Chapter 5: Managing Product

Chapter 5 overviews the issues and decisions involved in managing software product. The chapter discusses the following activities involved in managing product: proper product definition, development process management, quality assurance and control, configuration management, product delivery and installation, training, field service, and the application of the decision model to make product decisions.

Case studies:

- **New Technology—Is It Always the Best?:** In this case study, the project manager must make a decision regarding the adoption of new development technologies and techniques to create a product that is easier to maintain and less expensive to use.
- **Why Is This Product Wrong?:** In this case study, a software developer is faced with the dilemma that although it seems as though he did everything correctly, he still got the wrong answer.

Chapter 6: Managing Process

Chapter 6 emphasizes the importance of managing the processes for software development and software project management. The chapter discusses activities involved in managing process: defining, selecting, and understanding process; teaching process; measuring process; evaluating process performance; changing the process to improve its effectiveness; and using the decision model to make process decisions.

Case studies:

- **Bank on the Verge:** In this case study, a project manager asks two consultants to evaluate whether his team has made good decisions on process and whether there are things that the team can do better.
- **Damn the Process, Full Speed Ahead:** In this case study, a project manager is asked to review another manager's project that is having problems. The troubled project is behind schedule, and no one has been able to clearly identify what is causing the schedule slippage or what should be done to fix the project's processes. The manager must decide how he can help the troubled project.

Chapter 7: Managing Risk

Chapter 7 emphasizes the importance of managing risk across the project life cycle. The chapter discusses activities involved in managing risk: defining thresholds of success for the project, identifying project risks, formulating statements about risk, communicating information about risk to project stakeholders, mitigating risk, and conducting resource trade-offs in making decisions about how to manage risk.

Case studies:

- **SEWeb and Russoft Technologies:** This case study examines the decisions and risks faced by an academic institution in its attempt to use an offshore development firm, a Russian company located in Moscow, to develop a Web-based system. In particular, the case study exemplifies what can happen when the project stakeholders do only minimal risk management throughout the project.

- **Falcon Edutainment and the RiskSim Project:** This case study focuses on software project risks associated with client-developer interactions, communications, requirements elicitation, and the related decisions.

Chapter 8: Managing People Interactions

Chapter 8 discusses factors that influence interactions between people and shows how an understanding of these can help software professionals to manage their interactions with people on the job. The chapter specifically describes activities involved in managing project stakeholder interactions: understanding scenarios of interaction, understanding factors that influence interactions, deciding upon interaction objectives, evaluating factors that influence an interaction, deciding how to adjust controllable factors for an interaction, and reflecting on past interactions to improve performance in future interactions.

Case studies:

- **To Be or Not to Be: A Sense of Urgency at TestBridge:** In this case study, tough decisions have to be made with respect to the ability and willingness of specific players within the team to contribute as team members in light of an organization that is changing its focus and business direction.
- **A Friend or Foe at Hanover-Tech:** This case study focuses on the need to manage people interactions at the managerial level while balancing opposing constraints that are financial, strategic, personal, and temporal.

Chapter 9: Managing Stakeholder Expectations

Chapter 9 clarifies the nature of stakeholder expectations. The chapter introduces a model for understanding the mapping between customer expectations and solution provider expectations. The chapter discusses the activities involved in managing interactions between software project stakeholders: communicating with the customer stakeholder, managing multiple dimensions of stakeholder expectation over time, managing product and process to satisfy stakeholder expectations, understanding different types of customers, and managing stakeholder perception.

Case studies:

- **TCP Enhancements at Gigaplex Systems:** In this case study, the software project team encounters unexpected problems related to satisfying the customer's expectations as well as to internal team dynamics and the external relationship with the customer.

- **Tough Sell at Henkel Labs:** This case study presents a difficult situation in which stakeholder expectations need to be managed across a global organization with multiple subsidiaries and people from different cultures who reside in different countries and who sometimes have opposing organizational and business objectives.

Chapter 10: Managing Global Development

Chapter 10 discusses issues and decisions related to managing software engineering efforts that are geographically distributed. The chapter illuminates the challenges of communicating across geographical and time differences, understanding and handling cultural differences, managing distributed projects and software development, managing outsourced software development, managing software quality with distributed or outsourced development, and managing expectations across geographically dispersed stakeholders.

Case studies:

- **Globally Distributed Team: FibreNet Project:** This case study highlights issues of communication, collaboration, and trust when a project team is globally distributed. The software project manager needs to decide how to improve these aspects across the different globally distributed project sites.
- **Managing Global Software Development at FibOptia:** This case study looks at problems specific to global software development in managing process, product quality, and cost. A senior manager is trying to decide how she can help her global software development organization make process and product improvements.

How This Book Is Organized

In Chapter 1, "Managing Decisions," we discuss the nature and importance of decision making for software engineering. We present a decision model that we developed and have used in practice to assist software professionals in evaluating decisions. This chapter provides context information that will help you more easily identify and think about issues and problems that occur in the case studies. You will therefore benefit from reading this chapter before you read the other chapters in the book. The other chapters discuss decision making in the context of well-known management areas for software projects. These chapters broadly cover issues concerning people, process, and technology in the context of making decisions about them. Because evaluating risk should be an integral part of making decisions, all chapters discuss risk in the context of making decisions for a particular management area. Chapter 7, "Managing Risk," more generally covers risk management throughout the life of a software project. In addition, since process concerns how something is done, all of the chapters in some way discuss process issues when describing how software professionals manage a particular aspect of software engineering.

Chapters 2–10 have the same organizational structure. The first section of each chapter outlines the objectives for that chapter. The second section sets the context for making decisions in a particular software management area. The context material describes primary activities that software professionals perform to manage a particular project area. Alternatively, the context for Chapter 10, "Managing Global Development," explains that the activities for managing global development include those for the other management areas with added challenges, constraints, and opportunities. The chapter context also discusses key ideas, practical guidelines, or what-if questions for making decisions in the relevant management area. The context highlights example decisions with some analyzes that apply the PEAK decision model from Chapter 1. Some of the context information appears in tables to help you rapidly assimilate and reference it when needed. The chapters present concepts in the context of making decisions with respect to factors that influence stakeholder expectations for software projects: scope (requirements), time (schedule), quality, and cost (budget). The chapter context also includes references to publications that provide background in the software management area for interested readers. The authors recommend that you read or peruse the chapter objectives and context before reading the case studies.

The next section of each chapter presents two case studies whose scenarios highlight key issues and decisions related to the chapter topic. The first case study includes a full analysis of the case study issues and decisions with respect to the PEAK decision model. The case studies discuss decisions made by the stakeholders in the case scenarios and pose follow-on decisions that need to be made. Some case studies tell you what the stakeholders decide to do to solve the case problems and include the results of these decisions; others leave the evaluation of solutions for the case problems to the case study analyses. A set of questions to stimulate an analysis of the second case study concludes the case study. The last section summarizes important ideas to remember about the chapter. A list of references for all chapters appears at the back of the book.

We would like to help set your expectations regarding the references in the book. We do not intend for the book to be a survey of research and publication in the various software management areas. We have included some selected references that provide background for readers who are new to software engineering or to topics covered in the case studies or that provide supplemental information for interested readers. Some of the references are purposely dated because they provide the original and best definition of particular concepts or because the concepts discussed in these sources are still highly relevant for software projects of today. The referenced materials include books, conference and workshop proceedings, journal and magazine articles, and online information. They eclectically cover topics, events, or quotes from the subject areas of business management, civil engineering, communications, computer science, decision sciences, English literature, filmography, management and management sciences, networking, psychology, regulatory policy, software engineering, systems engineering, and others that provide background information for the case studies and example decision scenarios.

Some of our reviewers commented that a particular case study seemed to be relevant for different chapters or software project management areas. As you read the book, you too may recognize that a particular case study involves issues from multiple management areas. We purposely designed the cases to be multidimensional. After analyzing the cases in a specific chapter and management area, you might analyze the case studies in other chapters whose issues and decisions involve the same management area. For instance, all of the case studies entail issues and decisions involving scope, time, quality, cost, risk, stakeholder expectations, communications and other people interactions, or some set of these. As another example, case studies in Chapter 7, "Managing Risk," Chapter 9, "Managing Stakeholder Expectations," and Chapter 10, "Managing Global Development," encompass issues related to global software development. The scenario for one of the cases in Chapter 7 involves development by an offshore team, and one of the cases in Chapter 9 looks at establishing projects to be executed by globally distributed branches of a company. Both cases for Chapter 10 involve globally distributed software development teams.

The reviewers for our book requested that we provide full analyses for all the case studies. We talked with our editor about this and together decided that for space and cost reasons it would not be practical to include this additional information in the book itself. Our reviewers also gave us excellent suggestions for topics that they would like to see discussed in case studies. Therefore, we decided to offer a Web site where you can obtain supplemental information at www.andrew.cmu.edu/user/rosso/. This site will provide you with materials such as additional case studies and analyses as they become available. Depending on our time constraints, we will try as best we can to provide you with analyses for the second cases in the chapter.

We hope that you enjoy your journey through this book and that you will use the book as a guide as you encounter issues and decisions in your study and practice of software engineering.

Acknowledgments

We would like to acknowledge the people who provided information for the case studies or who provided critical assistance in reviewing our case studies or chapters. In addition to our anonymous contributors, we graciously say thank you in alphabetical order to Kanat Abirov, Dmitry Dakhnovsky, James Yinsey Hall, Kalyan Jakka, Dr. Chris Kemerer, David Kramer, Ron Lewin, Ron Lichty, Catherine Llopart, Frank Parth, Patrick Piemonte, David Root, Marco Schumacher, Orna Taran, Renuka Wariyar, and Dr. Eytan Wine.

The staff at Addison-Wesley was very helpful as we worked through the process of creating a book. We heartily thank Peter Gordon, the book's editor, and Kim Boedigheimer, editorial assistant, for their information about the publishing process, editorial advice, and ever present assistance. The production team included John Fuller, Anna Popick, Molly Sharp, Kim Wimpsett, Kelli Brooks, and Fred Brown. We offer our sincere thanks for their contributions to the transformation of our electronic files into a complete and marketable book. We especially appreciate their attention to quality issues. Thank you to Stephane Nakib for her contributions to marketing and advertising the book. Thank you also to Anne Jones for the classy and contemporary book cover.

Last, but certainly not least, our families offered significant encouragement and patiently waited for us to finish! Thank you for being you.

About the Authors

Dr. Carol L. Hoover
President and CEO, BiznessLegion, LLC

Dr. Carol L. Hoover has conducted software systems research and development for more than twenty years in industry and academia. Her focus has been on complex systems with real-time, high-assurance, and other quality-of-service requirements. Since 2005, Dr. Hoover has been the president and chief executive officer of BiznessLegion, LLC, a consulting company whose current mission is to help software development organizations manage software evolution in a cost-effective way through strategic planning and decision making, analytical software composition, and knowledge management. After coming to Carnegie Mellon University in 1992, Dr. Hoover held positions of director and senior systems scientist in the Institute for Software Research where she developed and taught a scenario-based, graduate-level software engineering curriculum including capstone courses on planning, managing, and executing consulting projects in the aerospace industry; project scientist and manager in the Robotics Institute; and lecturer for the Master of Software Engineering program in the School of Computer Science. Her research interest in automated software design, software knowledge engineering, innovative STEM education, and technology-related governmental policy originate from her prior experiences as a senior software engineer at the Allen-Bradley Company (now Rockwell Automation), a post-graduate intern at a NASA research center in Cleveland, Ohio, a computer manager in a U.S. congressional office, and an educator in the public schools. She earned a doctorate in electrical and computer engineering from Carnegie Mellon University, a master's degree in computer and information sciences from the Ohio State University where she was a University Fellow, and bachelor's degrees in computer science and education with minors in mathematics and music and specializations in science and engineering from the University of Akron. Dr. Hoover is a member of the ACM, IEEE, IEEE Computer Society, and Sigma Xi. She resides with her husband north of Pittsburgh, Pennsylvania.

Mel Rosso-Llopart
Associate Teaching Professor, Carnegie Mellon University

Manuel "Mel" Rosso-Llopart is currently the assistant director for the Master of Software Engineering program now in the Institute for Software Research, the director for distance education development in the Information Networking Institute, and an associate teaching professor for the Master of Software Engineering program, all at Carnegie Mellon University. With Carnegie Mellon since 2002, he has delivered executive education courses in project management worldwide, especially throughout Eastern Europe. He also does independent consulting on software management issues and software development programs. Mr. Rosso-Llopart has management and software development experience with large and small projects in a variety of computing environments. He has knowledge of large network configurations and database applications. Mr. Rosso-Llopart has developed complex, embedded systems for the aviation and rail-transit industries while working with the U.S. Department of Defense in California for fifteen years and later with Adtranz (now Bombardier) in Pittsburgh, Pennsylvania. He earned bachelor's degrees in physics, biology, and computer science at the University of California and a master's degree in software engineering from the School of Computer Science at Carnegie Mellon University. He is married with one son and lives south of Pittsburgh.

Gil Taran
Associate Teaching Professor, Carnegie Mellon University
Chief Executive Officer, iCarnegie, Inc.

Gil Taran is an associate teaching professor with Carnegie Mellon University's School of Computer Science, where he has been teaching in the Master of Software Engineering program (www.mse.cs.cmu.edu) since 2002. He is also the chief executive officer of iCarnegie (www.icarnegie.com), a Carnegie Mellon–owned educational affiliate whose mission is to provide high-quality, skill-based education and professional training programs to organizations and individuals around the world. Mr. Taran takes a special interest in setting up international collaborations in software engineering education and has been able to help initiate, facilitate, and develop programs in China, India, Kazakhstan, Korea, Portugal, and Russia, to name a few. Mr. Taran is an international speaker in the areas of software project management, software risk management, software engineering education, and managing technical people. He has trained thousands of engineers around the world from companies in the banking, defense, electronics, health care, and manufacturing sectors. Mr. Taran has spent the past fifteen years making project-based decisions as well as leading sales/marketing activities and technology/business operations globally. In the past, he has held management positions for international companies in Europe, the United States, and the Middle East. He earned bachelor's degrees in economics and English literature from the Tel Aviv University in Israel and a master's degree in information technology with high honors from Carnegie Mellon University. He lives with his wife and two daughters outside Pittsburgh, Pennsylvania.

Chapter 1

Managing Decisions

1.1 Chapter Objectives

This chapter introduces concepts about evaluating decisions for software development projects and other software engineering efforts. This chapter will help you understand the purpose, rationale, and application of a model for evaluating decisions. Succeeding chapters will illustrate how to apply the model to decisions being made to manage various aspects of software projects and to handle problems faced by the stakeholders in case scenarios. Managing decisions involves identifying a problem to be solved, formulating and evaluating alternative solutions to the problem, selecting among the alternative solutions, and executing the decision or implementing the solution. The model discussed in this chapter applies to the following phases: identifying the problem, formulating and evaluating alternative solutions, and selecting among alternative solutions or decision. The case studies in the succeeding chapters focus on these phases but may also include the execution aspect of managing decisions.

1.2 Context

A decision involves passing judgment on an issue under consideration. It is commonly understood to be the act of reaching a conclusion or of making up one's mind. All software projects involve making decisions. Even the act of not making a decision is a decision. For example, if a software project manager chooses to ignore a project member's request for more resources, the manager is making a decision not to act and must deal with the consequences of this noncommittal decision. Increasing a software professional's responsibility increases the number of decisions that the professional must make. This book will explore decisions made by different software project stakeholders and will shed light on how these decisions can be made.

The importance of managing the way in which project decisions are made is evident by the numerous publications that discuss decision making, particularly in the context of managing projects, of managing project risks, and more specifically of managing projects involving product development. The following references are just a few select examples of current publications in these areas. For more about decision making as an integral part of project management, see Cleland and Ireland (2007), McManus (2004), Pollack-Johnson and Liberatore (2006), and Verine and Trumper (2007). For more about the relationship between decision making and risk, see Chapman and Ward (2002), Dillon and Tinsley (2008), Hussey and Hall (2007), and Warkentin et al. (2009). For product development project decisions, see Barry et al. (2006), Gutierrez et al. (2008), Krishnan and Ulrich (2001), Messerschmitt (2004), and Schmidt et al. (2001) With the rise of global development, there is also an increasing interest in the effect of cultural, geographical, and time differences on how decisions are made within organizations and projects. For a current discussion of these issues, see Bourgault et al. (2008), Brett (2001), Espinosa et al. (2007), Mojtahedi et al. (2008), Shore (2008), and Wang and Liu (2007).

In general, software professionals do not understand how to *systematically* make decisions that result in software projects that are considered to be successful by the project stakeholders. One main problem is that decision makers for software projects often do not state or analyze the inputs and outputs of their decision processes specifically with respect to the needs and expectations of the stakeholders. They may recall that a solution was successful for a particular problem, but then they are surprised when the solution is not successful in solving a similar problem in which the stakeholders have different expectations. This book focuses on the viewpoints of different software project stakeholders to help you refine your decision-making processes so that the resulting solutions are more likely to satisfy stakeholder needs and values.

In general, software project stakeholders make decisions to satisfy their expectations regarding the scope of the project deliverables, the time for the project (schedule), the quality of the project deliverables or product, and the cost (budget). Figure 1-1 shows a model of the expectations that stakeholders have for software projects and the project deliverables.

The model shows that the dimensions of stakeholder expectation (scope, time, quality, and cost) are related. Stakeholders trade different values for scope, time, quality, and cost when establishing the requirements for a software project. Prioritizing their expectations can help stakeholders to make trade-offs more easily and effectively. Different software project stakeholders make different decisions to support their interests. They have different inputs feeding their decision process and different expectations about the outcomes of their decisions. For instance, stakeholders have different levels of tolerance for the risks associated with the decisions that they make.

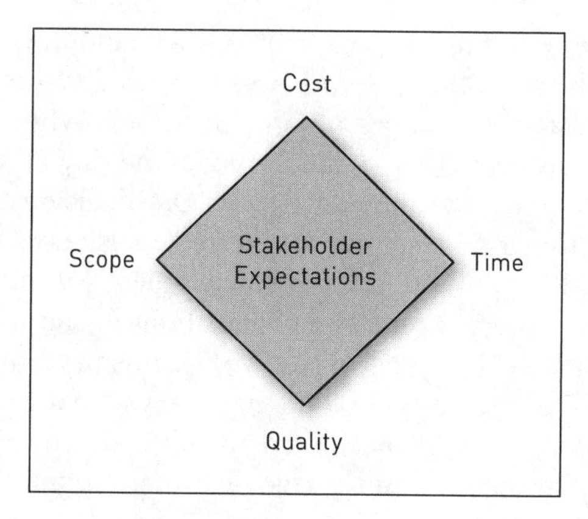

Figure 1–1: *Stakeholder expectation model*

Consider an example of how software stakeholders make decisions based upon their expectations with respect to scope, time, quality, and cost. Suppose a customer decides upon an acceptable budget for a specified work product, schedule, and quality. Likewise, the solution provider establishes a definition of quality to satisfy both the customer's expectations for the work product as well as the product standards set by the solution provider (who has a reputation in the market to maintain). The solution provider then determines an amount to charge that factors in the cost of developing the work product to satisfy the customer's expectations regarding scope, time, and quality.

But what happens if the customer's acceptable cost is lower than the amount that the solution provider wants to charge? This case would generate another set of decisions. Will the customer and solution provider agree to negotiate the amount to be charged? Will the stakeholders consider alternative scopes, schedules, levels of quality, and budgets? Or will the stakeholders decide that they are unwilling to negotiate an amount to be charged that is agreeable to both of them?

The customer may decide to pursue other solution providers and find that the costs posed by these solution providers are significantly higher than the amount asked by the first solution provider. The customer may then discover that the first solution provider in the meantime has taken on other projects and will not be available to perform the work until a future time that is not acceptable to the customer. What will the customer do now? Did something go wrong in the customer's decision-making process?

This customer–solution provider scenario highlights the interconnected or causal nature of decision making: One good or poor decision frequently leads to another good or poor decision. As the scenario described, a mismatch between the customer's acceptable cost and the solution provider's desired price may result in a cascade of successive decisions that eventually may leave the customer with the choice of selecting a solution provider who would charge a higher amount or abandoning the desired work to be done.

Therefore, it is important that stakeholders understand the factors that affect their decisions as well as the potential consequences of their decisions. Project delays and failures are usually related to a series of poor decisions. When asked how a project becomes a year late, Frederick Brooks answered, "One day at a time" (Brooks 1995, 160). We suggest that a more revealing answer is "One decision at a time."

One way to solve the problem of interconnected decisions is to disconnect them as much as possible, but this solution is not always applicable. For instance, a mismatch between customer and solution provider expectations is common. The issue is how to manage the stakeholder decisions to resolve the mismatch in a way that leads to the best possible outcome. The stakeholders need a systematic way to make software engineering decisions that are likely to lead to successful results. They also need a management strategy to monitor and correct less than optimal decisions before further harm is done to a project.

The purpose of this book is to help you refine your decision-making processes and decision management strategies. We examine the decision-making process with respect to the decision evaluation model presented in the next section. The model is a visualization of factors that are used to make decisions in software development and software project management. The model also provides decision makers with a systematic way to analyze the inputs and outputs of the decision-making process. The book shows how software project stakeholders use their expectations regarding scope, time, quality, and cost as inputs to making project decisions in case scenarios.

The model emphasizes that every decision incurs some amount of assumed risk and that the solution may not succeed in solving the stated problem. It is important for decision makers to understand the risk assumed when making a decision because it may be unacceptable to the project stakeholders. Assumed risk may accumulate over time to a level that is unhealthy for software projects. The objective is to recognize decision situations that need to be carefully managed because (1) the risk assumed in making these decisions is high or (2) the cost associated with unsuccessful outcomes to these decisions is high. The case study analyses in the book show how the model can be applied to make less risky decisions for critical software project management and engineering scenarios. In particular, the case study analyses show how stating the inputs and outputs of the decision model in terms of the stakeholder expectations helps reduce the risks assumed by alternative solutions.

The next section and the remaining chapters in the book will answer questions such as the following within the context of software projects:

- What do decision makers know when making decisions?
- Do decision makers use a process when making decisions?
- Are all decisions of equal value?
- Are software project decisions different from those for other projects? If so, how?
- What does it mean to manage decisions?
- Why is it important to manage decisions?

1.3 Decision Model for Software Engineering

For many people, the decision-making process consists of three basic (and usually vague) stages:

1. Information goes into a decision process.
2. A person-dependent miracle occurs.
3. A solution or decision comes out.

Professionals often consider people to be experts or gurus in their fields if they can make good decisions easily. This section gives an overview of a decision model whose purpose is to help software professionals manage their decision processes so that they better understand the solutions they generate.

The PEAK decision model presented in Figure 1-2 does not indicate "what a particular decision should be." It simply implies that stakeholders need to carefully examine their decision processes to help ensure that successful decisions are made. When making decisions, stakeholders should consider the inputs and their relationship to the solution as well as the risk assumed with alternative solutions. The model provides insight into how the inputs and outputs of the decision-making process influence the way in which decisions are made.

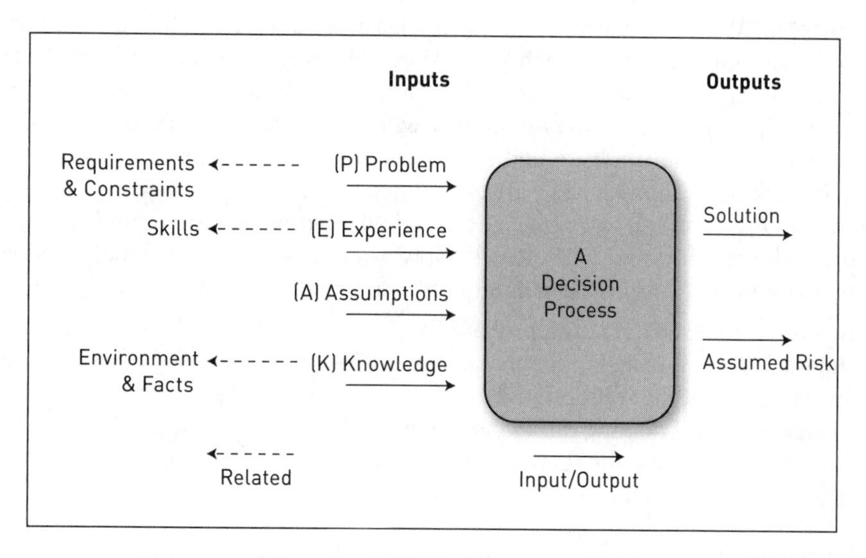

Figure 1–2: *PEAK decision model*

The *inputs* to the decision model are the following elements:

(P) Problem: What is the issue to be resolved or the problem to be solved? The problem statement should provide a clear representation of what needs to be solved.

(E) Experience: From prior events, what does the decision maker know or know how to do that might help with this problem? Has the decision maker seen or solved a problem like this one before? How appropriate and accurate is the decision maker's historical information?

(A) Assumptions: What information is accepted as fact without having evidence? What information about the problem does the decision maker abstract away because the information is not thought to be relevant to the solution?

(K) Knowledge: What conceptual understanding or factual basis can help the decision maker with the problem? What has the decision maker learned since last dealing with a problem like this? What facts does the decision maker have about the problem? What is the environment that surrounds this problem? For instance, when looking at military problems to be solved, soldiers might ask, "What is the current situation and terrain?"

The *outputs* from the model are the following elements:

Solution: What do the stakeholders need in order to solve the problem or to resolve the issue? What alternative solutions are feasible, and why? What are the benefits and cost associated with each alternative? Have the relevant stakeholders discussed the issues concerning the alternative solutions and expressed their preferences? The stakeholders may not know whether a solution is successful until they implement it. The results, whether successful or not, of implementing a decision feed back into the model as part of the decision maker's knowledge and experience. In response to a colleague who asked whether he thought himself to be a failure, Thomas Edison said, "Not at all. Now, I definitely know more than a thousand ways for how NOT to make a light bulb" (Rovira and Trias de Bes 2004, 1).

Assumed Risk: What is the probability that the solution will not work as envisioned? When a stakeholder makes a decision, the stakeholder assumes some level of risk that the solution or decision will not lead to a successful result. Risk is a consequence of making decisions. What are the risks associated with the alternative solutions? Have the relevant stakeholders discussed these risks with respect to their preferences for the alternatives?

Even if the decision maker is not aware of them, the inputs and outputs of a decision always exist when a decision is being made. To manage their decisions, stakeholders need to identify and manage these inputs and outputs when making decisions. The case studies in the book will describe situations in which most but not necessarily all of the inputs are known. Each case study will present the problem, the assumptions, and many facts. You will bring other knowledge and experience as inputs to the decision model. This book will help you use the inputs and feasible outputs of the model, as they occur in the case studies, to evaluate your decision processes.

So, why do decision makers need a model for evaluating decisions? A model helps decision makers think about the following aspects of their decision processes:

- Information that should be considered in making decisions
- The impact that the inputs to the decision process have on the outputs
- Solutions that are feasible with respect to the nature of the problem
- The assumed risk associated with alternative solutions
- Ways to improve the management of decisions

The remainder of this section provides four examples to illustrate how you can apply the model to the decision process. These examples clarify how to apply the model to evaluate alternative solutions and then to make a decision by selecting the best alternative. The first example, "Software Test Rerun Problem," shows how to identify the inputs and outputs to a decision regarding whether to rerun a software test. The second example, "California Bridge Problem," demonstrates how to apply the model to the more complex problem of building a bridge that can withstand earthquakes, a major issue for the California Department of Transportation. This example demonstrates how newly acquired knowledge feeds back into the decision-making process. The third example, "Unfamiliar Legacy Code Problem," highlights the risk that is assumed when making a decision. The last example, "Data-Processing Problem," clarifies why it is important to understand the nature of the real problem before working on a solution. The diagram shown with each story problem summarizes key inputs and outputs for the decision being made.

CASE STUDY

Software Test Rerun Problem

This example involves a testing problem that software developers often face. The scenario for the problem follows. Before leaving the office, Bob started a software regression test on the computer used for testing software products. He expected the test to complete and the test results to be ready sometime during the night. Bob came into the office the next morning and saw the login prompt on the test computer. He knew either that someone logged out the test account or that the machine rebooted. Bob quickly determined that there had been a power failure and that the machine had rebooted when the power resumed. The test that he had been running did not complete before the power failure, and the complete test results were not available.

Bob examined the incomplete test results and thought they did not provide sufficient verification of the software component being tested that would be needed to integrate this component with other software system components. He reasoned that the incomplete test results probably would not be useful to the software engineers who were depending on them. Bob estimated that running the entire test would take about four hours and that the complete results could be available by the afternoon if he reruns the test this morning. He rationalized that it would be better to have complete test results that are late by half a day than to provide the test stakeholders with incomplete results. Bob decided to rerun the test now because he did not want the delivery of the test results to be a day or more late.

Let's use the PEAK model to evaluate Bob's decision. Figure 1-3 outlines the inputs to and outputs from Bob's decision process. The risk associated with Bob's decision is also an output of his decision-making process.

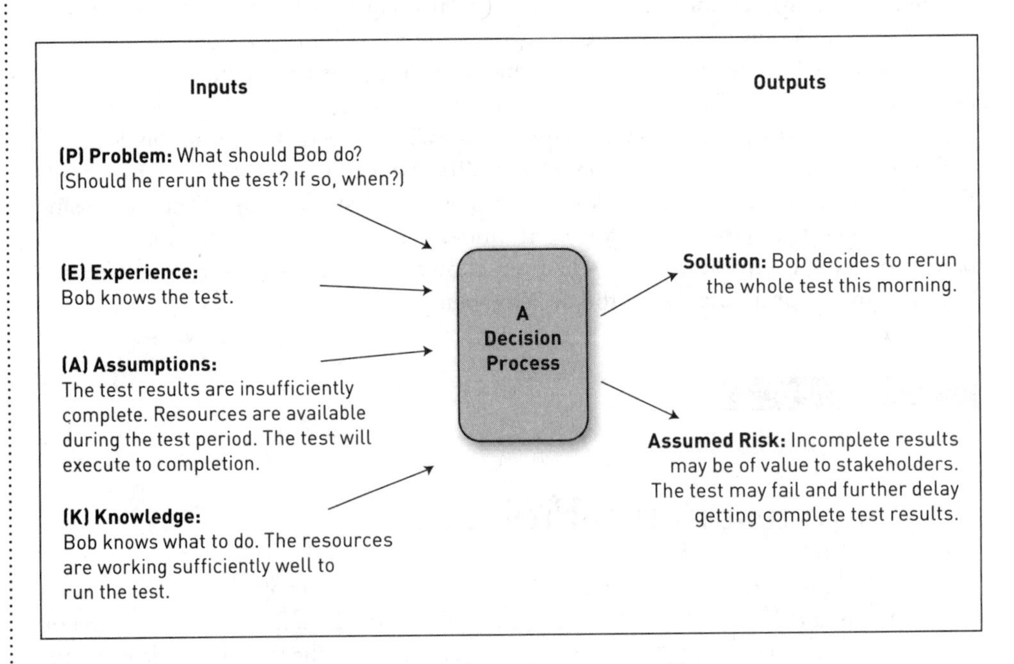

Figure 1–3: *Software test rerun problem*

Inputs

(P) Problem: The software test failed and yielded incomplete test results. What should Bob do?

(E) Experience: Bob knows the test. (He has run this regression test before. He can estimate the execution time and predict potential causes of failure. Therefore, Bob knows the test can be executed completely by noon if he starts the test now.)

(A) Assumptions:

- The test results are insufficiently complete. (Only complete test results are of sufficient value to the software engineers who will use them.)
- The resources are available during the test period (the next four hours).
- The test will execute to completion without problems. (The problem that occurred last night or any other problem will not occur.)

(K) Knowledge:

- Bob knows what test to run and understands the system well enough to run the test (fact).
- The resources are working sufficiently well to successfully run the test (environment).

Outputs

Solution: Bob did not give the first two alternatives in the following list much consideration and chose the last alternative:

- Do not rerun the test. (Deliver incomplete test results to the software engineers.)
- Rerun the whole test later. (The test results will be a day or more late.)
- Rerun the whole test this morning. (The test results will be approximately half a day late.)

Assumed Risk:

- Incomplete results that are available now may be of value to the software engineers who will use them.
- The test may fail, or the completion of the test results may be delayed for some other reason. (For example, another user may have already planned to use the computer for testing during the day. The execution of another test on the computer may delay or interfere in some way with the execution of the target test. The power outage may occur again.)

You may wonder whether each of the inputs is true. The assumption that "only complete test results are of sufficient value" is particularly suspect. If this assumption is correct, then failure of the test to complete would once again preclude the usefulness of the test results. This constraint would necessitate a more controlled test environment (for example, a battery backup for the test computer) including more extensive monitoring of the test execution. Bob could have assumed that any results up to the point where the power failure occurred might be valid. His actual assumption may have overly constrained the decision so that he did not consider other alternative solutions, such as delivering partially complete test results and rerunning only the incomplete part of the test or delivering partially complete test results and rerunning the entire test later after verifying that the test computer would be available. In addition, he is assuming that the power failure will not occur again when he reruns the test. What if the test is the cause of the power failure? An unproven assumption, such as the problem will not occur again, introduces risk for a decision based upon this assumption. If one of the assumptions is not true, the decision when acted upon may result in failure. Decision makers reduce the risk associated with assumptions by gathering the information needed to convert them to facts (knowledge inputs).

A critical aspect to understand about the decision model is that the inputs and outputs exist even if the decision maker does not acknowledge them. Bob made the implicit assumption that he has time to rerun the regression test this morning. Faced with the failed test situation, Bob did not explicitly, at least not yet, think about what tasks he might already have scheduled to do this morning. By explicitly identifying the inputs, decision makers have the opportunity to correct faulty information that they may otherwise use to make their decisions. The model encourages decision makers to explore the various kinds of information that they have about a problem and to carefully determine feasible solutions. The model also guides decision makers to consider risks that may be associated with alternative solutions or decisions. Faulty assumptions or incorrect knowledge about the problem environment introduces the risk that a chosen solution will not or cannot succeed in solving the problem.

CASE STUDY

California Bridge Problem

The California Department of Transportation, Caltrans, was very proud of the state's freeway infrastructure, which included thousands of bridges. Before the 1991 earthquake, the Caltrans engineers thought that they had the perfect model for freeway bridges in California. They used concrete, oblong, cylinder columns that they thought would withstand an earthquake of magnitude 8.49 on the Richter scale. The 1991 earthquake, of magnitude 6.2, changed the engineers' understanding of earthquake movement. Instead of moving up and down as engineers previously understood, this quake generated a side-to-side motion, which caused the bridge support columns to shear. The two-minute earthquake in 1991 collapsed many bridges in California, including part of the Oakland Bay Bridge.

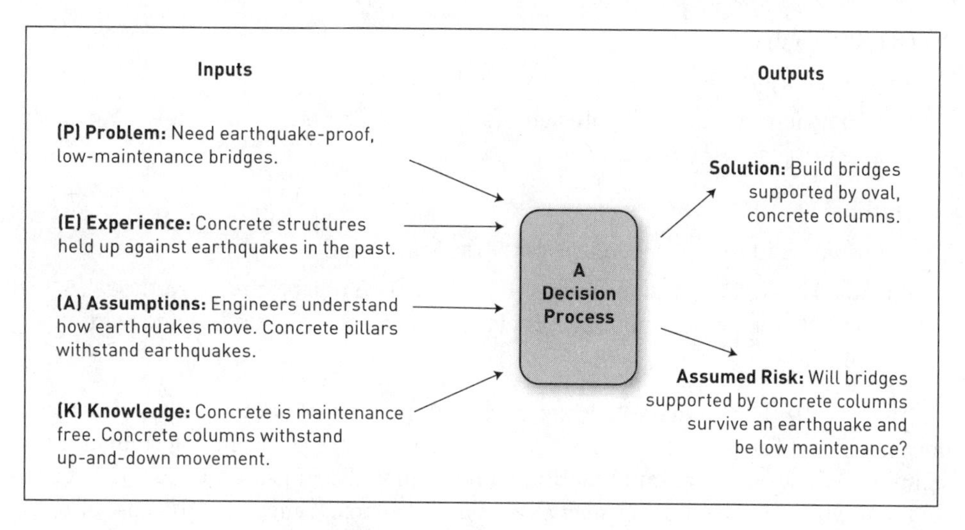

Figure 1–4: *California bridge problem*

Engineers studied the new models of earthquake movement and decided that the solution was to combine two materials to create a new "unbreakable" column. This column has the same concrete oblong structure in the middle as before but now has a steel sleeve on the outside. The steel sleeve holds the concrete in place against the shear, while the concrete columns still defend against an up-and-down motion. The problem is that the columns need regular maintenance because the steel sleeves rust. The original concrete columns were basically "maintenance free" (El-Azazy).

This scenario shows that some of the inputs can be based on faulty knowledge. Caltrans wanted a solution to bridge survival in earthquakes that was maintenance free. They based their solution on knowledge and experience that they thought was correct. The new earthquake model forced a new decision with the constraint of required bridge maintenance. The idea that knowledge remains fixed and is correct can create an environment in which the risk associated with decisions based upon this knowledge is unacceptable. As the Caltrans case illustrates, the inputs and outputs to making a decision can and sometimes should change. Figure 1-4 shows the inputs and outputs for the initial decision to build concrete supports.

Inputs

(P) Problem: Develop a mechanism for bridge support that is earthquake-proof and low maintenance.

(E) Experience: Concrete structures withstood earthquakes in the past.

(A) Assumptions:

- Engineers have a good understanding of how earthquakes move.
- Large, concrete pillars will withstand earthquakes.

(K) Knowledge:

- In California, concrete is basically maintenance free (fact).
- Concrete structures will withstand forces caused by the up-and-down movement of earthquakes (fact).

Outputs

Solution: Build round, concrete pillars to support bridges.

Assumed Risk: Will bridges supported by concrete pillars survive earthquakes that exhibit other types of motion? (Engineers may not fully understand earthquake movement.)

After the 1991 earthquake, engineers learned that earthquakes exhibit both up-and-down as well as back-and-forth movement. This knowledge led them to formulate a new solution to the problem of building bridges that can withstand earthquakes. The second solution, which involved using steel sleeves and concrete, came with the cost of maintaining the steel supports. The input to the second bridge decision included the new knowledge about earthquake movement as well as the experience of many California bridges collapsing during the 1991 earthquake.

As shown in its application to the California bridge problem, the decision model reflects a "semiclosed" system. There is a feedback loop from the outcome of the first solution into the knowledge and experience inputs for the revised solution. Some inputs are open ended in that they may be influenced but not determined by the outputs. For instance, the outputs from a decision may lead to but not necessarily constrain future problems. Likewise, the output from a prior decision can affect but not control a decision maker's assumptions. Decisions makers control their own assumptions. The output from a decision may impact the environment (knowledge) of a future problem, but it will not be the sole influence because many changing factors affect the environment for a problem.

CASE STUDY

Unfamiliar Legacy Code Problem

This short story helps illustrate how a decision maker's awareness of the risk assumed with alternative solutions may influence the decision that is actually made. The example also clarifies the role of the decision model in helping decision makers brainstorm about alternative solutions to a problem.

Iola is inspecting some "ancient" legacy code and discovers some unfamiliar routines. She asks her colleagues whether they know what the routines do, but most people reply that they don't know. The entire system is too large to rebuild and test as a whole, so she temporarily forgets about the code. But the mysterious code continues to bother her. What if the code performs no useful function and is just wasting space? Maybe she should comment it out or refactor it to be more efficient. She knows that the company is looking for ways to improve legacy code, but removing the code might cause another part of the system to fail or to produce bad results.

Iola decides that the risk of system failure is minimal. Therefore, she decides to comment out the unfamiliar code and to reload the component containing this code into the test environment. She has observed that changes to the other code in the component seem to affect the regression test results, so she assumes that the unfamiliar code will do the same. After three hours of regression testing, Iola detects no failures. She is not sure how to proceed because she has not seen the system respond to the removal of the unfamiliar code. In other words, there has been no smoke from the smoke test. Since the software developers have never built a whole-system regression test, Iola is concerned that she may never be able to know conclusively whether removing the code has a negative impact on the system. Iola decides that the risk of removing the code is too high because she can't determine whether the removal actually has an impact on the system. She uncomments the code and puts it back into the test system. Figure 1-5 shows the inputs and outputs for Iola's initial but not final decision.

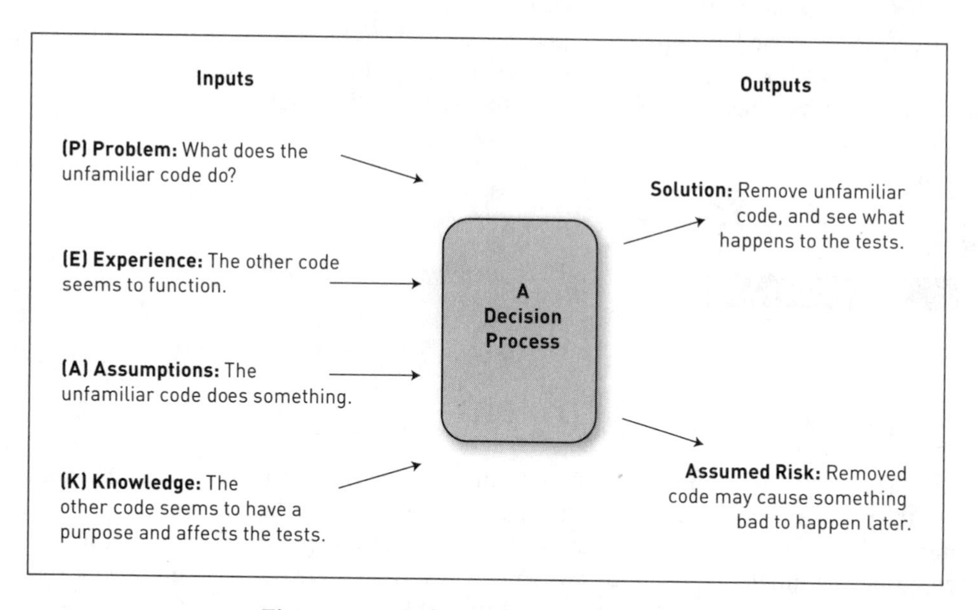

Figure 1–5: *Unfamiliar legacy code problem*

Inputs

(P) Problem: What does the legacy code do, and how should it be handled?

(E) Experience: Iola understands what most of the other code does and is able to test it.

(A) Assumptions: The unfamiliar legacy code should be there for a reason.

(K) Knowledge:

- The other code in the legacy component seems to have a purpose (fact).
- Other code changes seem to result in test result changes (fact).

Outputs

Solution: Comment out the unfamiliar legacy code, and see what happens.

Assumed Risk: Removing the unfamiliar legacy code may cause something bad to happen.

Through careful examination of inputs to the model, the problem solver may think of alternative solutions to the problem. Since Iola knows that other code in the component seems to affect the regression tests, maybe she could comment out the unfamiliar code and replace it with a message to indicate that the unfamiliar code would now be executing. She might also add some code to log the environment when the message code executes so that she can trace back to the caller of the routine containing the unfamiliar code.

The decision model is a convenient way to encapsulate factors that influence the result of the decision-making process. A model is more comprehensible than an abstract idea because it is a representation of reality. But since a model is not reality itself, it allows decision makers to examine and evaluate aspects of reality without altering them. Lastly, the model provides a frame of reference for studying information that people use to make decisions.

CASE STUDY

Data-Processing Problem

This last example will show how software project managers and software engineers can use the model to help manage their decisions. This story highlights the challenge of determining the real problem to be solved. If they are not currently overwhelmed, people who enjoy solving problems are curious when they hear that there is a problem. They expect the person with the problem to state very carefully all the facts concerning the problem. In the *Star Trek Voyager* television show, the character Doctor asks, "Please state the nature of the medical emergency" (CBS Studios). The doctor would not be able to help if the character with the problem responded by giving a life history or a synopsis of the next episode of *Days of Our Lives*.

Similarly, a software engineer may receive unhelpful information about a problem but still be expected to provide a solution to the person with the problem. The software engineer may not have a clear set of facts from which to start. Organizing the information one needs to solve a problem to make a proper decision can be difficult. The decision model will help problem solvers determine whether they have the information needed to determine appropriate solutions.

In particular, the model helps decision makers begin the process of "divide and conquer" in a systematic way. They start by perusing all the information (data) that they have received to find the four decision-making inputs. First, they ask themselves whether they have sufficient information to clearly identify the problem or issue that needs a solution. If they do, then they work on the other inputs needed for the decision. If they cannot clearly identify the real problem, then they will not be able to determine an appropriate solution.

In this example, an engineer came to the head of an engineering data-processing organization with a request. He wanted the latest and best-performing computer. The manager asked him why he needed the machine. At the time, the cost of this machine was at least seven times that of the standard machine being used within the organization. The engineer said that his processing system was too slow and was therefore causing him to fall behind in his analysis of data. He thought that the advanced machine would be five times faster than his current processor.

The manager knew the machine that the engineer wanted and agreed about its excellent performance, but she asked whether the engineer knew for certain that the processor was the cause of the slowness. The manager then asked the engineer whether the network could be the problem and explained that a faster data-processing machine would not help if the network was the bottleneck. The manager said that she could give the engineer three computers of the standard type today and that it would probably take 30 days for the new, nonstandard system to arrive.

The manager worked with the engineer and the networking people to determine whether the network was the bottleneck. They found that the network was responsible for the slowness in processing data needed for reports. With this new knowledge, the engineer explored ways to use the network more efficiently and discovered that he could improve the throughput of processed data by using multiple, standard machines working on parts of the data in parallel.

The story illustrates that software professionals need to clearly understand their problems as well as the other inputs before applying any decision process. If the inputs to the decision process are invalid, then the output is most likely to be an invalid solution. Software professionals intuitively know this, but because of time and other constraints, they do not necessary keep this in mind when they are solving problems. The decision model helps software professionals separate issues and ensure that they do not end up with "garbage in, garbage out."

Figure 1-6 shows the inputs and outputs for the engineer's initial solution.

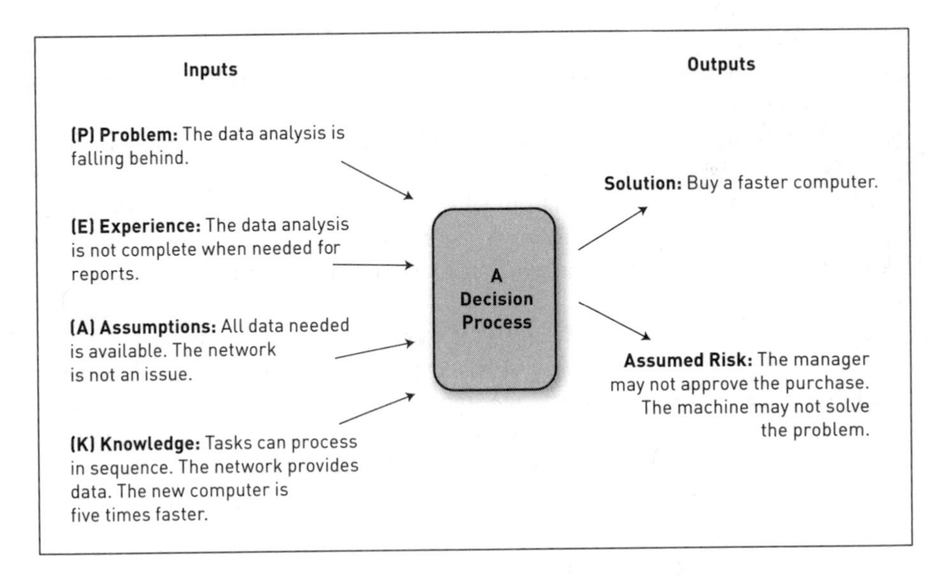

Figure 1–6: *Data-processing problem, initial solution*

Before Discussion with the Manager

Initial Inputs

(P) Problem: The engineer's data analysis is falling behind.

(E) Experience: The engineer has not been able to get the data analysis completed when needed for reports.

(A) Assumptions:

- All the data is available to be processed when needed.
- The network is providing the data as needed.

(K) Knowledge:

- The tasks are currently processed in sequence (fact).
- The network transfers data to be processed for reports (fact).
- The engineer sees an advertisement for a computer that is five times faster than the one he currently has (fact).

Initial Outputs

Solution: Buy the new machine that will process data five times faster.

Assumed Risk:

- The software engineer may not receive permission to buy the machine.
- The machine may not solve the engineer's processing problems.

Figure 1-7 shows the inputs and outputs for the engineer's final solution.

After Discussion with Manager

The engineer made the following changes to his decision inputs after talking with his manager.

Inputs

(P) Problem: The engineer's data analysis is falling behind.

(E) Experience: Multiple machines working in parallel can use network more efficiently.

(A) Assumptions: A number of tasks in the report process can be done in parallel.

(K) Knowledge:

- The network is the bottleneck. (The network was responsible for the slowness in processing data needed for reports.)
- While the network transfers data, it is possible to process report data. (Although many tasks are worked on in sequence, some can be processed in parallel.)

Outputs

Solution: Use a number of in-stock computers to work on parallel parts of the report at the same time.

Assumed Risk: The report processing tasks may not be sufficiently parallel.

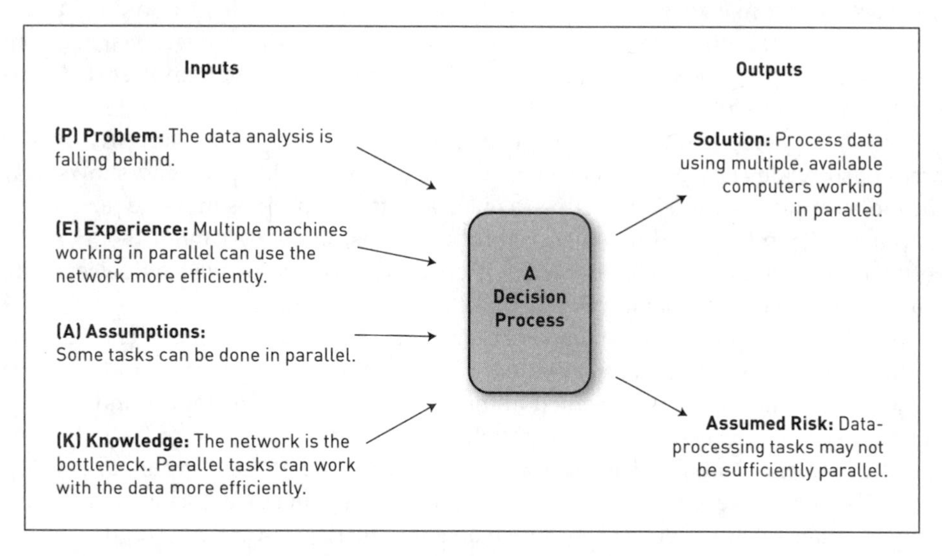

Figure 1–7: *Data-processing problem, final solution*

1.4 Summary

As shown in the example problems, the decision model presented in this chapter does not define your decision process. The model helps you better manage the inputs and outputs to your decision processes and thereby better evaluate your decisions. The case study analyses in the book will show how software professionals can achieve consistently good decisions by verifying that the inputs to their decision processes are valid and correct. You should be aware that there is no guarantee that decisions generated using the model will have successful results. Any one of the following events could occur:

- The decision makers may not apply the model correctly.
- The stakeholders may not implement solutions or decisions correctly.
- The decision makers may not understand reality and therefore may not identify valid or correct inputs.

If the results of the solutions or decisions generated using the decision model do not turn out as planned, the decision makers should review the process they used to make the decision to find any flaws in their understanding of the problem and other inputs. The decision model provides software project stakeholders with a way to analyze the results of their solutions or decisions and to check their understanding of how to manage the decision process. Software professionals can also use the model to reflect on decisions with good outcomes as well as those with poor results. Over time, software project managers and engineers will develop "patterns of thinking" about what constitutes a good decision for specific types of software project management and engineering problems. Knowledge acquired through reflection on past decisions can feed back into future decision making.

The book demonstrates how to apply the decision model to decisions in nine key areas of software engineering. Each chapter focuses on one key area and shows how the model applies to decision making to manage software projects in this area. Though its purpose is to help you make successful decisions, the book cannot model every software engineering decision that you will encounter. Therefore, we have selected the "high-value" decisions that frequently make or break software projects.

Lastly, we must emphasize that a decision process is individualistic. The purpose of this book is to help you better evaluate your own decision processes. The idea is for you to use the concepts presented in this chapter to model the inputs and outputs of your decision processes. Different people might need more or less of the inputs for specific problems, but all decision makers will need some of these inputs to develop solutions. Finally, we want you to understand the concept of risk associated with managing decisions. Managing decisions by managing the risk associated with these decisions is essential to successful software project management.

Chapter 2

Managing Requirements

2.1 Chapter Objectives

After reading and thinking about the concepts and case studies presented in this chapter, you will be able to do the following:

- Understand the activities that are essential to managing software requirements
- Identify key issues and decisions involving the management of requirements in the chapter case studies
- Use the chapter concepts to suggest feasible solutions to the problems faced by the case study stakeholders
- Recognize the importance of managing software requirements

2.2 Context

The ability of a software project team to deliver products or services that satisfy the user's needs and expectations depends first on the degree to which the requirements express the actual needs and perceptions of the user. The project deliverables can be only as "good" as the requirements that direct their development. Though determining appropriate requirements is essential, it is equally important that the software deliverables being developed satisfy these requirements and that the requirements do not change in an uncontrollable way as the software project progresses. When requirements are well managed, the resulting software deliverables are most likely to satisfy the user.

This chapter focuses on decisions that software project managers make to manage software project requirements. The chapter discusses these decisions in the context of activities performed by a software project team in managing requirements. It purposely does not delve into the details of specific techniques for managing requirements because many other people have written about this subject. Some insightful books that present techniques as well as practical advice for engineering software requirements are Hull et al. (2005), Jackson (2000), Wiegers (2003), and Wiegers (2006). IEEE Std. 830-1998 describes the content and qualities of a good software requirements specification (SRS) and provides several sample outlines for an SRS. Other suggested references related to managing software requirements appear at the end of the chapter context.

Before we talk about activities that compose the management of requirements, we should clarify some terminology. Practitioners use different terms to describe the activities involved in managing requirements. Some practitioners refer to the determination, documentation, and sign-off of the requirements as **requirements engineering** or **requirements definition** and to the activities after the requirements are signed off as **requirements management** (Borland 2006). We have chosen a more expansive use of the term **managing requirements** to reflect that stakeholders, including software project managers, make decisions regarding requirements throughout the life of a software project as well as throughout the life of the resulting software. Effective management of decision making and of the impact that decisions have on the requirements and resulting software deliverables is critical to the success of a software project.

Our discussion of managing requirements includes references to **functional** and **nonfunctional requirements**. Functional requirements are statements about the services that the software will perform for the user. Some software project stakeholders refer to these collectively as the required software behavior. Nonfunctional requirements are statements about **quality attributes** such as maintainability, performance, reliability, safety, security, or usability that the software should satisfy. Software project stakeholders generally describe and make decisions about **software quality** with respect to software quality attributes.

We'll start by presenting activities that software project teams perform to manage requirements; and while doing this, we will discuss decisions that software project managers make or should make during each activity. As you will note, managing requirements involves multiple activities, each of which involves multiple decisions to be made. Because decision making involves risk, the chapter briefly mentions risks associated with making decisions about requirements. Chapter 7, "Managing Risk," provides a more general discussion of risk in the context of making decisions for software projects.

Activities in Managing Requirements

Managing requirements is a process that usually begins with gathering requirements and should continue while the project team validates that the software deliverables satisfy their requirements. Primary activities in managing requirements include those such as the following (establishing the requirements for a software project includes the activities indicated by an asterisk):

- Eliciting and stating the requirements (specification)*
- Verifying and validating the requirements*
- Negotiating and contracting the requirements and project agreements*
- Managing requirements change and scope
- Validating software deliverables with respect to their requirements

Table 2-1 describes the activities that compose the management of requirements. Later, we will discuss example decisions that software project managers make when performing each activity. The example decisions are representative but are not intended to be complete or exclusive. You should talk with experienced managers about the decisions that they have made on the job and log the types of decisions that you encounter. Before embarking on a particular requirements activity, you might read the related discussion and peruse the corresponding table of example decisions.

Table 2–1: *Descriptions of Activities in Managing Requirements*

Activity	*Description of Activity*
Establishing the requirements	**Definition:** Process of eliciting and stating, verifying and validating, and negotiating and contracting the software and software project requirements. **Target outcome:** The sum of the target outcomes for the constituent activities described in the succeeding table rows.
Eliciting and stating the requirements	**Definition of *elicitation*:** Process of gathering ideas about what the software should do for the user in an identified context. **Definition of *statement*:** Process of specifying the software requirements in a format that is easily understood by the software stakeholders. **Target outcome:** A description that is understandable by the various software stakeholders of the functional requirements, the nonfunctional requirements, and the planned evolution of the software.

Continues

Table 2–1: *Descriptions of Activities in Managing Requirements (Continued)*

Activity	*Description of Activity*
Verifying and validating the requirements	**Definition of *verification*:** Process of determining that the specified requirements are clear, complete, consistent, correct, mutually compatible, and feasible. **Definition of *validation*:** Process of determining that the specified requirements satisfy the user's business objectives and expectations for the software deliverables and do not preclude the concurrent accomplishment of the specified set. **Target outcome:** A clear, complete, consistent, and correct requirements specification that is able to direct the development of software deliverables that can satisfy the user's business objectives and expectations.
Negotiating and contracting the requirements	**Definition of *negotiation*:** Process of trading off the scope and quality of the software deliverables with respect to their cost (budget) and time to delivery (schedule). **Definition of *contracting*:** Process of developing written, legally binding, and signed agreements regarding the expectations and responsibilities of all stakeholders for the software project deliverables, cost, schedule, and other interests or concerns. **Target outcome:** A signed contract that clearly states the software project stakeholders' agreements regarding their expectations, roles, and responsibilities for the software project deliverables to be provided (product), possibly for how the deliverables are developed or how the project is executed (process), and for the project cost (budget) and time (schedule).
Managing requirements change and scope	**Definition:** Process of managing requests for change to the software project requirements in a way that enables the software stakeholders feasibly to reach an agreement regarding the ongoing scope of the requirements as well as the cost and time to develop deliverables that satisfy any agreed upon changes to the set of contracted requirements. **Target outcome:** A stable set of requirements that directs the completion of software deliverables that satisfy the user's business objectives and expectations within the contracted (or possibly recontracted) cost and time for delivery.

Table 2–1: *Descriptions of Activities in Managing Requirements (Continued)*

Activity	*Description of Activity*
Validating the software deliverables with respect to their requirements	**Definition:** Process of determining that the software project deliverables satisfy the user's business objectives and expectations as stated in the software requirements that are outlined in the software project agreement or contract. **Target outcome:** Software project deliverables that satisfy the user's business objectives and expectations as outlined in the software project agreement or contract.

Establishing the Requirements

Considering the user's needs and the relevant stakeholders is paramount to successfully establishing the requirements. The software project requirements should support the user's business objectives. In other words, each requirement should map to a specific business objective. Determining and aligning the expectations of the customer or client with those of the developer or service provider is necessary to establish software requirements that will be acceptable to both types of stakeholders. Chapter 9, "Managing Stakeholder Expectations," discusses the alignment between the customer and software developer expectations.

Involving the appropriate stakeholders in effective ways at the right times is critical to successfully establishing the software requirements (as well as to the success of the software project). In particular, stakeholders with the responsibility or authority to sign off or approve the software requirements, software project, or software project deliverables including the budget or cost should be involved in establishing the requirements. Before eliciting the requirements, the leaders of the requirements establishment process should consult all key stakeholders regarding the nature of their preferred involvement in the process.

In general, projects with requirements that are unpredictable or that involve unknowns, such as the use of innovative technologies, should include feasibility studies in which the open issues are explored and resolved before the project requirements are established. Neglecting to identify and resolve uncertainties about the requirements can lead to software project failure. For instance, this problem may occur if the software developer decides to specify requirements that depend on the use of a software component to be developed by another vendor that ultimately does not provide the component on time or at all. One way to handle the uncertainty associated with this type of decision is to negotiate an agreement with the component vendor and to design a contingency plan in the event that the vendor is late or unable to deliver the component.

Likewise, if the stakeholders' understanding of and expectations for the requirements are still evolving, the process of establishing the requirements should include ways to explore alternative requirements. Time spent evaluating and resolving unknowns before deciding upon the requirements reduces the risk that the software deliverables or services will not satisfy the user's expectations or needs and that they cannot be rendered on time and within budget. Resolving uncertainties regarding the requirements helps reduce the risk of software project failure.

People who establish requirements make decisions such as those shown in Table 2-2. The example decisions are grouped by decision area. What other decisions have you encountered or do you think that you might encounter when establishing requirements?

Table 2–2: *Decisions to Make When Establishing Requirements*

Decision Area	*Example Decisions*
Stakeholders	Who are the key stakeholders? (Which stakeholders will approve the requirements or the software project?) What interest (stake) does each potential stakeholder have in the software project? With respect to expertise and interests, what role should each potential stakeholder take to ensure that the requirements most likely will satisfy that stakeholder's expectations? How does each stakeholder want to be involved in the elicitation of requirements? What are the agreed upon responsibilities of each stakeholder, especially those who will sign off on the agreement?
Business goals	What are the client's or customer's business goals for the software project deliverables(for example, software artifacts or services)?
Functional/non-functional requirements (scope and quality)	What functional and nonfunctional requirements best support the client's or customer's business goals? What scope and quality supports the business goals? What, if any, constraints or limitations are associated with the requirements?

Table 2–2: *Decisions to Make When Establishing Requirements (Continued)*

Decision Area	*Example Decisions*
Process and staff	What, if any, software development, project management, or other processes should the software project team apply? What, if any, are the requirements concerning the staff to be assigned to various project roles? What processes will the software project team follow to establish the requirements?
Time (schedule)	What is the desired time (schedule) for providing the software project deliverables?
Cost (budget)	What is the cost (budget) associated with the desired scope, time, and quality?
Legal issues	What, if any, disclaimers regarding the software project deliverables are needed? What, if any, compliancy or other legal issues should the software project deliverables or project satisfy?
Outstanding issues	What issues need to be resolved before establishing the requirements, and how should they be resolved?

Lastly, it is important to remember that managing requirements does *not* end when the requirements are established. The job of managing requirements is not complete until the software is retired!

Now, we'll cover the specific activities that compose the establishment of requirements. We will first discuss the elicitation and statement of requirements.

Eliciting and Stating Requirements

Eliciting both functional and nonfunctional requirements is critical to establishing requirements that will satisfy stakeholder needs and expectations. During the gathering of requirements, the software stakeholders frequently spend most of their time evaluating and deciding upon the functions to be performed by the software. Except for software qualities that are closely related to the functional behavior (such as the feedback loop rate for a control system), software stakeholders often wait until the end to consider the quality attributes that the software should exhibit. In an attempt to "wrap up" the requirements elicitation, they may quickly draft statements about the desired software qualities that are imprecise, inaccurate, incomplete, or simply incompatible.

For example, a common requirements mistake to is to state that the software system should "respond in real time and be fast" (whatever fast means). A real-time software system is not simply a system that responds quickly. A real-time system responds predictably with respect to events and time. The system may execute periodically (repeatedly every specified time interval) or aperiodically (only when a specific, noncyclical event occurs). The real-time system may need to satisfy hard deadlines (for example, it must respond within 20 milliseconds after an event occurs or else something undesirable will happen), may be allowed to miss a soft deadline by some specified amount of time (for example, it's preferable to respond within ten seconds after the event occurs, but it is sufficient to respond within one minute), or may be permitted to not respond at all to the event if the processing system is overloaded.

A quality attribute that software stakeholders often do not consider is the expected or likely evolution of the software. Decisions about software evolution are important if the software is to continue to provide value to the user over a lifetime beyond a single release. For software to be developed and released iteratively or incrementally in a cost-effective way, there needs to be a software release plan to indicate which requirements are expected to be developed for each release. The release plan may be flexible or change as the software developers receive feedback from users as with Agile development or other iterative approaches (Beck et al. 2001; Larman and Basili 2003). While establishing the requirements, the software stakeholders should consider and decide upon an overall plan for the evolution of the software to help the software architects and designers determine an appropriate composition for the software. See Ullah and Ruhe (2006), who present ongoing research in the process to develop a comprehensive and formalized model for planning and optimizing releases for software product lines.

Specifications of requirements should define the requirements from a user's point of view and should provide a system context. The requirements should fit into a "big picture" of where and how the software will be used. The objective is to specify the requirements in a way that enables the specification to be analyzed with respect to the ability of the requirements to satisfy the user's business needs. In other words, the specification enables the validation of the requirements. The stakeholders who review the statement of requirements need to develop a common understanding of what each stated requirement means.

The statement of requirements should be written in a way that enables the specification to be analyzed for clarity, completeness, consistency, correctness, and compatibility. Likewise, the requirements should be testable in that ways exist to determine that the software project deliverables satisfy them. For instance, stating that the software system should execute flawlessly in a weightless environment (such as outer space) is meaningless if there is no practical way on Earth to verify that the software does indeed execute as intended without the effects of gravity.

People who elicit and state requirements make decisions such as those shown in Table 2-3. The example decisions are grouped by decision area. What other decisions have you encountered or do you think that you might encounter when eliciting and stating requirements?

Table 2–3: *Decisions to Make When Eliciting and Stating Requirements*

Decision Area	*Example Decisions*
Users	Who are the intended users of the software? In what context will they use the software?
Functional requirements	Precisely what should the software do for the intended users? Which business objectives of the user are satisfied by each functional requirement?
Nonfunctional requirements	Which software quality attributes should the software exhibit? How should the software exhibit these quality attributes? Which business objectives of the user are satisfied by each nonfunctional requirement?
Other constraints or requirements	What are the constraints for how the software project deliverables are developed? What are the constraints for how the software project is managed or executed?
Coverage and consistency	To what degree are the user's business objectives satisfied by the functional and nonfunctional requirements or by the statements of other constraints or requirements? What degree of certainty is there that no requirement contradicts or makes it difficult or impossible to accomplish another requirement? What is the basis for this certainty?
Testability	How can the software developer determine that the requirements are testable? To what degree are the stakeholders certain that the requirements are testable? What is the basis for this certainty?

Continues

Table 2–3: *Decisions to Make When Eliciting and Stating Requirements (Continued)*

Decision Area	*Example Decisions*
Format	What are the formats for stating the requirements, and why? Do the chosen formats accomplish each of the following objectives? • Enable the meaning of each requirement to be stated clearly, completely, consistently, or correctly. • Enable the meaning of each requirement to be understood by stakeholders who will review it (possibly with assistance from the leaders of the elicitation and statement processes). • Support the analysis of the requirements for clarity, compatibility, completeness, consistency, and correctness (verification of the requirements). • Support the analysis of the requirements for their ability to satisfy the business needs and expectations of the users (validation of the requirements).
Process	What processes will the software project team follow to elicit and state the requirements? Who should elicit and state the requirements? Why?

Next, we'll discuss the types of decisions that software engineers make when verifying and validating requirements.

Verifying and Validating Requirements

Verifying the requirements ensures that the specified requirements are clear, complete, consistent, correct, mutually compatible, and feasible, whereas validating the requirements ensures that the specified requirements do indeed satisfy the user's business needs and expectations for the software project deliverables. It is particularly important that the software professionals who validate the requirements specification include stakeholders who represent the user's point of view. It may also help if the professionals who inspect requirements have university degrees in majors *not* related to computer science or have prior experience in writing requirements. See the report on a statistically controlled experiment at Microsoft Corporation involving 70 professionals who participated in a requirements inspection (Carver et al. 2008).

A critical process decision involves the techniques that will be used to verify and validate the software requirements. Software engineers often model the required software behavior and quality attributes to better analyze their correctness, accuracy, and compatibility. The premise for model-driven software development (MDSD) is that models of the software requirements can be verified, validated, and then mapped into software designs (which also may be expressed as models) and implementations that improve quality while reducing the time and cost associated with development. See *IBM Systems Journal* (2006) for an excellent collection of papers that give an overview of model-driven software development. A question to be asked when using MDSD is, how well do the selected models represent and clarify the required behaviors and qualities? In other words, how well will the selected modeling techniques enable the software developers to know whether the specified requirements are correct, sufficiently accurate, complete, compatible, and so on? Some additional references to techniques for modeling software requirements appear at the end of the chapter context.

Another important process decision, discussed earlier, is how the software developers will detect and resolve unknowns about the requirements. Identifying and resolving unknowns should be done throughout the life of the software project, but it is particularly important during the early stages of the software project when it is easier and less costly to make changes to the requirements and project direction. Even if the project stakeholders do not expect unknowns in the requirements, the verification and validation of requirements should determine whether any requirements may not be achievable or may preclude the achievement of other requirements.

People who verify and validate requirements make decisions such as those shown in Table 2-4. The example decisions are grouped by decision area. What other decisions have you encountered or do you think that you might encounter when verifying and validating requirements?

Table 2–4: *Decisions to Make When Verifying and Validating Requirements*

Decision Area	*Example Decisions*
Stakeholders	Who should verify the requirements specification? Why? Who should validate the requirements specification? Why?
Verification or validation criteria	What is the degree of certainty that the specified requirements are clear, compatible, complete, consistent, and correct? What is the basis for this certainty? What is the degree of certainty that the specified requirements completely or partially satisfy the user's business needs and expectations? What is the basis for this certainty?

Continues

Table 2–4: *Decisions to Make When Verifying and Validating Requirements (Continued)*

Decision Area	*Example Decisions*
Issues or risks	What, if any, are the unknowns, uncertainties, or other risks associated with the specified requirements? How should these issues be managed throughout the life of the software project?
Process	How should the verification and validation of the requirements specification be done? • For the functional requirements? • For the nonfunctional requirements? • For other constraints or requirements? How should errors found during the verification and validation of the software requirements be handled? Should the errors be corrected before the stakeholders finish contracting the requirements? Why or why not?

To explore the last activity in establishing the requirements, we'll next cover the types of decisions that software engineers make when negotiating and contracting requirements.

Negotiating and Contracting Requirements

In many organizations, the people who negotiate and contract agreements for software projects are not the people who eventually manage or lead these projects. Whether this separation of stakeholders hinders or promotes successful software outcomes probably depends on the degree to which the interests of all types of relevant stakeholders are represented in negotiating and contracting the software project agreements.

Negotiating the software project requirements is inherently a process of tradeoffs and decisions. Stakeholder discussion and agreement upon the trade-offs helps stakeholders to focus on elements of the requirements that they can actually control such as scope, time, quality, or cost. The negotiation process stimulates stakeholders to explore options that optimize the expectation space for all. In other words, it maximizes the win-win opportunities for "opposing" stakeholders.

Software project agreements (contracted decisions) should provide the stakeholders with a clear, compatible, complete, consistent, and correct description of elements such as those described in Table 2-5.

Table 2–5: *Elements of a Software Project Contract*

Contract Area	*Example Contract Elements*
Project objectives and deliverables	Statements of: • Project objectives • Project deliverables • Functional and nonfunctional requirements for the software project deliverables (These may be stated in a separate document that is to be developed as part of the project.) • Any constraints or limitations associated with the project deliverables or their requirements
Project execution constraints (process, staff, and so on)	Statements of: • Any agreements regarding technologies or processes to be employed as well as how, when, and by whom these are to be employed • Any agreements regarding the stakeholders who should be involved in the development of the software project deliverables
Other services	Statements of: • Any training to be provided • Any field service to be provided
Time (schedule) and cost (budget)	The schedule for delivery of the software project deliverables The cost associated with producing and delivering the software project deliverables Any cost associated with training Any cost associated with field service
Disclaimers, warranties, contingencies, and other issues of concern	Disclaimers regarding the use or application of the software project deliverables Warranties or guarantees in the event that the client or customer finds the software project deliverables to have errors, to not be applicable, or to be unacceptable in some way (what the software developer or service provider should do or not do to correct any problems that are found) Contingencies in the event that the software project deliverables are not delivered in full or if the delivery is late Other issues of concern identified and agreed upon by the stakeholders

In reading this section, you may view the contracting of requirements through a legalistic lens focused on the protection of stakeholder rights. Though software project contracts are intended to legally protect stakeholder interests, clarifying the expectations and responsibilities of the software project stakeholders is essentially a good business practice. The old adage "leave no stone unturned" is applicable to negotiating and contracting the software project agreements. Software project stakeholders should discuss, reach agreement, and document their expectations, concerns, and any other issues that they have regarding a software project. Making stakeholder expectations transparent is analogous to flushing out and resolving software project unknowns.

People who negotiate and contract requirements make decisions such as those shown in Table 2-6. The example decisions are grouped by decision area. What other decisions have you encountered or do you think that you might encounter when negotiating and contracting requirements?

Table 2–6: *Decisions to Make When Negotiating and Contracting Requirements*

Decision Area	*Example Decisions*
Stakeholder priorities and negotiable ranges	What are the priorities of the client or customer expectations with respect to scope, quality, time, and cost? What is the negotiable range in scope (requirements) that satisfies the user's business needs and expectations? What is the negotiable range in quality that satisfies the user's business needs and expectations? What is the negotiable range in time (schedule) that satisfies the user's business constraints and expectations? What is the negotiable range in cost (budget) that satisfies the user's business constraints and expectations? From the developer's point of view, what levels of technology, people, and process satisfy the negotiable range in scope and quality while staying within the negotiable ranges in time and cost? (For more information about developer stakeholder expectations, see Chapter 9, "Managing Stakeholder Expectations.") What set of requirements best matches the business needs and expectations of the client or customer with respect to scope, quality, time, and cost?
Stakeholder roles	Who should negotiate the requirements and software project agreements? Why? Who should contract the software agreements? Why?

Table 2–6: *Decisions to Make When Negotiating and Contracting Requirements (Continued)*

Decision Area	*Example Decisions*
Elements of software agreement	Which stakeholder expectations and responsibilities need to be expressed in the software contract? What are the other necessary elements of the software agreement? (See Table 2-5 for examples.)
Issues or risks	What are the risks of doing business with either the customer or the developer, and to what degree are these risks manageable? To what degree is there is a viable business reason for trying to formulate a software project agreement despite any risks associated with the software project?
Process	What processes will be used for negotiating and contracting the software project deliverables as well as the schedule and cost associated with their delivery?

We'll now progress to the types of decisions that software engineers make when managing requirements change and scope.

Managing Requirements Change and Scope

Some software project managers think that the requirements work ends when the requirements are established. In practice, project requirements need management throughout the life of the software project and across multiple projects for software that evolves iteratively or incrementally. The continuous and ongoing management of requirements is necessary because software requirements are not static. Software engineers may use techniques such as prototyping, simulation, and mock-ups to help users determine exactly what the software should do and how the interface to the software should look. But even by applying techniques to better understand the nature of the requirements, the user's (customer's) view and expectations still may change as the software project progresses.

The developer's view of requirements may also change for various reasons. Sometimes there is miscommunication by the stakeholders while eliciting the requirements. Other times, the developer viewpoint changes because of knowledge that is acquired through ongoing communication with potential users (especially with those who were not involved in establishing the original requirements), through applying the chosen technologies and development techniques, and through other forms of research or information gathering. For instance, the developer may discover unexpected technical issues that warrant changes in the requirements.

In general, changes in the requirements for a software project are beneficial when they improve the clarity, compatibility, completeness, consistency, or correctness of the requirements. But it is important that the software project stakeholders carefully consider the impact of a change request on the scope, time, quality, and cost of the deliverables before deciding to make the change. Obviously, changes that enlarge the scope of the requirements for the software project deliverables run the risk of overshooting the budget or schedule of a software project.

The main idea to keep in mind is that changing the software requirements involves a cost-benefit trade-off: there is a cost associated with the resources and time needed to handle the change as well as a potential benefit. The primary decisions that software project stakeholders must make are whether the software project budget can support the cost of a particular software change and whether the business benefit associated with the software change is worth the cost (including time). Stakeholders must weigh the benefit versus the cost associated with a particular change in the software requirements. The software managers should help the project stakeholders decide whether including the change later rather than in a currently planned release of the software yields better value. The stakeholders may need to reevaluate and make new decisions about the project agreements in order to accommodate changes in the requirements.

We'll now take a moment to apply the PEAK model when making a decision regarding a request to add a feature to the requirements for a software project's deliverables. Suppose that the customer for a robotic surgical assistant product requests the addition of a new software algorithm after the project agreements have been established. Using the PEAK model, the software developers can ask questions such as the following to help the customer decide whether the benefit of adding this feature outweighs the cost:

(P) Problem: Should the software project stakeholders expand or modify the project requirements to include the new software algorithm?

(E) Experience:

- How difficult or easy will it be to develop and integrate the new algorithm (with respect to process, staff, time, quality, and so on)?
- How difficult or easy will it be to verify and validate the software with the new algorithm (with respect to process, staff, time, quality, and so on)?

(A) Assumptions: What aspects of the algorithm should be established as facts rather than assumed? For instance, the project stakeholders should determine whether the following assumptions are factual:

- This algorithm will be the most appropriate one available for the foreseeable future. In other words, there is no other better algorithm that will be available in the near future.
- The algorithm will not interfere with or be incompatible with the other requirements.

- The performance, reliability, and safety of the algorithm have been sufficiently verified and validated.

(K) Knowledge:

- Considering the surgical procedures for which the robotic surgical assistant will be used, how will this new feature improve the performance, safety, or other quality attributes of the product?
- Does the addition of the new feature preclude the use of other requirements (is incompatible with other requirements)?
- What is the impact on the project time (schedule), quality, and cost (budget) of each alternative solution? Which of these scenarios is preferable to the software project stakeholders and why?

Solution:

- Add new feature in current software release.
- Add new feature in a future release of the software.
- Do not add feature in the foreseeable future.
- Are there other viable solutions? If so, what are they?

Assumed Risk: Given the current input information, what do the software project stakeholders know about the risks that they would assume with each feasible solution?

Ultimately, the software project stakeholders must decide whether the benefits of a particular solution outweigh the cost and risks associated with the solution and whether the cost-benefit relationship for a particular solution is better than that for the other solutions.

Another challenge involves scope creep that may occur when software developers implicitly expand or contract the requirements. The problem with implicit changes to scope is that they are less likely to be communicated uniformly to the project stakeholders who need to be aware of them. Uninformed stakeholders are likely to be surprised and possibly dissatisfied with the resulting validation test results or software project deliverables. The software project stakeholders should discuss, evaluate, and explicitly decide upon changes to the software requirements and their scope. The decision makers should communicate the changes to other software project stakeholders who need to know about them, such as the software analysts who can make certain that the changes are compatible with the ongoing requirements and the software engineers designing tests to validate the software project deliverables. Haphazard and implicit changes to requirements can lead to software development problems and ultimately to unsatisfactory software project deliverables.

People who manage requirements change and scope make decisions such as those shown in Table 2-7. The example decisions are grouped by decision area. What other decisions have you encountered or do you think that you might encounter when managing requirements change and scope?

Table 2–7: *Decisions to Make When Managing Requirements Change and Scope*

Decision Area	*Example Decisions*
Stakeholder roles	Who should manage the requirements change requests and scope? Why?
Impact on scope, quality, and value	How do particular software change requests impact the related scope and quality of the software project requirements? What is the benefit or value associated with each software change request? How, if at all, do particular changes in the software project requirements help maximize the overall benefits associated with the software project deliverables or help support other beneficial software changes that are expected or likely?
Impact on time (schedule, version for release)	How, if at all, would handling the requested change impact the current project schedule? What are the benefits and costs associated with handling particular software change requests in the currently planned release versus a later release of the software? Should particular software change requests be handled in the currently planned release of the software? Why should these requests be handled or not handled?
Impact on cost (budget)	How, if at all, would allocation of the software project budget for particular software changes enhance the opportunity for the software project deliverables to add value? How, if at all, would the budget outlay for particular software changes yield minimal value and, more seriously, preclude the opportunity to respond to other software change requests that would yield more value?
Process	How will the software project stakeholders handle interests in or requests to change the software project requirements after the original agreement and contract are in place? What processes will be used for managing requirements change and scope? Who should manage the requirements change and scope? Why?

Last, but certainly not least, we'll talk about the types of decisions that software engineers make to validate the software project deliverables with respect to their requirements.

Validating the Software Project Deliverables with Respect to Their Requirements

Software project stakeholders and managers often anxiously await the delivery of software project deliverables that demonstrate the success of the project and the culmination of a business venture. Validating the software project deliverables with respect to their requirements is the apex of their development. Project managers should consider validating project deliverables to be an integral part of managing requirements for several reasons:

- The reason for defining requirements is to help ensure that the resulting software project deliverables satisfy the needs and expectations of the user.
- The validation of software project deliverables with respect to requirements must be done from the user's point of view.
- The tests used to validate software project deliverables need to reflect changes to the requirements. Therefore, managing requirements involves managing changes to requirements as well as to the associated tests used to validate the software project deliverables.

Validating software project deliverables is best done by people who represent the point of view of the user, who are able to understand the various aspects of different types of software project requirements and deliverables, and whose observations are least likely to be clouded by detailed knowledge of how the project deliverables were developed. Validation experts should also be knowledgeable about problems that are likely to occur in the types of products or services being produced or delivered by the software project as well as about how to find obscure bugs that can occur.

When making decisions regarding the validation of software project deliverables, software managers need to remember that requirements should be tested from the user's point of view with respect to a system context. Validating software project deliverables ensures that the stakeholder expectations regarding the software project requirements and contractual agreements are met. Project managers also need to keep in mind that validating the software project deliverables with respect to their requirements is worthwhile only if the specified requirements and corresponding software system tests have been verified and validated. In addition, they need to remember that incorporating changes to requirements into the software requirements specification and corresponding software system tests is critical to ensure the complete and correct validation of software project deliverables with respect to requirements.

People who validate software project deliverables with respect to their requirements make decisions such as those shown in Table 2-8. The example decisions are

Table 2–8: *Decisions to Make When Validating Software Project Deliverables with Respect to Their Requirements*

Decision Area	*Example Decisions*
Stakeholder roles	Who should verify the software project deliverables? Why? Who should validate the software project deliverables? Why?
Verification or validation criteria	Verification: • When was the verification of the software project deliverables done, and who performed the verification? • Have the appropriate software project deliverables been sufficiently or completely verified with respect to the appropriate version of the software project requirements? • What is the degree of certainty that the software project deliverables have been sufficiently verified, and on what is the certainty based? Validation: • When was the validation of the software project deliverables done, and who performed the validation? • Have the appropriate software project deliverables been sufficiently or completely validated with respect to the appropriate version of the software project requirements? • What is the degree of certainty that the software project deliverables have been sufficiently validated, and on what is the certainty based?
Process	How should the requirements be kept up-to-date and properly associated with the appropriate software project deliverables? Which software project deliverables should be verified/validated with respect to which software project requirements? How, when, and why?

grouped by decision area. What other decisions have you encountered or do you think that you might encounter when verifying and validating requirements?

For readers interested in topics related to managing software requirements, we suggest the following references. Wang et al. (2007) discuss an automated approach for monitoring and diagnosing problems that occur with software requirements. For studies and discussions of requirements problems that contribute to software project or product failure, see Ebert and De Man (2005), Ebert and Hickey (2008), and Verner (2008). Some modeling techniques for functional requirements are the Unified Modeling Language (UML) included in the Rational Unified Process (Rational 2001; Object Management Group); problem frames (Jackson 2000; Jackson 2005; Cox et al. 2005), which includes a road map of problem frames research; and Jackson and Jackson (2006) for a formalized approach to separating concerns in requirements analysis. Bar-On and Tyszberowicz (2007) present a methodology for identifying conflicting functional requirements and potentially for deriving alternative, nonconflicting requirements. Raja (2009) overviews and highlights the pros and cons of current software requirements validation techniques, and Damian and Chisan (2006) discuss an empirical study that shows how requirements engineering can help improve other project processes with respect to productivity, quality, and risk management. Cao and Ramesh (2008) provide an analysis of data from 16 software development organizations that reveals 7 Agile requirements engineering practices, along with their benefits and challenges.

2.3 Case Studies

The two case studies in this chapter focus on aspects of managing requirements that are often overlooked by software project stakeholders and managers. In the first case, "The New Account Project at HBC," the software project managers encounter unexpected problems related to decisions made about selecting and involving the project stakeholders when establishing the requirements. The second case, "On Time, Within Budget, but Wrong" presents a "model" project. Everything goes well in the project until the stakeholders who represent the user decide that the finished software is not what is needed or expected. Read these cases to determine the issues and decisions that led to critical glitches in managing software requirements.

CASE STUDY

The New Account Project at HBC

Directions

When reading this case study, focus on the activities related to establishing the requirements for a software project. Identify issues and decisions associated with selecting and involving stakeholders in these activities.

Case Summary

DESCRIPTION

The Individuals Direct business unit of Hamilton Banking Corporation (HBC), a large financial institution, wants to increase customer usage of online banking services. In particular, managers have set a goal to increase the number of new accounts opened online by 50 percent within two years. To help do this, the business unit has requested the information technology (IT) group that services the unit to enhance the banking Web site for individuals. The case scenario involves the events that occur as the stakeholders try to establish the requirements for the software project and encounter an unexpected challenge to the project schedule and budget.

CASE STUDY OBJECTIVES

After reading the case study, you will be able to do the following:

- Understand the importance of the following decisions in establishing the requirements:
  - Which stakeholders should be involved?
  - How and when should the various stakeholders be involved?
- Identify the activities by which the organization established the requirements.
- Identify appropriate stakeholders in the case scenario who should participate in the activities to establish the requirements.
- Explain the problems that occurred in the case scenario, the causes of the problems, and the ways to reduce the likelihood that similar problems will occur in other software projects. Relate these to the decisions faced by project stakeholders.

SUBJECTS COVERED

Decision making, establishing requirements, eliciting requirements, verifying and validating requirements, and stakeholder selection and involvement in establishing requirements

SETTING

The setting is Hamilton Banking Corporation, which is a large, publicly traded financial institution that provides commercial and institutional banking services. The company maintains its headquarters in the city of New York and has a campus for business development and IT support in White Plains, New York (Westchester County). Branch offices are located in New York, Connecticut, New Jersey, Pennsylvania, and Rhode Island.

KEY CONCEPTS

- Successful establishment of the requirements depends on the appropriate selection and involvement of the stakeholders.
- When establishing the requirements, it is important to involve people who:
  - Understand the business goals of the client or customer
  - Are potential users of the software or understand what users need
  - Will approve the software requirements or software project
  - Will determine the time and cost associated with providing a solution that satisfies the required (and negotiated) scope and quality
  - Can verify the requirements with respect to clarity, compatibility, completeness, consistency, and correctness
  - Can validate the requirements with respect to the business goals of the client or customer and needs of the users
  - Have the knowledge and skills to negotiate a contract that satisfies the expectations of both clients or customers and solution providers
  - Are knowledgeable about compliancy, legal, and other corporate issues that are important to the client or customer and to the solution provider

TERMINOLOGY

CIO: Chief information officer.

HBC: Hamilton Banking Corporation.

IT: Information technology.

Use cases: A technique used in software and systems engineering to capture the functional requirements of a system. Use cases describe the interaction between a primary actor and the software system. Actors exist outside the system being studied and take part in a sequence of activities in a dialogue with the system to achieve some goal. Actors may be end users, other systems, or hardware devices. Each use case is a complete series of events from the point of view of the actor. See Jacobson (1992) for the foundational definition of use cases. See Kulak and Guiney (2003) for a practical guide to use cases as a primary tool for eliciting requirements.

VP: Vice president.

The Case

SCENARIO

Susan Calloway and Georg Johansson are puzzled and irritated. They wonder why upper-level management would consider delaying the New Account Project one month to satisfy a request by the "newly minted" Corporate IT group at HBC. Robert Caldwell, who heads this new group, has asked for his Web Strategy Team to be given one month to review the project requirements with respect to corporate issues such as branding, compliancy, privacy, and security. (See Figure 2-1, which shows the HBC organizational chart.)

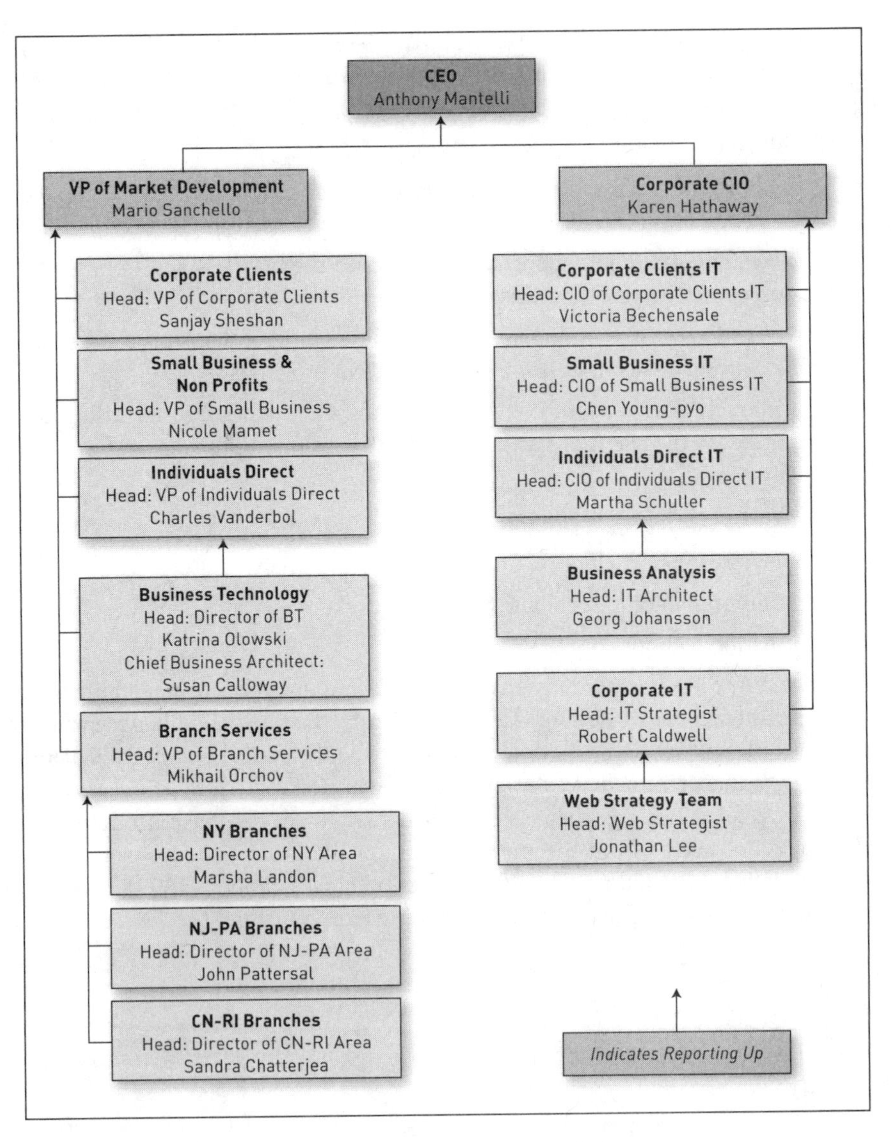

Figure 2–1: *HBC organizational chart*

Susan and Georg have managed the establishment of the requirements, including the initial sign-off on the project agreements by the stakeholders. They are anxious for the project to move forward into design. There are only ten months remaining for this tightly scheduled project. A slip of one month would incur not only the expense of the additional review but also other costs associated with the delay. Georg and Susan are worried that if the Web site enhancements (deliverables for the New Account Project) are not done on time, then the Individuals Direct business unit will not be able to meet its business goal to increase the number of new online accounts by 50 percent within two years. The market for Internet services to individuals is a high-priority business opportunity that would enable HBC to continue its record for steady growth.

As Georg and Susan reflect on the approach that they used to establish the requirements, Susan recalls, "Our approach worked well on previous Web-based IT projects. With a tight schedule, we barely had time to question the way we would establish the requirements. Besides, why should we have 'reinvented a wheel' that was successful in the past?"

Georg bemoans, "How were we to know that Corporate IT would be alive and 'chomping at the bit' to review business unit projects outside its immediate directive? I think that Robert Caldwell could do more good for HBC by reviewing and updating the corporate-level Web policies before becoming involved in unit-level projects."

Susan replies angrily, "We received a clear mandate from Katrina, Charles, and Martha that we are responsible for managing the project from beginning to end. I am surprised that they would give Robert's request consideration."

Georg agrees and then adds, "When Karen Hathaway speaks, the CIOs listen. I suppose Karen wants to establish the importance of her new Corporate IT group. But what should we have done differently? Perhaps we could have made better use of the extra time allocated in the schedule for the critical path . . . ."

Flashback to the Beginning of the Project

As experienced managers, Georg and Susan understood the importance of establishing the requirements. They had seen too many projects that went awry because the stakeholders had *not* established a common understanding of and agreement on their expectations for the scope and quality of the deliverables as well as the associated schedule (time) and budget (cost). Almost immediately, they agreed that the requirements would need to be established within about two months for the New Account Project to be completed in one year. From experience, they realized the importance of selecting a minimal number of stakeholders who could effectively determine the requirements and project agreements without becoming bogged down by "analysis paralysis" or endless dissension. They laughingly dubbed these the "necessary and sufficient" stakeholders.

To help them select appropriate stakeholders, they outlined the following kinds of stakeholders whom they thought were essential to establishing the requirements:

- People who will approve or audit the software project and its budget
- Users or people who can represent the user point of view

- People who can represent the software service provider or software developer point of view
- People who will manage the software project

In the past, the business units worked independently on their own IT projects and collaborated only when the projects involved corporate-wide business issues or opportunities. Georg and Susan understood that financial support for the project was coming from unit-level management. Charles Vanderbol (VP of Individuals Direct) and Martha Schuller (CIO of Individuals Direct IT) had announced that Susan and Georg would be directly responsible for managing the New Account Project. Susan and Georg expected little to no corporate-level involvement on this project.

Susan and Georg confirmed that Katrina Olowski, Charles Vanderbol, and Martha Schuller wanted to be involved in establishing the requirements, though Charles would most likely delegate the technical details to Katrina. In particular, Charles would validate the requirements with respect to the business objectives and keep an eye on the schedule and budget. Martha planned to oversee the development of the project agreements as well as the staffing on the development side of the project. Georg and Susan would assist Martha in establishing the project agreements and, of course, continually would report the project status to Charles. Katrina wanted to validate the scope of the requirements and the required software qualities. For this project, she intended to be less involved in auditing the schedule and budget and more involved as a backup technical manager.

On previous IT projects, Susan and Georg had observed that the branch managers and their staff have an excellent understanding of the needs of the bank's individual customers. The branches were also proactive in assessing and promoting the development of online banking services. Susan talked with Mikhail Orchov (VP of Branch Services) to determine whether his organization would be able and willing to represent the user's point of view in establishing the requirements. Mikhail enthusiastically offered the services of one of his regional branch directors.

Among the three directors, John Pattersal had the most recent and extensive experience with online services. Georg and Susan reasoned that current and relevant experience was a good indicator of a stakeholder's likely ability to contribute to their project. With this in mind, they decided that, of the three branch directors, John would probably be the most effective stakeholder. They planned to involve John in eliciting and verifying the requirements. Though his participation would be minimal, Susan and Georg thought that it was wise to keep Mikhail in the loop as a stakeholder. Mikhail would help "sell" the Web site to the branches in the future. He could also be involved in validating the requirements.

Likewise, Susan and Georg thought that marketing analysts who interface with customers would be best able to determine and validate the requirements. They scanned the resumes of senior marketing analysts within Individuals Direct and found Mary MacDonald, a senior analyst who headed up the requirements-gathering activity for a highly successful and visible Web project in the business unit. Susan was familiar with Mary's requirements work with customers and felt comfortable that Mary would be an asset in eliciting and validating the requirements for this project.

Because of the tight schedule for the project, Susan and Georg realized that the scope of the requirements would need to be controlled. Unlike many of the other marketing analysts, Mary MacDonald reportedly did not try to overload the requirements for a software project. She realistically knew that smaller-scoped projects generally had a greater chance for success. This was another reason why she would be good for the project. Since Georg and Susan had decided to limit the number of stakeholders who would participate in establishing the requirements, they did not consider adding other stakeholders to represent the user.

Both Georg and Susan had worked in the past with Tim Weber, a project engineer with the Business Analysis group within Individuals Direct IT. Tim had significant experience in leading the development of Web-based services and would be an ideal software development lead. They considered another project engineer with success in leading Web-based projects but chose Tim because his background included more work in estimating the time and cost of developing Web-based solutions. Georg was especially confident that Tim would be an excellent asset during the negotiation of the requirements and project deliverables. Tim's development team would create and verify the statement of software requirements.

To save time and money, Georg decided to serve as a stakeholder for both IT services/software development and project management. Susan would work with Georg on project management. Georg would lead the development of the time, staffing, and cost estimates associated with the scope of the requirements and the qualities that the project deliverables should satisfy.

In the end, Susan and Georg decided on the stakeholders shown in Table 2-9 to participate in establishing the software requirements for the New Account Project. Reflecting on their decision, they thought that they had some backup coverage for each stakeholder role in case a stakeholder had to leave the project for some unforeseen reason; but they knew that the coverage was not ideal. Susan and Georg consulted each "candidate" stakeholder individually to determine his or her interests and preferences for involvement in the project. Recognizing the excellent business opportunity that an improved Web site would offer and the visibility that the New Account Project would have within the Individuals Direct business unit and HBC, all the candidate stakeholders readily agreed to join the project.

Table 2–9: *Stakeholders Selected for New Account Project*

Software Project or Budget Approval and Audit	*User's Point of View*	*IT Services and Software Development*	*Software Project Management*
Charles Vanderbol (VP of Individuals Direct business unit) Katrina Olowski (director of Business Technology Group) Martha Schuller (CIO of Individuals Direct IT group)	Mikhail Orchov (VP of Branch Services) John Pattersal (director of NJ and PA branches) Mary MacDonald (senior marketing analyst for Individuals Direct business unit)	Tim Weber (lead project engineer for Business Analysis group) Georg Johansson*	Susan Calloway (chief business architect for Business Technology group) Georg Johansson* (IT architect for Business Analysis group)

* Georg Johansson represented two groups of stakeholders.

The stakeholders appreciated that Susan and Georg consulted their advice on how they should be involved, and even though they could not always attend all the scheduled meetings, the stakeholders provided the needed information in a timely manner and involved their own staffs in the requirements elicitation and validation processes. John Pattersal reported to his boss, Mikhail Orchov, "The new online features will make it much easier for our remote customers to open accounts. I appreciate the way that we have been involved in setting the requirements and am having fun with this project."

Subsequently, Tim Weber's Business Analysis project team produced a specification of the following aspects of the software system requirements:

- Business problem and purpose for the software to be developed
- The overall system context in which the new software features would be used
- Functional requirements including a set of use cases
- Requirements regarding nonfunctional software qualities including an evolution plan for future enhancement of the Web site
- Constraints and limitations associated with the use and development of the software

Meanwhile, Susan and Georg developed a software project plan that was reviewed and approved by the Business Technology and Business Analysis stakeholders. The stakeholders were aware of the tight, one-year schedule (which included establishing the requirements). They agreed that all the desired software features could not be developed in the first enhancement of the Web site, so they jointly developed a plan for releasing the features in successive versions of the Web site. The stakeholders thought the schedule for the first release of the Web site was doable but had minimal "extra" time allocated for the tasks on the **critical path** (a sequence of tasks in which the sum of the task completion times constitutes the time needed to complete a project). Georg and Susan had learned from experience to allocate some extra time, or **padding**, to the tasks on the critical path to allow for unexpected events that could impact the project schedule.

One week before the scheduled completion of the project agreements, Mary MacDonald had some questions regarding the way in which private information would be secured. In response to Mary's questions, Tim Weber replied that he would need to check with Pang Hwuang, who was the resident expert on Web-based privacy and security issues. Tim learned that Pang had moved to the Web Strategy Team within Corporate IT, a new group that had recently been created. Pang was on vacation and would not be available for a week. Tim told Georg that he would not be able to answer Mary's questions until Pang returned from vacation.

In addition, the stakeholders had found some errors while verifying and validating the requirements and, like Mary MacDonald, still had some unanswered questions. Therefore, Susan and Georg decided to use an additional week (from the extra time allocated for the critical path) to correct the errors and to find answers to the stakeholders' questions. They considered the fact that the number of errors and questions was minimal. Though they realized that the outstanding issues could probably be resolved while the project agreements were being finalized, Georg and Susan did not want the resolution of these issues or any other related issues to negatively impact the project agreements. They rationalized that it was best to take an extra week to resolve the requirements issues *before* finalizing the project agreements. Therefore, they decided to push back the finalization of the project agreements by one week.

Meanwhile, Tim's team diligently corrected the errors found in the requirements and had the corrections reviewed by the stakeholders. When Pang returned from vacation, he explained to Tim how privacy and security issues were typically handled for HBC Web sites. Hoping to impress his boss with his knowledge, Pang subsequently reported to Jonathan Lee that the New Account Project within the Individuals Direct business unit involved some interesting privacy and security issues that should be looked at across the company Web pages.

At the end of two months (which included one week of the extra time allocated in the project schedule), the software requirements and project agreements were finally complete. Susan and Georg were optimistic that the project could be finished within the next ten months. The upper-level managers Charles Vanderbol, Katrina Olowski, and Martha Schuller were pleased with the current project results.

Then Martha Schuller reported at a quarterly IT management meeting for the Corporate CIO and IT unit-level CIOs on the progress of the New Account Project. Robert Caldwell (IT strategist and head of the fledgling Corporate IT group) asked why he had not been consulted regarding this project, especially since his group had been chartered four months ago to oversee the development of HBC online services by the various business units and their IT support groups. He explained that he had hired Jonathan Lee to head up the Web Strategy Group that would provide the guidance and oversight needed to ensure that the company Web site satisfied standards being set by Corporate IT regarding branding, compliance, usability, and other corporate-wide business concerns.

Facing a wall of cold stares from the IT unit-level CIOs, Robert added defensively, "Six months ago you were eager to create a corporate-level group to establish and help implement IT policies to address issues that are important across the business units. The Web Strategy Group's input to any major Web site enhancement project is critical. Jonathan Lee and I should have been involved in establishing the project requirements. In fact, one of Jonathan's engineers was recently consulted regarding online privacy and security for the New Account Project."

After a lengthy pause, Martha Schuller replied, "We also decided that each business unit would handle its own enhancements to its Web pages in the period before the next corporate upgrade to the Web site. The New Account Project has followed the corporate-wide Web site policies set for the last major enhancement of the HBC Web site. The changes to the Individuals Direct Web pages are specific to the services that we would like to provide individuals online."

Martha continued, "I would be glad to provide Jonathan and you with copies of our requirements documents for your group to research ongoing Web site development issues.

I do not want to delay the New Account Project to address any new corporate policies that are currently under development. The cost of the delay and additional work will likely result in a budget overrun."

Considering that his group was still relatively new and that he wanted to be able to work productively with the IT unit-level CIOs, Robert said that he understood and had empathy for the budgetary and time constraints of the New Account Project. He requested that the Web Strategy Group be given just one month to review and make any needed changes to the requirements specification with respect to the development policies used for the last major release of the HBC Web site and to identify new issues that should be studied by his group. He looked to his boss, Karen Hathaway (the Corporate CIO), for support.

Everyone in the room took a deep breath and waited for Karen to speak.

Karen looked calmly around the group of CIOs and said, "Previously, we all agreed that it is important to look together at corporate-wide issues regarding the ongoing development of the company Web site. To implement this agreement, we decided to create a Corporate IT group that would study these issues and propose corporate policies and guidelines that we would review and approve via a majority vote."

She continued, "The issue is whether to delay an important project to enable a corporate-level review of the project requirements before they are released for design and implementation. Martha Schuller, Charles Vanderbol, and I will need to discuss this request further and make a decision together."

Karen then told Robert that she would need more information regarding the objectives to be achieved by the review as well as the estimated cost of the review. She asked her executive assistant, Jean, to set up a meeting with Martha and Charles as soon possible. Karen stated that Martha and Charles were welcome to invite any people whom they thought should be involved in the discussion, and then she moved onto the next item on her meeting agenda.

CASE PROBLEM

The New Account Project managers, Susan Calloway and Georg Johansson, were responsible for making a decision regarding the stakeholders for the project. They did not identify Robert Caldwell and Jonathan Lee, newcomers to the corporate-level management of IT Web development practices at HBC, as candidate stakeholders for their project. Later, Robert requested that the project be delayed by one month to allow his Web Strategy Team to review and possibly modify the requirements specification. The additional cost in resources and time needed for this review and the fact that one week of the project's extra time had already been used would likely preclude the completion of the project on schedule and within budget. The schedule slippage would further delay the timely achievement of Charles Vanderbol's goal for his business unit to increase the number of new online accounts. Charles Vanderbol, Karen Hathaway, and Martha Schuller must now make a decision regarding Robert's request.

Case Analysis

ANALYSIS ACTIVITY

Analysis Background

The case focuses on the following three problems and decisions:

- Which stakeholders should be involved in establishing the requirements for the New Account Project, and how should they be involved? (In the case, Susan and Georg made a decision regarding the solution to this problem.)
- What should be done when there are outstanding issues in establishing the requirements and only one week left to finalize the project agreements? (Georg and Susan decided upon a solution to this problem in the case.)
- How should Charles Vanderbol, Karen Hathaway, and Martha Schuller handle the request by Robert Caldwell to delay the New Account Project by one month to allow for a corporate-level review of the New Account Project requirements? (At the end of the case, no decision has yet been made.)

We'll analyze the first decision that Susan and Georg made by looking at the related PEAK inputs, solutions considered, and assumed risks. Then you can analyze the other two decisions on your own. The analysis questions should help to focus your analysis.

Decision 1 (Made by Susan and Georg)

(P) Problem: Which stakeholders should be involved in establishing the requirements for the New Account Project, and how should they be involved?

(E) Experience:

- Susan and Georg are experienced managers. They realize that it is necessary to minimize the number of stakeholders who work on establishing the requirements in order to complete the project agreements within two months.
- In the past, they observed that the business units usually work independently on their own IT projects with little to no involvement at the corporate level (also a knowledge element).
- From experience, they know that the branch managers have an excellent understanding of the online banking needs of individual clients (also a knowledge element).
- From having worked with Tim Weber, they know that he is a competent leader of Web-based projects and has significant experience in developing time and cost estimates for these types of projects.

(A) Assumptions:

- Georg and Susan assume that there will be no involvement at the corporate level on the New Account Project.

- They assume that they have identified all the types of stakeholders who should be represented in establishing the requirements.

(K) Knowledge:

- Susan and Georg know that the project must be completed within one year and that it is imperative that the requirements be established in a timely manner.
- They understand that they are responsible for managing the project from beginning to end and must make the decision regarding the stakeholders who will establish the requirements.
- They have received confirmation that the upper-level managers Charles Vanderbol, Katrina Olowsky, and Martha Schuller would like to participate in establishing the requirements.
- Having reviewed the resumes of the branch managers, they know that John Pattersal has the most recent and extensive experience with online banking.
- Having reviewed the resumes of senior marketing analysts within the Individuals Direct business unit, they identified Mary MacDonald as having led the requirements-gathering activity for a highly successful and recent Web-based project. Susan is familiar with Mary's work and is confident that Mary will be an asset in validating the requirements. In addition, Mary is known to be realistic about the scope for a software project.

Solution:

- Table 2-9 shows the candidate stakeholders that Susan and Georg selected. The table also indicates the point of view to be represented by each stakeholder. Based upon each stakeholder's interests and expectations, they planned for the stakeholders to be involved in the following requirements activities:
  - Charles Vanderbol: Validate the requirements with respect to the business goals. Oversee the schedule and budget.
  - Martha Schuller: Oversee the project agreements and staffing associated with the development side of the project.
  - Katrina Olowski: Validate the scope and quality requirements (focus on technical aspects of project).
  - Mikhail Orchov: Validate the requirements, and sell the new Web site to the branches.
  - John Pattersal: Elicit and validate the requirements.
  - Mary MacDonald: Elicit and validate the requirements.
  - Tim Weber: Lead the development team that would create and verify the requirements specification. Help in estimating the time, resources, and cost associated with the required scope and quality.

  - Susan Calloway and Georg Johansson: Manage the establishment of the requirements and assist Martha Schuller in creating the project agreements.
  - Georg Johansson: Lead the effort to estimate the time, resources, and cost associated with the required scope and quality.
- These are some alternative stakeholders that Susan and Georg considered:
  - Two other branch managers. They decided upon John Pattersal because he had the most recent and extensive experience in online banking.
  - The other senior marketing analysts in the Individuals Direct business unit. They decided upon Mary MacDonald because of her experience in leading the requirements elicitation for another Web-based project and because of Susan's familiarity with Mary's client work.
  - Another project engineer in the Business Analysis group of Individuals Direct IT with success in leading Web-based development projects. They decided upon Tim because of his experience in developing time and cost estimates for Web-based development projects.

Assumed Risk:

- Since the number of stakeholders for each role is small, there is a risk that one or more stakeholders may drop out of the project with the consequence that the remaining stakeholders may not be able to establish the requirements on time. (Georg and Susan considered this risk and provided some backup coverage for each activity. But the coverage is minimal.)
- There is a risk that the stakeholders selected by Susan and Georg do not represent all the types of stakeholders who should be involved and that an unidentified stakeholder who wants or needs to be involved in establishing the requirements and who has the authority to do so may later delay or stop the project. (In particular, their assumption that there will be no corporate-level involvement in this project led them to ignore this potential type of stakeholder. Their assumption turned out to be wrong, and corporate-level stakeholders did appear later and want to be involved in the project. It is yet to be decided whether the project will be delayed. Are there any other types of stakeholders who they should have considered?)
- There is a risk that the selected stakeholders do not, in fact, have the necessary experience or skills to perform their roles appropriately and that the requirements will not be established on time or that the resulting requirements will not express what is actually needed to satisfy the business goals.
- Are there other risks associated with the decision made by Susan and Georg or with the alternative stakeholders that they considered?

Analysis Questions

1. What was the problem that Georg and Susan faced one week before the completion of the project agreements? What decision did they need to make?
2. In addition to the problem, what were the other PEAK inputs that Susan and Georg used to make this decision?
3. What solutions did they consider? What are the risks associated with each solution?
4. What effect did this decision have on the problem concerning unidentified stakeholders that occurred later in the project?
5. Why do you think that Susan and Georg did not consider Robert Caldwell (from Corporate IT) and Jonathan Lee (from the Web Strategy Team) as candidate stakeholders for establishing the requirements?
6. What were the ramifications of not considering Robert Caldwell and Jonathan Lee as potential stakeholders for the project? What do you think could have been done differently to avoid this from happening?
7. What decision must be made by the upper-level management for the New Account Project?
   - What are the PEAK inputs for making this decision?
   - What are the potential solutions for this decision and the risks associated with each solution?
   - How might this decision impact the way other IT projects are handled by the HBC business units and their IT support groups in the future?
8. What decision would you make regarding Robert Caldwell's request, and why? What information, other than that provided in the case, would you like to make this decision?
9. Why might the decision makers for Robert Caldwell's request need to include the VP of Market Development, Mario Sanchello, or the other VPs of business units? (Hint: Consider related issues that might concern all HBC business units.)
10. What are some ways to reduce the risks associated with selecting and involving stakeholders in establishing requirements?
11. Review the key concepts listed at the beginning of this case. Now that you have read the case, are there others that you would include?

DISCUSSION

In general, the identification and selection of the stakeholders for this project was timely and effective. One potential flaw in the selection of stakeholders to help in establishing the requirements occurred when new project stakeholders "identified themselves" after the final review of the software requirements for the project. One of these new corporate-level stakeholders has requested a delay in the project that would be costly if upper-level management grants the request. This new stakeholder may or may not be able to "improve" the requirements.

The assumption that there would be no corporate-level involvement resulted in a decision to not consider stakeholders from the new Corporate IT group and Web Strategy Team. Likewise, the software project managers, Susan and Georg, assumed that they had sufficient knowledge to select the stakeholders who would be candidates for establishing the requirements. They might have reduced the risk that their assumptions were faulty by asking upper-level management as well as the other project stakeholders to review the list of candidate stakeholders and to suggest additional people who should be considered.

The case also presents the problem of allocating sufficient time to handle feedback from the verification and validation of requirements. The time scheduled for the verification and validation of the requirements was not sufficient. The time interval needed to correct errors and handle questions resulting from the review of the requirements overlapped with the week scheduled for the completion of the project agreements. Fortunately, in this case, the software project managers were able to add a week to the establishment of the requirements by using some of the extra time allocated to the project. But unfortunately, the project now has less "spare" time to handle other unexpected events that may arise in the future.

Lastly, this case raises issues regarding the corporate-level management of IT projects across independent business units. The decision to be made by upper-level management regarding the review of requirements for software projects that are "internal" to a business unit relates to these issues. In particular, the new corporate-wide focus on Web-based services highlights the need for policies regarding Web software projects to be undertaken within as well as across the business units.

CONCLUSIONS

Despite schedule and budget pressures, the software project managers decided upon a set of stakeholders who worked together effectively to establish the requirements for the New Account Project. The case problem involved the process that the software project managers used to make their decision regarding the selection of candidate stakeholders. They did not adequately consider the risks associated with their assumptions and did not have their decision reviewed by people who might have been able to find potential problems associated with their list of candidate stakeholders.

KEY IDEAS TO REMEMBER

- Selecting appropriate stakeholders for establishing software project requirements is critical.
- The appropriate involvement of stakeholders increases the likelihood that acceptable requirements will be established on time and within budget.

- Consulting upper-level management, people who are experienced in stakeholder selection within an organization, and other software project stakeholders helps ensure that appropriate stakeholders are identified and involved in an effective way.

CASE STUDY

On Time, Within Budget, but Wrong

Directions

When reading this case study, focus on the activities related to eliciting, verifying, and validating the requirements for a software project. Note how the software project managers handle requests to change the requirements. Identify issues associated with identifying and selecting the appropriate functional requirements and software quality attributes.

Case Summary

DESCRIPTION

NavEngineering specializes in navigational systems for the DoD. NavEngineering wants to leverage its global positioning system (GPS) technology and software assets in the commercial marketplace. Management has proposed a joint venture with Signals & Systems (S&S), a company that develops radio frequency identification (RFID) tracking systems for the shipping industry. The joint venture involves the development of a GPS-RFID system to enable the secure and reliable location and tracking of packages, containers, or other goods being transported. S&S has identified target customers who are excited about the product idea and are interested in field-testing the first version of the product. The predicted time to market for this product is 18 months. Software will be a primary component of the new product. The case scenario involves product development that is on time, within budget, but not what the customers in the field test group ultimately want.

CASE STUDY OBJECTIVES

After reading the case study, you will be able to do the following:

- Understand the importance of the following decisions in eliciting the requirements:
  - Which software quality attributes are important to the business needs and goals of the client or customer?

  - How can requirements regarding software quality attributes be verified and validated?
  - When and why should the evolution of the software be thought about and planned when establishing the requirements?
  - What risks are associated with the decisions made about the requirements, and how should they be handled?
- Identify the activities by which the organization elicited, verified, and validated the requirements.
- Identify the approach that the software project managers used to handle requests to change the requirements.
- Explain the problems that occurred in the case scenario, the causes of the problems, and ways to reduce the likelihood that similar problems will occur in other software projects. Relate these to the decisions faced by project stakeholders.

SUBJECTS COVERED

Decision making, functional requirements, managing requirements change and scope, nonfunctional requirements, requirements elicitation, requirements verification, requirements validation, software evolution, and software quality attributes

SETTING

The setting encompasses two privately held companies in the San Francisco Bay Area of California: NavEngineering in San Ramon and S&S in Santa Clara. NavEngineering develops GPS-based GIS systems for the DoD, and S&S develops RFID systems for the shipping industry.

TERMINOLOGY

DoD: Department of Defense.

Geographical Information System (GIS): Computer-based systems that are used to store and manipulate geographic information. See Aronoff (1989) for a foundational discussion of geographical information systems.

Geographical Navigational Satellite System (GNSS): A satellite system that is used to pinpoint the geographic location of a user's receiver anywhere in the world. Two GNSS systems are currently operational: the United States' Global Positioning System (GPS) and the Russian Federation's Global Orbiting Navigation Satellite System (GLONASS). A third, Europe's Galileo, is due to be fully operational in 2013. Each of the GNSS systems employs a constellation of orbiting satellites working in conjunction with a network of ground stations (SearchNetworking.com GNSS; British National Science Center 2008).

Global Positioning System (GPS): A "constellation" of at least 24 well-spaced satellites that orbit Earth and make it possible for GPS receivers to determine their geographic location, direction, and time. The location accuracy is anywhere from 100 to 15 meters for most equipment. Accuracy can be pinpointed to within one meter with special military-approved equipment (SearchMobileComputing).

Radio Frequency Identification (RFID): A method of identifying unique items using radio waves. Typically, a reading device communicates with a tag, which holds digital information in a microchip (RFID Journal).

Selective availability (SA): A DoD program that controls the accuracy of pseudorange measurements, degrading the signal available to nonqualified receivers by dithering the time and ephemeris data provided in the navigation message (National Park Service).

The United States removed SA on May 1, 2000, and currently has the capability to reintroduce the feature (Leopold 2000).

Software quality: The degree to which the software exhibits a desired combination of attributes (IEEE Std. 1061-1998; ISO/IEC Std. 9126-1:2001).

Software quality attributes: Characteristics that the software should exhibit. Some examples are functionality, modifiability, performance, reliability, security, and usability. See Barbacci et al. (1995) for a foundational definition of software quality attributes.

Note that functionality is a quality attribute that describes what the software is supposed to do. Nonfunctional quality attributes (such as performance and security) impose constraints on the design and implementation of software systems. Some practitioners refer to specifications regarding software quality attributes as quality of service (QoS) requirements. A requirements statement about a software quality attribute describes the degree (or the way in which) a particular attribute is to be achieved.

Software release plan: A description of how the software and its requirements are expected or likely to change over the life of the software. A product release plan outlines the functional requirements and nonfunctional requirements to be satisfied by each release of the software (Ruhe and Saliu 2005).

REFERENCES

See Finkenzeller (2003) and Garfinkel and Rosenberg (2005) for information about RFID technology and its use. Borck (2006) addresses RFID interoperability, which is important for the evolution of commercial products.

Lomer (2007) provides information to support the design of navigational systems that use both Galileo and GPS signals. For a comparison of Galileo, GLONASS, and NAVSTAR (U.S. constellation of navigational satellites), read Thurston (2002). Peruse *Proceedings of the IEEE International Conference on RFID* for a review of current GPS research.

The Case

SCENARIO

Having just talked with Sharon McPherson (the requirements and customer relations manager for the NavS&S Project) using his hands-free cell phone, Daniel Choi (general manager for the NavS&S Project) drove north along Interstate Route 680 toward San Ramon, California. He watched the fog blanket the East Bay as he reflected on his conversation with Sharon and on his ill-fated vacation plans.

After countless hours spent managing the NavS&S Project (a joint venture between NavEngineering and S&S), Daniel had been relieved when the new SecureLocTracker product was sent to the field for validation by a group of selected customers called the Customer Field Test Group. He had planned to use a few days of vacation to take his sailboat, the Zephyr, out for a jaunt in the bay. After hearing Sharon's report on the feedback from the Customer Field Test Group, Daniel grimaced and said to himself, "I might as well say goodbye to my vacation plans. This problem is too big to ignore for a few days. *C'est la vie!*"

As Sharon had explained to Daniel, the customers were pleased with most of the new product features; however, some of the customers had clearly expressed their disappointment with the product's ability to accurately and reliably determine difficult-to-locate geographical positions around the world. In particular, they said that they had doubts about the product's ability to handle locations in higher latitudes, city centers, and mountainous regions. The customers were also surprised that the product does not support the integration of GPS signals (from the U.S. NAVSTAR satellite system) and Galileo signals (to be sent from the European navigational satellite system under development) to enable more accurate and reliable positioning.

Daniel recalled that the Requirements Team had involved the customers in gathering and validating the requirements. But, as he and Sharon had discussed on the phone, maybe the team had incorrectly assumed that the existing GPS technology would be sufficient for the future of the product. The more he thought about it, Robert wondered whether the team had considered the Galileo satellite system being developed by the European Commission, European Space Agency, and private companies. In fact, he surmised that the team had focused solely on performance and security (quality attributes that had been identified as high priority by the Customer Field Test Group) without considering evolvability (the ability to easily change the product over time to satisfy new requirements).

Taking the exit for San Ramon, Daniel drove into the hills where the NavEngineering laboratories are located. His thoughts rolled back in time to the start of the project as he remembered the activities involving the elicitation of the requirements and the subsequent design and implementation of the product. Daniel recalled that the focus had been on the software because the project primarily involved developing software to integrate existing GPS and RFID technology into one system. Maybe they had not focused enough on the system that integrated both hardware and software components.

Flashback to the Start of the Project

Sharon McPherson and Daniel Choi are marketing executives with S&S and NavEngineering, respectively. In addition to their marketing work, they both had extensive experience in engineering and project management. They had carefully worked through the business issues. The integration of NavEngineering's high-performance GPS systems with S&S's secure RFID tracking systems was to provide a cost-effective solution for the real-time tracking of packages and containers. The shipping industry needed a solution to the security and reliability problems that plagued the transportation of goods worldwide. NavEngineering was looking to expand its business into the commercial marketplace, and S&S sought new product lines to leverage its engineering expertise. The joint venture, called the NavS&S Project, appeared to be an excellent business opportunity for both stakeholders. Some executives predicted a merger of the two companies in the future.

Sharon and Daniel provided general management for the project. Sharon managed the joint venture's relationship with a customer user group that will field test and provide feedback on SecureLocTracker, the product to be designed and implemented by the product development teams. She also managed the team to establish the product requirements, including both system and software requirements. Daniel managed the interface between the two companies and provided upper-level project management. He was also responsible for developing the overall project management plan. Through their work on the proposal for the joint venture, Daniel and Sharon had established effective communication and planning strategies. Sharon and Daniel had shared the goal to work together as a team to guide the project to success. (Figure 2-2 shows the NavS&S Project organization.)

Starting with the proposal for the NavS&S Project, the Requirements Team identified the various project stakeholders. Michael Long, the lead of the Requirements Team, assigned team members to serve as points of contact for the various stakeholders. Michael provided the interface to Sharon and Daniel (the executive project managers). The team outlined processes for eliciting, verifying, and validating the system and software requirements. Since the developers at both companies as well as the target customers were comfortable with use case diagrams, the team decided to apply this technique to help elicit and document the functional requirements. One of the Requirements Team members, Martina Costilla, had used a scenario-based approach in graduate school to characterize the requirements of software systems. She explained that these scenarios would help drive the development of a software architecture that would best satisfy the software quality requirements (Bass et al. 2001). The development lead of the Software Development Team, Sanson Chen, offered to work with Martina on the definition of scenarios for the target software quality attributes.

As a preliminary step in eliciting the requirements, the Requirements Team defined the environment and context in which the SecureLocTracker system would be used.

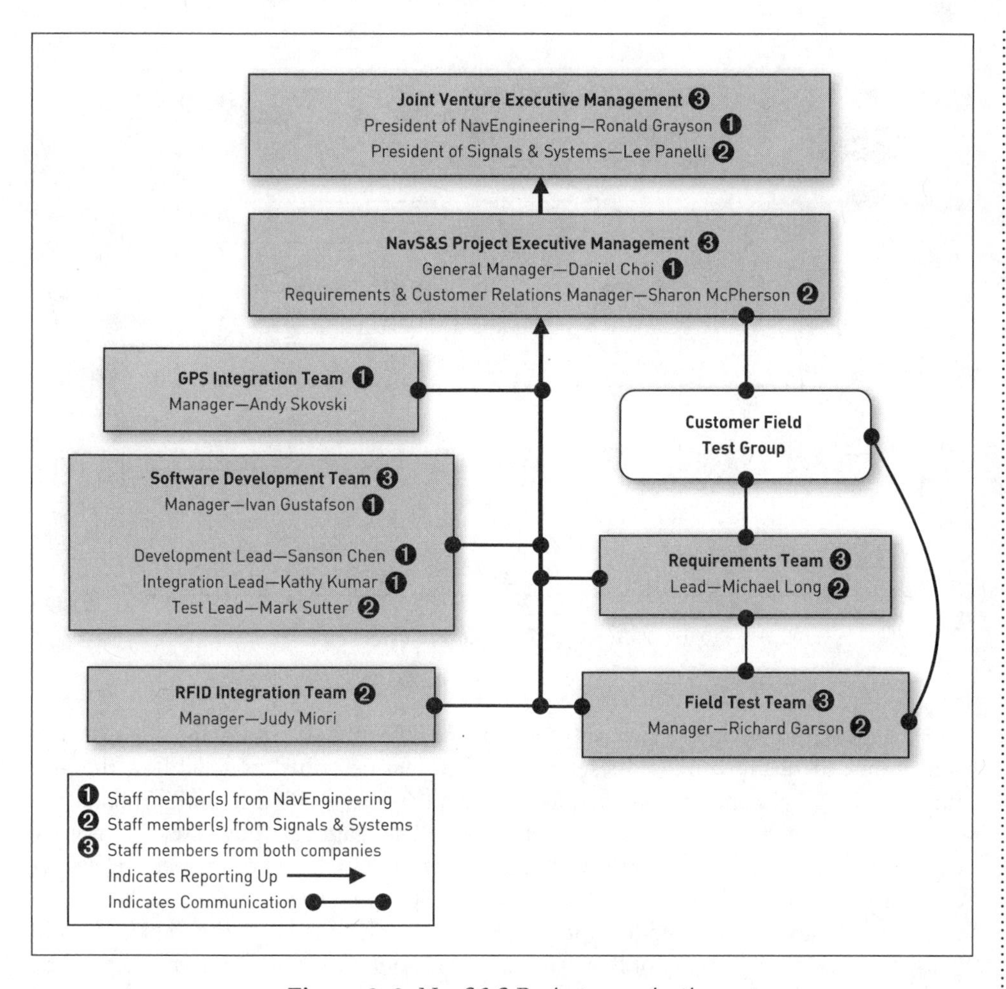

Figure 2–2: *NavS&S Project organization*

(Figure 2-3 shows the context diagram for the SecureLocTracker system.) At the time, Daniel had noted the Software Development Team's question as to whether there would be any problems with interference between the GPS and RFID signals. The software engineers at NavEngineering had seen how long it took to design a GPS receiver that could be integrated with a wireless cellular device (a device whose radio signals could interfere with the GPS radio signals). The software engineers wanted to known whether the GPS receivers and RFID transponders would need modification. They did not want the project to be delayed because of unexpected problems with the hardware components.

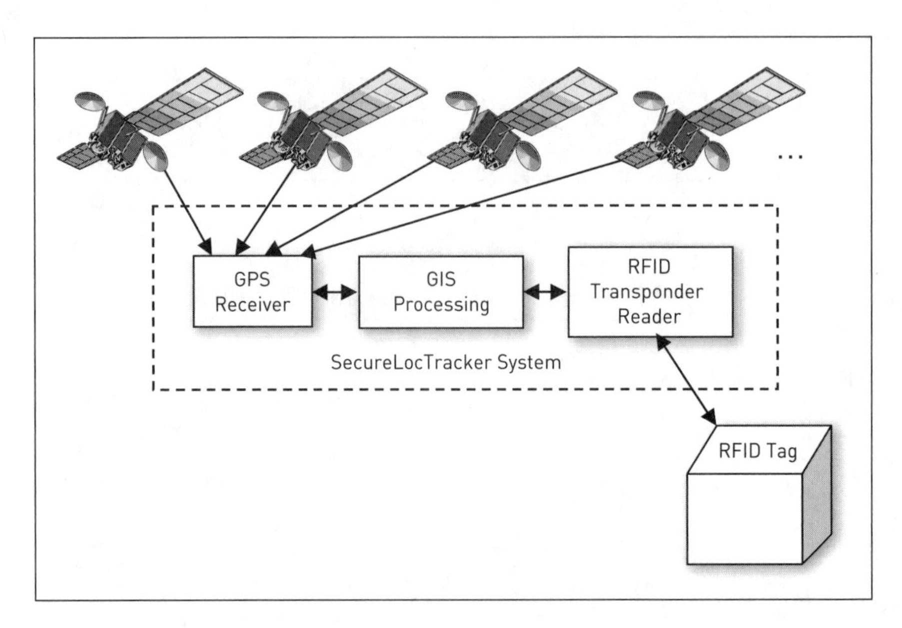

Figure 2–3: *SecureLocTracker system context*

Through extensive interviews with the Customer Field Test Group and the development teams, the team composed a set of use cases that described in detail how the user and other external components such as the satellites and RFID tags within containers would interact with the SecureLocTracker system. The team carefully considered usage scenarios that focused on the target qualities: interoperability, performance, reliability, reusability, security, and usability. They developed precise specifications based on concrete events that were expected to happen within the context in which the software would be used. Table 2-10 presents only a sample of the nonfunctional requirements that the Requirements Team elicited with respect to the business objectives for the project.

Table 2–10: *Sample of the Nonfunctional Requirements*

Business Objective	*Software Quality Attribute*	*Nonfunctional Requirement (Quality Attribute Scenario)*
B1.1 Conform to commercial communication protocols.	Interoperability	NF1.2 SecureLocTracker shall conform to Gen2, the EPCglobal Class-1 Generation-2 UHF RFID Protocol for Communications.

Table 2–10: *Sample of the Nonfunctional Requirements (Continued)*

Business Objective	*Software Quality Attribute*	*Nonfunctional Requirement (Quality Attribute Scenario)*
B2.1 Guarantee timely location and tracking service.	Performance	NF2.3 SecureLocTracker processing of location and tracking data should take no longer than: • X seconds without Selective Availability to yield horizontal accuracy within 1–15 meters. • Y seconds with differential code positioning to yield horizontal accuracy within 1–5 meters.
B3.2 Isolate SecureLocTracker system (including the RFID tags) from external or internal interference.	Performance	NF3.1 Noninterference with SecureLocTracker hardware components or devices: • External signals and distractions from devices (e.g., cell phone signals) shall not interfere with the operation of SecureLocTracker hardware components or devices, including RFID tags. • The SecureLocTracker hardware components or devices shall not interfere with the operation of each other. See the details outlined in the use case "Non-interference from External Signals and Devices."
B4.1 Maximize reuse of NavEngineering GPS and S&S RFID technologies.	Reusability	NF4.1 SecureLocTracker shall incorporate existing NavEngineering GPS and S&S RFID hardware components.
B5.1 Guarantee secured use of location and tracking service.	Security	NF5.1 Access to the SecureLocTracker services shall be password protected. See the use case "Access to Service."
B5.2 Protect data stored in RFID tags from malicious, fraudulent, or unauthorized access.	Security	NF5.2 Data stored in RFID tags shall be encrypted using a stream cipher approach.
B5.3 Ensure authenticity of data accessed from RFID tags.	Security	NF5.3 Data stored in RFID tags shall be authenticated using a tag authentication approach.

The nonfunctional requirement NF3.1 involved the operation of the SecureLocTracker hardware components without interference from external or internal signals or devices. Part of this requirement addressed the concerns raised by the Software Development Team regarding any potential interference between the GPS receivers and RFID transponders (hardware devices to be integrated into the SecureLocTracker system).

At the time, Daniel commented to Sharon, "The Software Development Team is concerned about NF3.1. The schedule for this project is based on the assumption that existing hardware will be used with little to no modification. I wish that we would have had time to verify the existing hardware's ability to satisfy NF3.1 before we set the project schedule. I certainly hope that this requirement does not cause problems in the future." (Fortunately, the electronics engineers had thoroughly studied the interference issue and had designed the GPS receivers to handle any potential interference from other devices in the area.)

The Requirements Team discussed the business goal to integrate the latest GPS and RFID information system technologies developed by NavEngineering and S&S into the SecureLocTracker product. The stakeholders understood that the project would involve integrating existing hardware with some new and existing software. The Customer Field Test Group, which consisted of current users of S&S RFID systems, were interested in access to real-time location data. They thought the idea to incorporate GPS data would increase their tracking capabilities. Location data that would be accurate within 15 meters seemed adequate. The Customer Field Test Group was particularly concerned about security issues and spent a significant amount of time defining the security requirements.

Noticing that the Customer Field Test Group did not spend much time discussing positional accuracy or hard-to-locate positions within indoor environments, urban canyons, or mountainous regions, Sharon said to Daniel, "The Customer Field Test Group does not seem to be concerned about positional accuracy. I assume that this is because of their familiarity with the performance of NavEngineering GPS systems. They are focused on security issues."

Daniel replied, "The stakeholders know that the new product will integrate our current GPS and RFID devices. I think this is why they are looking at integration and access issues such as security."

Within four months, the system and software requirements were specified. Then the Requirements Team verified and validated the requirements. They performed walkthroughs of the use cases and inspections of the quality attribute scenarios. Several members of the Requirements Team applied Rate Monotonic Analysis (RMA), a quantitative technique to analyze the ability of the target processing system to handle the task load of software modules needed to receive and process the location and tracking data in real time. See Klein et al. (1993) for a practical guide developed by the Software Engineering Institute to analyze real-time systems using RMA.

The Software Development Team helped by benchmarking existing GPS and RFID interface and processing software that were similar to software functions that would be needed. The development team created prototypes of new software functions to be developed and analyzed their execution-time characteristics. By the time the requirements were established, the Requirements Team was confident that the requirements would direct the development of a product to meet the stakeholders' expectations regarding scope (requirements), quality, schedule, and budget.

The development of the software and its integration with hardware took place with few surprises. The test engineers worked diligently to find bugs in the new product before handing it over to the Field Test Team. The Field Test Team had already prepared some preliminary user documentation and had briefed the customers on the functionality in the new product. The project was on schedule and within budget when the Field Test Team delivered the first release of the product to the target customers for the field test.

Daniel confided to Sharon, "Though the NavS&S Project is progressing well, I have this feeling that we missed something in establishing the requirements."

Sharon replied in jest, "If Murphy's Law applies to product development, a glitch will occur!" Then more seriously she said, "I think that we covered our bases well."

More than a year passed from the elicitation of the requirements to the field test. Sharon McPherson kept the Customer Field Test Group informed about the status of the product development. But other than status information and a few updates on new product features, there was little communication with the customers until the field test. The NavS&S Project members were anxious to receive the feedback from the Customer Field Test Group.

During the past year, several of the customers had been exploring the new Galileo satellite system that was being developed in Europe to complement GPS-based location techniques. Though they had not been concerned about positional accuracy when the requirements were established, they could now envision how they would use the increased accuracy that could be achieved by using GPS and Galileo data in combination. The customers were also concerned about the SecureLocTracker's ability to handle difficult-to-locate positions, especially places in northern latitudes (an issue of particular concern to Northern European customers).

In particular, the customers liked the idea that a dual GPS-Galileo system could provide better reliability. If the DoD decided to apply selective availability for whatever reason or if the data from either system was unavailable or degraded, backup calculations and corrections could be done more easily by having access to either GPS or Galileo data. The customers reported that by not having the ability to combine multiple signals from different navigational satellite technologies, the SecureLocTracker system would have a limited life. In addition to the European Galileo system, some of the customers were studying the Russian Global Navigation Satellite System (GLONASS) as well as the Japanese Quazi-Zenith Satellite System (QZSS), which is under development. The customers planned to explore other location-tracking systems that were to come on the market in the next six months before making their product selections.

Back to the Present

Now cloistered in his office, Daniel called back Sharon and explained, "I've been thinking. We need to determine how difficult it would be to evolve the SecureLocTracker product to handle multiple signals from different navigational satellite systems."

Sharon quickly responded, "Did you hear that the President just approved the recommendation that GPS III satellites procured in the future will not support selective availability? It appears as though this aspect of reliability will not be a concern" (U.S. Department of Defense 2007).

She continued, "As we discussed earlier, I think that the first release of the product has a viable market position today. But how long will this position last? I think we need a study group to help us determine how difficult it would be to evolve the product to incorporate new technologies on the horizon for both geophysical-based location and RFID-based tracking."

Daniel replied, "I agree, though the customers in the Customer Field Test Group seem to think that the product will soon be obsolete. How about asking the heads of the project teams to participate in the study group? We will also need to develop a proposal for the CEOs as to how to go forward with the SecureLocTracker product. We have our work cut out for us."

"And just when you thought that you could take the Zephyr out for a sail. Maybe next year . . . ," Sharon commiserated.

Along with a report of the results of the product field test, Sharon and Daniel are responsible for presenting to the company CEOs a proposal for how to proceed with the SecureLocTracker product. They think that the study group can help them develop a solution to the problem relating to the field test results. To start, they need more information before they can formulate a reasonable proposal.

What directives should Daniel and Sharon give to the study group?

CASE PROBLEM

A joint project team, from NavEngineering and S&S, has developed a new location and tracking system for the shipping industry. The software development was completed on schedule and within budget. The NavS&S Field Test Team has delivered the product for field tests at several key customers. The customers are disappointed that the product does not integrate multiple geophysical location technologies such as GPS and Galileo. The customers think that the system would be more reliable by having the ability to use data from different navigational satellite systems and would provide more accurate location information by combining data from multiple signals. The managers of the NavS&S project must now decide what to do in response to the feedback received from the key customers.

Case Analysis

ANALYSIS ACTIVITY

Analysis Questions

1. How did the NavS&S Requirements Team decide to focus solely on GPS signals rather than on a combination of navigation signals from satellites managed by different countries?
   - What were the PEAK inputs?
   - What alternative solutions were considered (if any)? Was the use of the Galileo technology considered? If not, why not?
   - What risks were associated with the solutions considered?
2. Which nonfunctional software qualities were specified in the software requirements? What technique did the Requirements Team use to specify these requirements? Why did they use this technique?
3. To what degree did the Requirements Team discuss and make plans regarding the evolution of the location and tracking product over its lifetime? How did this impact the resulting product and project outcomes?
4. To what extent did the Software Development Team consider product evolution when making software design and implementation decisions? How did this impact the resulting product and project outcomes?
5. Exactly what problem do the managers of the NavS&S project now face?
6. What information do you need to find a solution to this problem?
   - What are the PEAK inputs?
   - What are some alternative solutions?
   - What are the risks associated with these solutions?
7. What process improvements would you make to help prevent a similar problem from occurring in the future?
8. What key concepts have you identified for this case study?

2.4 Summary

The chapter focused on the following activities for managing requirements in the context of decision making for software projects. The asterisk indicates those activities involved in establishing the requirements.

- Eliciting and stating the requirements (specification)*
- Verifying and validating the requirements*
- Negotiating and contracting the requirements and project agreements*
- Managing requirements change and scope
- Validating software deliverables with respect to their requirements

The first case study, "The New Account Project at HBC," highlighted the importance of evaluating decisions about the appropriate stakeholders to establish the requirements for a software project and what their roles should be. The second case study, "On Time, Within Budget, but Wrong," focused on making decisions regarding the software quality attributes and other constraints that the software should satisfy. The case study also demonstrated the need to plan for the evolution of software products whose core assets are intended to be reused across similar products and applications.

Managing requirements does not end with their establishment. Software project managers must manage requirements change and scope to enable software projects to be completed on time, to be completed within budget, and to achieve their objectives. The highpoint of a software development project is the validation of the software with respect to the requirements.

Managing requirements, and therefore evaluating and making decisions about requirements, ends when the software is retired.

Chapter 3

Managing Estimates

3.1 Chapter Objectives

After reading and thinking about the concepts and case studies presented in this chapter, you will be able to do the following:

- Understand what estimation is and what it is not
- Understand when to estimate
- Understand the major approaches of estimation that can be used
- Understand what contributes to an estimation model and its successful use
- Identify key problems with estimation
- Understand key decisions to make with estimation
- Understand how to choose an approach to estimation

3.2 Context

This chapter will help you identify problems with estimation and ways to improve the estimation processes that you use. It will help you see how to gather information and apply that information to improve estimates in the future. Estimation should not be a black art (McConnell 2006) but should become a systematic, disciplined practice that you can use to better support your software development efforts. Estimation is *sometimes* considered as something that is done to get managers off one's back or to fill out the paperwork to start a project. We view estimation and evaluating decisions about estimates as essential components of successful software project management.

To begin our discussion of estimation, we need to define the concept of an estimate. Estimates are the information we use to evaluate the cost of a future decision. The following are some commonly used definitions for estimate and estimation:

Estimate: An approximate calculation of quantity, degree, or worth.

Estimate: A judgment of the qualities of something or somebody (Princeton University).

Estimation: The prediction of the quantitative result. It is usually applied to project costs, resources, and durations (Wideman).

Most of these definitions are similar statements about what is needed to make a best guess at a future value. Here we paraphrase the last definition to relate it more directly to software estimation:

Software estimate: An approximate calculation of the scope, time, quality, and cost of a software product (the four dimensions of project stakeholder concern).

The last definition works well for the models used in the book and for the purpose of managing estimates with respect to stakeholder expectations. See Chapter 9, "Managing Stakeholder Expectations," for further information on how to manage the four dimensions of stakeholder expectation.

So, what do software project managers do to manage estimates? People who manage estimates perform activities such as the following:

- Understanding requirements
- Conceptually designing a solution
- Performing element-wise decomposition (divide)
- Allocating resources from the bottom-up (conquer)
- Allocating overhead
- Estimating construction
- Estimating change management

Table 3-1 describes the activities to be performed when managing estimates in detail. Study the table, and think of any other activities that you may have performed when managing estimates.

Table 3–1: *Descriptions of Activities in Managing Estimates*

Activity	*Description of Activity*
Understanding requirements	**Definition:** Process of understanding the problem in sufficient detail to scope all the pieces needed. **Target outcome:** A sufficient understanding that the problem can be stated and the majority of the stakeholders believe the statement covers the problem.
Conceptually designing a solution	**Definition:** A solution that is sufficiently detailed to allow for partitioning the problem into smaller pieces, but not so detailed as to make commitments to a solution that cannot be changed. Might require prototypes to understand the major issues with a solution. **Target outcome:** Sufficient understanding of "a solution" that resources can be allocated to a problem.
Performing element-wise decomposition (divide)	**Definition:** Breaking down a problem into key parts that can be understood and estimated. **Target outcome:** A basic "work breakdown" structure that can be used for understanding dependencies and also relationships between logical elements of a solution.
Allocating resources from the bottom-up (conquer)	**Definition:** The assignment of resource needs for each component in a solution. **Target outcome:** All components are allocated a place in the solution and are understood in relation to other components in the system. The result is a relational hierarchy of how the system can be built.
Allocating overhead	**Definition:** The allocation of the resources needed to manage the overall development process for this project. This typically would include management cost and reserves and the cost of infrastructure modifications needed to support the project. **Target outcome:** The additional indirect costs associated with the project are understood and allocated to the project.

Continues

Table 3–1: *Descriptions of Activities in Managing Estimates (Continued)*

Activity	*Description of Activity*
Estimating construction	**Definition:** Creation of an estimate "plan" in which all the components of an estimate are identified, defined, and assigned values. **Target outcome:** All the values for the elements of the estimate are entered into the plan. The assumptions and risks associated with the decisions about estimates are identified.
Estimating change management	**Definition:** Changes to the estimate are tracked as knowledge is gained and assumptions are verified or decisions are invalidated. The changes are made, and new estimate components are created. **Target outcome:** An estimate that accurately reflects what is known in time and is usable as a model for future similar projects.

When performing the activities of managing estimates, you may need to consider multiple dimensions of stakeholder expectation at the same time. In other words, you may have to estimate aspects of projects that are related but not the same, such as scope versus quality or budget (cost) versus schedule (time). Trade-offs of the different dimensions of stakeholder expectation makes estimation decisions difficult and complicated.

Another helpful approach when managing estimates is to view estimates as snapshots in time. As soon as you have more information, you should consider updating your estimates. Even global positioning systems acquire information on a regular basis to update their estimates. With his famous "cone of uncertainty," McConnell (2006) explained that the only way to increase "certainty" in estimation is to move in time toward the solution. As McConnell suggested, you cannot improve the estimate by staying with your current knowledge. Likewise, Cohn (2005) stated that trying harder at the same point may actually reduce the value of your estimate. Therefore, we propose that you estimate early and often.

Figure 3-1 is a modification of McConnell's traditional "cone of uncertainty" diagram. It expands the cone to include the ideas of scope and quality so that all four dimensions of stakeholder expectation for projects are discussed.

Many practices can help narrow the cone and make estimation easier. Historical data, Wideband Delphi (to bring in experience), and even algorithmic models (estimation tools) can all help improve your estimates.

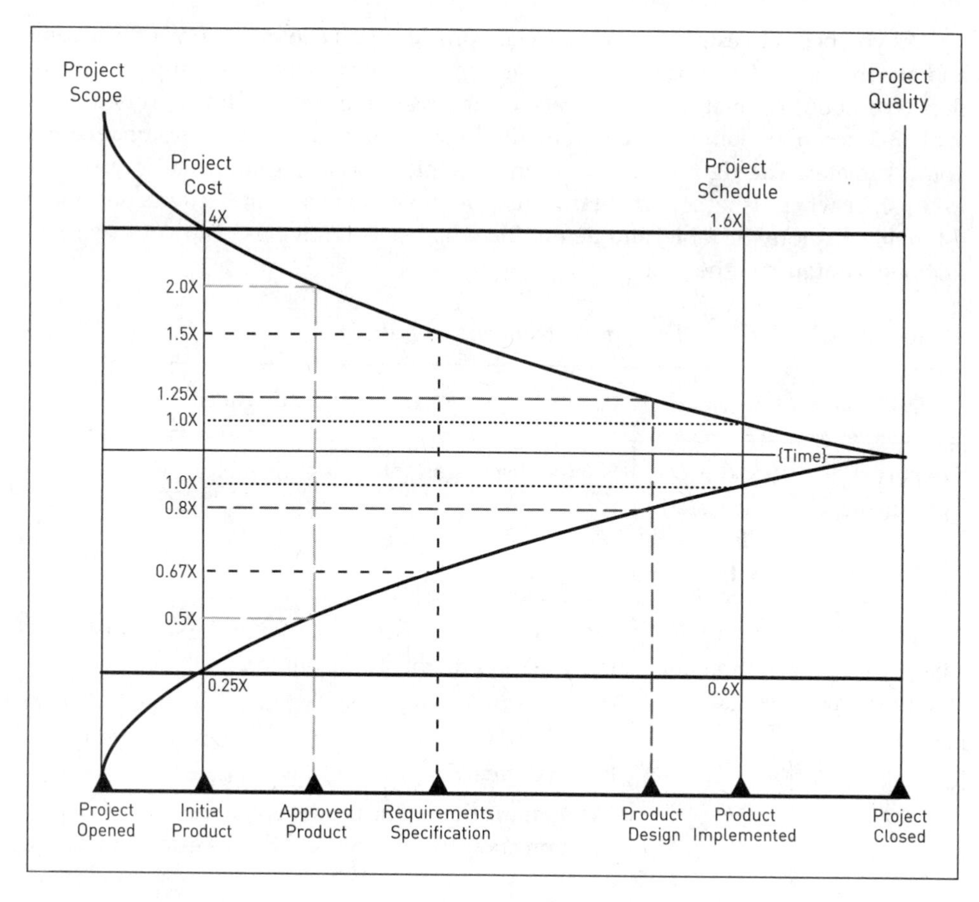

Figure 3–1: *Modified cone of uncertainty showing how estimates for the four dimensions of stakeholder expectation become more accurate as a project progresses*

Because of the sheer number of decisions that are dependent on estimates, any improvement in the estimation process can make for a significant improvement across the entire project. Examples of direct decisions that are dependent on estimates appear throughout this book. To understand the direct relationship and impact on project decisions, we will look at estimation decisions that concern the following dimensions of stakeholder expectations:

- Cost
- Scope
- Schedule (Time)
- Quality

As you begin to estimate your software projects, you can manage your estimates and ensure their proper use by understanding and documenting the inputs to your decisions about estimates and by tracking the results of your estimation decisions. Table 3-2 describes some estimation methodologies that can help you to understand your estimates. The rightmost column in the table describes some what-if questions to consider when using a particular technique to evaluate and make decisions about estimates. Explore the table, and determine whether you have used any of these estimation techniques in the past.

Table 3–2: *Using Different Estimation Techniques with PEAK*

Technique	*Reference*	*PEAK Inputs to Consider*
Expert judgment	See the discussion following the table.	See the discussion following the table.
Model-based (algorithmic)	COCOMO II (Boehm et al. 2000)	**(P) Problem:** The scope is larger, or the schedule is longer than previously encountered. **(E) Experience:** You have the data available for the model and have used the model before. (Is this a true statement?) **(A) Assumptions:** The model is calibrated for organization and projects. (Should this be established as a fact?) **(K) Knowledge:** You know the personnel, skills, and capabilities of the organization that are applicable. (Is this a true statement?)
Historical data	Estimation by Analogy (Pressman 2004)	**(P) Problem:** Can you use analogy to find a solution? **(E) Experience:** The proper data has been collected in the past and can be identified with projects. You have seen many types of projects for which you have data. (Are these true statements?) **(A) Assumptions:** The data collected is not garbage, and resources stay about the same. (Should these be established as facts?) **(K) Knowledge:** You basically can repeat your actions on a project. (Is this a true statement?)

Let's look at how you could use the PEAK model to make decisions about estimates that are based on expert judgment:

(P) Problem: Provide a reasonable representation of the scope, cost, schedule, and quality of the software effort for the organization that the customer will accept.

(E) Experience: This is the history the "expert" has with the type of project being proposed and the types of environments that will be used in the project.

(A) Assumptions: The project is similar enough to past projects that the experts in the company can relate the two efforts. Other assumptions might be the following:

- The expert understands *all* new technology on the project.
- The scope of the project is similar to the scopes of the other projects with which the expert is familiar.
- The company is not in a hiring phase and therefore not likely to add new people that the expert will not know.

(K) Knowledge: The expert has a very good understanding of the skills that people have and the resources that will be used to solve the problem. The expert clearly understands the problem.

As you can see from these inputs, the solution produced will be at risk if things are changing rapidly around the expert who has to make the decisions. You can think about many projects where people are changing, groups are moving between buildings, or new equipment and technologies are being adopted. You can see how these changes will greatly influence the risk associated with the solution produced by this decision process. As we proceed through the cases, we will discuss the four stakeholder expectation dimensions. You will note how the stakeholders' views about scope, time, quality, and cost affect their use of different estimation techniques as well as the PEAK inputs to their project decisions.

Estimating Budget (Cost) for Project

An old comic strip shows a scientist in front of a chalkboard with a massive number of equations. The last equation on the board shows the equation "time = $" with the caption "Oh my, time does equal money."

In the software field, we are expected to accurately estimate the time it will take to do a job that requires creative thought, that usually requires the team members to learn new concepts, and that pushes team members to provide undivided attention for long periods of time. These three factors are difficult to measure and even more difficult to estimate, but we need to deal with these concerns because estimation is a fact that we must handle to exist in the real world. The days of "Take as long as you need and here is a blank check" are over (if they ever existed).

Software is an integral part of systems, and dependency on software is increasing (Commander 2005). Therefore, it is also a significant part of the cost of the project. We not only have to estimate time, but we also have to estimate the resources needed to ensure the time is properly applied. Estimates for the cost of the project are generated from the very first moment a software person provides a value that can be related to time. Time is immediately multiplied by some "factor," and this generates a cost number. Loaded cost, engineering costs, and shop cost are all values, for example, that are derived from some number of units per hour multiplied by time.

You can apply the decision model to help you generate good estimates. You need to relate the PEAK inputs from the estimation process to the outputs needed from the estimate. Let's look at the inputs to see how they are tied to the estimation process and then look at the outputs. This will enable you to identify both in the case studies and later in your own projects.

(P) Problem: You need to allocate a value to the resources that will be committed entirely to the project or to any piece of the project. Therefore, if you estimate each piece, the decision process will be repeated multiple times. The allocated values can be time, money, or direct resources that you plan to use on the project.

(E) Experience: This includes what you have done in the past or estimates that you have developed for resource needs in the past that will help you with this estimation problem. How accurate were they, and do you still have the information?

(A) Assumptions: These are things that you assume are "facts" even though you do not have direct evidence to show them as facts. Examples might be availability of people, skill sets people have, or resource availability at the time it is needed. Others might be productivity of people, quality level of products, and reusability of components.

(K) Knowledge: This is what you know and can be confirmed that might help you determine what the project estimate would be. These are the facts you can apply to the requirements that will help you resolve the estimate.

These assumptions in turn tend to contribute to the assumed risks that accompany the solution. We assume a level of productivity that may not be achievable if people get sick, leave their jobs, or get hit by a bus!

Estimating Scope for Project

In addition to the effect of "development" time on cost, there is also the impact of the project scope. Our immediate response on a new project is to try to do everything, but the first thing that we do when the project falls behind is to cut scope.

The reality is that not all scope is of the same priority. You must consider how to prioritize the scope, or you can fall into the trap of thinking everything is of equal value. In fact, if you develop a "threshold of success," then you can see there are categories for pieces of the scope such as "must have," "should have," and "nice to have." (See Chapter 7, "Managing Risk" for more details.) These categories can quickly set the priority for the scope and help with estimation of the project.

These priorities for the scope determine the inputs into the decision process for estimation. Our decisions about what you can do are based on what you must have and what resources are available. A "must have" requirement that requires an engineer to go to training for a month is still a month away at best. The engineer should not be scheduled for tasks that occur during training, and training should be scheduled prior to when the engineer needs the skill to complete a task. This shows that estimation is also related to the planning decisions. See Chapter 4, "Managing Plans," for more details.

In estimation of scope for a project, reality, timing, and capability are all part of the decision process. One of the key issues when estimating scope is size. A number of estimation processes look at size or relative size. Some techniques for making decisions about scope (size estimation) are function points (Albrecht 1979), story points (Cohn 2004), and use case points (Schneider and Winters 2001). All support relative size estimation and provide a value for "scope." Other techniques provide for lines-of-code values, which also give you a feeling for size that can then be used to determine or justify scope.

Using the PEAK model, you can ask the following questions to make decisions about scope:

(P) Problem: What is the scope that is most likely achievable on this project within the constraints?

(E) Experience: What are the reusable components you know about from previous projects that will make this scope achievable?

(A) Assumptions: Should you assume that people currently working on other projects will be free to work on this project and that training will be available for any new technology needed to support the scope?

(K) Knowledge: What skills and resources do you have available for the project?

Estimating Schedule (Time) for Project

There is a difference between development time and clock time. In a sense, development time assumes an ideal world. Every hour will equal one hour of productive work produced. Reality is far from this.

When you estimate the schedule for a project, you almost always look at the things that have gone wrong in past projects. You see these as "unusual" events that affected the project. However, if you were to look over time, you would see that these unusual events are the norm for these types of projects. Things just happen. As you estimate, you are trying to evaluate the future environment. The analogy that best fits this is driving in a car from one place to another.

You have to be able to answer the following three questions in order to answer the age-old children's question on automobile trips ("When will we get there?"):

- How far did we have to go originally (problem)?
- How far have we traveled so far (experience)?
- How fast are we going now, or what is our average speed (knowledge)?

The first question in the trip analogy concerns the topic of scope. That is, how far do you plan to travel? The second question is a project-tracking issue. What have you done with the time you have already spent? In other words, what distance have you traveled? You can also use the distance traveled and time to generate your "average" velocity (assumption). Knowing the velocity, you can "assume" that if everything remains the same, then the distance left to travel divided by the velocity is the time you have left (solution). You can use this time to estimate the remaining schedule for the project.

Many of the Agile methods specifically call this "calculating the velocity of the team." These Agile methods combine the estimation, tracking, and planning steps into one action. This can be useful if it is understood.

The following is how to apply the PEAK model to determine a time estimate:

(P) Problem: How long will it take?

(E) Experience: How much have you done?

(A) Assumptions: You can keep doing things at the same rate.

(K) Knowledge: How much did you have to do when you started?

Estimating Quality for Project

Quality is the fourth dimension you need to estimate for a project. The question is, "What type and degree of quality is right for your project?" You need to consider the level of quality that your project can afford. People have a tendency in software to trade quality for time or scope. For example, people trade testing to ship a product on time. This is a direct trade-off. You also have indirect trade-offs such as cutting inspection or reviews from the development process to save time.

The following is how to apply the PEAK model to decide upon the right quality for a project:

(P) Problem: How much quality process is needed to support this project?

(E) Experience: What processes are in place to support the effort?

(A) Assumptions: You know that this level of effort is correct for this project.

(K) Knowledge: What have you done in the past that has worked?

Table 3–3: *Multiple Views on Estimation*

Dimension	*Estimation Technique to Use*
Scope	Size models such as function points, historical data, lines-of-code (LOC) counting
Time (schedule)	Algorithmic models and tools, expert judgment, and Wideband Delphi
Quality	Expert judgment and Wideband Delphi
Cost (budget)	Algorithmic models (COCOMO II, Slim, and so on), expert judgment

When considered individually for estimation, software project cost, scope, time, and quality have the added benefit of producing multiple estimation views. Table 3-3 summarizes applicable estimation techniques when the focus is each of these dimensions. Examine the table, and identify the techniques that you have used in the past.

3.3 Case Studies

These case studies will emphasis the key issues involved with estimation for software projects. In particular, they will look at overcoming entrenched estimation practices that affect decisions dealing with estimation either adversely or in a ways that are not well understood. The case studies will take a software project manager's point of view and show you how the software project manager identified, planned for, and corrected the estimation issues affecting their software projects.

The mini case study, "Estimation as a Tool," examines how people interested in improving their estimation process might begin to look for information that will help them with future decisions about estimates. Most of the techniques for estimation require historical information. Understanding this information and its origin will make using the data easier and more productive for estimating.

The full-length case study, "When a Team Runs a Race," examines how estimation can be influenced indirectly by aspects that need to be understood. It also examines the influence that multiple projects operating at the same time can have on a currently running project when there are interdependencies of resources, personnel, and developments.

CASE STUDY

Estimation as a Tool

Directions

You can read the case independently of the material from the chapter. If you choose to read the case study first, then read it once quickly in "story-reading mode" simply to set the context for the information in the chapter. Then read the chapter material thoroughly, and finally reread the case study in an analysis mode.

Case Summary

DESCRIPTION

A software project manager must make an estimate for a job and figure out what issues are influencing the estimate. He must figure out what are good inputs into the process so as to make a good estimate.

CASE STUDY OBJECTIVES

After reading the case study, you will be able to do the following:

- Understand examples of some estimation techniques
- Understand that there are different phases in which to estimate and how estimation during the planning phase might be improved
- Understand how some estimation techniques might be set up to better support an organization

SUBJECTS COVERED

Use of historical data to improve estimation, overall metrics in estimation, understanding metrics versus data issues, and how to look for similarity in projects

SETTING

This case will provide methods for estimating with minimal data, for obtaining base data that is usable in a software development environment, and for quickly collecting data and converting it into metrics.

TERMINOLOGY

Junior engineer: Engineers with less than five years of experience

Metrics: A relative understanding of how data can be used to evaluate some activities

Productivity numbers: A measure of how much project work the company gets

Senior engineer: Engineers with more than five years of experience

The Case

SCENARIO

Marvin Saymore was being asked to estimate his first full project after starting his new job with Transad. He had to give his boss an estimate, and he was not sure what the primary estimation issues on his projects were. The question was whether estimates were driven by events that were unavoidable or were because of mistakes in estimating past projects. He began to reflect on what he had learned back in school about estimation and what might influence the Washington Transit Authority (WTA) project.

Marvin thought that when people in the company tried to estimate, they tried, in some sense, to predict the future. Marvin was not sure whether this was really true as the new WTA project was being estimated. He thought that estimates were more based on the past and that they were a best guess of what might happen, not a prediction. With that "best guess" came some risk and some probability of success or failure. He had been taught that humans are creatures of habit and tend to do things more or less the same unless a major change occurs in the environment. In a sense, Transad had more or less been the same for the last 100 years of development, so change was not necessarily a big issue for the managers. So, based on this understanding, history should be a good predictor of future activities.

However, Marvin was still left with deciding what past, or, more accurately, what data from the past, he should use. There always seems to be much data, but if you do not know what the data means or represents, then it is hard to decide how to use it. For his purpose, Marvin would accept that data used to follow the progress of a project were valid measurements. Making his decisions more difficult on how to estimate the project was that Marvin had been taught to use more than one way of estimating. This, he believed, would allow him to compare estimates and see which ones seemed more reasonable and in some ways see whether he was aware of all the major issues on the project. Dramatically different estimates for the same project using different techniques might indicate hidden issues or future problems. Marvin realized that to understand the history for projects, he would have to understand the metrics the organization collected on projects in the past.

Marvin first discovered, as he took over the reins as the new software manager at Transad, that metrics were fine for other people but not necessarily for his group. He found out that a number of metric efforts had been proposed, but none had been maintained for a long period of time or were used to predict future performance. The company almost exclusively depended on the expert judgment of the senior engineers and the senior managers in the company for estimates. This would have probably been all right if historical data had been used independently to validate the estimates, but this was never done. In addition, the historical data that was available was mainly "bean counter" data, that is, number of hours on the project, hours preproduction, hours postproduction, and repair hours in the field. The preproduction did not specifically break out any software events, only how many hours were used.

One of the first issues Marvin had to resolve was whether the "bean counter" data was usable in some way. He needed to develop a way to obtain accurate data, which he could use to compare with the historical data he had available. He considered this accurate data, which was once related to his projects, as "metrics." He used a simple technique over a short period of time that would enable him to understand clearly how each type of engineer spent his time. Once he had enough of this information, he might then be able to use it to validate the overall estimates on the project. Marvin wanted to see whether he could establish a correlation between the bean counter data and real data on his development projects. Table 3-4 gives the resulting data that Marvin obtained.

What immediately became apparent is that accounting for all the time the engineer spent was something that would take a little work. Next, it was also apparent that there was a large difference between how much time the senior engineers and the junior engineers were getting to work on what people considered "real" project work. There seemed to be an inverse relationship between an engineer's experience and the length of time that the engineer was allowed to work on a project. Marvin wondered whether this interpretation of the data was correct or whether there was another reason that the experienced engineers spent less time on real project work.

Table 3–4: *Engineer Project Hours for Currently Operating Projects at Transad*

Engineer Title	*Project Work*	*Meetings*	*Other Support Issues*	*Field Work*
Sr. Engineer A	12.3	7.6	10.3	20.9
Sr. Engineer B	11.7	9.3	9.8	18.2
Engineer A	23.6	3.2	3.5	1.5
Engineer B	30.2	4.1	1.3	0.7
Engineer C	27.2	3.9	2.1	1.4

Without productivity numbers, these values may or may not have a major impact on the estimates, but Marvin's gut feeling was that something was very much out of "whack."

Just Like the Last One

Next, Marvin began to examine the company concept of "sameness" that was used by engineers to evaluate requirements. A number of recent projects had been bid to customers as being exactly the same with "minor" changes. As Marvin discussed this with his engineers, he found that this sameness was not quite the same for everyone involved. He decided to conduct a direct requirement-by-requirement examination of a new project compared with the "base" project, which was being changed. Requirements were directly compared by one of his senior engineers, and any differences other than syntax were noted. There was also an attempt to evaluate how different the requirement was from the original baseline project.

On one of the "same" projects, about half the original requirements had been modified, and about half of these modifications involved significant or moderate changes. In the eyes of management, this indicated a "same" project.

Significant Events

One other piece of information that Marvin began to put together for his projects was the idea of whether there might be some significant events during projects that were contributing to a large number of hours. In other words, Marvin was looking for the 80/20 effect on his project estimates. As he reviewed the data, he found that whenever the hardware group proposed a new hardware configuration for a project solution, there were a certain number of hours needed to integrate the software and new hardware and to integrate the new hardware into the system. Table 3-5 has a number of the data points that Marvin was able to develop from the historical data.

Table 3–5: *Group Hours Spent on New Hardware Implementations for Transad Projects*

Project	*Hours for v1.0 of Hardware*	*Hours for v2.0 of Hardware*	*Other Hours**
Baltimore	3,120	753	1,012
Dallas	2,999	1,001	576
Los Angeles	4,230	2,017	423
San Francisco	2,100	1,423	1,018

* Some of these hours were used for integration and testing the software and hardware together.

Marvin now felt armed with a number of new elements to help with his estimation efforts. He planned to update his estimation process so that he could incorporate his new knowledge. He had to figure out how best to explain to his boss that he had a new tool to better estimate the WTA project. He thought that by using the information in Table 3-5 he could produce at least two if not three more techniques to help the expert judgment that had been used by Transad to estimate projects in the past. Now all he had to do was convince Enrique, his boss, that this was the right thing to do.

CASE PROBLEM

Marvin encounters the following problems in the case study:

- Are the decisions to use the estimation techniques or the information that Marvin has at his disposal effective?
- What issues are most affecting the estimation decisions Marvin has to make?

Case Analysis

ANALYSIS ACTIVITY

Analysis Questions

1. What are the major decisions that the manager must make to help him with his estimation problem?
2. What would you have done differently if you were in the manager's place?
3. What estimation techniques from the case can you identify that are being used? Were the decisions for these techniques supported in the case?
4. What information about estimation did you gather that you did not already know?
5. What are the decisions that Marvin needs to make?
   - What are the PEAK inputs for these decisions?
   - What are the alternative solutions and risks associated with these decisions?

CONCLUSIONS

As you look at the decisions that were made concerning estimates in the case, one of the key concepts is that your best estimates must be based in accurate metrics. To ensure accurate metrics, you must make sure to verify that the data feeding the metrics is valid. Although decisions concerning estimates can be evaluated with PEAK, the knowledge can be corrupted if the metrics being used are not correct. "Garbage in, garbage out" is a well-understood concept. But garbage can be hidden in metrics very easily, and the impact on estimation along with the consequences is severe.

KEY IDEAS TO REMEMBER

The PEAK model can help clarify the inputs and show that a decision based on faulty input data is also likely to be faulty.

The decision to put new functionality in hardware rather than in software is not the best decision because it is based on faulty input data. The experience and the assumptions are flawed in the decision:

(P) Problem: New functionality is needed.

(E) Experience: It's easy to add hardware to the system.

(A) Assumptions: It's easier and less costly to add hardware than to add software to a system.

(K) Knowledge: Basically, for a hardware company, software is harder to manage.

Solution: Add a new hardware component to the system to meet the functionality.

Assumed Risk: The cost to get software running on new hardware is not well understood and may be greater than expected. The recent cost model shows the cost to be about 5,000 hours to integrate software with new hardware.

The estimation decision to split the engineers' time also needs to be reviewed. The information being used shows all time being equal, but the concept of context switching is ignored. Machines can switch jobs back and forth, but humans cannot easily do this. Application of the PEAK model reveals the flawed assumptions associated with this estimation decision:

(P) Problem: Projects are late because engineers are overloaded.

(E) Experience: The company has many projects all in different phases of development.

(A) Assumptions: Engineers can support more than one project without much impact.

(K) Knowledge: Senior engineers will most quickly resolve problems with products in the field.

Solution: Split the engineers' time as needed to solve problems.

Assumed Risk: Junior and senior engineers may not actually get the same amount of time on a project, and therefore using senior engineers to solve field problems may be an issue.

The PEAK model helps you evaluate the estimation decisions that were made and look for where problems with the inputs can contribute to issues with the solutions.

CASE STUDY

When a Team Runs a Race

Directions

You can read this case independently of the material from the chapter. If you choose to read the case study first, then read it once quickly in "story-reading mode" simply to set the context for the information in the chapter. Then read the chapter material thoroughly, and finally reread the case study in an analysis mode.

Case Summary

DESCRIPTION

The manager Halley realizes that a project is going to be late well in advance of the date when the project is due. He has to figure out whether the data is accurate enough to make his claim, what he can do about the problem, and what made it happen. He wants to understand the decisions that were made that created the problem in the first place so that he can improve his decision making in the future.

CASE STUDY OBJECTIVES

After reading the case study, you will be able to do the following:

- Identify a number of estimation techniques used in this case study. You will also be able to state whether the techniques were used correctly or incorrectly and what the people in the case study did wrong.
- Understand how to identify "the haze" of data that normally surrounds a project and what you have to do to get the proper information for correct estimates.
- Provide mechanisms to build your case for improving estimation within your own organization.

SUBJECTS COVERED

Estimation bias, perception, and delivery schedule

SETTING

A software project manager cannot figure out why his projects seem to be off schedule. He is being asked to provide status but thinks he does not understand the key issues that govern his estimates. He has to do a better job of explaining his estimates.

KEY CONCEPTS

Many factors influence the decisions around estimates:

- Looking at the problem from multiple directions can help with understanding.
- The problems are seldom easy, or they would have long ago been solved.
- First impressions seldom provide you with enough information for in-depth analysis.

TERMINOLOGY

Loaded cost: The organization cost per unit of time, which includes not only salary but also infrastructure support for engineers, such as benefits, building, and environment

TC: Train control

WTA: Washington Transit Authority

The Case

SCENARIO

When a relay team runs a race, the last team member always seems to get the blame for the team being late. It does not matter that everyone before him dropped the baton or took their time. There is an expectation that the last person, the anchor, can make up for anything. In the development of complex integrated systems, this last "person" usually seems to be software.

Halley Anderson had a tough day ahead. He knew that today he was going to have to tell his manager that the Washington Transit Authority (WTA) project was going to be late. This might sound unusual because the project was not due for another six months, but nonetheless it was going to be late.

This all started back when the WTA project began. Halley had done a detailed estimate of the project after the Train Control (TC) group had received a notice to proceed on the contract. He wanted to make sure that the proper resources were assigned and that the proper risks were observed in the project. Halley had used a number of techniques to estimate the cost of this project, but the assumptions made in one of them were now being reviewed.

The estimation had accounted for the fact that every time new hardware was used on a project, there appeared to be a fixed number of engineering hours needed to get the software operational on the hardware. This additional time almost seemed like a constant and had to be verified a number of times by Halley, but he started to believe it was not only the software but the time to get the software installed and working in these new hardware environments that made this development time constant. In other words, Halley thought the problem was with the hardware group.

The hardware group was where Halley's boss, Enrique Wattsman, had come from. Enrique had a "soft spot" for the hardware group. How could Halley blame the hardware group for the problem when Enrique's view of software was put to him as follows?

Enrique said, "Here is what I view about software," while drawing on the board (Figure 3-2).

Halley replied, "But at least we might want to break it down into design and then implementation (code) and test. Design is the creation of the solution."

Enrique then said, "Well, I guess we could add that, but the percentages would stay the same."

This left Halley with a problem and maybe a solution. Enrique had the view that software was "easy" and not related to the other things that the company did. For example, Enrique did not say that requirements followed availability of hardware. He assumed they were independent. Was this an opening for Halley to explain to Enrique the relationship, or was this just another "thing" the last runner (software) would have to overcome?

Halley had calculated that it would take about 5,000 engineering hours to get software operational on a new hardware board. He had used this information for the WTA estimate but had not made his manager aware of this number. It was somewhat scary to tell Enrique that every time his engineers decide to add a piece of hardware, it cost the company $500,000 dollars. (The loaded cost for engineers at Transad was about $100 per hour.)

The question was how he could make his manager and everyone else aware of this so that basically the "last runner" was not blamed again for always being late.

Halley had made friends with the head of the hardware group. Calvin Smith was nice but knew his department was contributing to some of the problems that recent projects had experienced at Transad. He always had engineers in the field debugging problems and always seemed to be in Enrique's office explaining why this or that was late. His engineers were overworked, and he could not see any clear way out of his problem. Calvin's problems and Halley's problems were related. If the hardware were late, the software would be late.

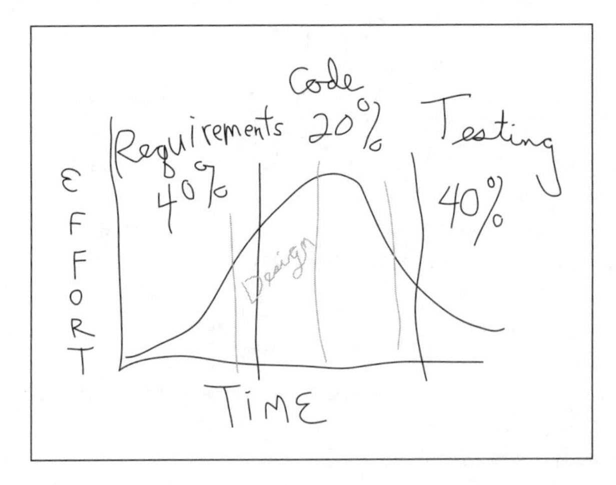

Figure 3–2: *Halley's boss's view of software development*

One issue in particular bothered both managers. They both understood that they had about 11 months to develop the system; however, a couple of months before the end of that period, if they needed to make changes, it became more and more difficult. Although the number of changes usually decreased during the life of the project as the product was being integrated and finalized, changes could become more frequent. When the engineers understood the most about the product, they were being allowed less and less opportunity to implement changes that would improve the product.

Halley and Calvin came in on a weekend and decided to look at the data. A diagram that Halley and Calvin put together made the problem immediately clear (Figure 3-3). Although technically the managers were given a certain amount of time to produce their solutions, in reality the time was much shorter. This was because the time needed by manufacturing overlapped with the time needed for development. This overlap had probably started occurring in response to the company needing to win more projects by shortening the overall time to deliver a product to the customer. Although on paper this looked good and probably meant that overall development schedules could be compressed, the reality was that new development time overall had been cut from the understood 10 to 11 months down to 8 to 9 months. This began to explain why projects were coming in later and later at Transad. However, of course, the bidding was showing the same amount of time as before, and the costs were holding—to some extent.

The need to overlap manufacturing with development was a logistical need to meet the demands of new contracts. If you have to build a thousand units and it takes you a fixed amount of time to build each unit, then divide the number of units by the time and back up the calendar. Transad was still thinking in a mode that is common to many hardware manufacturing companies rather than with an awareness that hardware depends on software as well as on creative processes such as hardware and software design.

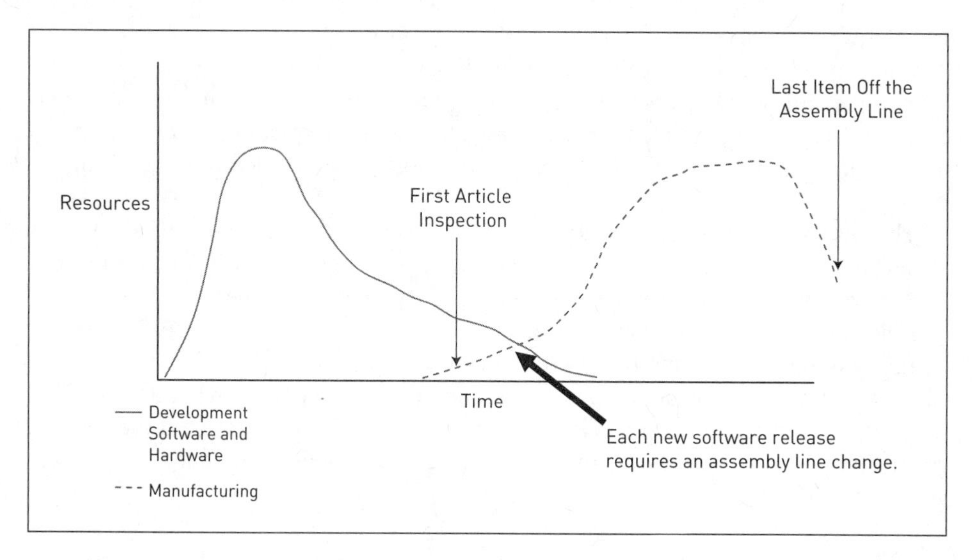

Figure 3–3: *Manufacturing and development relationship*

Calvin now understood why he was in so much trouble. His normal lead time on parts and development of boards was longer than the time he could make changes. He was expected to deliver new hardware before he could have it fully tested. Halley used this opening to let Calvin in on a secret, the 5,000-hour cost. If Calvin was having trouble getting parts and if when he finally did get the components built it would take another 5,000 engineering hours to load the software, project delay was inevitable.

Halley suggested that the problem was that the system had to be product-lined. The company could not afford, except for highly specialized conditions, to add new hardware. The cost would be too high to get the new component in place. The specifications would have to be available and the interfaces would have to be defined by the second or third month of the project for the TC group to be able to make the new board work. Two to three months seemed too short for the hardware group. Even with this understanding, there was still a problem in making this newly discovered internal deadline of an eight- or nine-month delivery to meet the manufacturing issues. Halley would have to assign approximately five or six engineers to work on the software for any new board.

In some ways, Transad had limited its options. If Halley could convince the systems engineers to use "off-the-shelf" hardware, then projects could begin to be on time. It was too late for the WTA project, but Halley would insist on the change for the future.

The WTA project had a new component in the form of a board the company had never made before. It was called the Brake Feedback Monitor (BFM). The device might make a nice product-line element in the future, but on this project, it created a deadline that Halley needed the hardware group to meet.

At the kickoff meeting, Halley announced the need for the new BFM hardware by March 27. At the meeting, this date was some three months away.

Halley said, "In the planning phase of WTA, it has become apparent that this new board is going to be difficult to handle. Historically, it has taken a lot of time to install software on new hardware, so can we make sure to get the boards we need for test, by March 27?"

Calvin quickly replied, "Yeah, sure, no problem."

Enrique said, "Calvin, let's make sure. Your guys have not been doing very well lately."

Calvin responded, "What are you talking about? I have three guys in the field right now. We are handling more than our share of the work. They are doing pretty damn good in my eyes . . . ."

This discussion between Calvin and Enrique was typical. It came to a head when one evening after most of the engineers had left. Enrique came into Halley's office and asked, "One year! How can it take someone one year and still not get it done?"

Halley replied, "I am not sure I understand."

Enrique then said, "Calvin's guys have been working on a board for the Fusser project, and they have had an action item to fix it for a year. They know what the solution is but have not worked on it, and it is due tomorrow. So, a year after we tell the customer that the problem will be fixed, I am going to have to tell them, "A little longer, please.' A year . . . a whole year!"

Halley realized how all the projects in the company were to some extent interrelated, and this meant that problems on one project could impact development on another project.

Shortly after this, Calvin left the company. He did not think he could deal with the hardware group problems logically or in an objective fashion anymore.

In his last conversation with Calvin, Halley said, "Calvin, I understand you are leaving. I am sorry to see you go."

Calvin replied, "Save your self, man; this place is never going to get better."

The important day had come. How was Halley supposed to approach his boss and tell him that today, March 28, represented a one-day slip in the WTA schedule? And the day after that would represent another day's slip. As of today, the WTA project was going to be late. Halley thought about the famous Fred Brooks quote, "How does a project become one year late? ...One day at a time" (Brooks 1995, 153).

CASE PROBLEM

Halley encounters the following issues and decisions related to project estimates:

- What are the major issues impacting the WTA project that may cause Halley's decisions concerning estimates to be wrong?
- What decisions might Halley have made to try to deal with the impacts to his estimates when software is embedded in a larger hardware system?

RESULTS

The hardware for the WTA project was delivered a day late. The project was able to get the software into production roughly on time, after all the issues, about a week late because of other issues also found on the project. The project overall was about 14 days late because of a subcontractor on a subcomponent that interfaced with the main motor control system. In general, the estimation decisions were some of the best seen on any new project at the company in some time.

Case Analysis

ANALYSIS ACTIVITY

Analysis Background

First Case Problem

(P) Problem: What does Halley have to do to ensure that the project is not late?

(E) Experience: The Transad standard development process was in place, and they were in the middle of an 11-month effort.

(A) Assumptions: Everything will arrive on schedule because even if the hardware is delivered late, they can make up time in software.

(K) Knowledge: Because software is waiting on the new hardware, software appears to be running late "as usual."

Solution: They need to work harder in software.

Assumed Risk: They may not be able to make up time in software and get the project back on schedule.

Second Case Problem

(P) Problem: What can Halley do to minimize the impact to his estimates when the software is embedded in a larger hardware system?

(E) Experience: Halley understands the Transad production environment for hardware or software integration.

(A) Assumptions: Software is just like hardware and does not cost as much as the hardware to change.

(K) Knowledge: Hardware takes a certain amount of time to manufacture. Halley knows the 5,000-hour cost to integrate hardware and software.

Solution: They can build the hardware and fit in the software as needed.

Assumed Risk: Software problems, especially those associated with integration or the need to change, may affect production schedules. The estimates may not account for this possibility.

Analysis Questions

1. Why is Halley concerned about the WTA project? What key issues should Halley be aware of that would help him understand the issues that affect his estimates?
2. Whose fault was the one-year failure to deliver the hardware solutions, Calvin (the head of hardware) or Enrique (the head of the division)? Why?
3. What makes it one or the other's fault, or would you blame it on someone or something else?

CONCLUSIONS

As you examine the assumptions that you have to make to produce estimates, you need to be aware of when assumptions are directly in opposition to the solutions or options produced by your decisions. You want to minimize the assumptions that increase the risks to the solutions or verify the assumptions and convert them into knowledge. The chapter discussion shows that assumptions are the largest generator of bad decisions. You are forced to make the assumptions because sometimes you don't have the needed data until later in the project. Although, for estimation, the PEAK model will mostly show that assumptions are a problem, other factors such as the availability and accuracy of knowledge are also issues.

An example might be the one-year problem in the case. The risk was that free time might not be available, but the assumption was that free time would be available sometime within a year. When the original estimate of one year was put forth, everyone assumed that the time would become available. No one verified this assumption, and the knowledge that this issue was pending was probably not provided to the engineers who had to work on it. The project went forward with an estimate decision based on an assumption that may not hold.

The main principle that Halley learned that would influence his decisions about estimates in the future is that some costs, such as the 5,000 hours needed to integrate software into new hardware, are fixed. If these fixed costs were better understood, his estimation process could be improved. Halley increased his knowledge for future estimate decisions. He also learned that his knowledge about the production process, actual costs, and estimation needed to be made available to everyone in the organization if the group was going to be successful.

KEY IDEAS TO REMEMBER

At first glance, it seems that the problem for many project managers is that software is always late. As the title of the case indicates, the software people "run the anchor leg" of the project race. They usually handle the integration of the product and, in doing so, are the last people to work on it. Therefore, they may be expected to make up for any previous deficiencies that have occurred earlier in the project. The estimation decisions made early in the project might be completely invalid if this is not taken into account.

In practice, being 14 days late on an 11-month (220 working days) project is a very small amount, but understanding what might make a project late is critical to knowing how to keep the project on schedule. Many factors can influence this understanding, and taking the time to reflect can be critical to making the right decisions.

When Halley and Calvin stepped back from "running the race" of managing their projects and reflected, they began to understand a much deeper issue that was influencing their projects. Their reflection effort increased their knowledge for future PEAK decisions about estimates. They learned that one of the problems they had thought was the fault of the software engineering organization was actually related to the manufacturing requirements and the order of performing the related tasks in the compressed schedule. This issue, which was not completely under their control, indicates the complexity of factors that can influence estimation and schedule planning for a project. After this experience, Halley was better prepared to defend his estimate decisions.

3.4 Summary

This chapter focused on the following activities for managing estimation in the context of decision making for software projects. The items marked with asterisks are involved in making decisions about all types of estimates.

- Understanding requirements (see Chapter 2, "Managing Requirements")*
- Conceptually designing a solution
- Performing element-wise decomposition (divide)
- Allocating resources from the bottom-up (conquer)
- Allocating overhead
- Estimating construction
- Estimating change management

The case studies in the chapter presented decision issues associated with managing the estimates of current and future projects. The first case study, "Estimation as a Tool," discussed how you can use the decisions made when gathering information to defend future estimate decisions. The case concerned estimates of overhead allocation and estimate change management. The second case study, "When a Team Runs a Race," covered the issues of estimate construction as well as divide and conquer.

As you increase your experience in estimation, your PEAK analyses can show you how to better evaluate your decisions about estimates.

Chapter 4

Managing Plans

4.1 Chapter Objectives

After reading and thinking about the concepts and case studies presented in this chapter, you will be able to do the following:

- Understand the activities that are essential to managing software project plans
- Identify key issues and decisions involving the management of plans in the chapter case studies
- Use the chapter concepts to suggest feasible solutions to the problems faced by the case study stakeholders
- Recognize the importance of managing software project plans

4.2 Context

A **project** is commonly understood to be an undertaking requiring concerted effort that is synonymous with a plan or proposal (TheFreeDictionary by Farlex, Project). A **plan** is a scheme, program, or method worked out beforehand for the accomplishment of an objective (TheFreeDictionary by Farlex, Plan). In practice, the software project objectives (scope), schedule for completion (time), quality attributes to be achieved (quality), and budget (cost) need to be finite. These four dimensions relate to the expectations of the project stakeholders (as discussed in Chapter 9, "Managing Stakeholder Expectations"). Also, a project is usually characterized by a clear start and end.

You would probably agree that most projects could not be accomplished without planning. Imagine trying to construct a new home, to develop an extensive travel tour for a group of tourists, to organize a technical conference, to put together a trade show, or to develop a large software system without a plan. Projects, regardless of their scope or complexity, need a plan of attack. The project plans should be inputs to daily decisions made about project execution.

Project plans address any aspect of a project that will be managed, such as development plans for managing how a product is developed; work plans for managing tasks, schedules, resources, and project progress; budgetary plans for managing project cost; quality and process plans for managing product and process quality; and support plans for managing tools needed to execute the project (configuration management system, development tools, issue-tracking system, and so on). Humphrey (2000) defines a comprehensive software team process in which members of the team assume these types of management responsibilities in the roles of development manager, planning manager, quality or process manager, and support manager, respectively. He adds a team lead role and does not assign a specific role for the management of project costs.

The chapter discusses activities and decisions that compose managing software project plans and gives overviews of fundamental principles for evaluating and making decisions about project plans. This chapter focuses on helping you develop a practical understanding of basic project plans that specify the software project purpose and objectives, work, organization and responsibilities, constraints, and budgetary aspects. Other chapters discuss planning related to product, process, and risk. It provides basic ideas to keep in mind when planning the scope (objectives), time (schedule), and cost (budget) for your projects. Chapter 5, "Managing Product," and Chapter 6, "Managing Process," discuss quality constraints in more detail. Chapter 2, "Managing Requirements," more comprehensively discusses the issues and decisions associated with managing software requirements change and scope.

Because software projects rarely proceed exactly as planned, the need for replanning is inevitable. The client wants to increase the project scope midstream, there are unexpected requests for help from the field service organization, project members leave the company, the project estimates are too low, the project is behind schedule or over budget, and so on. At some point, for most software projects, the plans will not reflect the actual status of the project. Questions arise regarding the need to replan as well as regarding the aspects of the project to replan. Software project managers usually decide to replan when the current plans no longer help them in directing the project to completion of the objectives on time, within budget, and according to specification. Replanning usually involves changes to the scope, schedule, quality, or budget for the project. See Rönkkö et al. (2005) for an empirical study of the necessary means that need to be provided within a company in order to cope with situations when software plans do not work out. Deleris et al. (2007) from the IBM Research Center discuss a two-pronged approach to adaptive project replanning that involves the analysis of risks affecting activities in a project plan (that is, the root factors leading to cost and time overruns) and an optimization of the resources allocated to each activity in the project plan.

Managing plans entails ongoing attention to the details of the plans. Projects frequently fail, not necessarily because the project plans are faulty but because the project managers do not pay attention to details or do not systematically use the plans to evaluate their project decisions. Project managers who are continuously fighting fires often fail to execute to plan or do not replan when the plans are no longer valid. For instance, small slips in the schedule that accumulate to significant delay, mounting cost overruns, or software features that do not exactly satisfy quality requirements can cause well-planned but poorly managed projects to fail. Much has been written about why software projects fail. Some insightful resources about this topic are Johnson (2006), Mangione (2003), McManus and Wood-Harper (2008), and Taimour (2005).

We'll now apply the PEAK model when making decisions that impact the software project plans. A project manager is struggling to keep a software development project on schedule, within budget, and according to specification. Field service has requested that some of the software engineers on the project help repair a defect that was found by an important customer in the latest release of the software. Meanwhile, the business analysis part of the project is behind schedule, and the actual cost associated with the performance of the data modeling tasks exceeds the planned cost because more outsourced staff were needed than what was originally estimated. The project manager is under pressure from the director of software development to get the project back on schedule and within budget as soon as possible. Using the PEAK model, the software project manager can ask questions such as the following to decide how to handle issues that together impact the schedule, budget, and resource plans:

(P) Problem: What should the software project manager do to resolve the issues regarding schedule slippage, cost overruns, and overlapping demands for project resources? Is replanning needed?

(E) Experience:

- What policy does the software development organization have in place for handling a field service request that would interrupt an ongoing project? How has the project manger or software development organization handled such requests in the past?
- How has the project manager or the software development organization handled schedule slippage in the past?
- How has the project manager or the software development organization handled the underestimation of cost in the past?
- In the past, what have been the important customer's expectations for repairing defects in the field? If applicable, has the customer been willing to wait for the next release of the software or demanded that the repair be done immediately?

- What issues, if any, relate to managing interactions (relationships) with the customer, field service, or director of software development? How will these impact the alternative solutions?

(A) Assumptions: What, if any, inputs to the problem should be established as facts rather than assumed? For instance, the software project manager could ask questions such as the following:

- Does the reported defect actually exist and prevent the software from achieving the quality expected by the stakeholders for the current release and next version of the software?
- Would repairing the defect interrupt the development of the next version of the software with respect to schedule, budget, or quality?
- Does the important customer, in fact, expect to have the defect repaired immediately?
- What does the director of software development really mean by "fix the project now"?

(K) Knowledge:

- What is the cause of the schedule slippage for the business analysis tasks?
- In what way, if at all, does the slippage impact the critical path of the schedule? (See the schedule planning activity in Table 4-2 for a definition of critical path.)
- What can be done to alleviate the slippage without impact to the critical path?
- What can be done to reduce the cost of the data modeling tasks?
- What other project costs could be reduced to keep the total project cost within budget?
- Which other available software engineers, if any, could handle the field service request?
- How might the defect repair be done as part of the current project deliverables?
  - What would be the impact on the project schedule and budget?
  - Who would pay for the added cost (field service, development project, customer, and so on)?
  - What would be the impact on the quality of the project deliverables? What additional testing would be needed to ensure the expected quality?

Solution: The alternative solutions involve answers to the following questions:

- When will the software defect repair be done?
  - Repair the defect as part of the software release currently under development.

- Repair the defect as a special software release for the customer.
- Do not remove the defect if it does not prevent the software from satisfying stakeholder expectations regarding quality. (The customer's perception may not match reality.)

• Who will do the software defect repair?
  - Software engineers currently working on the project who have the necessary skills, experience, or knowledge
  - Software engineers not currently assigned to the project (if there are engineers who are sufficiently skilled to do the repair and are available)

• How will the schedule slippage for the business analysis tasks be handled?

• Who will pay for the software defect repair?

Assumed Risk: Given the current input information, what do the software stakeholders know about the risks that they would assume with each feasible solution?

For the remainder of this section, we discuss activities involved in managing plans and provide practical guidelines for making decisions concerning project plans. This material serves as a review or checklist for experienced project managers and we hope as a stimulus for thought to new managers. The guidelines are based on the actual experiences of project managers. We encourage you to log your own software project planning experiences and to develop your own decision guidelines based on your experiences and those of your colleagues. The guidelines presented in this chapter should appeal to your common sense, but do not be fooled. As you may already know, what makes sense is not always easy to practice.

The ensuing discussion includes the following terminology commonly used by project managers:

Software: Is composed, in general, of a variety of entities involved in the creation, execution, and maintenance of computer programs and data. Each one of these entities is a **software artifact**. Some examples of software artifacts are requirements specifications, architecture and design specifications, source code, executable code, test plans, documentation, databases, data files, and so on.

Software project deliverable: Is (1) a software artifact that is an outcome or result of work done by machines or humans for a software project, or (2) a software product created or a software service provided within the context of a software project that yields some defined value to the project stakeholders (notably to users, clients, or customers).

Software product: Consists of a group of software artifacts that together perform a computerized purpose. Often they are integrated, packaged, and sold as a single entity. They usually consist of one or more computer programs and documentation. The documentation typically contains information regarding the authenticity of the software, legal statements about the allowable distribution and use of the software, system requirements for executing the software, and directions for installing and using the software.

Software service: Is an activity performed for a user, client, or customer that involves the creation, definition, delivery, design, execution, maintenance, and so on, of one or more software artifacts.

Task: Is an activity that is performed by a machine or human in the development or delivery of software project deliverables, including software services. A task usually requires the allocation of staff, equipment, budget, time, or other resources for its completion.

Milestone: Is (1) an event or outcome of a software project activity that is observable and therefore able to be tracked, or (2) the completion or delivery of a software project artifact, software service, or constituent part of a software project deliverable that is useful for tracking purposes.

Software project: Involves the allocation of budget, time, staff, and other resources for the production of software artifacts or for the performance of software services on behalf of a user, client, or customer.

Software project plans: Describe what should be produced or done (scope), who should do what and when (staff and schedule), what other resources should be used (equipment, supplies, and so on), how much should be spent on what (budget), what constraints or properties should be satisfied (quality attributes), how something should be produced or how the project should be managed (process), or any other aspect of a project that is to be managed.

Software project plans are multifunctional: They describe the details of scope, schedule, quality attributes, and budget. Software project plans specify how the status of the project will be tracked and how success will be measured with respect to each of the stakeholder expectation dimensions. A basic software project plan specifies the objectives and scope for a software project. It provides estimates for the tasks, staff, and other resources needed to accomplish the project objectives and indicates an approximate schedule and budget for the completion of the project tasks or deliverables. The plan provides an organizational view of the project and a description of the roles and responsibilities of the people in the project. Likewise, it describes any specifications or constraints on how the project will be executed. The project plan includes the work plan and sometimes the budgetary plan. The software project manager, with input from the project members and possibly a planning assistant, usually develops the software project plan.

Software project plans typically provide the types of information shown in Table 4-1. The example information is grouped by project management area. Review the table, and think about other information that you have included in your software project plans or that you have seen in project plans written by other people.

Table 4–1: *Example Content of Software Project Plans*

Project Management Area	*Project Plan Information*
Project overview	Project objectives, context, and scope Project policies and constraints
Project stakeholders and organization	Identification of project stakeholders and their responsibilities Project organization including staff positions, reporting structure, and so on
Work planning	Project milestones (for example, intermediate or final project deliverables) Tasks to be done to accomplish the project milestones Staff assignments to accomplish project tasks and milestones Schedule estimates for completing tasks and milestones
Budget planning	Budget detailing cost estimates for staff, equipment, supplies, and other resources to complete the tasks and milestones
Risk planning	Identification of project risks Strategies for managing risk (also listed under process planning)
Process planning	Process plans for the following project management areas: • Managing audit and control of project plans • Managing communications between project stakeholders (see Chapter 8, "Managing People Interactions," and Chapter 9, "Managing Stakeholder Expectations") • Managing development of project deliverables and quality (See Chapter 5, "Managing Product") • Managing project decisions • Managing project issues • Managing project meetings • Managing project objectives and scope (See Chapter 2, "Managing Requirements," and Chapter 9, "Managing Stakeholder Expectations") • Managing project risks (See Chapter 7, "Managing Risk") • Managing project status with respect to plans • Managing replanning • Managing staff assignments and other resource allocations

We'll now explore the activities that software project managers perform to manage plans as described in Table 4-2. To manage your project plans, you might start by thinking of how you would perform each activity. The main idea is to understand why you are doing a particular activity (the target outcome) and how the activity contributes to accomplishing the project objectives. Study the table, and then think about other activities that you have performed or think you might perform when managing software project plans.

Table 4–2: *Descriptions of Activities in Managing Plans*

Activity	*Description of Activity*
Defining project objectives, policies, and scope	**Definition:** Process of determining what the project should accomplish as well as any constraints on how the project satisfies the objectives. The project plan may include a diagram and explanation of the software system to be developed and its context of use. **Target outcome:** Clear, complete, consistent, and correct statements of the project deliverables with respect to scope, time, quality, and cost as well as statements of any policies to be followed by the project. The project stakeholders should have a common understanding of these statements.
Task and milestone planning	**Definition:** Process of determining the step-by-step activities needed to complete the project deliverables and of decomposing project deliverables into partial deliverables that are useful for budget, resource, and schedule planning. It also includes defining any other tasks that are needed to execute the project. **Target outcome:** Clear, complete, consistent, and correct list of the tasks and milestones to be used in developing the project schedule and budget. The relevant project stakeholders should have a common understanding of these statements.

Table 4–2: *Descriptions of Activities in Managing Plans (Continued)*

Activity	*Description of Activity*
Schedule planning	**Definition:** Processes of (1) estimating the amount of resource units (for example, man-hours) needed to complete the project tasks, (2) laying out the tasks and milestones on a timeline so that tasks/milestones are done before those that depend on their completion, (3) assigning dates to the completion of milestones, (4) identifying the critical paths (the longest paths of dependent tasks/milestones), and (5) refining tasks/milestones as feasible to reduce the critical paths or to better use the resources. **Target outcome:** A timeline that indicates accurately, clearly, and precisely the time interval for completing each task/milestone, the resource units allocated to each task/milestone, the dependencies between the tasks/milestones, the critical paths, and the available slack times. The project stakeholders should have a common understanding of the schedule plans.
Budget planning	**Definition:** Process of estimating the cost of each task/milestone to be completed as well as other costs that are not directly attributable to specific tasks/milestones. **Target outcome:** An accurate, clear, precise, and complete description of planned project costs along with discretionary allocations to handle unplanned costs that impact project execution. The relevant project stakeholders should have a common understanding of the budget plans.
Staffing and other resource planning	**Definition:** Process of determining, locating/obtaining, and allocating resources to the task/milestones to be completed. **Target outcome:** An accurate, clear, precise, and complete description of the resources that will be needed to complete the project tasks/milestones and other project efforts, a description of the source of the resources, and a schedule of when the resources will be used during the project.

Continues

Table 4–2: *Descriptions of Activities in Managing Plans (Continued)*

Activity	*Description of Activity*
Tracking and controlling the budget and schedule	**Definition:** Process of gathering and analyzing information to determine the state of the project with respect to the budget and schedule. It also includes making adjustments as needed to stay within budget and on schedule. **Target outcome:** At any point in the project, an accurate understanding of the project accomplishments and expenditures. It ensures project deliverables are complete on schedule and within budget.
Estimating the budget and schedule	See Chapter 3, "Managing Estimates."
Managing midstream changes to project plans	**Definition:** Process of adjusting plans in order to achieve the project objectives or, when needed, of modifying the project objectives to satisfy the stakeholder expectations. **Target outcome:** Modified plans whose successful execution will enable project results that satisfy the stakeholder expectations.
Managing software development with respect to project objectives, policies, schedule, and budget	Managing product quality is a goal of development management. See Chapter 5, "Managing Product."
Managing processes with respect to project objectives, policies, and other project plans	Managing process quality is a goal of process management. See Chapter 6, "Managing Process."

People who manage software project plans make decisions such as those shown in Table 4-3. The example decisions are grouped by decision area. As discussed earlier, the decisions focus on the basic elements of a software project plan such as objectives, organization, and work and budget planning. Because a project plan specifies what should be managed and how it should managed, the related decisions naturally concern content as well as process. Explore the table, and then think about other decisions that you have encountered or think you might encounter when managing software project plans.

Table 4–3: *Decisions to Make When Managing Software Project Plans*

Decision Area	*Example Decisions*
Project overview	What are the project objectives, context, and scope?
Project stakeholder expectations	What are the stakeholders' expectations regarding the scope (requirements), time to delivery (schedule), quality, and cost (budget) for the project deliverables?
Project resource allocations (schedule, budget, staffing, and so on)	What tasks and milestones, schedule, budget, staffing, and other resource allocations will enable the software project objectives to be achieved with the expected time, quality, and cost?
Project constraints	What specified software development or project management processes are needed to satisfy the stakeholders' expectations? What specified staffing or other resources are needed to satisfy the stakeholders' expectations?
Project organization	What organizational structure for the software project assigns responsibilities in a way that increases the likelihood that the project objectives will be achieved? For large or complex software projects that must be divided into subprojects, how will the individual software work plans be organized and related to each other?

Continues

Table 4–3: *Decisions to Make When Managing Software Project Plans (Continued)*

Decision Area	*Example Decisions*
Project quality and risk management	What is the degree of certainty that the software project plans will enable the software project objectives to be satisfied on time, with the specified quality, and within budget? • On what is this degree of certainty based? • What are the risks associated with each aspect of the project plans? What tracking and audit processes will be used to identify the following risks to the success of the software project? • The planned tasks and milestones, schedule, budget, staff, and other resources are inadequate to achieve the software project objectives. • The status of the software project with respect to tasks and milestones completed, schedule, budget expenditures, staff, and other resource decisions do not match or satisfy the project plans. • The software development plans do not adequately ensure that the project deliverables will exhibit the expected or required quality attributes. • The project deliverables do not satisfy their functional or nonfunctional requirements. • The specified processes and their definitions do not properly ensure the accomplishment of the software project objectives, or executing the software processes does not accomplish the objectives defined for these processes.

Table 4–3: *Decisions to Make When Managing Software Project Plans (Continued)*

Decision Area	*Example Decisions*
Project replanning	What processes will be used to modify software project plans midstream when needed to enable success of the project? • How will managers of plans know if and when replanning is needed? • How will the satisfactory completion of tasks and milestones be ensured? • How will the project schedule be kept on track? • How will project costs be controlled? • How will the staff and other resources be selected and assigned at the appropriate times to achieve the project objectives and plans? • How will the project deliverables be verified and validated?

Table 4-4 shows some practical guidelines when making decisions about software project plans. The left column of the table describes the issue or decision that a project manager faces, and the right column presents some practical guidelines to consider when handling the corresponding issue or decision. Scan the table, and develop guidelines from your own experiences in managing software project plans. If you are new to project management, now is a good time to start logging and reflecting upon your experiences.

Table 4–4: *Practical Guidelines When Making Decisions About Project Plans*

Manager's Issue or Decision	*Guidelines*
What should be in a project plan?	Make the plan as complete but as simple as possible. A project plan should enable the manager to know what to manage and how to manage it. See Table 4-1 for examples.
What project characteristics should be tracked?	Identify the measurable "vital signs" that clearly indicate the health of the software project with respect to scope, time, quality, and cost.

Continues

Table 4–4: *Practical Guidelines When Making Decisions About Project Plans (Continued)*

Manager's Issue or Decision	*Guidelines*
How should project plans be regularly evaluated?	Determine how the project vital signs can be monitored easily, quickly, and regularly in order to make adjustments to the plans as needed.
How should the project vital signs be used?	Develop "pulse points" regarding how much adjustment needs to be made with respect to the amount of deviance that a vital sign is from the related project plan.
What should be the tasks and milestones for the project?	Task identification should enable the manager to do the following: • Determine the activities that need to be done to achieve the project objectives. • Determine task dependencies and the appropriate order of task execution. • Schedule the completion of each required task. • Allocate the staff and resources needed to perform the required tasks. Work activities that exhibit the following properties are candidates for tasks: • They are distinct and can be done concurrently. • They must be done in a particular order. • They result in milestones or project deliverables whose completion should be tracked. • Their performance requires specific skills that may restrict their assignment to staff members who have those skills. Milestones that exhibit the following properties should be defined separately: • Tracking of their individual completion helps ensure project success. • They are required software project deliverables. • They are prerequisites for the completion of required software project deliverables and should be tracked. • Their completion requires highly specific tasks that may restrict their assignment to staff members who have the required skills.

Table 4–4: *Practical Guidelines When Making Decisions About Project Plans (Continued)*

Manager's Issue or Decision	*Guidelines*
When developing a project schedule, what are some important ideas to remember?	Be certain that the end date for the critical path satisfies stakeholder expectations for when the project deliverables will be available. Adjustments to the tasks or schedule may be needed. Pay attention to the task or milestone dependencies. Be certain that the estimates for effort or time are realistic, include appropriate error factors, and allow adequate time for the resolution of problems. Allocate time for meetings, administrative duties, and other nondevelopment but necessary activities.
When developing staff and other resource allocation plans, what are some important ideas to remember?	Validate that the human skills, effort, equipment, and other specified resources are indeed necessary and sufficient to achieve the project objectives. Adjustments may be needed. Verify that the people and other resources being assigned actually satisfy the skill, effort, and other resource requirements.
When developing a project budget, what are some important ideas to remember?	Be certain that the project budget satisfies the stakeholders' expectations. Verify that the budget allocations associated with staff and other resources represent the actual costs of these resources. (For example, verify that the actual cost associated with a resource fits within the budget allocation. Adjustments to the resource or budget may be needed.)
When managing large software projects that are divided into subprojects, what are some important ideas to remember?	Carefully consider the tools that will be used to create the work plans as well as the skills of the people who will manage these plans before deciding how to organize the master and subproject plans. (One issue is that tools frequently have limitations regarding the identification of dependencies and cross-references between plans.) Be careful to check the staffing and other resource dependencies between the subprojects.

The Software Engineering Institute's (SEI's) *Capability Maturity Model Integration for Systems Engineering, Software Engineering, Integrated Product and Process Development, and Supplier Sourcing* (CMMI) defines project planning as one of several fundamental process areas that compose project management. The CMMI, which models software project management processes, is an excellent reference for how to define your project planning processes (CMMI Product Team 2002). When defining processes for planning and tracking projects, you will find it helpful to read the material in this chapter before delving into the CMMI guidelines.

Other software project planning resources are IEEE Std. 1058-1998 for guidelines on writing software project plans; McConnell (1997) for a classical example of a basic software project plan; Pfleeger and Atlee (2006) for how to plan and manage a software project; Bennatan (2000) and Stellman and Greene (2005) for advice on best practices in software project planning areas such as estimating, scheduling, and budgeting; and OGC to learn about a process-based, standardized, and comprehensive approach to managing projects developed by the U.K. government.

For readers who want to learn more about managing plans, we suggest the following references. Muñoz-Avila and Cox (2008) analyze research in case-based plan adaptation that helps set the groundwork for reusing project plans across similar software projects. Xu and Muñoz-Avila (2008) present the prototype for a knowledge-based system designed to assist with project-planning tasks using case-based reasoning. Ceschi et al. (2005) studied 20 managers from software companies who employed either plan-based (traditional) or Agile approaches to project management. They found that managers who use Agile methods focus more on people and process than other managers. Pikkarainen et al. (2008) found that while Agile software development practices facilitate team and organizational communication of the dependencies between product features and working tasks, the team and organization also must use plan-driven practices to ensure the efficiency of external communication between all the stakeholders of software development.

4.3 Case Studies

The case studies in this chapter emphasize the not so glamorous but important activities of replanning and managing the details of plans. The "To Replan or Not to Replan?" case study discusses the issue of when and why to adjust the budget, schedule, or staffing plans. Stakeholders in the case study have to decide whether replanning is needed. The second case study, "Management Is in the Details," looks at the details of planning and tracking software projects that share resources with other projects and engineering groups. A special Process Analysis Team (PAT) investigates and determines reasons for why the software organization consistently has problems in planning and managing software projects and resources. The team must decide recommendations for improvement to give to the director of engineering. Read these cases to understand better the nuances of managing software project plans.

CASE STUDY

To Replan or Not to Replan?

Directions

When reading this case study, focus on the activities and decisions that are part of planning and tracking a software project. In particular, note the issues associated with the need to replan. The case refers to a few standard but specific metrics that are used in practice for project planning and tracking. Therefore, it is particularly helpful to review the terminology for the case study before reading it.

Case Summary

DESCRIPTION

Nordic Petro has adopted an enterprise approach to managing its business operations. All business and management decisions will be based upon company-wide information accessed in real time. With this goal in mind, Nordic Petro converted its core business systems to a centralized SAP suite of software to manage human resources, finance, and sales and distribution. The software conversion yielded significant savings in operational expenses as well as increased revenues. The company now wants to add the SAP enterprise software for customer relationship management, supplier management, and asset management. The company's goal is to reduce the costs of managing customer service and the supply chain as well as the expenses associated with the maintenance and use of plants, equipment, and other capital assets. The estimated cost for the Renaissance Project is 300 million Norwegian Kroner (approximately 50 million USD in June of 2007). The estimated rollout of all new systems is 2.5 years from the start of the project. The company has contracted a large consulting firm, IT Sphinx, to help with project planning and management, business and integration process planning, and software development and integration. The case scenario focuses on the project-planning phase.

CASE STUDY OBJECTIVES

After reading the case study, you will be able to do the following:

- Understand better the following issues when managing software project plans:
  - Determining when and why replanning is needed
  - Selecting project management metrics and data to be collected
  - Managing risks associated with project plans

- Identify the activities and decisions by which the software project managers manage the budget, schedule, and staffing plans.
- Explain the problems that occurred in the case scenario, the causes of the problems, some plausible solutions to the problems, and ways to eliminate the problems in the future or to reduce their impact. Relate these to the decisions faced by project stakeholders.

SUBJECTS COVERED

Budget planning, managing project plans, managing project risk, project planning, project replanning, project staffing, project tracking, and schedule planning

SETTING

The setting is the information technology (IT) center at the global headquarters of Nordic Petro in Oslo, Norway. The company focuses on the exploration, development, and production of oil and natural gas from the Norwegian Continental Shelf but has recently ventured into renewable energy production. The company has business operations in more than 40 countries and operates four business segments: Oil Exploration and Production, Natural Gas, Renewable Energies, and Manufacturing and Marketing. Nordic Petro is publicly traded on the Oslo Stock Exchange.

KEY CONCEPTS

- Making appropriate decisions about when and why replanning is needed is important to the successful management of software projects.
- Deviating from software project plans is a common occurrence. Knowing the reasons why deviance typically occurs can help software project managers develop plans that are less likely to be impacted by deviance and can help them more effectively prepare for, recognize, and handle deviances when they occur.
- Software project managers need to collect project management data that will help them develop benchmarks for estimating the resource needs of similar projects in the future.

TERMINOLOGY

Actual cost of work performed (ACWP): The sum of costs actually incurred in accomplishing the work performed (U.S. Department of the Navy).

In practice, ACWP is the sum of the hours (cost) actually used for all tasks that are complete by the end of the reporting period.

Budgeted cost of work performed (BCWP): See *Earned value (EV)*.

Budgeted cost of work scheduled (BCWS): See *Planned value (PV)*.

CEO: Chief executive officer.

CFO: Chief finance officer.

CIO: Chief information officer.

COO: Chief operations officer.

Cost Performance Index (CPI): The ratio of work accomplished versus work cost incurred for a specified time period. The CPI is an efficiency rating of work accomplished for resources expended (U.S. Department of the Navy).

In practice, CPI is BCWP/ACWP. (See the definitions for BCWP and ACWP.) CPI ≥ 1 means that the budgeted cost of work performed by the end of a reporting period is equal to or greater than the actual cost for this work. In other words, current project costs are within or below budget.

More detail: CPI is calculated as BCWP divided by ACWP (BCWP/ACWP). The budgeted and actual costs may be expressed as monetary values (for example, in dollars) or in another unit of measure such as hours. As a ratio of two values having the same unit of measure, CPI has no unit of measure. A CPI ≥ 1 is a preferred situation in which the budgeted cost of the work performed is greater than or equal to the actual cost for this work. On the other hand, a CPI < 1 suggests a less desirable situation in which the actual cost for the work performed exceeds the budgeted cost for this work. Also, a CPI that is much greater than 1 indicates that the original plan grossly overestimated the cost (in hours, dollars, and so on) needed to accomplish the planned tasks. The managers in the case study track the CPI for their project over time to determine how well their project stays on budget. A project's CPI value does not reflect a project's performance with respect to schedule. A project may be on budget while being on or behind schedule.

Earned value (EV): The amount or volume of work completed to date, commonly referred to as the budgeted cost of work performed (BCWP). When compared to the planned value (budgeted cost of work scheduled) and actual cost (actual cost of work performed), EV provides an objective measure of schedule and cost performance (U.S. Department of the Navy).

In practice, EV is the sum of the hours assigned to each task that is actually complete by the end of the reporting period.

More detail: Calculations of earned value typically consider units of work that are entirely complete, such as the completion of an entire task. Earned value calculations usually do not consider tasks that are partially complete. The related SPI and CPI indexes use EV to measure schedule and cost performance, respectively. EV may be expressed as monetary values (for example, in dollars) or in another unit of measure such as hours. Each unit of work (task) in the schedule is assigned a cost, as in hours, needed to complete it.

IT: Information technology.

Planned value (PV): The assignment of the budget for each reporting period for each work component, also called budgeted cost of work scheduled (BCWS) (U.S. Department of the Navy).

In practice, PV is the sum of the hours assigned to each task that is scheduled to be complete by the end of the reporting period.

More detail: Calculations of planned value consider the tasks that are scheduled to be complete to date. PV may be expressed as monetary values (for example, in dollars) or in another unit of measure such as hours. Each unit of work (task) in the schedule is assigned a cost as in hours needed to complete it.

Schedule performance index (SPI): The ratio of work accomplished versus work planned for a specified time period. The SPI is an efficiency rating for work accomplishment by comparing work accomplished to what should have been accomplished (U.S. Department of the Navy).

In practice, SPI is EV/PV. (See the definitions for EV and PV.) SPI ≥ 1 means the actual amount of work performed by the end of a reporting period is equal to or greater than what is scheduled to be complete. In other words, the project is on or ahead of schedule.

More detail: SPI is calculated as BCWP divided by BCWS (BCWP/BCWS). This is the ratio of earned value to planned value (EV/PV). The budgeted and actual costs may be expressed as monetary values (for example, dollars) or in another unit of measure such as hours. As a ratio of two values having the same unit of measure, SPI has no unit of measure. An SPI ≥ 1 is a preferred situation in which the work completed to date is greater than or equal to that which was scheduled. An SPI < 1 suggests a less desirable situation in which the actual work performed is less than the scheduled work. Also, an SPI that is much greater than 1 indicates that the original plan grossly overestimated the amount of time (cost) that would be needed to perform the planned work. The managers in the case study track the SPI for their project over time to determine whether their project stays on schedule. A project's SPI value does not reflect a project's performance with respect to budget. A project may be on schedule while being over or under budget.

Slack time: The amount of time a noncritical path task can slip before it affects another task; or, the amount of time between the latest finish time and the earliest finish time of a noncritical task.

The Case

SCENARIO

Project Proposal and Start (Late Spring and Summer 2007)

As the days lengthened in late spring, Henrik Holmann (a vice president of operations for Nordic Petro) and Bernard Rothstein (a partner with IT Sphinx) drafted a proposal for the next step in moving Nordic Petro toward a complete enterprise approach to managing its business operations. This next step, officially called the Renaissance Project, would involve integrating the SAP enterprise software for customer relationship management, supplier management, and asset management. The Renaissance Project would take about 2.5 years with a budget of 300 million Norwegian Kroner (approximately 50 million USD in June of 2007).

Figure 4-1 shows the organizational chart for the Renaissance Project as well as the related corporate-level committees.

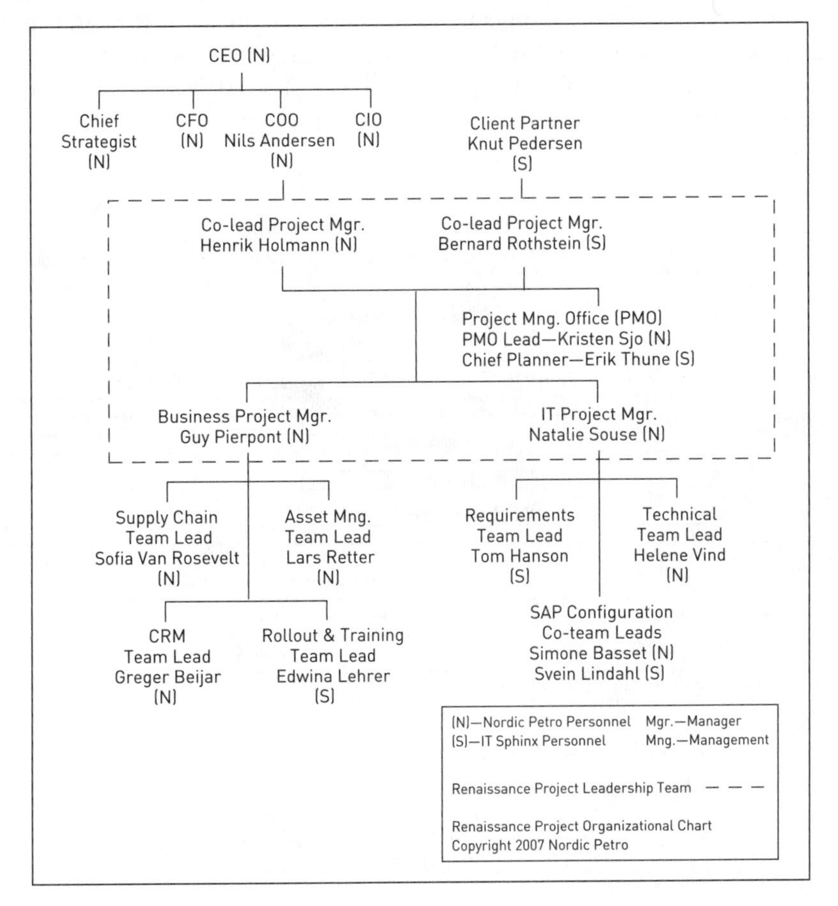

Figure 4–1: *Renaissance Project organizational chart*

From their experience with the first integration project, Holmann and Rothstein knew that the Nordic Petro investment committee was more receptive to large projects that were composed of distinct planning and execution phases with separate budgets. The committee carefully managed its investments and preferred to provide seed funding for a planning phase that can be meticulously reviewed before approving the budget for an execution phase.

Holmann and Rothstein had used their own discretionary funds to recruit help in developing a proposed work breakdown and schedule for the Renaissance Project planning phase (Phase I). The Gantt chart in Figure 4-2 provides an overview of the high-level tasks for Phase I, which was scheduled for completion by late August 2008. Two key members of the team that helped plan the proposed schedule for Phase I were Guy Pierpont, a Nordic Petro executive in operations, and Natalie Souse, a Nordic Petro IT executive. Everyone understood that if the proposal were approved, Guy and Natalie would stay on the project to provide the needed business and technology planning expertise.

The Nordic Petro investment committee was enthusiastic about the Renaissance Project and readily agreed to allocate 60 million Norwegian Kroner (approximately 10 million USD in June of 2007) for the planning phase (Phase I). Their willingness was based upon the cost savings achieved by the prior SAP integration project.

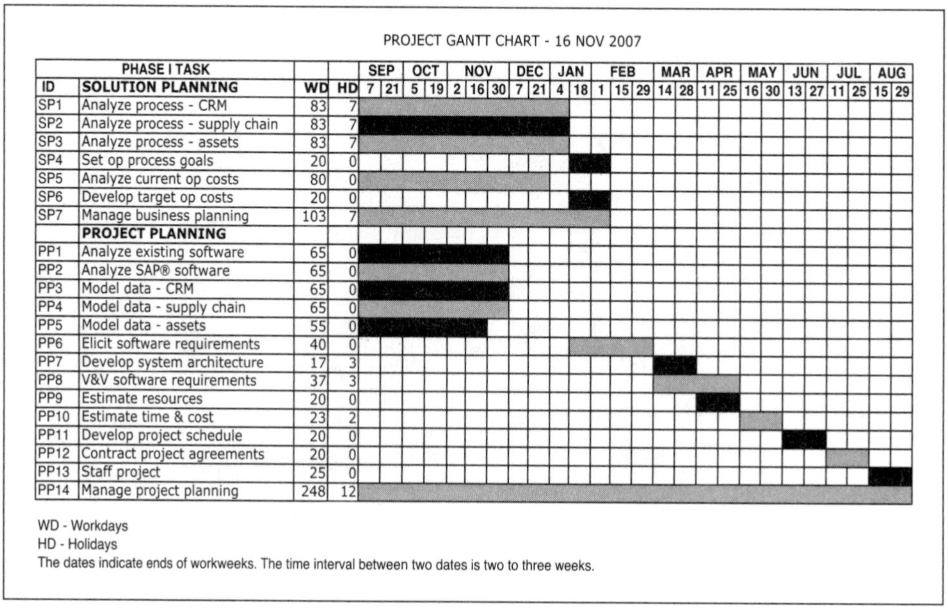

PROJECT GANTT CHART - 16 NOV 2007

SEP 7 21 | OCT 5 19 | NOV 2 16 30 | DEC 7 21 | JAN 4 18 | FEB 1 15 29 | MAR 14 28 | APR 11 25 | MAY 16 30 | JUN 13 27 | JUL 11 25 | AUG 15 29

ID	PHASE I TASK	WD	HD
	SOLUTION PLANNING		
SP1	Analyze process - CRM	83	7
SP2	Analyze process - supply chain	83	7
SP3	Analyze process - assets	83	7
SP4	Set op process goals	20	0
SP5	Analyze current op costs	80	0
SP6	Develop target op costs	20	0
SP7	Manage business planning	103	7
	PROJECT PLANNING		
PP1	Analyze existing software	65	0
PP2	Analyze SAP® software	65	0
PP3	Model data - CRM	65	0
PP4	Model data - supply chain	65	0
PP5	Model data - assets	55	0
PP6	Elicit software requirements	40	0
PP7	Develop system architecture	17	3
PP8	V&V software requirements	37	3
PP9	Estimate resources	20	0
PP10	Estimate time & cost	23	2
PP11	Develop project schedule	20	0
PP12	Contract project agreements	20	0
PP13	Staff project	25	0
PP14	Manage project planning	248	12

WD - Workdays
HD - Holidays
The dates indicate ends of workweeks. The time interval between two dates is two to three weeks.

Figure 4–2: *Gantt chart for Renaissance Project planning phase (Phase I) (Copyright 2007 Nordic Petro)*

Guy and Natalie would need help with the numerous activities involved in planning and managing the Renaissance Project. Therefore, Holmann and Rothstein organized a Project Management Office (PMO) to provide project planning and management guidance for the Renaissance Project. Kristen Sjo (a senior manager with Nordic Petro) would head the PMO. Rothstein recruited Erik Thune, who had significant project planning experience, from IT Sphinx to be the chief planner. Figure 4-1 shows that the PMO reports directly to Holmann and Rothstein.

Henrik Holmann also set up a Renaissance Project Leadership Team to "set a course, navigate, and steer" the project. See the dashed line in Figure 4-1 that denotes the Renaissance Project Leadership Team. Holmann (a former naval commander) was determined that by August 2008 the project would have completed Phase I and have received its next round of funding for Phase II (the execution phase). This would be about one year after the official start of Phase I on September 3, 2007.

Holmann's rationale for wanting the Phase I tasks (up to the contracting of the project agreements for Phase II) to be complete by the summer of 2008 was based on advice from his boss (the Nordic Petro COO Nils Andersen). Since the Nordic Petro investment committee met quarterly, Nils had advised Henrik to submit the funding request for Phase II during the investment committee's summer meeting in 2008. As Nils and Henrik had discussed, missing the summer meeting would result in at least a three-month delay in receiving the approval and therefore the funding for the execution phase of the project. The lapse would not only delay the rollout of the new business systems but would also cause continuity problems. It would be difficult to find alternative projects for all the project staff that would span only three months (the delay time).

During the first meeting of the Renaissance Project Leadership Team, Henrik gave his management crew this direction: "Full speed ahead. Project agreements and funding for Phase II must be in place by July 25, 2008!" Staffing for Phase II would be done in August 2008, as shown on the Gantt chart in Figure 4-2.

The Renaissance Project Phase I started officially on September 3, 2007. The Renaissance Project Leadership Team held weekly meetings to review the project status and to convey information that needed to be communicated to the various project teams.

Conversation Between Guy and Natalie (November 16, 2007)

"Ugh, no improvement. The SPI for our project is still around 0.88," exclaimed Guy. "We are 11 weeks into the project, and we have not been able to catch up." (SPI < 1 means that the project is behind schedule.)

"I know. I just got the bad news from Kristen Sjo. At this rate, we will never have the project agreements for Phase II, which is on the critical path, in place by July 25, 2008," bemoaned Natalie.

"How did we get into this situation?" Guy asked. He then commented, "In the past, I might have suspected poor estimation, but I don't think that poor estimation is the problem because the estimates were based on our experience with the first integration project. We should have the team leads check the actual expenditures of effort for the Phase I tasks that have been finished or are near complete with the effort that was planned for these tasks."

Guy continued in an animated voice, "At first, we thought that the low SPI values reflected some problems that we had getting ramped up, but we have had all the staff in place for several weeks now. From our prior experience with the way our staff works, we thought that the actual work accomplished would catch up with the planned work. It's as though there is a gremlin in our project that is wrecking havoc with the completion of tasks as planned!"

"Henrik and Bernard are not going to be happy at our leadership meeting on Monday when they hear that the project progress has not improved. They are adamant about the date when the agreements and funding for Phase II should be in place. Do you remember what Henrik said when we were working on the project proposal?" Natalie asked Guy.

Guy quoted Henrik with authority, "Full speed ahead. The project agreements and funding for Phase II must be in place by July 25, 2008!" Then he added, "I don't think we can accomplish this with the current schedule."

Weekly Project Leadership Meeting (November 19, 2007)

Attendees: Henrik Holmann, Bernard Rothstein, Guy Pierpont, Natalie Souse, Kristin Sjo, and Eric Thune

The meeting started briskly with a quick review of old action items. Henrik Holmann queried the others regarding the move that the project had made to the new headquarters building on King Harald Street. "Were all of the teams settled? Did they have the physical resources that they need?" he asked. Everyone reported that the move was going smoothly, though there had been some minor delays in the transport of computing equipment.

Next was the review of project status. Guy reported that the project SPI was still running about 0.88. Natalie explained that a major data modeling effort that was to have been finished yesterday was significantly late. (The data modeling effort is task PP5 on the Gantt chart in Figure 4-2.) Guy added that the tasks for business process analysis were also behind schedule (tasks SP1–SP3 on the Gantt chart).

Henrik Holmann looked very serious when he said, "What is the likelihood that the current schedule slippage will negatively impact the completion of the project agreements for Phase II on time?"

Kristen replied, "With the current rate of schedule slippage, the project will not start contracting the project agreements for Phase II as planned on July 7, 2008, and therefore is not likely to be on schedule in completing this task."

Holmann barked, "Do we have a plan in place for handling schedule slippage? What would it take for the project to catch up?"

Kristen cautiously answered, "We had planned to bring in more people if schedule slippage occurred, but this may not solve the problem. We need to look at the root causes for the slippage and study the current schedule, budget, and staffing plan to determine a good solution."

Guy added, "The problems that we had in ramping up the project were solved weeks ago."

"Well, I want you to find out what is causing the schedule slippage and to determine some ways to fix it. I would like to hear back with your proposed solution at a special leadership meeting to be held in three days," Holmann ordered.

"If the CPI is still running around 1.04, we might have unused budget to expend on a solution," Bernard Rothstein stated quietly but firmly. Bernstein had been closely monitoring the budget and knew that the outsourcing deal that they had negotiated for the data modeling tasks had come in below budget. The planned costs were more than the actual costs to date.

Holmann moved to the next items on the agenda, which were issues and risks. Natalie reported that the team analyzing the existing software did not have sufficient access to the Nordic Petro business systems. Natalie explained that the team was behind schedule because of this situation. She wanted some help in getting the CIO to provide more access to these systems.

Natalie also reported that the project might not be able to obtain a software package being developed by Asset Management & Solutions, LLC, that they planned to add onto the SAP asset management software in time for integration. She had read in a reputable trade journal that the release of this module was likely to be significantly behind schedule. Natalie said that with the current plan to use the module, the schedule for Phase II (to be developed in Phase I) would be dependent on the release date of this module. She requested that the risk management group look into and propose ways to manage this situation. (The risk management group is composed of people from various teams and is not shown on the project organizational chart.)

During the report on human resource management, Guy said that Lars Retter, the lead for the Asset Management Team, would be leaving the company in a month. Tartan Renewable Energy, a Scottish company that focuses on the exploration and development of alternative energies, had hired Lars to head up their asset management operations.

Holmann responded, "Lars will be difficult to replace. I will ask Human Resources to work on finding a replacement as soon as possible, but I am concerned that the project could be further delayed while we look for a replacement. In the meantime, Guy, I would like for you to fill in for Lars until we find a replacement." Guy smiled but looked stressed. Guy thought they could manage for a while without a replacement but knew that as the project progressed he would not have time to provide adequate leadership to the team.

Next, Kristen announced that the project Christmas party was set for the second Friday in December, starting at 6 p.m. The party would be held at the Aurora Borealis Restaurant that overlooks the Oslo Fjord.

The leadership meeting ended with a review of the new action items. The highest-priority action item was Holmann's directive for Guy, Natalie, Kristen, and Erik to determine the root causes of the schedule slippage and to propose ways to bring the project back on schedule. They had three days to work on this problem.

Special Project Management Meeting (November 20, 2007)

The PMO held a special project management meeting to explore the root causes of the schedule slippage. Guy, Natalie, Kristen, Erik, and the team leads attended the brainstorming session.

Leading the meeting, Guy said that their goal was to determine what was causing the schedule slippage and to brainstorm ways to fix the problem. He suggested that they start by reviewing the task areas that were behind schedule. Guy then projected the schedule for the high-level tasks of Phase I on an overhead screen.

The business manager and his team leads were managing the tasks listed under "Solution Planning," while the IT manager and her team leads were heading up the tasks shown under "Project Planning," as indicated previously in Figure 4-2. The staff working on many of the tasks consisted of people from business and IT. The special project management team looked at the current SPIs and CPIs for the high-level project tasks in progress, shown in Table 4-5. The SPIs in bold are 0.8 or less. (SPI < 1 means that the task is behind schedule. CPI ≥ 1 means that a task's budgeted cost is greater than or equal to its actual cost.)

Table 4–5: *Current SPIs and CPIs for Phase I Tasks in Progress*

Renaissance Project Phase I Task	*SPI*	*CPI*
SP1: Analyze process—CRM	0.95	1.12
SP2: Analyze process—supply chain	0.85	1.07
SP3: Analyze process—assets	**0.75**	1.1
SP5: Analyze current op costs	1.0	1.06
SP7: Manage business planning	0.95	1.0
PP1: Analyze existing software	**0.8**	1.03
PP2: Analyze SAP software	0.83	1.04
PP3: Model data—CRM	0.87	1.0
PP4: Model data—supply chain	0.85	0.98
PP5: Model data—assets	**0.78**	0.97
PP14: Manage project planning	0.98	1.0

Each high-level task is composed of multiple lower-level tasks whose progress is tracked by the project team working on them. The SPI value for a particular high-level task is determined by the progress made on the constituent lower-level tasks.

The team leads grimaced when they saw the SPI values. Guy waited a moment and then said, "The numbers are poor, which indicates that the work efficiency is much less than planned, but I do not think that the speed of at which work is done *when work is being done* is the main problem.

He then explained, "I spoke with each of the business team leads and found that their staff members are not getting the information that they need from the business operations personnel. Team members are often working on other projects while waiting for information from the field."

Guy continued, "The problem is *not* that the business analysis task work is being done more slowly than planned. The problem is that the business analysts are not able to work on their tasks. That is one reason why the CPI numbers for the project have been good for the last 11 weeks, while the SPI values during the same interval were dismal."

An SPI value reflects the tasks that were finished with respect to the tasks that were planned to be completed within a given time period. A CPI value shows the budgeted cost of the tasks that were finished for a given time period with respect to the actual cost of completing those tasks. Figure 4-3 shows the plots of the project CPI and SPI values for week 1 through week 11 of Phase I. Note that though they are the ratios of cumulative values, CPI and SPI values are not cumulative values. Ideally, their values will be around 1.0 or better at the tracking points in time for a project.

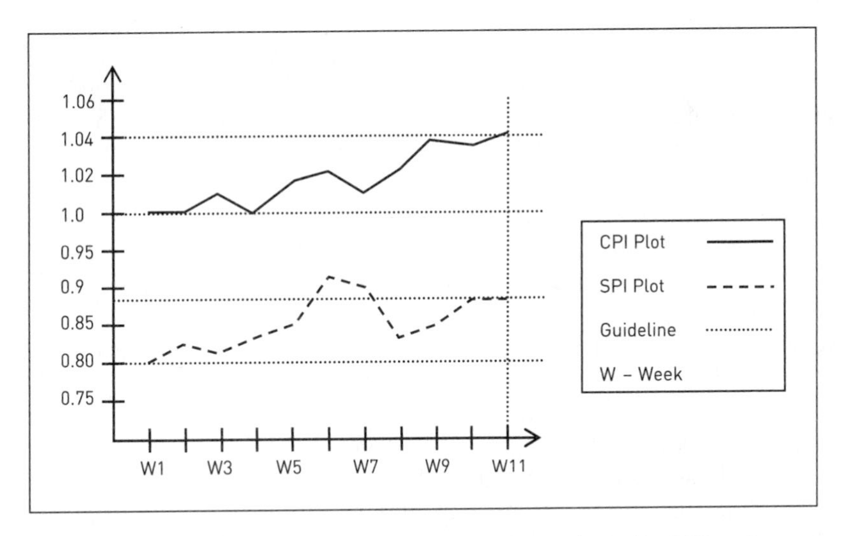

Figure 4–3: *Project CPI and SPI values for weeks 1–11 of Phase I (Copyright 2007 Nordic Petro)*

The lead for the Asset Management Team, Lars Retter, then lamented, "My team has personally visited the people in business operations and still cannot get them to commit time to work on the Renaissance Project. When Henrik recruited me for this project, he promised that he would get commitments from the business operations people. I should have escalated this issue sooner. Before I leave, I will introduce you, Guy, to the key people who you need to help analyze our asset management processes. I didn't expect this job offer and do not like leaving you with this problem!"

The other business team leads agreed that their teams were having the same problem. The one bright spot was the process analysis for the CRM area. Apparently, the operations personnel in this business area were excited about the timesaving aspects of using an enterprise SAP CRM system. Therefore, they eagerly set aside time to work with the Renaissance Project staff.

"I have also heard that the data modeling people are having some of the same problems getting information from the business operations people. So, one root cause of schedule slippage is the lack of information and help from the business operations people who do not have scheduled time commitments to work on the Renaissance Project when needed," Natalie concluded.

Helene Vind, the IT technical lead, then commiserated, "My team has had a related problem. We have not had adequate access to the existing business software. We are continually in a 'beg and borrow' mode that has delayed our progress. I understand that Natalie reported this issue at the last Project Leadership meeting. What is going to be done about it?"

"I asked for help in getting the CIO to provide us with more access to the business systems that we need to analyze. I will certainly follow up at the next Project Leadership meeting," Natalie offered.

"Even if productivity is not the main cause of the overall project schedule slippage, I think we need to look at the productivity of the staff working on the data modeling tasks. The outsourced staff is less skilled than we expected when we negotiated the outsourcing contract. That may be why the bid came in lower than the budgeted amount," Kristen commented.

Helene Vind quickly added, "The outsourced team members are good workers, but they require lots of guidance about how the data modeling should be done. This lowers the productivity of all the project staff working on these tasks. I think that the productivity of the data modeling teams is causing some of the schedule slippage."

"We have identified lack of access to information and help from business operations personnel as well as limited access to business system software. We have agreed that these factors in addition to the low productivity of the data modeling staff [because of the lower than expected skill level of the outsourced staff] are root causes of the schedule slippage. I think we should also compare the actual effort to the planned effort for the completed tasks to verify that our effort estimations are appropriate. Are there any other root causes for the schedule slippage?" Guy asked.

No one offered other suggestions. Therefore, Guy stated, "I think the question is whether we can make up the schedule slippage without replanning or if we need to replan.

In particular, can we make up the schedule slippage with the current schedule, or do we need to revise it? With the current schedule, we would need to increase the productivity of the data modeling staff that we have said is working more slowly than planned or possibly add more people. We have some unused budget that could fund this approach."

Erik Thune then commented, "Consider task PP5, model data for assets, with an SPI value of 0.78. Getting back to an SPI of 1.0 would require about 29 percent increase in productivity [0.78 x 1.29 is about 1.0]. If this could be done immediately, we would not incur any additional schedule slippage, but to 'catch up,' we would have to increase the productivity by more than 29 percent. Training the outsourced data modeling staff to help them be more productive would incur more time and cost."

Erik continued, "Adding people may or may not help. Brooks' Law says that adding people will make a late project run even more behind schedule because of the additional coordination, communication, and other management issues. In any event, we should look more closely at the data modeling tasks to see whether there is another solution" (Brooks 1995).

Eric paused and then stated, "We also have the problems associated with lack of access to information and resources. I think we are beyond the point at which we can make the current schedule work. I think we must replan. This will probably involve the schedule and staffing plans as well as the budget allocated to each task."

"I agree with Erik that adding more staff often does not solve a schedule slippage problem. I noticed in the project PERT chart that there is slack time for some of the noncritical tasks and that most tasks do not overlap," said Kristen. A program evaluation review technique (PERT) chart indicates the dependencies between the tasks and shows the critical path or series of dependent tasks, each of which must be completed on time in order for the project to finish on schedule. A task in the critical path has no slack time.

Eric replied, "We scheduled many of the Phase I high-level tasks without overlap because upper-level management is more comfortable with a waterfall schedule. In addition, dependencies between tasks that overlap are more difficult to manage. However, I think there are some high-level tasks that could start before the tasks on which they are dependent end. For example, we could start to verify and validate the requirements before the elicitation of the requirements ends, and the development of the system architecture could start earlier."

"OK. We need to replan. What should the replanning entail? Is there slack time that we can use? Can we overlap more of the tasks? Would adding more people actually help? What else should be done? Will we be able to contract the Phase II project agreements by July 25, 2008?" Guy summarized the questions still to be answered.

"At our next meeting, I would like for us to develop revised plans that we could present to the Renaissance Project Leadership Team. Please bring your task, staffing, and cost plans with you to the meeting," Guy requested. "Also compare the actual effort with the planned effort for the tasks that are done or near done. I want to verify our effort estimates for the tasks in Phase I as we replan. We will meet off-site at the company retreat center starting 'pronto' at 8 a.m. tomorrow. I will reserve the Elk Room for our replanning session."

CASE PROBLEM

The Renaissance Project is behind schedule. The actual work accomplished is 88 percent of the planned work (SPI = 0.88) and does not appear to be improving. Henrik Holmann, a lead manager for the project, has asked the project managers and planners to determine the root causes for the schedule slippage and to propose a way to bring the project back on schedule. At a special meeting, the project managers and planners identify some root causes for the schedule slippage. They discuss the problem of whether to replan and make a decision to replan the schedule, staffing plans, and budget.

At the upcoming replanning session, the PMO will work on the problem of adjusting the schedule, staffing, and budgetary plans so that the project can complete the Phase I tasks on time and within budget.

Case Analysis

ANALYSIS ACTIVITY

Analysis Background

(P) Problem: In the case study, the project managers and planners must identify the root causes of the schedule slippage and decide whether replanning is needed. In particular, they must decide whether adjustments to the schedule are necessary.

(E) Experience: The project managers and planners communicate their understanding that adding more people to the project may actually cause the schedule to slip further because of the extra communication, coordination, and management that would be needed. Their understanding of this phenomenon may be from experience, or it may simply be that they have studied and agree with Brooks' Law (Brooks 1995).

(A) Assumptions: The project managers and planners assume that the estimates used to schedule the tasks and allocate resources are good since they were based upon a similar project from the past.

(K) Knowledge: At the special project meeting, the managers and team leads identified the following factors that they think have caused the schedule slippage and are related to the decision of whether replanning is needed.

- The business process analysis and data modeling staff have not been able to complete their tasks because of a lack of information and help from business operations personnel.
- While waiting for information from the business people, some project members have worked on tasks outside the project.
- The staff members analyzing the existing software have had inadequate access to the software.
- The skill level and productivity of the outsourced staff working on the data modeling tasks is lower than expected.

- The productivity of the Nordic Petro staff working on data modeling is lower than planned because of the extra time that the staff must spend guiding the outsourced project members whose skill level is less than expected.
- The increase in productivity needed to make up the schedule slippage for the data modeling tasks is more than can be practically achieved.
- There is slack time in the schedule for some of the noncritical path tasks.
- The schedule for the high-level project tasks exhibits a waterfall pattern with minimal overlap between tasks.

Solution: The project managers and planners discuss the following factors as root causes of the schedule slippage and consider whether replanning is needed.

Factors considered as root causes:

- Lack of information and help from business operations personnel
- Limited access to business system software
- Low productivity of data modeling staff because of the lower than expected skill level of the outsourced staff who are working on data modeling

Approaches considered regarding whether to replan:

- Do not replan. Simply increase productivity of the data modeling staff.
- Use current schedule and adjust the staffing and budgetary plans. Catch up by adding people.
- Replan the schedule and adjust the staffing and budgetary plans.
    - Adding people may or may not help and will be considered with caution.
    - Effort estimates for tasks will be checked and revised if needed during the replanning session.
    - Tasks with slack time and tasks that could overlap offer opportunities to adjust the schedule so that Phase I might still be able to complete on time.

For all approaches, the Renaissance Project Leadership Team must ensure that the project obtains the needed information and help from the business operations personnel as well as sufficient access to the business systems software. In addition, Guy will lead the Asset Management Team until a replacement for Lars Retter is found.

Assumed Risk:

- The project managers and planners have assumed that the task estimates are good. In fact, some of the task estimates may not be good. Using faulty estimates for replanning is likely to result in a new schedule that does not provide appropriate allocations of time for tasks and a repeat of the schedule slippage problem. The managers and planners can help mitigate this risk by verifying the estimates for completed tasks at the replanning session.
- Lars Retter, the lead for the Asset Management Team, is leaving the company in a month. Guy Pierpont will lead the team until a replacement for Lars is found. This

may work for a while, but as Phase I progresses, Guy will not have time to provide adequate leadership to the team. A replacement for Lars may or may not be found quickly.

Analysis Questions

1. Consider the reasons that the software project managers and team leads have given for the schedule slippage. What other factors, if any, *not* identified by these stakeholders do you think might be contributing to the delay?
2. Explain why the stakeholders think that replanning is needed. Do you agree or disagree with their decision? Explain your reasoning, and describe any additional information that you may like to have before making this decision.
3. Now suppose that you have been asked to lead the all-day, off-site replanning session. What replanning options would you like the stakeholders to consider? Identify issues that you think should be discussed as potential action items or for which special action plans may need to be developed.

DISCUSSION

At the special project meeting, the managers and planners first identify factors that they have determined are causing the schedule slippage and discuss a few approaches to solving the problem. The factors (such as inadequate access to information, help, and software) highlight issues associated with obtaining and enforcing time and resource commitments from business operations personnel. Another factor is the lower than planned productivity of the data modeling staff that is a result of the extra time spent guiding the outsourced project members whose skills are lower than expected. The solution to the schedule slippage problem must ultimately address these issues.

As a second step, the project managers decide whether they need to replan. They discuss two commonly considered strategies for making up schedule slippages: adding more people to project tasks and increasing the productivity of the people working on tasks. The managers and planners reason that adding more people or increasing productivity will not resolve the delays because of lack of information, help, and resources. They are also aware that adding more people may or may not speed up task completion. They calculate that the necessary increase in productivity, in particular for the data modeling tasks, to "catch up" is unrealistic. Increasing the productivity of the data modeling teams would require extensive training or replacement of the outsourced staff, which would require increased expenditures of time and money.

The project managers decide that there is no way that contracting the project agreements for Phase II could be complete by July 25, 2008, without replanning. They decide to meet again to adjust the project plans as needed to achieve the target completion date. The project managers and planners identify some features of the schedule that offer replanning opportunities, such as using the slack time of noncritical path tasks and overlapping more tasks. At the end of the case study, the question remains as to what the replanning should entail and which project plans (for example, schedule, staffing, and budget) and policies (for example, obtaining and enforcing time commitments from the business operations personnel) will be adjusted.

CONCLUSIONS

The arguments that the project managers and planners make for replanning are reasonable. They think that strategies such as increasing productivity and adding people are impractical or may not solve the problem. At the replanning session, the managers and planners will adjust the schedule as well as the staffing and budgetary plans to be used in guiding Phase I to completion on time and within budget. Part of the replanning will include the verification of estimates used for the tasks that are done or near done. This may help the managers determine whether they need to adjust the estimates for the tasks that still need to be completed. The managers should also develop plans for how to obtain time commitments from the business operations personnel as well as sufficient access to the business software.

KEY IDEAS TO REMEMBER

- Project execution frequently does not proceed as planned.
- Replanning is necessary when the current plans no longer help managers guide their projects to completion on time and within budget or help them achieve project objectives.

CASE STUDY

Managing Plans Is in the Details

Directions

When reading this case study, focus on the activities and decisions that are part of planning and executing software projects that share resources with other projects or activities. Observe the points of view taken by people who manage software development projects in comparison to those who manage field service activities. You may find it helpful to review the terminology related to earned value for the first case study in the chapter ("To Replan or Not to Replan?").

Case Summary

DESCRIPTION

SmartElectronics is a company that has fine-tuned its technical expertise but has limited management expertise. Managers struggle to plan projects in a timely fashion and often find that their projects deviate from the plans. The resource needs of different projects and software activities frequently conflict. The company's director of software development, Alice McCaddish, creates a Process Analysis Team called PAT to study these problems and to propose ways to improve the management of software projects and resources. The case study gives an overview of the PAT discoveries and lets you decide what improvements should be made.

CASE STUDY OBJECTIVES

After reading the case study, you will be able to do the following:

- Understand issues, problems, and decisions related to the following activities:
    - Planning and tracking projects
    - Managing dependencies between plans and subplans
    - Managing software projects that share resources
    - Selecting and using software project management metrics and tools
- Explain the problems that occurred in the case scenario, the causes of the problems, some plausible solutions to the problems, and ways to eliminate the problems in the future or to reduce their impact. Relate these to the decisions faced by project stakeholders.

SUBJECTS COVERED

Managing projects that share resources, project management data and metrics, and project planning and tracking

SETTING

The setting is the software development center for SmartElectronics in Adelaide, Australia. The company specializes in the research and development of medical devices. SmartElectronics is a privately held company founded by professors from Southern

Australia University. The company employs more than 500 people, including a large proportion of software engineers.

KEY CONCEPTS

- Software project planning and tracking requires attention to detail.
- When making decisions about using techniques and tools for project planning and tracking, software project managers should consider the following:
  - The capabilities and limitations of the techniques and tools
  - The nature of any tracking data that will be collected as well as how it will be analyzed and used to manage the project with respect to the project plans
  - The ease by which the project staff can use or learn to use them
  - The ease by which they can be used across projects that share resources

TERMINOLOGY

Earned value (EV): See the definition provided in the "To Replan or Not to Replan?" case study.

Planned value (PV): See the definition provided in the "To Replan or Not to Replan?" case study.

The Case

SCENARIO

Alice McCaddish, the director of software development, has gathered the following software project managers for a weekly status meeting:

- Alan Brown, manager for Release 2 of the Robo Surgeon Assist (RSA) product
- Sansan Chin, manager for Release 3 of the Robo Nurse Assist (RNA) product
- Deepak Patel, manager for Release 1 of the Robo Home Healthcare (RHH) product

"Good morning, and welcome to our weekly status meeting," Alice greeted the project managers.

"As shown in the meeting agenda, we are going to spend some time today discussing project planning and management issues or problems that you think are affecting our ability to deliver quality software on time and within budget. Our objective is to find areas for improvement that will help us to keep our products competitive in the market," she continued.

"But first, we will review the status of our projects. Alan, how is your project going?" Alice asked.

"My project is still behind schedule. The earned value is running about 95 percent of the planned value. Our actual costs are about 98 percent of the planned costs. One problem is that we are short-staffed. Two of our key software engineers are currently fixing an 'unacceptable feature' that was detected in the field for Release 1 of the RSA product. We need these engineers to help complete the requirements and effort estimation for Release 2," reported Alan.

"What is the feature, and why is it unacceptable?" Alice asked.

"The feature involves calibration information that was used when designing Release 1 of the RSA software. The customer reviewed and approved the calibration requirements for Release 1, and the software passed the system tests based on this information. Now the customer has different assumptions about calibration that invalidates some of the earlier calibration requirements for the software. The software does not perform in the field as the customer expects. This is why I call the feature unacceptable rather than defective," Alan explained.

"This must be the issue that you called me about last week, the one regarding the robot arm that jerks when being calibrated. Are the customer's assumptions valid?" Alice inquired.

"That is the one. Though the customer's environment is not typical, the customer's assumptions are valid. Robert Davis [the director of field service] has made it clear that this customer will purchase more RSA robots once Release 1 passes the customer's tests. The unacceptable feature is not a safety issue but is considered important by marketing and sales," Alan replied.

"Are there other staff members who can temporarily replace the software engineers who are modifying the calibration software?" Alice asked.

"Probably, but it would take more time and money to find qualified staff and to bring them up to speed on the product than it will to modify the software. We're trying to shorten the planning time for Release 2 by using a more systematic approach to effort estimation based on an analysis of the historical data from Release 1. This will help if we are not bogged down in resolving issues regarding the requirements and modifications to the architecture for Release 2. I have encouraged the project planners to move forward by defining tasks with time allocated for the exploration and resolution of open issues instead of waiting for the requirements and architectural issues to be resolved," Alan explained and sighed.

Alice raised her eyebrows and then asked, "How is the RNA Release 3 progressing?"

Sansan reported, "The project is almost on schedule with the earned value running about 99 percent of the planned value. There were fewer defects reported in the field for Release 2 than for Release 1, so we can spend more time on new features for Release 3."

Then she added, "The field service organization has once again [with emphasis] requested our help in providing a feature enhancement between releases for a very important customer. The additional feature involves the tracking and reporting of patient vital signs over time. The staff members who are most knowledgeable about the tracking and reporting parts of the system related to the enhancement are currently needed for the detailed design of Release 3. Their expertise is particularly important for the review of the detailed design, test plans, and test cases. Most notably, I have only one software engineer working on creating graphical displays, which the customer wants to be part of the report."

"Robert tried to convince me that the enhancement was critical to the customer and that the feature upgrade could then be offered to other customers in Release 3. He is asking us to expand the scope of Release 3 in order to satisfy his service request," Alice stated. "Can we split the time of the software engineers so that they could perform the review tasks while working on the enhancement?"

Sansan cautiously answered, "Yes, but we would still take a hit on the Release 3 schedule." Then she asked, "Who will pay for the additional development cost?"

Alice said, "Please provide me with an estimate of the projected impact on the schedule and budget. Meanwhile, I will talk with the marketing and sales people to learn more about the need for this feature between releases."

"How is the RHH project coming along, Deepak?" Alice inquired enthusiastically.

Frowning, Deepak replied, "Well, we have the typical new product challenges. Project planning is slow with the earned value at about 93 percent of the planned value. There has been some confusion in tracking progress. For instance, some people count tasks that are complete or nearly complete to determine the earned value; others count only the tasks that are complete. I have asked the team leads to count only tasks that are complete and to be certain that their teams do the same. The software engineers working on the architecture are slow in reaching a consensus, which is holding up task planning. Because RHH is a new product, we do not have any historical data for estimating the effort for tasks."

Deepak lamented, "Many of the software engineers who worked on my past project are currently involved in other projects. I am finding it difficult to find suitable staff members for my project. The employee profiles in the Human Resources (HR) database are not complete, and the terms used to describe employee skills and knowledge vary a lot. I wish that we had a more effective way to recruit staff members for our projects. For instance, I am looking for a software engineer who has developed software to interface with radio frequency identification (RFID) devices. We want to use RFID technology to sense and track items in a person's home."

"A thorough search of the HR database yielded no results. Then yesterday in the cafeteria, I overhead a colleague, Joe Montgomery, mention that the company has hired a few software engineers with experience in developing RFID applications. Joe is helping me locate the new employees. It should not be so difficult to find qualified staff within the company," Deepak complained.

Alice replied, "Let me know if you need my help in obtaining time for one of the new employees to work on your project."

She waited a moment and then said, "We have some common project management problems to solve. Let's list a few that you highlighted in your status reports. I'll start with an obvious one: the way in which we handle field service requests is interfering with our development projects. What others do you see?"

Alan contributed, "We have problems in planning development projects. We are slow in making decisions about tasks and resource needs. Estimating the resources that we will need for project tasks is difficult."

Sansan added, "I think we could improve our estimates if we would systematically compare past project estimates to the actual data and make suitable adjustments. We do not have access to historical data for products other than the ones on which we have worked, and we do not fully understand how to use historical data across products and projects."

"Project planning is delayed by our slowness in architecting the software for new products. We are plagued by analysis paralysis," Alan said. "Project planning is also delayed when planners wait for the resolution of requirements issues rather than planning for the exploration and resolution of these issues."

Sansan commented, "My teams also find it difficult to plan tasks and schedule staff when tasks go across subplans and when staff members work on tasks that are described in multiple plans. Our project management tools do not help us to coordinate tasks and resources across plans."

Deepak suggested, "I think we should add to the list the problem of staffing our projects. When the company was small, the project managers knew all the staff and could easily recruit project members with the needed knowledge and skills. As the company grew, the employee profiles became important for locating new project members, but these profiles are not adequate." He expounded, "To add fuel to the fire, there is the competition between field service and development for software engineering and product expertise that Alice mentioned."

Alan explained, "The reason for this competition is the way in which we handle problems found in the field. In the past, defects involving safety and reliability issues took precedence over product enhancements; but because of increased competition, marketing and sales is pressuring us to handle more customer requests between product releases. Our competitors are catching up with us in their acquisition of core robotic technology and will start to compete on features such as user interfaces and report generation."

Sansan added, "After the first release of a product, we must conduct a trade-off between new features and bug fixes for successive releases. We are slow in establishing the requirements for a product release, which in turn slows project planning. This will certainly hurt us down the road."

"OK, here is the next step," Alice said. "We are going to quickly ramp up a small team of experienced software engineers to study these problems in more depth and to identify others that we may not have mentioned today. I will bring in a consultant to lead this study and to help us develop and execute a plan for resolving our project planning and management problems. I would like each of you to recommend a team lead who is interested in these issues and who is also available to work on a process analysis team that we will call PAT. Please send me your recommendations by next Tuesday."

PAT Study and Approach

Alice McCaddish hired a consultant, Georgiana Howard, to lead the PAT study. The three lead software engineers selected for the team were Michelle Bowman (Robo Surgeon Assist product), Chakra Neil (Robo Nurse Assist product), and Rob Lin (Robo Home Healthcare product).

To kick off the first meeting of the PAT team, Georgiana asked, "What area of project management do you think needs the most improvement?"

"Project planning," Michelle, Chakra, and Rob quickly replied in unison.

"Especially task planning and estimating the effort and resource needs for tasks. I dread this part of project planning," Chakra said.

Michelle added, "We spend a lot of time developing a project plan, and then we have to replan because of an 'urgent request' from the field service organization. These requests always seem to take the wind out of our sails just as we ramp up a project. We eliminate most defects through extensive review and testing, but there are always some 'high-priority' requests from the field for every product release."

"I wish that I had time to attend a project management class or a training seminar on project planning," Rob commented.

"It sounds as though you agree on a major area for change. However, before we can suggest changes to be made, we need to understand better the problems that exist. To start, we have the list of problems identified by the project managers of the RSA, RNA, and RHH products. To gather more information, I suggest that we interview all the managers of software development projects as well as the team leads. We can also interview the director of field service, Robert Davis. We should develop a list of questions to structure our interviews," Georgiana explained.

"That sounds like a good idea. How extensive should these interviews be?" Rob asked.

"Since you all agree that project planning is a key problem area, I suggest that we focus at first on project planning and tracking. We can review the results of the interviews to see whether we need to make any adjustments to our approach before we move on to other areas of project management. We can start by outlining some of the major tasks involved in planning and tracking," Georgiana said.

"We could ask the interviewees how their projects accomplish each task and what problems they encounter in doing these tasks," Chakra reflected.

"That's what I had in mind," Georgiana replied.

"I would like to know more about the metrics and tools that our projects use. I think we could be more effective in project planning and tracking if we could use metrics and tools appropriately. Maybe we also need some new tools," Michelle said.

"At this time, we know that Deepak Patel reported confusion in the way people on the RHH project were reporting earned value. In addition, Sansan Chin said that the management tools do not help project planners coordinate tasks and resources across plans. We should learn more about these issues and determine whether there are any other problems or issues involving the use of metrics or tools. We might also look for opportunities to improve project planning and tracking through the use of metrics or tools," Georgiana replied.

The PAT team listed activities involved in software project planning and tracking. Then the team composed directives for the people being interviewed.

For software project planning and tracking, the PAT team asked the interviewees to explain how their projects perform each of the following activities:

1. Determining an appropriate task breakdown
2. Determining the human skills and nonhuman resources required for tasks
3. Estimating the effort and cost required for tasks
4. Developing a schedule and budgetary plans
5. Selecting and scheduling staff (staffing plan) and nonhuman resource usage
6. Creating and working with subplans
7. Tracking project status with respect to plans
8. Handling customer service requests
9. Measuring project success

In particular, the team asked the interviewees to describe any issues or problems that their projects had encountered when performing these activities. To gather information about issues involving the use of software project management metrics and tools, the team asked the interviewees to describe the following:

- Metrics and tools that your projects use to measure status and success with respect to scope, time (schedule), quality, and cost (budget)
- Issues or problems that their projects have encountered in using project management metrics or tools

In particular, the team asked the interviewees to explain how these issues or problems have affected the ability of their projects to achieve project objectives.

Results of the PAT Study

Over the next three weeks, the PAT team conducted the interviews and summarized the results. You may want to scan the results for each planning and tracking activity now and read them in more detail later when you work on the analysis activity.

1. Determining an appropriate task breakdown:
    - Establishing the requirements is frequently slow and delays task planning.
    - Developing a high-level architecture for a product or system delays task planning (especially for the first release of a product or system). The software architects are prone to analysis paralysis.

- Planners wait for the resolution of requirements or architectural issues rather than move forward by planning for the exploration and resolution of issues.
- Creating and tracking tasks across plans and subplans is tedious and errant.
- Product teams differ in their development approaches and documentation. There is almost no reuse of knowledge about tasks across products.

2. Determining the human skills and nonhuman resources required for tasks:
   - This is particularly challenging for the first release of a product because no staff has worked on previous versions of the product.
   - There is limited reuse of knowledge across product lines with similar product features.
3. Estimating the effort and cost required for tasks:
   - Different approaches to estimation yield inconsistent estimates within and across projects or field service activities.
   - There is no transfer of knowledge when staff members leave the company.
   - There is limited reuse of historical data across product lines or projects.
4. Developing a schedule and budgetary plans:
   - Project planners struggle with how to schedule tasks that are dependent on the resolution of issues such as those related to requirements or architecture.
   - Some project planners allocate extra time to tasks to allow for estimation errors and other unplanned events, while others do not. In the first case, project managers frequently argue with marketing regarding the need for a longer time to product release; and in the second case, project managers often must defend the need to extend the product release date.
   - The project planners do not effectively use product scope and quality (through iterative product releases) to control the time to market.
   - SmartElectronics does not have standard cost models to help in determining the budget for projects or field service activities. (There is a standard overhead to cover expenses such as building maintenance, utilities, employee benefits, and so on.)
5. Selecting and scheduling staff (staff planning) and nonhuman resource usage:
   - It is difficult to find appropriate staff using HR's employee profile database.
     - The terminology that employees use to describe employee skills and experience varies and is not consistent.
     - Hiring of new staff occurs even when there are available, qualified staff members in-house because it is difficult to locate them.
   - Employees tend to stay on the same product line for a long time. It is therefore difficult to share experience across product lines and projects.

6. Creating and working with subplans:
   - Scheduling and tracking tasks that go across plans or subplans is a tedious and manual process with no assistance from project management tools.
   - Scheduling and tracking staff whose tasks go across plans or subplans is also a tedious and manual process.
7. Tracking project status with respect to plans
   - Project members are inconsistent in collecting data to track project status.
   - Staff members on the same project may vary in their approach to tracking project status (for example, some project members use partial earned value, while others use the traditional approach of counting only completed tasks). This leads to confusion.
   - Project managers are reluctant to "abandon" plans that are not working.
8. Handling customer service requests:

   See the "Synopsis of Key Resource Management Problems" section on the following page.
9. Measuring project success:

   See the discussion that follows.

Software development projects measure success with respect to scope (completion of planned project deliverables), time (days ahead or behind schedule), quality (passing system tests), and cost (percentage below or above budget). Completion of a product release that demonstrates the required quality attributes on time and within budget constitutes success.

Although the field service group also measures success with respect to scope, time, quality, and cost, the field service definitions for these dimensions of stakeholder expectation are different from those for software development projects. Some example definitions are the following: scope (number of customer service calls closed per reporting time period), time (average response time to handle a customer service request), quality (weighted average of customer service ratings with the weights dependent on the importance of the customers), and cost (average cost per customer service request).

Their different views of success make it difficult for software development projects and field service to share resources. For instance, a software development project may determine that the additional time and cost associated with having project staff work on a particular field service request does not add sufficient value to the scope and quality of the next product release. Meanwhile, the field service group may perceive that the field service request has high value because the request is from an important customer. Likewise, servicing a field request often involves the issue of whose budget will cover the cost of work done by software development staff. There is currently no company policy for how to budget the cost of shared resources.

The PAT team discovered the following issues or problems regarding the use of project management metrics or tools:

- Software engineers must learn "on the job" how to collect and use data that can help them plan and track their projects.
- The use of project management metrics and tools depends on the interest of the project managers or team leads. There is limited sharing of knowledge.
- Software engineers are reluctant to spend time collecting data about their work and how they do it. The tools do not make data collection easy and automatic.
- The tools being used do not provide automated help with effort estimation, which is a particular problem for project planners.
- The tools do not help in coordinating tasks or staff across plans or subplans.

The PAT team members also drafted a synopsis of two key resource management problems that they identified through their interviews. Their synopsis appears next.

Synopsis of Key Resource Management Problems

Problem 1: After a new product release, conflicts frequently occur between the staff needs of the software development and field service organizations.

In general, field service engineers are able to handle customer service requests on their own. They receive training after the release of a product and continually increase their own knowledge as they help customers use the released product. "Low-priority" defects found in the field are typically not repaired until the next release of the product and therefore do not usually place demands upon the development organization between product releases.

The conflict occurs when the knowledge and skills of software engineers who developed a product are needed to repair "high-priority" defects detected in the field or to enhance a product between releases. These engineers are usually working on the next release of the product and must be taken away from their current development activities to produce interim versions of the software. Software project managers must first determine the overall impact of the time spent on interim bug fixes or enhancements and decide whether they can accommodate these field service requests. Delays in responding to field service requests often occur. As a result, the field service engineers take their requests for help from the development organization to the director of field service, who in turn takes them to the director of software development. The overall process of coordinating bug fixes and handling special enhancements between product releases is slow and disruptive.

The problem is complicated by the fact that software engineers tend to move on to similar development assignments in successive product releases. Software developers become experts on particular aspects of products and become the "owners" in some sense of product features. Software engineers are rewarded for high productivity and low error rates, a policy that motivates them to focus their knowledge and expertise within a particular product and on specific product features. This specialization makes it difficult to find alternative staff members who can work on field service requests. It also constrains the staff planning for a project.

Problem 2: Resource planning across software projects for different products, as well as across development projects and field service activities, is difficult to manage.

The tools for software project management do not automatically take into account the use of staff members and other resources across different software development projects and field service activities. There are currently no master plans other than the HR employment records that show staff allocations. Software projects to support product-line development tend to invest in and reuse their own project members and equipment. There is minimal sharing across product lines. Software development managers have discussed the need for master plans across product lines and projects to track staff and other resource allocations. To date, the development organization has not addressed this issue with the field service organization.

Recommendation for Project Planning and Tracking Improvements

The next step for the PAT team is to draft a recommendation for process improvements that would alleviate the issues and problems outlined in the results of their study.

What recommendations do you have for solving the problems outlined in this case study?

CASE PROBLEM

The SmartElectronics software development organization is not able to manage its projects effectively. Most notably, project planning is frequently behind schedule, and diverting development staff to handle high-priority field service requests results in project delay. Managers find it difficult to staff their projects because accurate and complete information about employee knowledge, skills, and experience is not available. There is little sharing of historical data across products and projects.

Case Analysis

ANALYSIS ACTIVITY

Analysis Questions

1. What are the primary problems that plague the SmartElectronics software development organization?
2. After a careful review of the PAT study results, draft some recommendations for improving the way in which the software development organization plans and

tracks projects. Include some recommendations for managing resources across products, projects, and field service activities.

3. If you were a software project manager at SmartElectronics, how would you decide to implement your recommendations for improvement? Is there other information that you need to know to make this decision? Use the PEAK model to evaluate your decision.
4. What do you think are the training or educational needs of the software development organization?

KEY IDEAS TO REMEMBER

- Project management requires attention to multiple details in a timely manner.
- Successful project planning and tracking depends on the appropriate use of metrics, tools, and processes. It is worthwhile to study how your project performs project planning and tracking to make any needed improvements.

4.4 Summary

The chapter focused on the following activities involved in managing plans as they relate to decision making for software projects. The activities marked with an asterisk are discussed in more detail in other chapters.

- Defining project objectives, policies, and scope
- Task and milestone planning
- Schedule planning
- Budget planning
- Staffing and other resource planning
- Tracking and controlling the budget and schedule
- Estimating the budget and schedule* (see Chapter 3, "Managing Estimates")
- Managing midstream changes to project plans
- Managing software development with respect to project objectives, policies, schedule, and budget* (see Chapter 5, "Managing Product")
- Managing processes with respect to project objectives, policies, and other project plans* (See Chapter 6, "Managing Process")

The case studies in the chapter presented practical ideas for planning and tracking project work and budget. The "To Replan or Not to Replan?" case study illustrated that software projects rarely proceed exactly as planned and that software project managers often need to carefully evaluate their decisions about whether to make adjustments to plans. The second case study, "Management Is in the Details," focused on the challenge of managing the various details of developing and tracking plans, especially when resources are shared across projects while information about how to plan and execute projects is not shared across the organization.

Software project plans should enable project managers to understand and make decisions about what is to be managed and how to manage it.

Chapter 5

Managing Product

5.1 Chapter Objectives

After reading and thinking about the concepts and case studies presented in this chapter, you will be able to do the following:

- Recognize the key issues involved with product management
- Understand the relationship between the process and the product
- Understand the key factors that influence the product in the eyes of the customer
- Recognize factors that can significantly increase product quality with minimal cost

5.2 Context

This chapter will give you insight into the issues that affect the software product. These issues are typically highly customer dependent because the customer judges the product for value. Many times in the software development domain, we refer to the key set of characteristics that the customer expects of the product as **quality attributes**. Product decisions frequently relate to issues concerning the required quality attributes.

The following are two definitions for **product management**:

- "Ensuring over time that a product or service profitably meets the needs of customers by continually monitoring and modifying the elements of the marketing mix, including the product and its features, the communications strategy, distribution channels, and price" (PDMA 2006).
- "The organizational structure within a business that manages the development, marketing and sale of a product or set of products throughout the product life cycle. It encompasses the broad set of activities required to get the product to market and to support it thereafter" (BusinessDictionary.com).

The second definition better matches the software management concepts described in this book.

The domain of software product management concerns a number of issues. The primary issues involve product development, product delivery, and product support. Although product marketing is also important, it is beyond the scope of this discussion and could easily be a topic of another chapter. Product management also involves issues of services used to deliver the product to the customer. You can use the PEAK model to help you evaluate and make product decisions, as shown in Table 5-1. The rightmost column of the table contains what-if questions that you can answer to better manage a particular issue. For each what-if question, you can determine whether the PEAK input statements are true. Study the table, and think about how you would answer these questions to manage product for your current software project.

Table 5–1: *Managing Product Decisions Using PEAK*

Issue	*PEAK Inputs*
Product development	**(P) Problem:** What can you get done constrained by cost and schedule? **(E) Experience:** Have you done anything like this before? **(A) Assumptions:** Do the people whom you assume will work on the project have the required knowledge and skills? Will these people be available when they are needed as assumed? **(K) Knowledge:** Is there a known timeline for the product to be ready? Is the software developer's understanding of the customer's business objectives, expectations, preferred communication style, and other helpful facts about the customer accurate and complete?

Table 5–1: *Managing Product Decisions Using PEAK (Continued)*

Issue	*PEAK Inputs*
Product delivery	**(P) Problem:** Which stakeholders should receive the product? **(E) Experience:** Does the software developer understand the systems on which to deploy the product or the systems to which the product must interface? **(A) Assumptions:** Will all elements needed to demonstrate the system be available as assumed? **(K) Knowledge:** Is the documentation available for the new system?
Product support	**(P) Problem:** Can the people who work with the system properly maintain the system? Is the action really a support action or a change to the original intent of the system? **(E) Experience:** Can the software developer satisfy the software project objectives by using the original delivery as a baseline and trying to duplicate issues in-house? **(A) Assumptions:** Is the assumption that people on-site can maintain the system true? **(K) Knowledge:** Is the only known configuration the original configuration delivered to the customer?

This chapter focuses on the following product management activities because they appear to be the ones that give software managers the most difficulty:

- Proper product definition
- Development management (including product-line development)
- Quality assurance and control
- Configuration management
- Product delivery and installation
- Training
- Field service

Product maintenance frequently occurs in conjunction with field service or as part of successive product releases. Therefore, we do not list it as a separate activity, though you might prefer to do this. Table 5-2 describes the activities in managing product in detail. Read the table, and think about other activities that may be involved in managing product.

Table 5–2: *Descriptions of Activities in Managing Product*

Activity	*Description of Activity*
Proper product definition	**Definition:** Establishing the requirements, quality attributes, and expectations that the customer has for a product early in the project life cycle. **Target outcome:** All stakeholders in the project have a common understanding of what "done" means for the product.
Development management (including product-line development)	**Definition:** Selecting, applying, and managing processes that enable the development of a product that will satisfy project stakeholder expectations with respect to scope, time, quality, and cost. Product-line development involves the production of evolvable software. **Target outcome:** A set of development processes that enable production to satisfy the expectations of project stakeholders.
Quality assurance and control	**Definition:** The process of ensuring that the product delivered to the customer satisfies the required quality attributes (both functional and nonfunctional). **Target outcome:** A set of process filters to ensure that the smallest possible number of noncompliances with the requirements is found by the time that the product is ready for customer delivery.
Configuration management	**Definition:** The process by which a particular version of a product can be delivered whenever the need arises. **Target outcome:** The ability to guarantee that a product that is delivered can be redelivered and that anything within the product can be tracked to its source and included in the final product.
Product delivery and installation	**Definition:** The process of putting the product in the customer's environment in addition to turning over control of the product to the customer so that the customer is independently using and working with the product. **Target outcome:** The product is integrated into the customer's environment, and the customer performs the functions of starting up and shutting down the product.

Table 5–2: *Descriptions of Activities in Managing Product (Continued)*

Activity	*Description of Activity*
Training	**Definition:** Teaching the customer how to properly configure, use, and possibly maintain the product within its operational environment. **Target outcome:** The customer understands how to operate the product from start-up to shutdown as necessary.
Field service	**Definition:** Providing the support needed to ensure that the product functions properly while the customer takes control of the product and uses it. **Target outcome:** The product maintains it reliability and availability attributes while supporting customer operations.

Even though product management is the crux of developing a software product, you cannot really consider product without considering process. Product management also involves aligning the processes used to develop the product with the stakeholder expectation dimensions of scope, time, quality, and cost. At different times in the life cycle of the product, these dimensions alternate in prominence. Early in the project, the stakeholders may consider schedule, scope, and cost to be most important. As the product begins to mature, the quality issues begin to dominate. As the project nears its end, the budget may once again become prominent because it is nearly exhausted (sometimes despite the scope that has been attained). You can use the PEAK model to ensure that you have the correct information about the relevant dimensions of stakeholder expectation to make the best project decisions possible. In the end, your decisions will be bounded by these four dimensions.

"Price is no object" is a famous saying that everyone likes to hear but that usually should have the addendum "for the next *N* minutes or until the end of the project, whichever comes first." In software product development, you must always be concerned with critical aspects of the product, even if you remove cost from the stakeholder expectations. You still have to consider what you are going to make, how long it will take, and of course how well it will meet all of its requirements.

Some people think that the customer is interested only in the software product. This is sometimes true, but at other times, the customer is also concerned with the maintenance and support that comes with the product or even the process by which the product is created. Some people use the phrase "Quality, not questions" about how the product should work when referring to the service associated with a product. This phrase is enlightening when you consider how you want to manage support of the product. Think about the last time you were involved with product management. Did you deal with quality or questions?

Software product and service cannot be separated, because they represent the same thing to the customer. This might refer to sales service as well as service after the sale. If you deliver a perfect product with lousy service or if you deliver a lousy product with perfect service, you still have not met the customer's needs. As mentioned earlier, product and process are tightly coupled. You cannot easily develop a perfect product if you have poor processes, and you are less likely to develop a poor product with good processes. You might view process and product as two sides of the same coin: independent but related. This mind-set sets the context for the reference to process concepts presented in Chapter 6, "Managing Process," during our discussion of product issues in this chapter and in the case studies. Likewise in that chapter, we discuss process management with respect to managing product quality.

When considering product management, the idea of cost has two key concepts: customer's price and development cost. You'd seldom price products at development cost unless you are a nonprofit organization. You'd normally want to make a profit. It is beyond the scope of this book to discuss how to set the price for products. One key concept that many people forget about when it comes to software product management is that this is a business; if you don't make money at the business, you don't stay in business (Goldratt and Cox 1992).

It may seem that the cost of managing the product is trivial. Unfortunately, this is not the case. Cost permeates all of the stakeholder expectation dimensions as well as all of the inputs to the decision process. Though you would like for "cost to be no object," every product has cost bounds (in other words, cost drivers for a project). Many of the decisions you'll make concerning product management are rooted in how the decision will affect the cost of the product and its profit to the organization.

Cost is so pervasive that sometimes it becomes invisible. Like the air around us, it is needed but not seen. If you want to learn the value of air, learn how to scuba dive. The first rule of diving is to answer the question, "Are you breathing?" If the answer is yes, then you have time for the next decision. If it's no, then you have a problem that needs an immediate solution. Cost, like air in diving, can be treated the same way by answering the question, "Do you have the budget to complete the solution proposed?" The subject of this chapter is not the economics of product management, so we will stop here, but each product management decision that is made assumes the budget for the decision is available to complete the solution.

As you read the case studies to examine product issues, such as quality assurance and control, change management, and product testing, you need to consider the four stakeholder expectation dimensions: scope, time, quality, and cost. Let's look at scope, time, and quality with respect to the PEAK decision inputs for product management.

Schedule is a dominant dimension when you consider factors such as time to market or fixed-price contracts. Many companies, in particular start-up companies, fall into the trap of bidding a minimum schedule to create a product so that they can win the contract. Product management sometimes forces them to make decisions about the schedule that impact the other dimensions of scope, quality, and cost. When managers decide whether to ship the product, they look at the impact on schedule. The following is an example of the PEAK inputs for this decision:

(P) Problem: The customer needs a change to the product that is contained in the next software release as soon as possible, which is a situation that creates a very tight schedule for the development group.

(E) Environment: The development group has only a small number of computers running the new software release.

(A) Assumptions: The change is believed not to affect the rest of the software application.

(K) Knowledge: The specific change requested by the customer has been heavily tested with regression tests.

Solution: Install the new version or a patch to the software to meet the customer's need on time.

Assumed Risk: The new change will affect some nontested component of the system, or the regression tests do not sufficiently cover the system functionality and thereby force the team to deal with undetected problems that would impact the future product schedule.

When product managers are considering product decisions that deal with scope, they are normally looking at whether there are sufficient features ready to be presented to the customer. The "build" must represent a valuable enough "scope" for the customer. Many companies today regularly release new versions of a product to add features and repair defects in older versions.

As software developers, we have learned to deliver the product in shorter cycles to the customer so as to avoid "the big bang" or the big surprise of over budget, under quality, or over schedule. This means the scope of each delivery must be sufficient enough to maintain customer expectations. We can ask what-if questions, such as the following, to formulate and evaluate our product scope questions using the PEAK model:

(P) Problem: Is there sufficient scope available in the product to warrant delivery?

(E) Experience: Does the system allow for incremental delivery? Will the next cycle to be delivered adversely affect the data, environment, or software already delivered and installed?

(A) Assumptions: Is the assumption that the features that are not added to the product can wait or are not a high priority to the customer at this time true?

(K) Knowledge: Do we know everything that has been built? Do we know everything that is left to be built as well as the relative priority of the features not yet added to the product?

When the product managers decide whether the product should be shipped, they look at the quality of the product. Product quality with respect to satisfaction of requirements is the critical aspect by which the customer judges the value of the product.

(P) Problem: Is the product of sufficient quality to ship?

(E) Experience: Do we understand all the defects that have been found in the product and their severity, and have we agreed to an acceptable defect level?

(A) Assumptions: Is the assumption that the defect density for a shippable product is known and understood true?

(K) Knowledge: Did we expect to find x defects at this point in the process and instead find y?

We do not intend for this discussion of managing product to be exhaustive but rather to set the context of how you can evaluate product management decisions by using the PEAK model. In particular, the examples show you how to use the PEAK model to evaluate the decisions that the characters in the case studies make in trying to manage product. We want you to understand our point of view for evaluating and making product decisions.

We recommend Clements and Northrop (2001) for a comprehensive discussion of the practice of software product-line development. You may also want to refer to the Software Engineering Institute's Web site that discusses its software product-line practices and resources (Software Engineering Institute).

5.3 Case Studies

This chapter has two case studies: one in which a major decision is to be made that will determine the direction of the product and one in which decisions were made that affected the eventual outcome of the product in an unplanned way.

In the first case study ("New Technology—Is It Always the Best?"), the engineering manager must decide on the adoption of new development technologies and techniques to create a product that is easier to maintain and costs less to use. Both the new technology and new concepts incur a number of risks that must be addressed if the product is going to be successful.

In the second case study ("Why Is This Product Wrong"), the developer is faced with the dilemma that although it seems that he did everything correctly, he still got the wrong answer. For example, PEAK information was not available or not considered when decisions were made. The result was a project that focused on the repair of product defects rather than on developing a clean solution.

CASE STUDY

New Technology—Is It Always the Best?

Directions

You can read the case study independent of the chapter background, because it will still be useful; however, you might benefit from reading the background material before reading the case study. If you choose to read the case study first, then read through it once quickly in "story-reading mode" just to set some context for the information in the chapter. Then read the chapter material. Finally, reread the case study in an analysis mode.

Case Summary

DESCRIPTION

This case will discuss the decisions a software product manager working for Transport must make regarding using a new technology component for a project. The product manager must make decisions regarding how much additional new technology can be incorporated into a transit component. This new technology involves new techniques for the development group that might require staff training and other issues. The manager must decide whether the benefits outweigh the risks.

CASE STUDY OBJECTIVES

After reading the case study, you will be able to do the following:

- Understand examples of product management issues
- Understand that there are different aspects of product management that govern decisions made on the project
- Understand the long-term impact of product and project decisions
- Understand the impact of the development techniques you can use on your own projects

SUBJECTS COVERED

Product management, quality issues, product-line development, and change management

SETTING

A decision regarding using new technology on a development project is imminent. The decision will determine to some extent how and if new technology can be integrated into future projects and how the new technology will affect the future development efforts for the group and possibly the entire Transport organization. If the new technology effort fails, future use of new technologies will be rejected because this product will be used as an example of what might happen. The key issues behind the decision are how much "new technology" is enough on a project and how to know when you have too much new technology. The manager must keep in mind the key tenants of product management to ensure that the delivered product meets the customers' expectations in the time needed.

KEY CONCEPTS

These are the questions project stakeholders must answer when making product management decisions:

- How much newness can a project take?
- Who is affected by decisions made in development?
- What are the best ways to integrate new technology?
- Who is responsible for change?

Some principles for managing product are the following:

- Product management involves the consideration of long-term issues. The product you deliver today is the product you have to maintain tomorrow.
- Different project stakeholders affect product management in different ways and to different degrees.

TERMINOLOGY

BFM: Brake feedback monitor.

Greenfield development: Completely new development; interfaces to older systems but internally starting from a clean design.

OO: Object-oriented. This is the use of software structures that model physical structures in the product or system context to implement a new product.

QA: Quality assurance.

Reuse: The idea that software components or features are reusable in future products.

TC: Train control.

The Case

SCENARIO

The Wabash Project for Transport was an 11-month software development effort. Sal Altery, the software engineering manager, had to make a major decision. A new hardware platform was being proposed by the hardware group to solve the brake feedback requirements on the Wabash transit system. Sal knew that each new hardware component in a system required some 5,000 engineering hours to design, implement, and install the software to run on the new hardware. He had obtained this information by looking at historical data for the last eight years of projects. Sal knew that the new component was being proposed as a product-line component, so that it could be used on other similar projects across existing transit systems.

The Train Control Group in which Sal worked was in charge of both the hardware and the software that provided propulsion to the train. The group was in charge of all the control logic, implemented both in hardware, which initiated braking on the trains, and in software, which directed the motors on the train to start and stop. This included an energy saving/recycling feature in which the motors could be reversed, when the train wanted to stop, to regenerate rather than use power. In effect, this feature involved converting a train's kinetic energy into power that could be used by other trains in the network. The train system either used brakes to reduce the velocity of the train by friction or put the excess electricity generated from reversing the motors into resistor banks on the train. Have you ever felt a big blast of hot air in a subway station when a train stops at the station? That blast is from the resistor banks as they heat. The new hardware was supposed to help the operator of the train provide just the right amount of braking pressure to stop the train without wasting energy.

Because this new component was an innovative "greenfield" development, it created many opportunities to be considered and required many decisions to be made. Bill Madley, the lead engineer for the Wabash Project, asked whether the new software could be developed using object-oriented (OO) techniques. Until now, all development on projects at Transport had been highly structured. This was probably because Transport originated from a hardware-based background and the people were very familiar with that type of environment. The software had always been "structured" to make the hardware components work. For example, the engineers thought that the software ran on hardware components that did all the work. As technology changed, the software was performing more and more of the logical operations on the hardware components. The decision of what method would be used for development might determine the future success or failure of the Wabash Project as well as the future of this new hardware product, called the brake feedback monitor (BFM).

The Wabash Project had the advantage and disadvantage of working with a new customer for the company. The customer, Facilidades Automaticos de Carril (FAC; a European company), had never worked with Transport before but had great expectations for the product and for what could be done in a train development project. The customer expected that everything would go "very well." This was a potentially great opportunity with some associated risk. If the customer's expectations for the product were not met, then Transport could lose a customer, and Sal might get blamed. However, if the product met the customer's expectations, then this could be "the beginning of a beautiful friendship" (IMDb.com, *Casablanca*).

FAC was a heavy-industry manufacturer in Spain. Transport had primarily been bidding contracts with a Japanese partner but had decided that it needed another partner as a safety valve. FAC also had production facilities that were closer to the Wabash Project than the Japanese partner was. Crossing the Atlantic would cause a two-day reduction in shipping time for vehicle bodies to the project site. FAC was also more receptive to the idea that new techniques might be used to save money on contracts as well as on future jobs. FAC was a heavily standards-driven group with pride in its ISO certification for quality products.

The person from FAC who was in charge of the Wabash Project was Arturo Llopart, and he visited Transport a number of times during the reviews and during the early phases of the project. He was also the person who expressed the most interest in seeing how things were done at Transport. It was obvious that he wanted to see how well integrated the Transport processes were in product development.

Project Environment

The BFM was considered a safety-critical component. This had a significant impact on the development process. Care had to be taken on how the component was interfaced to other components, and the development process had to be more disciplined than was normally used when developing new components in the group. Sal also had the idea that, since the BFM was a safety-critical component, the project might not only create a new reusable component for the company but also define new practices that could be used for safety-critical development in the future. Safety-critical requirements made the brake feedback component for the Wabash Project highly visible and a critical development in the Train Control (TC) Group. Figure 5-1 shows the Transport organizational chart.

Sal had many issues to consider before making his decision on using "new technology" for this new product. Many of the issues affecting the TC group would directly affect the engineering hours spent on the project. With the fact that too many of the recent TC software projects had been running overtime and therefore over budget, this was a serious consideration for Sal. In addition, the issues of object-oriented development would affect the Quality Assurance (QA) group and even the customer, who also participated in code reviews. Using the customer in the reviews was a little odd, but it was in response to previous problems on another project. By involving the customer, the hope was that the customer expectations would be properly set for this product. Sal had to decide whether these outside groups would accept the decisions that he would make regarding the techniques used to develop the BFM.

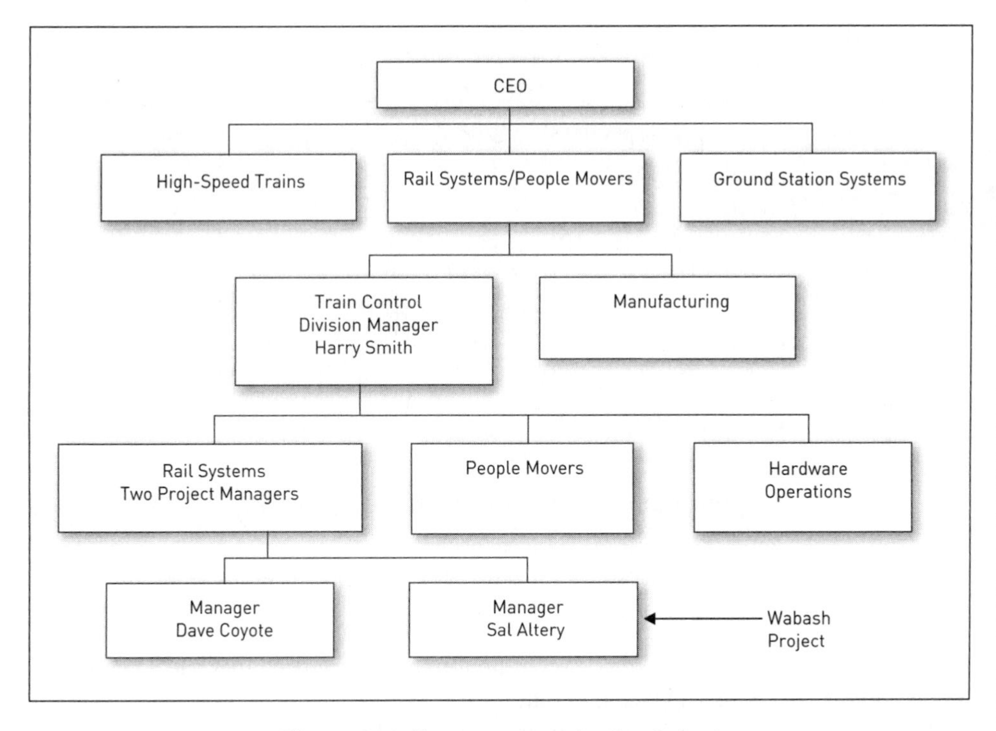

Figure 5–1: *Transport organizational chart*

Sal was concerned with how to make the best decision. He wanted to make sure that the decision he made was the best for the project.

Sal's boss, Harry Smith, did not have educational background or practical experience in software engineering. Having come up through the hardware ranks, he did not have a positive view of software and did not understand the issues and problems involved in developing software. Sal remembered one conversation where Harry drew a bell-shaped curve on the board and said, "Software development is 40 percent requirements, 20 percent coding, and 40 percent test. What else is there?" (see Figure 5-2).

Sal, on the other hand, had a software background both from his education and from a number of years of practice in the software industry. Sal was finally able to help Harry realize that a significant part of the software development process involves design, but Harry still had his idea that software was "easy." Sal knew the value of object-oriented development and reusability and thought that the organization's structured development methodology was creating maintenance issues for the TC group. He could not possibly propose changing the basic software programming languages that were used at Transport, but he might be able to affect the elements of design. The key languages being used in the TC group were C and Assembler code. Most systems had been designed using the Intel 80386 processor, which was soon going to be phased out of production.

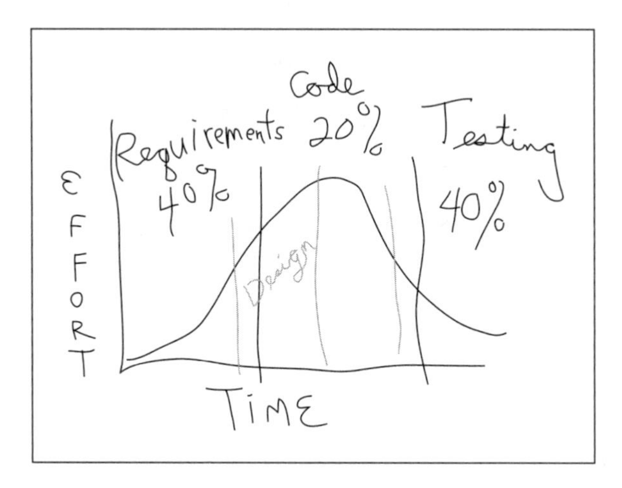

Figure 5–2: *The boss's view of software development*

Another Problem

As Sal was considering his decision, a serendipitous event occurred that had a bearing on his decision. Harry came and talked to him.

Harry said, "We must make our software more reusable."

Sal replied, "OK, that will probably require some additional work to set up reuse libraries."

Harry then stated emphatically, "No! You don't understand. Just make our current code reusable!"

This was another example of Harry's simplistic understanding of software; for Sal, it also indicated an opportunity that might help with the decision he had to make. From his past education, Sal knew that the cost for reusable code was about 25 percent more than for regular code. Therefore, if the decision was made to create reusable code, the code needed to be reused to gain the benefit.

Sal continued to weigh the issues for the BFM project. Sal considered that the BFM was only one piece of the Wabash Project. Other controllers and train management functions had to be built and tested for the Wabash system. The TC group was responsible for everything involved with moving and stopping the train. All of the code had to be "embedded" in system ROM, and this created some constraints for the decision Sal had to make.

Project Bidding

Transport bid on projects six months in advance of any work being done on them by the development group. Projects were significant and from start to finish could represent two years of work for the company. The development portion of the project alone could represent payment for 20,000 engineering hours at a loaded cost of $100 dollars per hour. For the Wabash Project, Transport had bid the effort with a new supplier with whom it had never worked. This was unusual for this industry because everyone knew everyone else. It was a small family of suppliers that provided all the components for the transit systems across the world. Occasionally, the primary contractors would change as some new country would try to get into the industry. This was the case on this project.

What Sal Knew

Sal was responsible for six projects at the time he was considering his decision for Wabash (see Figure 5-3). Sal had initiated an effort for general software process improvement on some of the projects about three months earlier. This effort had begun after Sal had been with the company for about six months. The Wabash Project had been selected to try one of the new techniques for software development improvement. The project had been slated to use software code reviews on all software produced for the project. Sal had decided to use this technique to improve the quality of the products that the TC group was producing. In reality, Sal had a hidden reason, which was that he did not want the senior engineers in the TC group to have to keep fixing defective products in the field on older projects. It appeared to Sal that defects might be keeping engineers from completing their new projects on time.

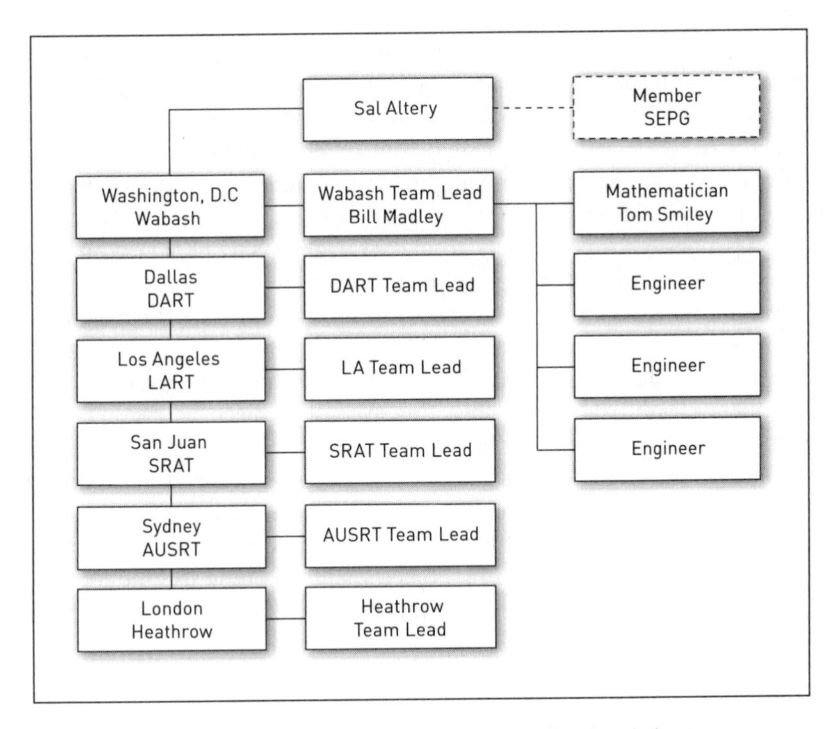

Figure 5–3: *Rail Systems Group organizational chart*

One of the critical considerations for Sal on the project was that a new BFM algorithm would need to be validated to determine whether it was going to be safe. Assigned to the project was one of the newer engineers in the company, Tom Smiley, and the lead engineer from the Wabash Project, Bill Madley. The designation as a safety-critical device made the BFM a component that had to be isolated from all other parts of the system. Safety-critical devices have a tendency to make the software embedded in them as well as other components that communicate with them safety critical simply because of association or contact. This created a mind-set of minimizing exposure to this "new" component.

Tom Smiley was a mathematician, and he was intrigued by the required BFM algorithm. The original design for the BFM algorithm required seven inputs. Usually for an embedded system, each input to a hardware-based system represents a wire connected to the component. The software group was proposing a new algorithm that could be tested in the new BFM, and it required only three inputs. Reducing the number of inputs would incur a cost savings for the company and simplify the configuration for the Wabash system. These advantages all depended on getting the new algorithm to work with the inputs provided by the Wabash hardware engineers.

To test the waters for the new object-oriented development concept, Sal identified the person in the QA group who would be supporting the Wabash Project. Albert Quinn would be heading up the QA efforts of the Wabash Project, so Sal decided to take him to lunch to float the idea of object-oriented development.

Sal inquired, "Albert, have you heard about object-oriented programming?"

Albert replied with a sigh, "Yes, I wish we had time to learn it, but we don't have time to learn anything new. Besides, my manager never wants to pay for training."

Sal then asked, "Have you ever thought about anyone using it at work?"

Albert explained, "It would never happen. Management is too stuck in its ways. They are all hardware guys, you know."

The conversation set the parameters, from the QA group's point of view, of what would be minimally needed to do an object-oriented development project. They need training and approval from a higher level of management for object-oriented development to be allowed.

The last factor in the decision was the customer. With a new customer on the project, management clearly wanted to have this Wabash Project hit its scheduled dates. Management always had the philosophy, "If you take care of the schedule, the budget will take care of itself." The customer would have to be receptive to the idea of object-oriented development for this to be a consideration for this project. The maintenance, monitoring, and verification of the system by the customer meant that the customer must be able to read and understand the code. Using object-oriented coding techniques would help with future projects by making reuse easier but might make this project more difficult to manage.

Attitude . . . Attitude . . . Attitude

There had been efforts in the past to try to make the structured code base used by the development group more reusable, but these efforts had not succeeded. These efforts failed because of the attitude at Transport that software was simple (shown in Harry's comment "Just do it" when talking to Sal about reusable code). Sal wanted this effort to succeed and to be done so that the code would be reusable, but he needed to convince all the parties involved, including the customer, that it was the right thing to do.

Sal therefore was actually thinking about a number of new technologies and efforts for the Wabash Project. They were considering a new algorithm, a new development approach and programming language, new techniques for the QA group, and a new interaction with the customer. From everything Sal had been taught, creating too many "new things" for a project was always a big risk. Many projects had died on the "bleeding edge," and Sal did not want his project to be one of them. Sal was confident about the new development approach and programming language because, though new for his company, they were well understood and used successfully by the software industry.

Sal wrote down a set of issues so that he could clearly understand the decisions he had to make:

- He has to get his engineers training in OO.
- QA needs to read and understand the code during the testing phase, especially for the safety-critical code.
- Customer involvement in code reviews means the customer needs to understand the OO methodology used.
- Compliance with standards would be difficult since there were none set for the company in OO methodology.

It just so happened that a project review for the Wabash Project was going to be conducted. All interested parties would be present, and this might offer an opportunity to field the idea of object-oriented development for this new and exciting component called the BFM. Sal talked over the issues with the lead engineer, Bill Madley, and they discussed how the idea could be addressed. Since Sal was a graduate of a software engineering program, he knew that the analysis of requirements could be represented in a number of ways. Some ways contribute to OO, while others contribute to structured views. The decision was made to represent the analysis for the BFM component using an object-oriented technique because Sal knew this would not significantly impact a structured development if they decided not to pursue OO, while it would enhance the use of an OO approach.

Looking for dual-use methodologies was a standard that Sal had been pursuing in projects since he was hired as a development manager. Sal even had to provide the engineers in his group with books on how to do OO analysis, design, and development in C. This was again a hedge against critics if C++ was not portable to the new hardware configurations. At this time, an effective real-time C++ was not available, so C was the language of choice and was well entrenched at Transport.

During the review, the customer asked about the different representations the Wabash Project had used. In particular, the customer indicated a preference for the OO analysis format used on the BFM, rather than for the more structured "flow-chart-like" format. The Wabash Project customer said during the review, "Your diagram showing the object that does the operations on the BFM helped us understand the need for very clean signals and straight paths on the links to the monitor."

Sal's boss asked to meet with him after the Wabash Project meeting. Harry's comment was, "Good job on the presentation, but we need to talk about the BFM."

The time to make a decision on the Wabash Project development methodology had come. Sal thought he understood enough about the product to make this critical decision. He would now have to convince Harry that the BFM idea was based on his idea regarding reusable code. Sal was prepared to handle the questions he knew that Harry would ask, at least most of them.

CASE PROBLEM

The case study has a number of problems in addition to the main one concerning the use of a new technology in developing a product for the company. There were transition problems between the development and quality groups and trust issues that had to be managed. Chapter 8, "Managing People Interactions," can shed more light on these issues.

The expectations of both the internal and external customers had to be properly managed, or the project could fall apart. Pitting one group against another group works only for so long before the issue impacts the development of the product. Managing an evolving product is always challenging in a software development environment. You might also look at how the relationship between the people on the project might interfere with the proper management of the product.

Case Analysis

ANALYSIS ACTIVITY

Analysis Background

First Case Problem

(P) Problem: Sal has to decide whether he will use new OO development techniques on the BFM project.

(E) Experience: The BFM is already a new piece of hardware that Sal knows will take some 5,000 engineering hours to develop and install the software to run on the new hardware.

(A) Assumptions: The BFM will be ready on time, and the only issue Sal's group will have to worry about is getting the software operational on the new board.

(K) Knowledge: Using OO development techniques would imply less risk because these techniques are well understood in the industry.

Solution: Develop the new BFM software using OO techniques.

Assumed Risk:

- The hours might exceed the 5,000 hours allocated for the job.
- The project team, the QA team, and the customer are not in practice able to adopt OO technologies seamlessly and on time.

Second Case Problem

(P) Problem: Sal has to decide whether they should be updating the algorithm while building the BFM to cost the company less for future brake modules.

(E) Experience: The BFM is already a new piece of hardware that Sal knows will take some 5,000 engineering hours to develop and install the software to run on the new hardware.

(A) Assumptions: The BFM will be ready on time, and the only issue Sal's group will have to worry about is getting the new algorithm operational on the board.

(K) Knowledge: The mathematician can solve the algorithm reduction problem from seven inputs to three. Solving this problem should imply a simplified and well-understand algorithm, which means simpler code to understand in the final product.

Solution: Use the new algorithm on the new BFM board, and make the product even more attractive by reducing costs.

Assumed Risk:

- The project team does not find a solution to the input problem associated with the BFM algorithm.
- The configuration of the system cannot in practice be modified to minimize the cost by using three inputs versus the seven inputs that were required for the old algorithm.

Analysis Questions

1. What decision would you make as the project manager?
2. What issues of product management do you think Sal needs to handle to ensure the success of the Wabash Project?

3. Do you think that Sal really does understand the problem thoroughly and is ready to make the decision? If not, what else might he need to know to help him with the decision he has to make?
4. Is the issue with OO development the real decision that has to be made?

RESULTS

The BFM was built using OO development techniques. The new standards established for reviews during the development process made this possible and allowed the QA group enough understanding of the process that it was able to conduct significant testing on the BFM prior to its successful implementation on the Wabash Project. The most significant event for the Wabash Project was the revolt by the engineers when they were asked whether they wanted to stop reviews to speed up delivery. Their unanimous answer was no. They agreed that the only way the team would make the scheduled delivery date was by continuing reviews. The team knew the quality they were producing on the code was keeping them on schedule. The final product delivered on the Wabash Project had only minor defects that could be attributed to the software from the TC group. A number of defects were found, but all were quickly shown to be from other components in the system.

DISCUSSION

As you can see from the results, the product was successful. Not only was the product delivered as expected, but the processes used were integrated as standard practices for the teams to ensure product quality. The normal testing time for a new development in the test lab was one to three months. The new Wabash system took only three weeks to clear testing in the lab. The team was able to use the new techniques to develop the software as expected. But what can also be seen is that Sal had to do some product development analysis prior to making the final decision. Sal also had to involve the key stakeholders in the effort to ensure that everyone was receptive to the idea of the new development technique.

There were many problems to overcome even after the decision was made. Training the engineers to use OO techniques in conjunction with a non-OO programming language was probably the most difficult. New concepts such as OO can help in understanding and developing reusable components, but the environment, such as embedded systems for trains, might preclude the actual use of OO languages. OO concepts existed before OO languages, and on this project they were used even though an OO language was not available for the embedded development. It required the use of "brown-bag lunch" training and many lectures by the lead engineer Bill Madley who explained key concepts.

The other issue was that there were many other ongoing environment issues (a new customer, a new process improvement effort, and new engineers coming into the company) that had to be handled. This created opportunities and problematic conditions that had to be dealt with to ensure that the product was properly managed and delivered to the customer. As you can see from the case study, the customer was interested not only in the product but also in the product production process.

Product management begins with the development of the product and continues with the transition of the product to the customer. In this case, Sal used code reviews with the customer as a way to help with the final product transition. The new customer on the Wabash Project gave Transport the opportunity to try new techniques and appear competent in what they were doing.

CONCLUSIONS

You must recognize the decisions associated with the product when they come into your projects. These product decisions normally surround the quality issue of the project but can also be tightly coupled with the process decisions you make to support a development effort. Sal had the advantage of an education in software engineering. We hope this case study has given you the ability to recognize product decisions when they are needed as well as provided you with the understanding to get the information you need to use PEAK to make a product decision to support your project.

KEY IDEAS TO REMEMBER

The key idea here is that each product decision you make will impact the product. If these are not managed, then you are not managing the product. Product management in software development involves not only the final product being built but also how the product being built is represented to the customer and all stakeholders.

CASE STUDY

Why Is This Product Wrong?

Directions

Read this case study after reading the chapter material. Look at how you might think you have all the information you need but some critical aspect is missed that directly affects the usability of the product.

Case Summary

DESCRIPTION

A developer is pondering how his company got the product wrong after having done everything right, at least from his perspective. He is wondering where things went off track and why he couldn't deliver a customer's product on time, on schedule, on budget, and in a way that meets all the customer's needs.

This case study will present the idea that although things appear to be "easy" in the product definition, this doesn't always mean that you will get them correct. There are hidden assumptions, issues, and expectations that, if not properly understood, will lead to poor product management decisions and possibly project failure. This case study illustrates that the failure of the product was set by the very first decision that was made for the Three-Tech phone search product. By the time the developer is brought on to the project, decisions have been made that have a lasting impact on the final product and that may not be recoverable.

CASE STUDY OBJECTIVES

After reading the case study, you will be able to do the following:

- See how decisions made early in the life of a product can have a dramatic impact on the product management to be done later
- Understand how various product management decisions affect the product and why
- Understand that scope and time are not all that matters
- Show that early bad decisions can create poor customer expectations

SUBJECTS COVERED

Product versus process issues, what makes a good product in the eyes of a customer, quality attributes, and perceptions of product

SETTING

The case study occurs in a garage with a start-up company that always wants to take shortcuts. "You can figure it out" and "Doing things for fun" are common phrases that usually present risks in a project. The environment is a small project. But the case product is interesting and has enough technical challenge to leave you saying, "I could have made that mistake." The case study should help you see that a dumb question is simply one that is not asked. The product is managed correctly, but the influences of the environment determine the project's success or failure.

The Case

SCENARIO

Three-Tech is a consulting company that was in its customer-building phase. The CEO, John Smith, was on the East Coast of the United States with most of the administrative offices, while most of his development team was on the West Coast. Fred Moresay had been hired by John and sent to training on how to build software for phone switches. The other developer on the West Coast was Tom Billings. Tom was a hardware guy and knew how to get systems to work. He had run his own small company but was essentially "doing this job for fun." Tom was more of a systems engineer than purely a hardware engineer, and he thought software was "foo-foo," although he did know what it was supposed to do. Tom was like the professor on *Gilligan's Island*; he could make a satellite reflector out of coat hangers, but if it had software, he wanted someone else to do that part.

Fred had gone to work for this small company called Three-Tech after leaving his old job in a large government organization where he had worked for more than ten years. While working for Three-Tech, Fred found that the projects were smaller in scope than those he had handled in his old job, but they appeared to offer some interesting opportunities to learn new technologies. The pay was better than that for the old job, and one of the nice things was he got to work from home. He remembered waking up one day and telling his wife Ann that he was off to work. Fred put on his slippers, got a cup of coffee, went to the desk on the other side of the room, and sat down. He logged in and was at work.

Project Activation

On January 25, 1999, the day began for Fred with a phone call from John:

John started the conversation by saying, "Fred, I have a project for you. Maybe I can get my money's worth out of that training I provided you."

Fred replied with a laugh, "Sure . . . what is it?"

John stated in a matter-of-fact way, "The project is a phone switch answering service with automated menu selection and advertisement playback. You have two months to deliver it."

Fred replied, "Sounds interesting. Are there requirements for the software?"

John abruptly answered, "Call Tom. He got all the details from the company while you were at training. He is already getting some of the parts for the system. Let me know if you need anything." <click>

When the hour became decent, Fred called Tom who lived about three miles away, and they made arrangements to meet on the new phone lookup project that afternoon.

Team Initiation

Fred drove to Tom's house in the hills near San Diego. It was a typical California day, and he was eager to get all the details of the new project. The first meeting went something like this:

After briefly explaining what he knew about the new project, Tom concluded, "Well, it looks pretty straightforward, as long as you can make the software work."

Fred replied, "Thanks, Tom. Do we understand the requirements? Are they written down?"

Tom did not answer Fred's question but said, "I talked to the customer, and they want to have someone call an 800 number service. The customer is then given a basic list of restaurants. The list is broken down into categories by cuisine such as Mexican, Italian, American, and so on. The users can then go through a category menu and try to locate restaurants that interest them."

Fred then asked, "Sounds neat, but who is going to enter all the restaurant information?"

Tom answered, "The customer has some ideas about this. We just have to provide them with a format that they can use."

Fred did not say anything for a while and then quizzically replied, "Hmmmmmmm."

From Tom's description, the product seemed straightforward, but of course, from Fred's point of view, there appeared to be a few holes that still needed to be filled. In general, any time Fred heard the phrase "The customer has some ideas," the hairs on the back of his neck stood up. Tom was not a software person; he was a hardware guy who put systems together. From Tom's point of view, all they had to do was to install a new phone switch server and create the database to provide information to a user who accessed the server. Tom always felt that software was "easy." Then the system would have to allow the user to navigate through a menu of options as specified by the customer. The menus had to be simple, intuitive, and easy to use. Fred was a little concerned, especially about the format of the menu, but the overall product seemed simple enough.

Fred had been sent to school to learn how to set up the phone system. Fred and Tom quickly experimented to create a server that basically could answer the phone with the new phone switch hardware. They tested the system online and used Fred's cell phone to call Tom's home phone and test the basic switch. It seemed that this part of the product was going to be easy. Next, the server was set up to turn control over to the software, which Fred would program to do what the customer wanted. The phone switch server and the interface software were implemented as commercial, off-the-shelf software that had to be integrated to function together. Most of this work was done in Tom's living room.

Fred took a copy of all the software to create a duplicate server in his home environment so that they had two systems with which to test software and to get the system operational.

The option selection software Fred was supposed to use consisted primarily of a database that also appeared to be simple; after a few experiments, the basic system was in place. The project had been scheduled for two months; after the experiments, the schedule appeared as though it would not be an issue for Tom and Fred. There were still some requirements that were a little unclear, but everything was on schedule or a little ahead of schedule.

Problems Appear

The first problem came when the customer asked whether the information that was played back to the user could come from the database. In other words, could the database feed the sound system of the phone server? The problem was to find a format for the audio data that could be stored in the database and used without conversion by the phone switch. After some questions to the switch company and some more experiments, Fred and Tom found an audio file format that could be stored in the database and used by the phone switch. Prior to this, text-to-voice information was all that was supported by the phone switch. This is the normal type of information that phone switches use when "passing a call to Phil in accounting." However, this "suitable" format would result in some consequences later in the project.

Some sample files were created using a simple recording technique, and the entire system was ready for a demo. The issue of who could provide the data for the database and the audio files came up, but the customer had an idea and said he would take care of it.

As it turned out, the database that pleased the customer was Microsoft Access. The system was installed at the customer site two days ahead of schedule. Fred and Tom decided that this would give them a buffer if something went wrong. The system worked perfectly when activated, no defects appeared in the code, and the customer loved some of the added features that had been provided.

Then a major issue appeared. The customer asked what other audio file formats the phone system could accept. This put the development team back into the search mode. The team was forced to research what formats were available to play messages to users on the phone system. There were compatibility issues with the database and with the phone system's ability to digitize and convert the information for the switch. This all resulted in a phone call to the phone switch company and Phone Switch Customer Service (PSCS):

The PSCS representative asked, "What are you guys trying to do with this system?"

Fred explained, "Well, the customer says the sound does not have the 'fidelity' he wants."

The PSCS representative replied, "Well, I'm sorry, but as of right now, the only audio format we accept is 8-bit format. Most people just want to record a short message such as, 'Hi this is Julie, leave your message.' It sounds like you need more than this."

Fred then asked, "Maybe. Are there any options we can buy?"

PSCS regretfully replied, "My boss says development might be interested in the task, but he doesn't know of anything else. The person to contact in development is . . . ."

The answer was none. The famous story about Henry Ford selling the Model T came to Fred's mind: "You can have it in any color you want, as long as it is black."

The issue was that the customer wanted to use commercial-quality sound files on the system. The minimum bit storage requirement was 16-bit data, but when the files were converted to the format that the phone system needed, the greater fidelity of the commercial recordings was lost because the data was changed to 8-bit. The customer said this made the files that were called up sound "tinny."

There appeared to be no fast technical or other solution to the problem with the system being used. Three-Tech could ask the switch provider to enhance the system, but the cost would be prohibitive and would make the system one of a kind. This was not very attractive to the customer, who was already starting to think that he did not want to "throw good money after bad."

From Three-Tech's point of view, it had delivered the system on time, on schedule, and with everything that the customer wanted. The customer viewed the system as if it didn't work. Fred thought about how to avoid this problem in the future. He asked himself, "What were the mistakes?" This project was a nightmare. How could the product not be acceptable when it did what was agreed on?

The next day started with a phone call from Fred's boss, John. Fred was thinking that many people have a tendency to measure the quality of their product by the presence or absence of calls from upset customers. Software has the ability to bring out the worst in people. There is always the view that it should be easy to develop a product that involves only software. His boss was asking how things were going with the phone switch project.

CASE PROBLEM

Will the product satisfy the information needs of the customer?

Case Analysis

ANALYSIS ACTIVITY

Analysis Questions

1. What are the major issues that are affecting the product?
2. What would you have done differently if you were in the developer's place?
3. What key issues about product management did the developer fail to consider when dealing with the product?
4. What were the decisions that Fred had to make?
   - What are the PEAK inputs for these decisions?
   - What are the alternative solutions and assumed risks associated with these solutions?

KEY IDEAS TO REMEMBER

The product is more than just the set of functions that the customer says they want the product to do; it is greatly influenced by how the functions do their job. The quality with which the functions are delivered determines whether the product meets or exceeds the customers' expectations. When you look only at the requirements as a set of functions that must be accomplished with no care of the quality with which they perform the functions, you have an infinite number of choices of what you can do. However, when you must consider the quality with which the functions are delivered, you are left with only a few solutions that will deliver the correct product.

In software, since you deliver something that is not very tangible, that is, a disk or a download of electronic bits, the idea of quality is paramount and highly integrated with the product. Early requirements were met with decisions that later impacted the final product being delivered. You must manage the product by managing the quality that goes into the product. The quality is directly measured by the requirements used to establish the product being delivered.

5.4 Summary

This chapter focused on the following activities for managing product in the context of decision making for software projects:

- Proper product definition
- Development management
- Quality assurance and control
- Configuration management
- Product delivery and installation
- Training
- Field services

The case study "New Technology—Is It Always the Best?" examined many aspects of product management but focused particularly on development management, quality assurance, and proper product definition. The case study "Why Is This Product Wrong?" covered training, field service limitations, and proper product definition. The case highlights that sometimes projects cannot recover from poor decisions made early in a project.

Product management is the crux of developing a software product, but because process and product are tightly coupled, you cannot really consider one without the other. Product management involves aligning the processes used to develop the product with the stakeholder expectation dimensions of scope, time, quality, and cost. You can use the PEAK model to ensure that you have the correct information about the relevant dimensions of stakeholder expectation to make the best project decisions possible.

Product management requires that you continuously make decisions that will affect one or more of the four dimensions of scope, cost, quality, and time.

Chapter 6

Managing Process

6.1 Chapter Objectives

After reading and thinking about the concepts and case studies presented in this chapter, you will be able to do the following:

- Recognize the key issues involved with process management
- Understand the relationship between product and process
- Understand the key factors that influence process in the eyes of the stakeholders
- Recognize factors that can significantly improve the development process with minimal cost
- Understand that process is not a dirty word

6.2 Context

A **process** is a set of steps with a purpose. A process is a framework for action whose purpose is to achieve a well-understood goal in a repeated fashion. A process consists of a set of actions or tactics to achieve the goal. A process is also a set of steps that standardizes the production of a product. Humphrey (1989) defines process as a set of tasks that, when properly performed, produces the desired result. In other words, a process can help you produce a product and also can serve as a filter to ensure that defects do not get into the product we are creating.

Viewing process as a filter enables a project to remove defects early when the cost is lower. We all know about the 10-to-1 cost when software defects are allowed to migrate into later phases of development. It is important that defects are encapsulated or removed before they spread out. If not contained or removed, they "infect" other code and therefore are harder to remove. The processes that you use can serve as a uniform, disciplined way to remove these defects so that the later phases of the project are not delayed because of the need for bug fixing. The process can save the engineer from having to expend time doing rework.

To use the software development process as a quality filter for the results of your software project tasks, you need to be able to perform the following activities to manage the processes used by the project members: define or select the process, teach the process, measure the process, evaluate the process effectiveness, and change the process to improve its effectiveness. Each project member who uses a process should be able to perform the following activities: understand the process, execute the process, evaluate the results of executing the process, and understand how to change the execution of the process to improve results.

As you examine process in this chapter, you will look at the decisions that a manager must make to influence or instantiate process in a software development effort. You can use the basic PEAK model to make decisions that will impact the activities performed by the project team. Table 6-1 presents what-if questions to answer when evaluating and making process decisions. For each what-if question, you can determine whether the PEAK input statements are true. Study the table, and think about how you would answer these questions to manage process for your current software project.

Table 6–1: *Managing Process Decisions Using PEAK*

Activity	*PEAK Inputs*
Understand the process	**(P) Problem:** How will the process benefit the project? **(E) Experience:** Is this the right process for the people working on the project? **(A) Assumptions:** Is the assumption that there is not a better process to use true? **(K) Knowledge:** Do you know whether the process will lead to the generation of a product that is usable?
Execute the process	**(P) Problem:** What has to be done to make the process work? **(E) Experience:** Do you know how this process works and whether the target product can be produced by using this process? **(A) Assumptions:** As might be assumed, do you have everything you need to run the process? **(K) Knowledge:** Do you know whether the people are properly trained in doing the process?

Table 6–1: *Managing Process Decisions Using PEAK (Continued)*

Activity	*PEAK Inputs*
Evaluate the results of executing the process	**(P) Problem:** What shows the process was successful? **(E) Experience:** Do you know the signs that indicate whether processes are working well? **(A) Assumptions:** Is the assumption that a good product means a good process true? **(K) Knowledge:** Does the end justify the means when it comes to process? Why or why not?
Understand how to change the execution of the process to improve the results	**(P) Problem:** Can you make the process more effective? **(E) Experience:** How do you know whether there is room for improvement when it comes to process? **(A) Assumptions:** Is the assumption that the users of the process are the best people to make changes to the process true? **(K) Knowledge:** Do you know if there is a more efficient way to do things?

Software project managers or software engineers can better eliminate defects by managing the decisions that they make about how they do their work. To manage these decisions, software engineers need to understand the way in which they complete tasks (or the processes that they use) and to be able to perform them in different ways if needed to achieve fewer defects. Changing the way you perform a process to improve its outcome is called **process improvement**.

Process improvement is a way to improve efficiency through the recognition of better ways to perform actions. When you write things down and are able to evaluate what you are doing systematically, then you can see "better" ways to do things. Many of the decisions you make with respect to process involve making the process more efficient or less error prone when applied. In a sense, process is a tool like any other development tool. It can be used badly or well. For software engineers, process is essential because the work they do is detailed and requires their best efforts. One guideline to remember in making decisions about process is that the process should serve the user. The user does not serve the process. Another guideline when making process decisions is to consider whether the process or the tools should come first. When these get reversed, teams get into trouble.

Activities of Process Management

Process is fine for other people. To paraphrase a line from the film *Blazing Saddles*, "Process? We don't need no stinking process!" (IMDb.com, *Blazing Saddles*). Some people view process as a necessary evil. They think that it is needed because someone else wants visibility into the project. This is the wrong reason for process, although sometimes it used as the "stick" to get engineers to listen.

A useful way to view process is as a mechanism by which defects can be filtered from a work product throughout its creation. This is sometimes at odds with some people's view of process, in other words, "process for the sake of process." Process without value for the user is useless. Process is not an end in itself but a means of guiding and planning software project actions to achieve project objectives.

A decision to *not* have a defined process or a disciplined process is still a decision to have "a process." In this case, the process is not managed to improve a project. So, another truism for process is that unless you manage it and define it, you cannot improve what you do.

Managing process requires planning, discipline, and proper decisions. Processes must be based on the business goals and needs of the organization, the project objectives, and "best practices" for the domain. Basic activities to be performed in managing process are the following:

- Defining, selecting, and understanding the process
- Teaching the process
- Measuring the process
- Evaluating the process
- Changing the process to improve its effectiveness

Table 6-2 describes these activities in more detail. Explore the table, and consider other activities that you think may be helpful in managing process.

Table 6–2: *Descriptions of Activities in Managing Process*

Activity	*Description of Activity*
Defining, selecting, and understanding the process	**Definition:** Establish the objectives, quality attributes, and expectations that the users of the process need so that they can understand the reasons and uses of the process. **Target outcome:** The users of the process understand the process objectives and expected outcomes, how the process applies to them, and what they are expected to do in the process.

Table 6–2: *Descriptions of Activities in Managing Process (Continued)*

Activity	*Description of Activity*
Teaching the process	**Definition:** Show the process to new members joining the organization, and be able to verify that people are doing the process correctly. **Target outcome:** The process used by the organization must be defined and have the supporting information to make it teachable to anyone who is expected to use it (for example, notebooks, workbooks, presentations, documentation, and so on).
Measuring the process	**Definition:** Build into the process the data collection points where information is uniformly and consistently collected for evaluating the effectiveness of the process with respect to the process objectives. **Target outcome:** The process stakeholders understand the values being collected, who and how they are used by the project (organization), and how they will use the values to evaluate the execution of the process.
Evaluating process performance	**Definition:** Evaluate the process for its ability to satisfy the business, project, or product objectives of the users. **Target outcome:** The process must be measured against standards and goals for performance.
Changing the process to improve its effectiveness	**Definition:** Provide the mechanisms by which the process can be adapted to changing environments and to the needs of the stakeholders (for example, people who execute the process, people who use the results of the execution of the process, and so on). **Target outcome:** Groups are created that evaluate processes regularly and periodically to verify that the processes still achieve their objectives and that the process objectives are still valid for the stakeholders.

Making Decisions About Process

You cannot control what you cannot measure (DeMarco 1982). Process goes hand in hand with improvement. If your projects are running perfectly and you see no need to change anything, then you don't have to worry about process because obviously you have good processes. But if your project is like many other software projects, the results are not always acceptable, and things are always changing. As the saying goes, "The only thing consistent is change." Therefore, if you are making changes, you want to make sure the changes are improvements; and you can't improve your process if you can't measure it. So, decisions made about process usually focus on how to evaluate its effectiveness.

An important concept is that process and product can be viewed as two sides of the same coin. For this discussion, product consists of the artifacts that compose the output of a project. They can be customer or management focused. The execution of a process results in a product. Most of the time, the quality of the product is highly dependent on how the process is followed. People who insist on focusing on only product or only process are cheating themselves. As people who deal with software know, a software development effort involves compromise. The software project stakeholders make decisions regarding one alternative or another because of a slight advantage. The choice of how much effort goes into managing the process and how much goes into managing the product is a compromise at the project level. Project managers are constantly making decisions regarding the resources needed to manage process and regarding what and how much to measure to ensure that the project delivers the right product to the customer. The process resources include variables such as people's time, reports, and reviews. Every project must decide which and how many resources to expend.

Schedules are key factors in making project decisions and are likewise dominant in making process decisions regarding how to execute the project in order to produce acceptable project deliverables on time. Process can serve as a defect filter that can reduce completion while improving quality. When selecting processes to be followed for a project, project managers are primarily deciding how many "issues" they would like to filter out as soon as possible within the project. The right amount of process is always a balancing act to manage effort and time while attaining the proper effect on the product. Usually this balancing act is directly related to quality (that is, zero defects), but most project managers have given up on the idea of process nirvana and strive for minimal rather than zero defects.

Process decisions often involve the search for ways to improve project speed through efficiency and productivity. One of the major decisions a project manager has to make is how much new process technology the team can handle. Many projects have suffered from the introduction of new support tools, languages, and hardware that is supposed to make the team more efficient, faster, smarter, and able to leap over buildings in a single bound. The project management always seems to be surprised when the team is slower than normal and spends all of its time "learning" these new systems. Project managers need to balance process changes with respect to the impact that they will have on the efficiency of the team. This is one decision area that can benefit highly from the application of PEAK, which makes transparent the statement of the problem to be resolved as well as the assumptions being made. One of the case studies addresses this issue directly.

Next, you'll examine the process in the context of making decisions to achieve project objectives and to satisfy stakeholder expectations. You will consider the effect of process on the four dimensions of scope, schedule, quality, and cost. The following example applies the PEAK model to examine the impact that process can have on quality:

> **(P) Problem:** A team sees it might be late for a delivery. The team members are deciding whether they should eliminate code inspections to reduce the time needed to get the software out the door.
>
> **(E) Experience:** The software being delivered in this release contains only the GUI code. The complete software application will be delivered in the next release.
>
> **(A) Assumptions:** If the team eliminates code inspections, the code will be "ready" for delivery sooner.
>
> **(K) Knowledge:** The team understands that the software tests provide sufficient verification and may be willing to deal with the impact of releasing software with "less quality" more quickly.
>
> **Solution:** The team would release a software version that consists only of the GUI code, which would not be fully inspected. The next software release would contain all code and be fully inspected.
>
> **Assumed Risk:** The team assumes that the consequence of delivering lower-quality code is not as severe as the consequence of delivering late code because the customer knows that this is an interim release. If this assumption is not accurate, then the consequence of releasing lower-quality code may be more severe than the team expects.

Cost is frequently a concern when project managers are considering the process that is best to use. The next example applies the PEAK model to clarify the impact that process can have on cost:

> **(P) Problem:** Do you use the lab to test the software when the cost of usage is $1,000 a day, or do you use the simulator, which is less expensive but not as "complete"?

(E) Experience: The lab is a fixed-cost, highly utilized resource in which the entire new system environment is established with all hardware and connection configurations. The simulator has only some of the hardware features.

(A) Assumptions: The simulator produces test results that are as useful (with respect to accuracy and reliability) as those produced when using the lab for "certain" tests.

(K) Knowledge: We understand what tests are best suited for the simulator and which ones are best suited for the lab. We can clearly identify these in a project.

The use of process is a people issue. Businesses don't perform processes, but people do. Process influences people to produce or not to produce higher-quality products that meet stakeholder expectations (Microsoft 2007). Refer to Chapter 8, "Managing People Interactions," and Chapter 9, "Managing Stakeholder Expectations," for more information regarding the relationship between people and process. See also Crosby (1995) for a discussion of how to achieve quality through satisfaction of customer expectations, and see Goldratt and Cox (1992) for information regarding how to use process improvement to improve the business of software development.

6.3 Case Studies

This chapter has two case studies. One case study focuses on the process decisions that have been made for a project and analyzes whether they were the right decisions for the project. The second case study examines decisions about processes that can directly impact the quality of the project deliverables and therefore the schedule.

In the first case, "Bank on the Verge," two consultants are asked by a project manager to evaluate the project that he is working on. The project manager wants the consultants to evaluate whether his team has made good decisions on process and whether there are things that the team could do better. In particular, the project manager wants all the members in his group to work on the product to help ensure that it is the best that they can produce. He is concerned that if all of his team is not involved in this effort, then the expected product features cannot be delivered in the time allocated, and the product will not be the best that his team could achieve.

In the second case, "Damn the Process, Full Speed Ahead," one project manager is asked to review a project with problems that is being run by another project manager to determine what can be done to improve the situation. The troubled project is behind schedule, and no one has been able to clearly identify what is causing the schedule slippage or what should be done, if needed, to fix the project's processes or to help the project stay on schedule.

CASE STUDY

Bank on the Verge

Directions

You can read the case independently of the chapter background, but you might benefit from reading the background material before reading the case study. If you choose to read the case study first, then read through it once quickly in "story-reading mode" to set some context for the information in the chapter. Then read the chapter material. Finally, reread the case study, and look for opportunities in which you can analyze and apply the chapter concepts.

Case Summary

DESCRIPTION

This case deals with consultants who have been called into a bank to help with general software engineering principles for all the developers. The person who asked the consultants to come and who was a former student of the consultants asks them to evaluate one of his projects and provide ways to "improve" what they are doing. The bank has evolved through an era in which traditional, though now outdated, software development practices became standard at the bank. For example, the bank's software projects usually follow the traditional waterfall-like view of software development (Royce 1970) with the "added benefit" that developers work alone. The developers do not see projects as team efforts but as individual efforts that collectively make the project successful. New Agile methods that emphasize intense cooperation among developers are being adopted slowly, but some of the senior developers are resistant to process changes. The organization's culture of working alone has been difficult to change, especially when project managers try to introduce new processes, such as Agile approaches, in which two people work together on one console (Beck 1999).

In particular, the sponsor for the consultants wants to know how he can get more of his senior engineers involved in process improvement efforts and whether the processes that his team are using can be improved to help all engineers better participate in the effort. He can see that the "senior" engineers are not as comfortable with the techniques being proposed as the "new" engineers.

CASE STUDY OBJECTIVES

After reading the case study, you will be able to do the following:

- Understand the decisions associated with the introduction of new process technologies
- Understand that there are different stakeholder points of view regarding process
- Understand how process decisions can affect a group of engineers

SUBJECTS COVERED

Process management, quality issues, life-cycle development, and buy-in from rank-and-file engineers

SETTING

A software consultant must help a development manager decide how new processes can be taught to all engineers in a development group while continuing to produce project deliverables on time and with the right quality. In particular, the consultant must assess the development group's processes and help develop an effective way to measure the successful introduction of new Agile processes to traditional development engineers and management. The company is hiring many new engineers who are comfortable with Agile development processes. The decision to use these new processes is being reviewed with respect to what the consultants have learned about the developers in the company and about how management makes decisions.

KEY CONCEPTS

The following are basic concepts to keep in mind when making process management decisions:

- How much process change can a project handle?
- Who is affected by the decisions about development processes?
- What are the best ways to integrate new processes into a development group?
- How do you ensure that process changes meet expectations?

Process management involves the consideration of long-term issues. The processes used today must be able to deliver expected development information for the past and the future. (The process must enable the use of metrics to evaluate how well the process is working.)

Different project stakeholders view process management in different ways and to different degrees. For example, management views it with respect to schedule and budget, and customers view it with respect to quality and cost.

TERMINOLOGY

ATM: Automatic teller machine

The Case

SCENARIO

Tom Moresay is a consultant and, as part of his job, was visiting a bank in a former Soviet-bloc country. In 2006, the country was moving quickly in the direction of modern information management. Software project managers were experiencing the issues typically found in immature organizations developing software.

Tom's client was one of the largest banks in the region. The bank was embarking on a number of development and modernization efforts to improve its position as a bank of choice among the clients looking for banks in that region. With a changing consumer society, the bank was positioning itself to be a major player among banks in the new society evolving after Soviet rule.

The client knew Tom and his consulting partner, Wil Narat, through their relationship as instructors at a major university in the United States. The contact at the bank, Tanak, was a former student who had returned to his country after completing his degree. Tanak understood the concepts of process improvement from his studies but lacked experience in leading improvement efforts. He asked whether Tom and Wil could support his effort and asked how they might do this. Tanak wanted to know whether the efforts he had already begun were worthwhile and whether they were improving the state of the software development practices at the bank, in particular those used on his project.

To understand how the management at the bank viewed key software problems, it is important to understand how the consultants got involved. The request for software process support provided the opportunity to work with the bank and to help with its software development process improvement effort. The effort had been running for about three years and had begun when both Tom and Wil taught their first class on-site at the bank. The consultants could provide solutions to the bank as they discussed issues from the bank projects during their classes. In addition, the software developers and project managers taking the courses could ask the consultants for advice on how best to deal with problems on their projects.

Tom and Wil put together the following questionnaire in an e-mail to set the context for what needed to be done to improve the bank's software development processes. (This series of e-mails followed some online discussion and other e-mails in which Tanak indicated that they were having issues that "plain old hard work" could not seem to resolve. The e-mails that follow set the context in which the process decisions were being made.)

```
Tanak,

I am repeating what I told you over MSN last night (morning for
you). Now that our previous discussions have shown that you are
interested in process improvement, we would like to make sure we
provide you with the best service possible and teach the things
that:

1. Are applicable for the bank

2. Provide the best result for your immediate needs

3. Help in uncovering other needs

We can come in and teach anything, but we try to be a lot more
service oriented and meet our client's expectations. To do that,
we need to know what those expectations are and would like to
conduct a short mini-assessment (free of charge) to help iden-
tify the bank's areas of pain and where we think we can offer
some education to help with it.

Please ask the following questions of your department head and of
several key project managers in your department:

1. What are some of the things that are being done well (or done
correctly) on current software projects?

2. What are some of the things you need improvement on (or things
not going well) on existing software projects?

Please send us the information. We will assess it, provide our
input on how we can help, and then schedule things from there.

Let me know if you need more information to proceed.
```

After Tanak answered the questions in the previous e-mail, Tom and Wil followed up with these questions:

1. The available number of personnel does not satisfy the huge number of projects. Is it a problem in getting the *right* people or a problem in getting *enough* people into the bank?

2. What kind of painful problems are you having because of lack of documentation?

```
3. Do people leave the company often, looking for other jobs? Or do
they get fired?

4. Is there a training plan for new people hired? From your
previous answers, you are using busy human resources to get new
hires ready to work. What training do you give these new recruits?

5. Why is there no clear distribution of roles/responsibilities in
your project teams?

6. Is any risk management done in your projects?

7. Why are project slippages (in schedules) common? What are some
of the things that you are doing to stop that from happening?

8. A lot of rework can be caused by a number of things. What is the
main reason for your rework? Is it a quality issue (not getting the
right quality the first time), or is not understanding exactly what
the customer needs/wants causing you to have to do some rework to
get it right.

9. Is someone measuring quality? How many bugs do you have to fix
per 1,000 LOC on average? Is quality getting any better?
```

The answers to the original and the follow-up questions provided insight into an organization that was divided into three main areas. Each of these areas had its own development processes and issues, as explained in Table 6-3.

Table 6–3: *Software Development Groups in the Organization*

	Function/Group	*Process Focus*
1.	The computation and data storage group (Data Warehouse Unit*)	Hierarchical, disciplined, and approved processes in place for years. This group has to deal with government regulation. Quality and policy are critical to this software.
2.	The automated teller machine (ATM) software developers (Support Division*)	PC versus mainframe mentality. Process is good for other people. Innovation is important. Little process definition. "Hacker" approach to development. Time to market is dominant even if the "quality" is not the best.
3.	The bank interface group (Corporate Systems Unit*)	Some disciplined processes used "if there is time," but a lot of ad hoc rapid processes are used to "fix things" quickly. There is the concept of "core" code that deals directly with the money and "other software."

*See the organizational chart for the bank shown in Figure 6-1.

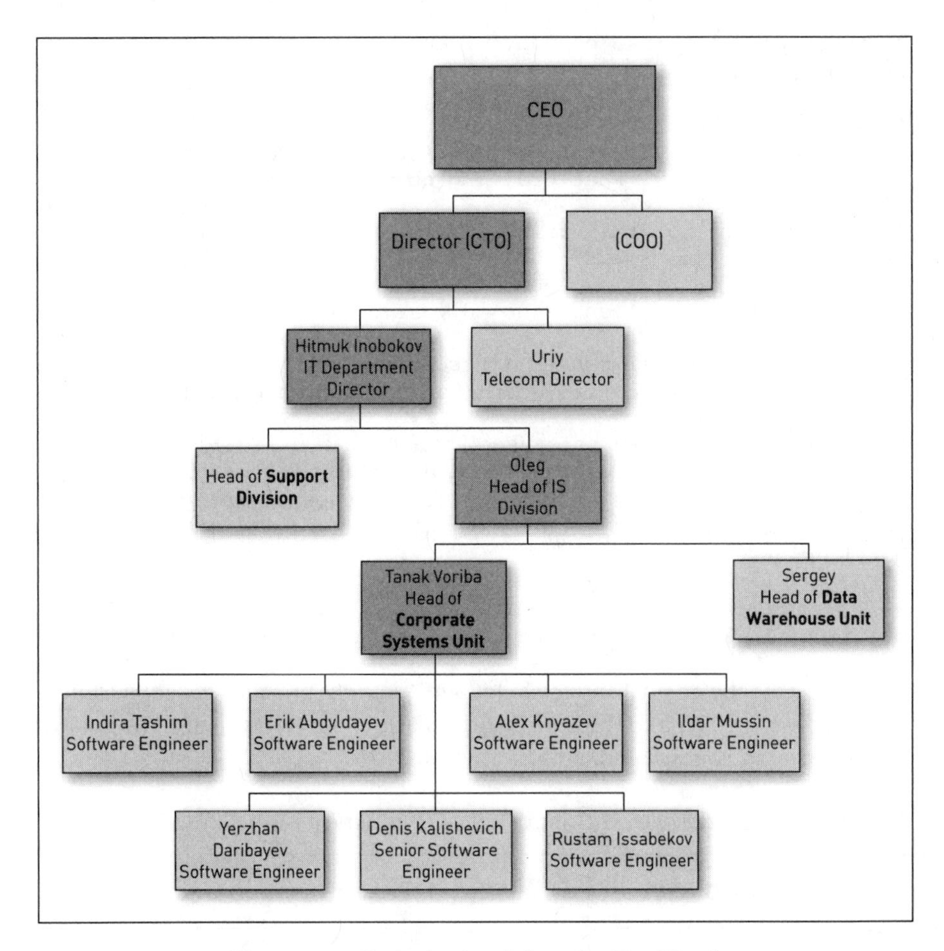

Figure 6–1: *Organizational chart for Kossi Bank*

The three groups were distinct from each other, and although they used the same information base and customer information for all their development, they all viewed this information differently. Some developers viewed this information with respect to the customers of the bank, while others viewed it simply as account numbers that they had to maintain.

The first group had a significant legacy program that was primarily in maintenance mode and needed few major changes other than to rehost the system on a new hardware platform when the old system became obsolete. This represented the main computational model approved by accounting to perform transactions on accounts. This was the area that was governed by laws of the country to maintain proper accounting practices. The quality had to be highest in this area. Development in this area followed a waterfall life cycle: Requirements were well defined before proceeding to design, changes to requirements or design were written and approved, coding was done with inspections, and the transition and turnover process occurred after exhaustive testing. The software quality was paramount, with zero defects being the goal.

The second group dealt with the most novel software and was "pushing the envelope" to support online banking at an ATM kiosk. They were looking for new ways to generate revenue for the bank. These kiosks could do everything from selling stamps to paying the electric bill. They did not reliably enable the users to access their bank accounts and get money, which was supposed to be their primary function.

The third group was somewhere in the middle between hardcore, disciplined, waterfall-like processes (Royce 1987) and the "hacker-like" processes of the ATM group. They were maintaining old legacy software while implementing new software to replace the old proprietary code that was no longer fully supported. They had to interface with other banks and with the largest clients of the bank. Their job was to make sure that the system provided enough visibility into the transactions so that issues could be reported quickly and reliably to the customer.

Tom and Wil had been working with another company in the Soviet bloc and had delivered a number of software management seminars. The slides for these seminars had been translated into Russian, which was good and bad for this new client. It was good in that obviously the people who attended the seminars from the bank could easily understand the slides, but it was bad in that it made making any changes to the slides difficult. This was important because the consultants could not adjust the slides to compensate for issues they identified in the bank projects. This slowed down the effort in transferring new ideas that would help the bank's software developers improve their projects.

Tanak had requested that all the seminars be performed with translation. This created a new situation for Tom and Wil in which lectures actually took 50 percent longer than in English. So, a two-day seminar now took three days, and the presentations and exercises had to be adjusted accordingly. The additional time resulted in the developers having to work on weekends because the bank did not want to give up two or three days of development time. This put extra pressure on the developers compared to the seminars that Tom and Wil delivered in other parts of the world.

After the answers to the questions came back, it was decided that Tom and Wil would deliver a number of seminars over a two-year period as time permitted, usually every six to nine months for bank software developers. Each time, another seminar and topic was delivered to keep the interest up among the software developers in the bank. The manager of the development group who was responsible for all three of the software areas, Hitmuk, tried to attend the seminars with his engineers. This showed buy-in from management for the time that the engineers were spending on the seminar work. Because the seminars were conducted in the bank, many of the engineers performed their "regular" days of work after the seminars were completed. This put a large strain on the engineers.

The bank was hiring software people as quickly as it could but found, as many other companies have, that if you don't have clear written processes, then it becomes hard to integrate new engineers into an organization. The new engineers were fresh out of school with little experience but with a great deal of software engineering knowledge. This allowed Tom and Wil to teach more and to concentrate on examples from their experiences managing software efforts. The primary topics that were provided as courses to the engineers were the following:

- Risk management
- Managing technical people
- Quality assurance
- Planning and tracking
- Change management
- Estimation
- Requirements management

As the final lectures were being given at the bank, Tanak Voriba, Tom, and Wil had a conversation. Tanak was the person who originally had established the need for the training at the bank and had asked the consultants to come and teach.

Tanak commented, "I am not sure if my project is going well. Can you guys take a look at it?"

Tom replied with a smile, "Sure, what makes you think there is a problem?"

Tanak said, "Well, only the youngest developers want to work on it, and I can't seem to get good advice from anyone."

Wil then asked, "What are you looking for us to provide you?"

Tanak sighed and said, "I don't know. You guys are smart. You will see what I mean and can probably help."

Tom and Wil exclaimed quizzically, "OK?!?"

The project that Tom and Wil reviewed had been in the works for three months and was planned to launch in another three months. The product was intended to replace a proprietary and aging system that was not being supported anymore by the original Russian company that had developed the software. The reasons for the project appeared to be sound, and the project was far enough along that many of the decisions about the product were already validated. But some process decisions were still left to be made. Life-cycle processes were still in flux. Tools to support the development process were being introduced in an ad hoc fashion. A mix of technology, people, and processes were being used to address many of the process issues identified in the seminars.

Tanak wanted to know whether an object-oriented development process that was being used by the team for their project was the right choice. The primary issue was that many of the more senior developers in this group and in other groups were unable to help with the project because they didn't understand the processes being used. Agile techniques, such as Scrum (Takeuchi and Nonaka 1986), had been practiced by the junior engineers in school, but the senior engineers were still waiting for "all the requirements" to be written down so that they could plan their work. The junior engineers were already coding. The architecture was straightforward, but it was obvious that the legacy systems were having a major influence on some of the components. Understanding the legacy systems required a systematic and disciplined method that the senior engineers knew how to do, but the junior engineers were less familiar with this method. Deciding how much of the legacy system with which to work and at what level was an issue.

Tanak wanted to know whether they should change some of the developer information to be more similar to a traditional development approach or whether there was something else that the team should consider doing to help with this transition and support.

Tom and Wil discussed the techniques that the team was using to control the project. The processes that the team was using were, in general, Agile techniques (Scrum-like). The main characteristics of the processes were the following:

- Pair programming among the younger developers.
- Burn-down charts for status reporting that were posted on white boards for all developers to use. (Burn-down charts show the units of work that have been completed against a prioritized set of tasks. They provide a view of how fast the team can complete work assigned.)
- Tight interaction with the customer and use of interviews and surveys to make sure the customer expectations were understood.

The project they were working on was a critical banking application (see Figure 6-2). It was the core for all large client interactions between major customers and the bank. Many of the customers had been with the bank since the days of the Soviet Union. The interactions included the following:

- Making payments in local currency
- Making exchange rate operations
- Transferring money between international accounts and local bank accounts
- Sending service request messages
- Getting account balance information and statements
- Getting exchange rate information
- Transferring payroll to large companies

This application had great visibility and importance to the continued operations of the bank.

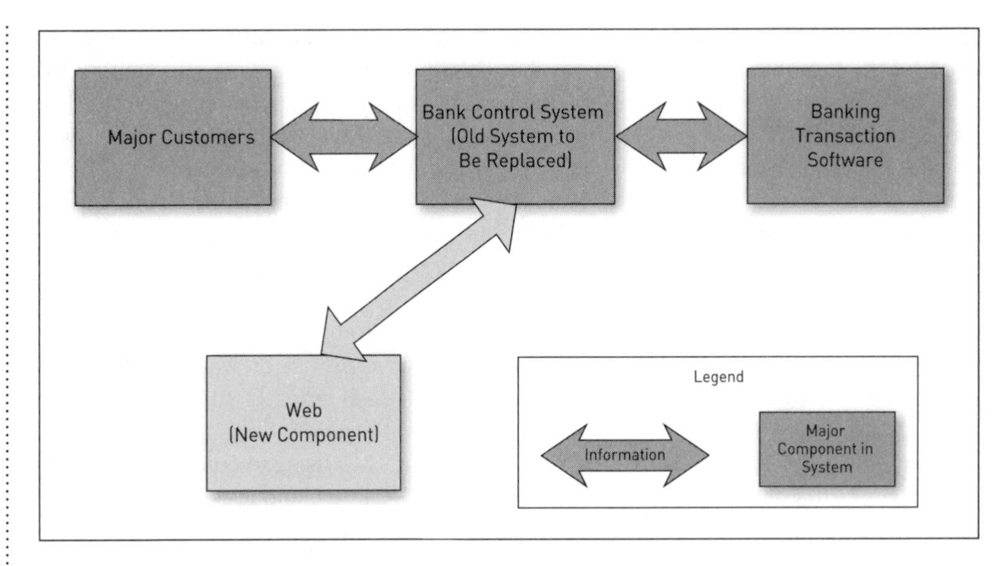

Figure 6–2: *New project under development*

As Tom and Wil talked over the decisions being made on the project with some of the developers, it was evident that everyone who was a stakeholder had a good understanding of the decisions that had been made. The question of whether the process being used on this project was the right thing do was not really the question they wanted to answer. The primary concern was how to show management that the process they were using was the right one.

Tom and Wil referred to the questionnaire that the bank originally had completed. It was evident that management at the bank judged the success or failure of the process being used by its ability to guide software developers in delivering the product on schedule and with minimal defects. Using these as criteria, Tom and Wil began to question the team on how it could show this to management. The team broke down the problem into the following decisions to be made about their processes:

- How could they show management that they were going to deliver the software on time with the process they were using?
- What would be evidence that the quality of the software was better than the old system in spite of the fact that the team also was tasked with maintaining the old system?
- What was a clear indicator of the improved quality of the system over the previous system that management would understand?

Tanak seemed to understand what needed to be shown to management and how he could present the process information to show that his team was meeting its expectations.

CASE PROBLEM

Managing the process is more about finding the right type and amount of process rather than being a "taskmaster" to make the people fit the process. Understanding that the process should help the users is critical in understanding how to manage process. Process for the sake of process probably will not result in higher product quality. Also, process that is not embraced by the users creates a problem for management. Everyone needs to buy in to a process, or there will be a problem in getting people to use the process that is proposed. In the case, finding the right level of process is critical for success. If there is too much, the young people will quit, and if there is too little, the more senior developers think they are just "hacking" the code. We'll leave you to judge whether the manager does a good job of balancing the right amount of process.

RESULTS

The reengineering project was initiated on June 30, 2006, after a horrific week of updating the legacy system for the bank to a new version. The total number of developers at the time of reengineering was eight, including Tanak. The system had not been updated for three to four years, and it missed a couple of critical updates because of some issues with the cost of updates. (That is, the bank was not willing to spend extra money for an "old system.")

To the developers, it was evident that the old system was going to die some day. The support engineers had to make regular reboots of the system, once a day on average. Corporate customers were very angry with the bank (the bank was considered a corporate bank since its customers were mainly corporations and firms).

The vendor of the system was a Russian software company that sent one of their software consultants to do the system update. While updating the legacy system, the development team and the consultant realized that the system would continue to cause problems even after the update. The consultant discussed the system condition with her company, and the company advised the bank's developers to consider reengineering the system.

The process of acquiring an understanding of the legacy system along with requirements elicitation and analysis started on July 15, 2006, and ended on September 15, 2006. The effort invested for this stage was 8 developers × 2 months or 16 man-months. The new system design and architecture started on September 15, 2006, and ended on November 30, 2006. The effort for this stage was 8 developers × 2.5 months or 20 man-months of effort. The new system prototyping started on October 15, 2006, and ended on November 30, 2006.

The new system development for the corporate bank market started on December 1, 2006, and ended on February 28, 2007. The new system was integrated and tested using ten offline customers. The system included one simple security policy and supported only five types of business documents. The integration included only one back-office system. The system for the bank was rolled out on March 30, 2007.

The new system development for a corporate market started on January 30, 2007, and ended on May 31, 2007 (three months later). This system would support 10,000 customers and provide the following features:

- Ten types of business documents
- Offline and Web client interfaces
- Three complex security policies for the offline client
- Two complex security policies for the Web client
- One complex security policy for the offline and Web client
- Integration with five back-office systems

The new system for the bank was rolled out on June 8, 2007. The system displayed no significant defects after the rollout. The system was delivered nearly on schedule.

Case Analysis

ANALYSIS ACTIVITY

Analysis Background

First Case Problem

(P) Problem: The software development process is creating a gap between groups of engineers on the project, and Tanak wants to prevent the gap from causing problems on the project.

(E) Experience: The previous projects in the bank have used a software life cycle and process that force a great deal of documentation and that focus on quality as the primary aspect of the new system no matter how long it takes. New development processes are not understood or trusted by many of the senior engineers in the organization.

(A) Assumptions: The engineers have the skills needed to deliver the new system on time and with the right quality and features.

(K) Knowledge: The project is developing critical software to be used by some of the bank's most important clients. The project team will be composed of senior engineers and new hires from the bank.

Solution: Use some new Agile techniques, and through training attempt to persuade more senior engineers to learn and adopt these new techniques. Use this project as a learning model for other projects in the bank.

Assumed Risk:

- The senior engineers have not been trained and may not be able or willing to adopt Agile methods, which would have a negative impact on the team and cause the project to be late.
- The new engineers engineers are using Agile techniques and may not be able to deliver a project that meets the quality expectations of management.

Second Case Problem

(P) Problem: The new development process being introduced on the project is not being tracked well by the old tracking methods. Tanak needs a new tracking method for the Agile processes being introduced.

(E) Experience: The other projects at the bank, except for those in the ATM group, were using a traditional method that bank management understood. The management could easily ask the question, "Where are you?" and the project could answer with a phase name.

(A) Assumptions: Tracking information is universal to software projects. If Tanak could find the right "metrics," then he could report the status in a way to meet management's expectations.

(K) Knowledge: All projects appear to measure themselves by size and features developed.

Solution: Tanak needs to develop a measurement method that reflected how the output of the Agile method was meeting the requirements of the project.

Assumed Risk:

- Management would need to trust that what Tanak was saying about the features being delivered was true and that the features represented management's expectations for the software.
- Management may focus on the traditional artifacts from projects as a method of measuring progress on a project and therefore may not be open to understanding Tanak's new metrics for representing project progress.

Analysis Questions

1. What were the major concerns that Tanak had about the software development processes being used by the bank, and how might he improve those processes?
2. How did the software processes affect the quality of the software system, and how could these processes be changed to ensure that the right quality was produced for the system?
3. What were the dominant environmental drivers working against the use of new processes, and who was providing the drivers?

DISCUSSION

Tanak, the key character of the story, thought that the main objective of the project was to increase the number of customers (in other words, to increase sales). Was this evident in the story? Sometimes what we want and what the people who work for us understand that we want are two different things. Management in the story had a perception that the objective of the new system was to provide new features, but the developers knew the system was "unreliable." Was this evident? Sometimes quantitative evidence about the project and project deliverables understood by all the stakeholders is needed to ensure that everyone is working toward the same goal. Otherwise, the project stakeholders must draw their own conclusions about the project deliverables. See the Chapter 9, "Managing Stakeholder Expectations," on managing stakeholder expectations to develop a better understanding of this concept. The customers thought that the software system was unreliable, but in a new environment, this view can sometimes be mistaken because customers do not know what they want. Once again, quantitative values can help determine what the process should change to make what is being done better. So, even though Tanak had to appease management by adding features, he also had to appease the customer by making the system more reliable and to appease the developers by giving them more control. The processes that were used seemed to achieve all of these requirements. To management and to Tanak, the project was a success.

CONCLUSIONS

As you can see from the results of the project, the process seemed to deliver the right quality, to meet stakeholder expectations, to handle the requirements, and to deliver a product that worked. This shows that process crosses many of the domains discussed in this book and is sometimes hard to separate from other aspects of software management. Decisions concerning process affect not only the development team but also everyone involved with the project. As a process manager, you must not only make a process visible but also teach, use, and measure it to ensure that the process is always improving or doing the job that is expected. People often have the attitude that because something has always been done a certain way, they are going to do it the same way. Process needs to evolve in a systematic, disciplined manner to satisfy project expectations.

KEY IDEAS TO REMEMBER

- Process and product are related, but they are not the same thing.
- Decisions to introduce the right amount of process are dominated by the needs of the project. The solutions must be measured against success criteria for the project as well as the processes.
- Process without measurement cannot be improved.

CASE STUDY

Damn the Process, Full Speed Ahead

Directions

You can read this case study independently of the chapter background, but you might benefit from reading the background material before reading the case study. If you choose to read the case study first, then read through it once quickly in "story-reading mode" to set some context for the information in the chapter. Then read the chapter material. Finally, reread the case study, and look for opportunities in which you can analyze and apply the chapter concepts.

Case Summary

DESCRIPTION

This case study will review the decisions a software project manager working for Transad must make regarding the use of quality process techniques to ensure that the project deliverables meet the customers' expectations.

CASE STUDY OBJECTIVES

After reading the case study, you will be able to do the following:

- Understand how to make decisions when it comes to process versus schedule management issues
- Learn to recognize process-induced problems and the decisions to address these issues
- See how you can identify ways to better manage processes

SUBJECTS COVERED

Process management, quality issues, process involvement with product delivery, and process choices

SETTING

A project manager is asked to help with another manager's project after some successful project deliveries. The project has been unable to deliver on schedule, and no one is really clear on what the problems are with the project. The project involves a great number of variables that appear to be impacting the project indirectly and the schedule for delivering the product directly. The project manager who is asked to help does not want to create a bad situation by suggesting processes that will be viewed as either wasteful or not usable on a "late" project.

KEY CONCEPTS

The decisions a team makes when they encounter trouble provide evidence of the real processes that the team is using, no matter what they say:

- How does a team perceive the value of process?
- How do software project managers make decisions to handle process problems?
- What are the cost and benefits of process at the team level?
- How can you show people that the decisions they are making about their process are not yielding good solutions?

TERMINOLOGY

Fault tolerance: The ability to handle faults in a graceful manner

Redundancy: Multiple systems doing the same job with a main system and backup systems

The Case

SCENARIO

Fred Montana started the day thinking about how the process changes that he had instituted on his projects were beginning to show signs of working. He was happy to see the first indicators that the heavy price he had paid at the beginning of some projects was paying off as rapid progress in the test process and in the Transad project demonstration lab.

The following are examples of process changes that he had begun to use on the pilot projects:

- Code reviews on all critical code in the system
- Use of configuration management software and a development process followed by all engineers
- A new process handbook being used by all engineers
- A new process for the task folder that had been used for years but only recently updated to support the software development processes

- New time card tracking that worked for current project tasks
- New stand-up meetings where team leads would update status first thing in the morning and spend the rest of the day working on product

The process changes were distributed among the different projects that Fred had to manage. This allowed the piloting of process changes and the ability to see improvements as the new processes were adopted. Prior to the process changes, most projects were taking between two and three months to complete testing in the lab. The first project on which Fred had changed some of the processes had completed testing in three weeks, and the second project had completed 98 percent of the tests in only two weeks. These results were signs of improved quality but also of improved efficiency for the projects.

After the first project, Fred's manager, Enrique, had called him "lucky." Now as the second project neared completion in the lab, Enrique asked Fred what he was doing. It's hard to argue with success, unless it gets rewarded with failure.

There were two software engineering managers at Transad, and each was responsible for four or five projects. Danny Walton was the other manager who worked with Fred, and both worked for Enrique. Danny was in trouble. One of his projects was extremely late. The ATRAM project was supposed to be easy, even though it had never been done before.

When the ATRAM project had been proposed, the solution to one of the requirements seemed simple. If you want to make something fault tolerant, "You simply make it redundant." Fred understood that redundancy was one tactic among many that could be used to support fault tolerance, but it was not the only one. He also knew that redundancy in real-time systems was not an easy solution.

Because of Fred's "success," Enrique asked him to take a look at the ATRAM project. Enrique suggested that Fred might be able to make some recommendations to Danny that might get the project back on track. This put Fred into what he considered a bad position. He had the problem of having to "help" Danny without making him angry or jealous and without creating a rivalry.

The first conversation about the ATRAM project went something like this:

Fred asked, "Danny how are things going?"

Danny answered with a grimace, "Fine, except for ATRAM. I don't know what to do. The engineers are just not able to get rid of all the problems like on your projects. We fix one thing and break two more."

Fred commiserated, "Ouch! What have you been trying? Can I help?"

Danny abruptly replied, "You are as overloaded as I am. I'll figure it out."

From Fred's point of view, it seemed that Danny recognized there was a problem but did not necessarily invite help for a solution. Fred would have to consider carefully how to approach the issue.

Fate sort of intervened when Danny had to go on a multiweek business trip. This temporarily delegated the project management function to Fred. Fred decided that the situation created an opportunity for him to help the ATRAM project.

Fred had to decide what to do first to deal with the project issues. The general issues on the project seemed to be identifiable. The team lead, Randy Berger, was inexperienced. He had been with Transad for a little more than a year, but this was the first project on which he had been a team lead.

Four other engineers were working on the project, which meant they spent the majority of their time on the project. One engineer was senior to Randy in his tenure with Transad, but the other engineers were all junior to him. As the team lead, Randy did not really appear to have any issues with the other engineers; however, as noted, there were many problems with the product. In addition, all the ATRAM project engineers were starting to work many overtime hours to try to complete all the needed features and to fix the features already delivered.

The project was unique to Transad in that for the first time the company was building a "fault-tolerant" system using redundancy as the solution. The solution consisted of two independent computer systems with each monitoring the functions of the vehicle. One system would serve as the primarily propulsion controller, and the other would serve as a backup if problems were detected with the primary controller. When this solution was originally proposed, it was stated that the solution should be simple because it was basically a copy of the same system twice.

Since it was just a copy of the same system twice, the project manager decided that no additional hours were needed for testing the dual configuration. Additionally, the processes that were used to design the system did not allocate time to understand the concepts of "standby" and hot spare, features that were needed by the system to successfully allow the transitions to occur. The testing processes for the dual state system required more extensive test generation than had been planned and more expertise than was immediately available at Transad. In retrospect, Danny had indicated that this was his biggest mistake.

When Fred had time, he talked to Randy to ask how things were going. They had the following dialogue:

Randy said, "OK, I think. It's sort of hard to tell."

Fred then queried, "Why is that?"

Randy explained, "Well, we got in the lab when we were supposed to. I mean, we were a little late but almost on schedule. Then we installed the software on the hardware for the vehicle because Danny said Enrique said we had to."

Fred prodded, "And?"

Randy replied with a cautious note in his voice, "Well, I assume Danny and Enrique read my testing reports, so they know what they're doing."

Fred started thinking about what process changes he might make to enable the ATRAM project to get back on schedule. Decisions would have to be made about the testing processes, the development process with respect to quality, and the overall development process status and tracking. Fred could see from Randy's comment that Randy did not think management had a clear view of what was happening.

Fred considered many of the processes that he had instantiated on his projects as viable candidates to be used on the ATRAM project. He began to identify a number of problems, for which decisions would have to be made, that he might present to Danny and Enrique.

CASE PROBLEM

How can you help someone who does not know that they need help? The first step to successful change begins with recognizing there is a problem. This case portrays one person trying to help another person see that process can help him with his "problem." In one sense, the problem is not "how do you help a project" but rather "should you help it." This problem permeates many of the case studies in the book. In this case, making the decision of whether you should help is not the main problem. The problem is how to introduce process management changes without having unintended consequences.

Case Analysis

ANALYSIS ACTIVITY

Analysis Questions

1. What problems does the project have for which PEAK might be used to help evaluate the decisions?
2. What are the key process areas that you would suggest to be changed if you were in Fred's place?
3. What is the most important process decision that should be made?
4. How can Fred help the troubled project make changes without hurting the other engineering manager's feelings or job?

6.4 Summary

This chapter focused on the following activities for managing process in the context of decision making for software projects:

- Defining, selecting, and understanding the process
- Teaching the process
- Measuring the process
- Evaluating the process
- Changing the process to improve its effectiveness

The case study "Bank on the Verge" looked at decisions concerning process definition, teaching the process, and process measurement. "Damn the Process, Full Speed Ahead" covered decisions related to evaluating and changing the current process.

Many people view process as a necessary evil. They think that it is needed because someone else wants visibility into the project. This is the wrong reason for process, although sometimes it is used as the "stick" to get engineers to listen. Software developers can view process as a filter that enables them to remove defects early when the cost is lower. They can also see process as a way to improve efficiency when they recognize better ways to engineer software.

Process and product are two sides of the same coin. Software project managers must decide how much resource to expend so that the amount of process improvement yields the desired product improvement. They also need to look for ways to make the project processes more efficient while making them more effective. Managing process for the sake of process is a waste of time.

Process decisions are particularly important when they affect the project's ability to save time, reduce cost, and improve quality.

Chapter 7

Managing Risk

7.1 Chapter Objectives

After reading and thinking about the concepts and case studies presented in this chapter, you will be able to do the following:

- Identify major risks as they pertain to software projects and the decisions about risk that will impact a project
- Identify key issues and decisions involving the management of risks (or lack thereof) in the chapter case studies
- Use the chapter concepts to suggest feasible solutions to the problems faced by the case study stakeholders

7.2 Context

Risk management activities are an integral part of what project managers and team members should practice and make decisions about on a software project. Since risk is inherent in projects, the question is not whether risks will materialize but rather when will they do so. Experienced managers recognize the need to systematically identify, analyze, and mitigate the risks faced by their project. They need to communicate with the project stakeholders (for example, their team, the client, and management) to apprise them of project risks, the actions to be taken to mitigate these risks, and the potential consequences associated with these risks. In particular, they need to be aware of and consider the risks associated with their project decisions.

In the PEAK decision model, risk is one of the outputs of decisions that are made for a project. In a way, managing risk means managing the level of risk that is tolerable to the project as each project decision is made. The basic risk management activities discussed later in the chapter apply to the management of general project risks, but understanding that risk is inherently part of making choices is also key to managing risk. The fastest way to get people to think about what they are doing is to ask them the simple question, "Are you sure?" Having to face the risks involved in making decisions stimulates people to question or evaluate their choices.

Using the PEAK model to make transparent the risk associated with each decision (or chosen solution) is one way to make risk management an integral part of a project. Decision makers can ask what-if questions about the inputs to the decision model to identify and verify the factors that contribute to the risk associated with each alternative solution. They can verify that the risks associated with the alternative solutions are valid and can more confidently use this information to make a decision.

Many of the common software project risks originate from decisions that are made about the topics discussed in this book, such as requirements, estimates, plans, product, and so on. But some software project risks specifically have to do with issues involving scope (S), time (T), quality (Q), and cost (C), which we have discussed throughout the book as the four STQC dimensions of a software project. Table 7-1 contains a suggested set of questions to help you evaluate the risk associated with the STQC dimensions of a software project via the inputs to the PEAK decision model. By answering these questions, you can determine how well the risk associated with each STQC is being managed for your project. You can incorporate these evaluation questions into your process for managing software project risk. Now examine the table, and think about how you would answer these questions for your current software project.

Table 7–1: *Risk Management of STQC Dimensions Using PEAK*

Dimension	*Risk PEAK Review*
Scope	**(P) Problem:** Is the scope stable as stated? **(E) Experience:** Has this customer been reliable in keeping the scope stable? **(A) Assumptions:** Is the assumption that the specified scope is doable with the available resources true? **(K) Knowledge:** Do you understand the relationship between scope and resources on software projects?

Table 7–1: *Risk Management of STQC Dimensions Using PEAK (Continued)*

Dimension	*Risk PEAK Review*
Time	**(P) Problem:** To meet the time for this project, how much of a change will be needed in your current development processes? **(E) Experience:** What have you seen recently that can impact the schedule (time) being allocated to complete this project? **(A) Assumptions:** Is the assumption that the needed resources will be available for completion of the project on schedule true? **(K) Knowledge:** Is this project similar enough to other projects for you to consider this schedule to be reasonable?
Quality	**(P) Problem:** What level of quality is acceptable for this type of project, and what is the impact on quality of the variability in resources that can be applied? **(E) Experience:** For this customer, can the project team achieve the needed quality? **(A) Assumptions:** Is the assumption that the QA organization will have the resources necessary to complete this effort to the level necessary for this customer true? **(K) Knowledge:** Is the quality for this type of project attainable in your organization?
Cost	**(P) Problem:** Can the project be done at the specified cost with the available resources? **(E) Experience:** Is this customer strict on cost and likely to fight for every penny of value? **(A) Assumptions:** Is the assumption that there is a sufficient reserve provided to make this project achievable on budget true? **(K) Knowledge:** Do you have a good understanding of the costs that will be associated with this type of project for your organization?

Both practitioners and students should understand and perform the activities critical to managing project risk. These activities are listed here and described in Table 7-2 in detail. Study the table, and think about how you would perform these risk management activities for your software project. Are there any other activities that you have performed to manage project risk?

- Defining a threshold of success
- Identifying risks
- Formulating risk statements
- Mitigating, tracking, and controlling risk
- Communicating about risk
- Trading off resources when making decisions about how to manage risk

Table 7–2: *Descriptions of Activities in Managing Risk*

Activity	*Description of Activity*
Defining a threshold of success	**Definition:** Decision makers often fail to specify the key elements required for achieving success on a software project. These elements might include factors such as meeting the "must-have" requirements, finishing the project within a certain percentage of budget, or following a certain software development process. Defining these elements helps the project stakeholders (customers, developers, managers, and so on) establish a common understanding of the threshold of success (ToS) in terms of product, process, and people. The ToS serves as a catalyst in identifying risks that, if they were to materialize, might prevent the project from being successful. **Target outcome**: The project stakeholders have and understand the definition of what success means for the project. The definition of threshold of success serves as the basis by which project managers can sort out those concerns that require action (potential risks) and those that do not (events that might happen but would not prevent the project from being successful).

Table 7–2: *Descriptions of Activities in Managing Risks (Continued)*

Activity	*Description of Activity*
Identifying risks	**Definition:** Key to managing risk is the decision maker's ability to identify the "right" set of risks (right being those actually faced by the project stakeholders). Although activities such as analyzing, prioritizing, mitigating, and tracking project risks are also important, they all require a correct identification of risk. Without knowing what should be your real concerns, you might haphazardly expand energy and resources dealing with a subset of items—some that might be relevant, some that might not be relevant, and some that are not even considered. **Target Outcome:** The project managers continuously identify actual risks associated with their project decisions and with other existing project conditions.
Formulating risk statements	**Definition:** The typical way of phrasing a statement about a project risk is to use an "if-then" format. This common practice may result in failure to properly identify risk because these types of statement are simply hypotheses about things that might happen rather than statements about existing conditions that could lead to failure. Therefore, a better way of describing project risk is to use a condition-consequence form (Gluch 1994; Williams et al. 1999). By identifying and describing existing conditions, which are observable and current, decision makers can analyze and determine how current conditions might negatively impact their projects (the consequence). **Target outcome:** The project managers continuously develop fact-based statements of existing conditions that have the potential to negatively impact the project.
Mitigating, tracking, and controlling risk	**Definition:** Decision makers need to analyze the conditions associated with identified risks to determine the way in which the conditions could lead to negative consequences for the project. They also need to consider the impact of these potential problems with respect to scope, time, quality, and cost. Likewise, decision makers should determine how the conditions might be removed or controlled to remove the risks or reduce the potential negative impacts on the project. They should conduct resource trade-offs to determine the most cost-effective way to handle the risks. **Target outcome:** The project stakeholders understand the potential negative consequences of identified risks. The project managers have developed plans for eliminating, controlling, or monitoring the risk conditions and their potential negative impacts.

Continues

Table 7–2: *Descriptions of Activities in Managing Risks (Continued)*

Activity	*Description of Activity*
Communicating about risk	**Definition:** The process of communicating to appropriate stakeholders relevant information is an integral part of efficient risk identification, risk mitigation, and risk tracking and control. Risk is a team activity. All project stakeholders are part of this team, though individual stakeholders may be involved in managing different types of project risk. It is paramount that risks be identified, analyzed, and worked on as a team and that people share responsibility for the risk management life cycle. Likewise, project stakeholders share responsibility for the consequences associated with improper risk management. **Target outcome:** There are continual and effective communications among appropriate project stakeholders regarding project risk.
Trading off resources when making decisions about how to manage risk	**Definition:** Decision makers must understand how to balance the cost of managing risks with the benefit it provides. Resource allocation has to take into account potential negative consequences of the risks faced in the project with its associated utility of mitigation. Typically project managers want to know how much they should spend on managing risks. They want to know the cost in terms of budget as well as the potential impact on the schedule. They hope to achieve a cost-benefit analysis that they can justify to management. Doing this analysis is not as simple as it seems, but spending resources on risk management is worthwhile when the potential negative outcome outweighs the expenditure. **Target outcome:** The project managers perform cost-benefit analyses of the resources needed to manage project risk with respect to its value (which may be expressed in terms of the cost associated with project failure because of a lack of risk management).

Software project managers need to be aware that managing risk is done throughout the life cycle of the project. Identifying risk conditions early in the project enables project managers to mitigate, track, and control potential risks before they can result in problems for the project. That is why exploring and resolving unknowns in the requirements should be done before the requirements are finalized, a topic that is discussed in more detail in Chapter 2, "Managing Requirements." But even after the requirements are established, project unknowns may arise and should be resolved as soon possible if they are considered to be risk conditions with a potentially high impact on project success. An effective risk management approach involves all the risk management activities and is applied consistently and continuously from the beginning of the project until the end.

Managing risk is an integral part of managing decisions. Evaluating and making project decisions should encompass the assessment of risk associated with alternative solutions. Therefore, all the chapters in the book discuss risk in the context of making project decisions.

For information about managing project risks as an approach to decision making, see Chapman and Ward (2002). Gluch (1994) and Williams et al. (1999) provide additional information about stating risks for software development projects in a condition-consequence form. Mojtahedi et al. (2008) discuss a group decision-making approach to perform risk identification and analysis concurrently. Dillon and Tinsley (2008) discuss how prior mistakes are opportunities to learn how to better manage risk in future decisions. To learn about managing risk in global development, see Hussey and Hall (2007). Warkentin et al. (2009) present an integrative framework for analyzing systems development project risks.

7.3 Case Studies

The two case studies in this chapter focus on aspects of managing risk that are often overlooked by software project stakeholders. In the first case study, "SEWeb and Russoft Technologies," the software project managers encounter unexpected problems related to their work with an offshore development team located in Russia and the cross-cultural differences that arise. The second case study, "Falcon Edutainment and the RiskSim Project," presents a project whose troubles stem from the client-developer interaction. Decisions made on both projects appear to have led the developers and customers down paths none of them wanted to take. Minimal risk management was applied in both cases. Read these cases to determine the risks and decisions that led to project problems.

CASE STUDY

SEWeb and Russoft Technologies

Directions

When reading this case study, focus on the risks encountered in the project as well as any risk management activities taken to minimize or mitigate them.

Case Summary

DESCRIPTION

Gene Fisher, one of the faculty members in the University of Madison's School of Computer Science, is facing multiple challenges while working with a Russian company for developing the departmental SEWeb project. To take advantage of the low-cost offshoring opportunity, Fisher had outsourced software development to Russoft Technologies and is now faced with multiple issues involving communications, culture, language, and others.

CASE STUDY OBJECTIVES

After reading the case study, you will be able to do the following:

- List the risks and the decisions faced by clients working with remote development teams
- Recognize the consequences of not performing risk management activities explicitly on a project
- Review risks taken and decisions made on a global development project and to explore various alternatives

SUBJECTS COVERED

Risk management, decision making, offshore development, requirements management, customer communications, project estimation, planning and tracking

SETTING

The setting is the United States and Russia during the 2002–2003 time frame. The software project involves Web-based system development, an academic client, a small budget, and a short time frame (less than one year).

KEY CONCEPTS

- How to handle remote development teams to minimize project risks
- The risks faced by project teams working in today's global environment of offshore development
- The effects of decision making on project risks and on successful project management

The Case

SCENARIO

Gene Fisher was staring outside and watching as people left their offices for the day. It was November 2003, and he had just returned from another frustrating meeting with his technical project lead, Alex Rau, a meeting in which they both struggled to understand the mixed messages from their Russian counterparts 6,000 miles away in Novye Cheremushki, a little suburb 15 miles southwest of the center of Moscow. With the time difference and the cultural issues, it seemed that this project was continuously moving one step forward and two steps backward. Fisher wondered whether his recent trip to Moscow, ten days ago, had affected the situation at all.

The meeting with Russoft, in a local Moscow restaurant on a late November afternoon, was good yet tense. Russ Laughlin, Russoft's CEO, and the newly assigned project manager, Mark Urlanski, were present. Fisher decided not to push the envelope too far and risk alienating his service providers—yet he was adamant that some major changes were going to have to be implemented in Russoft's software development management process for this project to be successful. The project was over budget, at least over the one originally discussed. It had certainly exceeded the time frame suggested by Russoft for project completion in August (the finish date was already sliding into November with no end in sight), and the project still did not include some of the pieces requested by Fisher and his staff. Fisher now felt as if that discussion had never taken place. Fisher was certainly at a loss.

The Setting

Almost a year earlier, in fall 2002, Peter Johnson, the new director of the Master of Software Engineering Program at the University of Madison (UW Madison), had given the green light to start working on a massive redesign and implementation of a new student-faculty-staff Web site to expand the national and international reach of the program. With increased costs of marketing, application processing, and content management, Johnson wanted to replace the obsolete systems they were using and adjust the working procedures to maximize efficiency and reduce cost. He gave the project to Fisher, who had joined the department only a few months before, because of Fisher's previous experience at successfully designing and implementing such a system for a different department on campus and because of his willingness to take on the project.

The budget was small, and Fisher had the responsibility, with minimal approval and oversight required, to select a local development team or to outsource the project. As the high-level requirements were being finalized by a team of dedicated individuals within the department (assisted by program manager Jane Weber and system administrator Al Molsters), Fisher conducted a search to understand both the technical capabilities that the potential service provider would need and the costs associated with implementing the system. Figure 7-1 shows the UW Madison project team.

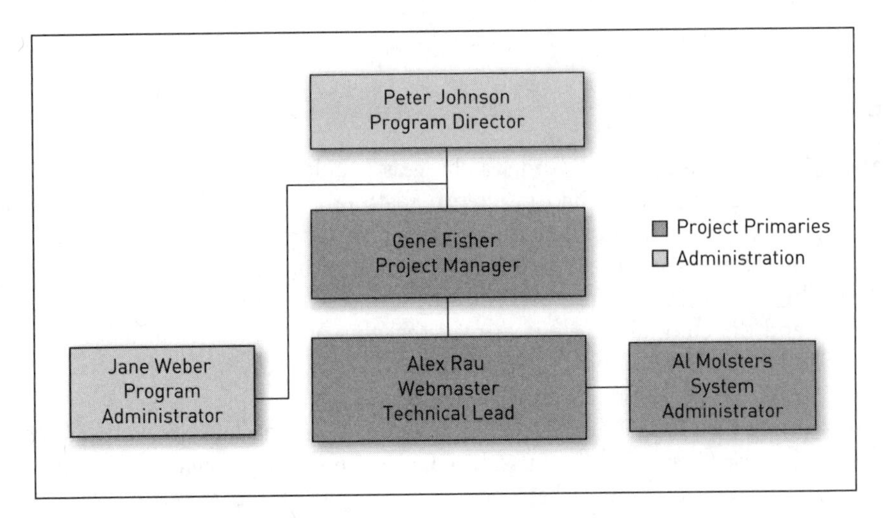

Figure 7–1: *UW Madison project team*

Fisher recalled what had led to the decision to look for an offshore development team instead of one in the United States:

> Hourly rates in the United States for Web development were ridiculously expensive. It was as if the dot-com meltdown had no impact on what people or companies were charging for their services. A typical development hour for a U.S. software house was close to (if not more than) \$100. The same development hour would cost \$6 in China, \$8 in India, and \$12 in Russia. For someone with a constrained budget of roughly \$5,000, who was willing to compromise on the location but not necessarily on the design, there was no beating offshore development. Yes, I was concerned with some of the offshoring issues, but the local stakeholders seemed willing to accept and work through them.

Some members of the program's staff and faculty at UW Madison were not as enthusiastic about the decision Fisher had made. To cover all his bases and to get a good look at the "whole picture," he decided to send out requests for proposals to four other companies (none of which had worked with academic clients before), besides Russoft, whose proposal he already had. He asked for bids from LogicArt, a New York-based company with Russian operations; Wisto Technologies, a large India-based company headquartered in Oakbrook, Illinois; Grapple Effects, a Cleveland-based company; and DesignIT solutions located in San José, California. Even though formal criteria for deciding among them were not explicitly defined, a simple analysis including cost, references or reputation, location, and experience convinced Fisher to go with Russoft Technologies Corporation, a decision that confirmed his initial "gut feeling."

Vendor Selection: The Russian Connection

The choice of going to Russia was not taken lightly or done randomly despite how it appeared. The decision was primarily a result of a trip that Fisher and Emillio Arroyo-Lopez, the Argentinean-born director of the department's distance education program, took to Moscow and St. Petersburg a few months before, in early 2003, at the request of a UW Madison alumnus.

Yuri Kashnovsky, who had just founded LearnIT, Inc., a software training consultancy in the Russian capital, wanted to collaborate with the university by having UW Madison software engineering faculty conduct executive education and training seminars in software project management for project managers in Moscow. Fisher had received that assignment in August 2002, and his first trip was arranged for early March 2003 during one of the school's spring semester breaks. Fisher remembered:

> People at UW Madison seemed apprehensive when we told them we might go to Russia. Emillio and I saw this as an excellent opportunity to watch a country in growth and to get a close look at what the market was like and what software development houses were doing. We were certainly curious to see their ability to compete in the global economy with the Israelis, Indians, and Chinese. We were very much aware of the cultural issues and the potential communist-type mind-set, but we were going with open minds to explore and bring back some knowledge.

As part their trip preparation, both Fisher and Arroyo-Lopez took the opportunity to see who among the UW Madison faculty had previously traveled to Moscow and could give them useful tips and recommendations on what to pack, how to behave, what to see, and what problems might arise. They also discussed the trip with the following students in the software engineering program: Mukhit Ashgirov, a student from Kazakhstan; Natalya Girienko, a student from Russia; and Oksana Milov, a student from the Ukraine. The students reassured them that traveling in Russia was quite safe and that they would have an enjoyable time in the former Soviet Union.

The visit lasted more than a week and took Fisher and Arroyo-Lopez to two main Russian development centers, the capital city Moscow, and the city of St. Petersburg (formerly Leningrad) on the Baltic Sea. They met, through what seemed at the time to be an endless number of meetings, people from Motorola, HP, IBM, and Oracle. Sparing nothing during their visit, the Russians took them to the best restaurants and were gracious and generous hosts. Emillio Arroyo-Lopez reported:

> We landed in Moscow on a flight from Spain where we had attended a conference. The Russians took us around and showed us the charms of their city. Their hospitality was impeccable. We even got a chance to see the magnificent Kremlin and Red Square. We really had a good time. Our week in Russia seemed to run too short, and we very much looked forward to coming back a second time to continue what we started. While in St. Petersburg, we met with Dr. Viktor Polutin, who was

> the managing director of Motorola's R&D center in Russia. The facility was rather impressive. We toured a facility that looked like an American laboratory with high-end equipment, extremely motivated engineers, and experienced management.

While teaching project management concepts to a large group of 50 software project managers gathered from all over the country, Fisher and Arroyo-Lopez also met prominent Russian professors, local industry leaders, and representatives of the two leading IT trade organizations, Fort Ross and Silicon Taiga.

Through these meetings and the lengthy discussions that followed, some lasting well into the night, both Fisher and Arroyo-Lopez had an interesting firsthand glimpse at what it was like to develop software in this new and growing Russian economy. In a country that only a few years before was mass producing things primarily for government use, the spirit of capitalism and entrepreneurship was certainly at full swing. It was interesting to gain a better understanding of the practices used in Russia, of how the Russians were currently developing software, and of whether they had any gaps in their ability to work with U.S.-based clients using industry best practices.

Toward the end of their visit, Fisher and Arroyo-Lopez also met with the two co-chairs of the Information Technology and Telecommunications Committee of the American Chamber of Commerce in Moscow. Russ Laughlin and Peter Kower had been partners in a few business initiatives. The biggest one was Russoft Technologies Corporation, a company Laughlin had founded in Canada in the late 1980s as a software development house.

Russoft Technologies Corporation

Founded originally in 1989 by Russ Laughlin, a Canadian residing in Toronto, Russoft Technologies Corporation was a small software development house that specialized in custom development for the local North American market with a small established clientele in Canada and the United States.

In early 1992, Laughlin, a savvy entrepreneur with an acute business sense and a flare for adventure, was able to capitalize on an opportunity to work on a project developing software in Russia. Laughlin observed that the country was in dire need of experienced project managers and an "Americanized" style of doing business, because it was still in turmoil following Mikhail Gorbachev's failed attempt at perestroika. He knew that those skills, coupled with a strong English-speaking ability, would give him and his company a substantial competitive advantage and a niche position in the market. The Russian industry back then had just started to convert from a government-centric provider to a private-sector-driven industry that did not know how to win foreign business, especially business coming from the United States and Canada.

Laughlin decided to relocate his entire technical operation to Moscow and to leave a small staff contingent in Toronto, Canada, in what later became his "official" headquarters for Russoft. Legally speaking, the company was based out of Toronto with offshore operations in Russia. Technically speaking, the company operated out of the fifth floor of building 219 on Profsoyuznaya Ulista, in a quiet, old, working-class neighborhood on the outskirts of Moscow.

By 2001, Russoft had four working offices worldwide, with Toronto and Moscow as the big centers and with Phoenix and Almaty as field offices to run projects in the United States and in the oil-rich country of Kazakhstan, respectively. With more than 50 full-time employees and a solid track record of delivering outsourced projects internally within Russia and externally to customers in Europe, Canada, and the United States, Russoft was fast becoming a noticeable player in the Russian outsourcing landscape.

Dennis Bramer, Russoft's U.S. managing director, explained:

> I joined Russoft Technologies in 2001 as the U.S. managing director. I was extremely impressed with Russ Laughlin, the company's founding partner. In a country that wasn't known to forgive business mistakes, Laughlin guided Russoft through more than ten years of market turmoil and grew it into a formidable second-tier provider of international software development.
>
> Russ Laughlin was not only business savvy but also showed integrity. He was someone who was serious, didn't joke around, and yet seemed like a real people's person. He certainly knew how to network, was very involved in the local chapter of the American Chamber of Commerce, and knew the foreign business community quite well. In Kazakhstan, he was working on a very large project for one of Russia's top oil producers, and people thought very highly of him and his services.

Commenting on the Russian operations, Dennis added:

> In a country where only a handful of software companies had more than 100 full-time employees and where most development houses consisted of young entrepreneurs working out of their own backyard garages, Laughlin's office was bustling with 50 to 60 full-time employees and was certainly something to notice, by any Russian standard.

The SEWeb Project

It all started more than a year before, in late summer 2002, as Prof. Peter Johnson was taking over the position of program director from Prof. Ed Schubert. Johnson, a pioneer in the field of software architecture, decided to increase the Web presence of the professional programs in software engineering through a rollout of a new Web interface.

As an analytical person who did not like to make fast, impulsive decisions, Johnson was concerned about what his staff was telling him regarding the way prospective applicants were now searching for software engineering graduate programs and what appeared to be the lack of the program's readiness to address this trend.

John Foote, a faculty member, reflected:

> We were witnessing a growing trend of people learning about our programs mostly through online searches and connections with program alumni. We typically polled incoming students at the start of the first term to gauge how and where they heard of us. Fewer and fewer people seemed to indicate that they used print ads, the famous Peterson catalog of colleges and universities, or even conferences where the program had an advertising booth. The World Wide Web was gaining momentum in how people searched for education, and this wasn't just in the United States alone. We were a global program with more than 70 percent of the applicants coming from outside the United States. Naturally, having an outdated Web site didn't make us look good, especially since we were one of the premier programs in the world in software engineering.

Seeing three different Web sites, all saying different things at three different locations, Johnson had every right to be concerned, and he thought that his decision to simplify and coordinate this online information was justified.

The project was more complicated than a simple graphical user interface (GUI) design because the requested system had to be linked to a content management system (CMS) to help with maintainability. The program also wanted a system that could tie into existing legacy databases used by the department; provide dynamic content generation of elements such as news, events, and announcements; and be documented to enable ease of future maintenance by providing a clear understanding of how and what went into its design and implementation. The department had never done anything like this before.

Al Molsters, the department's system administrator, stated:

> This project wasn't just about designing and implementing a system for a typical "techno-phobic" kind of client. This system must support a premier program in the United States for teaching software engineering. People around here not only knew what they wanted but also knew how the developers should develop the system. They wanted specific documentation that would help them extend the system in the future. They wanted maintenance to be a task that a support person without HTML skills could perform. In addition, the system must have reliability built in as a standard operating procedure.

Gathering Initial Requirements

It only seemed logical that gathering internal requirements would easy to do in a place where most people were technical experts who are familiar with both software processes and software project management. Unfortunately, the task proved to be anything but easy.

The world of academia was very different from industry and the public service with which Fisher was familiar. In typical "university" projects, the notion of "getting things done" did not get in the way of "getting things right," and the word urgency had a different meaning. Fisher recalled:

> It was very frustrating to have to collect requirements when you were given the responsibility and not the authority to do so. Decisions were typically made as a committee where consensus was highly desirable. If we had a project "champion," I was supposed to be it. Don't get me wrong, people did want to contribute, but people were so busy with their own work that I literally had to plead and cajole them to provide me with their input. This project just wasn't a high enough priority. I really didn't feel that we were working on this as a team.

Fisher received the assistance of Alex Rau, a new person with very little experience who had just been hired for the Webmaster position, to help with requirements. Rau was tasked to help coordinate, test, and monitor this offshoring development project under Fisher's supervision. Rau said:

> I was very excited to work for UW Madison. Having just returned from Africa where I taught English with the Peace Corp, I really didn't have a lot of experience. I certainly had a lot of Web coding experience; but at 23, I had never done any of this before. With a year in Namibia under my belt, I was very comfortable working with other cultures. I was happy to assist where I could and to have Fisher, who was experienced, mentor me along the way.

To get the list of requirements, Fisher and Rau interacted for more than three months with Johnson and Arroyo-Lopez (program directors for the on-campus and distance education programs, respectively), the other full-time faculty, the department support personnel and program managers, current students, some of the program alumni, program mentors, and so on. Fisher remembered:

> We used a list of questions given to us by Russoft as one of the tools to gather requirements. (See Tables 7-3, 7-4, and 7-5.) The list was long and comprehensive and covered various areas of design, technology, need, and system characteristics. Russoft gave it to us well before any contract was signed to allow them to estimate the scope of the work based on our answers. Again, this action made us feel like we were working with a team of professionals and not with just a mom-and-pop operation. This was a standard way of doing business for them, and they used our input to make the final proposal.

Table 7–3: *Original Requirements Questions and Answers: Current Site*

Questions	*Answers*
Do you think your current site promotes a favorable user experience? Why or why not?	No, it is very static and is not updated currently. There are no news items and no "user experience."
What specific areas of your current site do you think are successful? Why are they successful?	None. The site has some of the right information, but it is so old that it is not even funny.
What shortcomings exist with the current site, and what are the three most important elements you want to change on the site today?	We want to make it dynamic (with current information always being injected), easy to update (incentive to keep it new and fresh), and with a nice design that is simple to navigate.
Have you conducted usability tests or gathered user feedback for your current site?	We did this about three months ago as part of a general survey. Unfortunately, the feedback did not say much.
How important is it to maintain your current look and feel, logo, and branding?	Very important. The university and our program depend on our names. Branding is important for people to recognize us.

Table 7–4: *Original Requirements Questions and Answers: Content*

Questions	*Answers*
Will this site use existing content from the current site? If so, what is the source, who is responsible for approval, and has the content been audited? If not, will you be creating content in-house or using an outside provider?	We will use a combination of what exists right now (packaged differently) and create new content per the relevant information architecture. We will create it in-house and have a technical writer review it.
What is the basic structure of the content, and how is it organized? Is it a complete overhaul of the current site, a modification, or an expansion?	It is a complete overhaul. We will have to come up with our own information architecture to lay it out.

Table 7–4: *Original Requirements Questions and Answers: Content (Continued)*

Questions	*Answers*
Describe visual elements or content that should be utilized from your current site or marketing materials (logo, color scheme, navigation, naming conventions, and so on).	Our current Web site is not something of which we are proud. We can use the university logo (we don't have our own) but are looking for you to come up with design ideas.
How will the content of this site (along with functionality and navigation) expand or differ from your current site? Do you have an existing site map for the outgoing site structure? Do you already have a site map or outline for the proposed redesign?	We do not currently have a site map.

Table 7–5: *Original Requirements Questions and Answers: Technology*

Questions	*Answers*
What is your target platform and browser?	All browsers; Windows, Unix, and Mac users.
Are there specific technologies (Flash, DHTML, JavaScript, and Real Audio) that you would like to use in the site? If so, how will they enhance the user experience?	We would like to have some Flash in the back, scripts when forms are displayed, dynamic content as much as possible, and have it be database driven.
Will you have database functionality (dynamic content generation, search capabilities, personalization/login)? Do you already have a database in place?	Yes to all of the above. No database is installed now. We would prefer going with an open source platform like MySQL.
Will you have a need for secured e-commerce? Do you already offer transactions online? Please describe in detail.	No.
Will you require other specific programming needs (such as personalization or search capability)? Please describe in detail.	Additional information about required components and their functionality are contained in the "Requirements for the Web Site Modernization" document.

The interviews, answers, and interactions of Rau and Fisher with the program faculty and staff resulted in a rough requirements document that divided the project into two phases. Phase 1 involved all the static informational pages and a temporal part that included events, news items, and an announcement calendar. Included was a student planner to help organize classes, course schedules, and prerequisites. Lastly, Phase 1 also included the functionality to allow students to download, fill out, and submit surveys and forms online for course grades, change requests, course adding and dropping, and so on.

Phase 2 of the project focused on creating an intranet that could be accessed securely through the Web site to enable access to various levels of information to program staff, faculty, existing students, and alumni. Because requirements for Phase 2 existed only at a rudimentary level, it was agreed that currently only Phase 1 would be contracted, estimated, and budgeted. When time and budget permitted, a business arrangement would be further negotiated to the satisfaction of both the client and the software developer (see Figure 7-2).

The Work Begins

With the development contract signed in late June 2003, the project plan was laid out, at least on a basic level, by Dennis Bramer, the account manager located in Phoenix, Arizona. The plan called for spending some time to do more requirements gathering to understand the client's needs and the state of current Web site designs before proceeding to database design and coding work in Russia. Dennis Bramer reflected:

> We had a budget of only 400 working hours for this project. Fisher had negotiated our hourly cost down to the bare minimum for a fixed-cost contract. I thought that he might have gotten the price he wanted but that we were left with "no fat on the bones" from a profit perspective. Russ Laughlin [Russoft's CEO] must have really wanted this project to allow the negotiations to go this way. Having the University of Madison's name as a client reference was a major opportunity for a company like Russoft, even if this was a small-budget project.
>
> Since this was important for Russ, I didn't want to spend too much time collecting requirements. There wasn't enough time in the plan anyway for it. We already had what was needed as part of the plan that Fisher approved. We needed to get into design fast so that we could use most of our hours for coding rather than talking. I was hoping we could get everything done that was needed in the time we had.

The design, or the "look and feel," seemed to be one of the big-ticket items for the system. Fisher wanted to make sure that people were "happy" with what the Russians came up with because this was going to be the system of choice for a few years to come. He knew that Johnson and the other full-time professors were very particular in how they thought the system should look. Fisher said at the time:

> The designers in Russia provided us with a few potential designs that I had shared with my internal team. I didn't think that I needed to discuss every little detail with every member of the staff. When we finally picked a design we liked, we presented

> it to our general committee.* It was then that we got a lot of flack from one of the professors.

Alex Rau recalled:

> For some reason, one professor adamantly did not like having the site page in a three-column template in the center with equal margins on both sides. He must not have realized that this was how most companies back then chose to design their Web interfaces. I pushed back and might have been a little too "animated" in how I responded to his questions, but then, I did not know who he was at the time.

Rau's hiccup with Levin, the Norbert L. Graf professor of computer science, was just another wrinkle in the project as far as Fisher was concerned. It did raise some questions regarding the readiness of people to commit to a GUI design that was otherwise "imposed" on them. To speed things up and clear any misunderstandings, Fisher instructed Rau to search for samples from known Web sites with a similar look and feel to get some of the faculty comfortable with the particular design they had chosen. Fisher said:

> I wasn't about to change our entire design just because one professor objected to having a three-column layout. That seemed foolish to me. I knew that we would not be able to please everyone and that we would have to live with this.

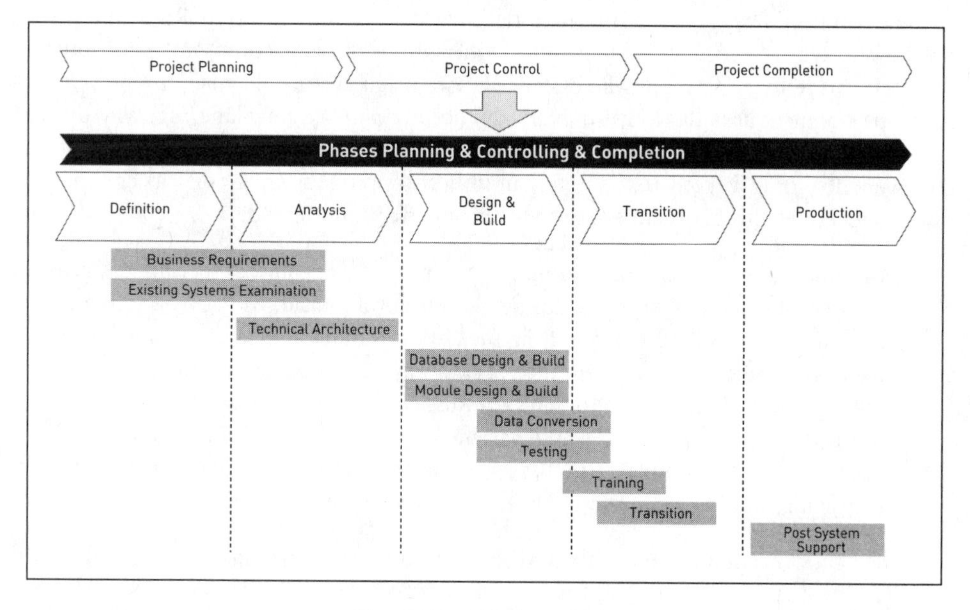

Figure 7–2: *Project phases*

* The software engineering program held a monthly meeting for people involved in teaching, assisting, or interacting with the program (dubbed the "general meeting").

Fortuitously, Fisher was scheduled to be in Moscow the following month (September) for a teaching seminar. He was always concerned that they had not budgeted for travel in this project to meet their vendors. Luckily, it worked out that he could use the business excursion to also meet with Russoft and discuss how things were going. He approached Sergey Nizamov and Russ Laughlin from Russoft to arrange a meeting to see their office firsthand and to discuss project specifics. To get ready for the trip, he asked Rau to identify ongoing and open issues that needed to be addressed. He also spoke to Bramer in the United States to learn how the project was going from his perspective and to obtain a detailed account of the hours spent, though the later information was not provided.

Visiting Russoft Technologies in Moscow

As usual, Fisher traveled to Russia directly from the United States via Delta Airlines, where LearnIT's CEO, Yuri Kashnovsky, picked him up at the airport. Kashnovsky was a young (23), well-connected entrepreneur with a remarkable track record of start-up companies in Silicon Valley, where he resided after graduating from UW Madison's School of Computer Science at the age of 19 in 1999. For someone so young, he was impressive in how he always seemed to know what the latest business buzz was, where to get it, and how to bargain for it. He never let go of an opportunity when someone from UW Madison was in town to "arrange" a meeting with potential investors, existing clients, or managers in companies he was considering as targets for merger or acquisition.

The trip from Shermetyevo International Airport, a gloomy old-style Russian terminal on the outskirts of Moscow, was a traffic nightmare in the late hours of the morning. A three-hour ride to cover a 15-mile distance was a usual event. Likewise, the gray "train-like" apartment houses lined up in every direction along the four-lane highway did not add much to the charm of the trip. When Fisher landed, he was surprised to find out that they were not going directly to the hotel but rather stopping to "knock off," as Kashnovsky put it, a meeting with Laughlin at Russoft. Kashnovsky commented:

> Gene had asked me to arrange a meeting with Russ [Laughlin] at their offices near Cheremushki market sometime during his visit. It was outside Moscow and the easiest way to do it was on our way from the airport. I didn't have a car, and going via the metro would take us an hour at least each way. I knew Fisher was tired, probably hungry, and still unadjusted to our local Russian time, but he played along with it. It wasn't his first trip to Russia, and we generally packed his schedule with meetings from dawn to dusk to maximize the use of his time in the country. Usually, he was easy going, and I figured we might take advantage of the opportunity.

When they reached the building and Russoft's offices on the eighth floor, Fisher had mixed feelings about what he saw. Fisher reflected:

> On the one hand, everyone was very courteous, spoke English, and treated me with the utmost respect as a guest of the CEO and as a professor from the United States.

> On the other hand, the office had a haphazard appearance, with confused-looking people working out of every available nook.

Russ Laughlin remembered the meeting quite well, "We brought in Sergey Nizamov and Mikhail Pisarev, the project leads, to discuss the specifics on GUI design, ongoing issues that needed to be resolved, and the planning that lie ahead of us. Fisher was very business-oriented and seemed very happy with our designs." Figure 7-3 shows the Russoft project organization.

Sergey, the project lead on the Russian side, was just about done discussing the various design options when Laughlin and Pisarev were called to a phone conversation with a client who needed some help. Fisher stayed on to discuss the project progress one-on-one with Sergey. Sergey recalled:

> I gave him a few color schemes from which to choose. He said that he would get back to me with an answer after he showed it to some of his people in the United States. He also wanted to know how many hours we had spent on this design so far. I really didn't have an exact answer for this. I said I thought we had spent about 30 to 40 hours so far. Fisher was very pleased with my answer and reiterated that we need to make sure we didn't spend too much time in design because we won't have enough left for implementation. I didn't really understand what he meant. Didn't he want a good GUI for his system? My designers were working extra hard to custom tailor the graphics. Fisher gave us some guidance on what he wanted, but he must have known these were going to take time to complete. Overall, I think he was happy with what we produced so far.

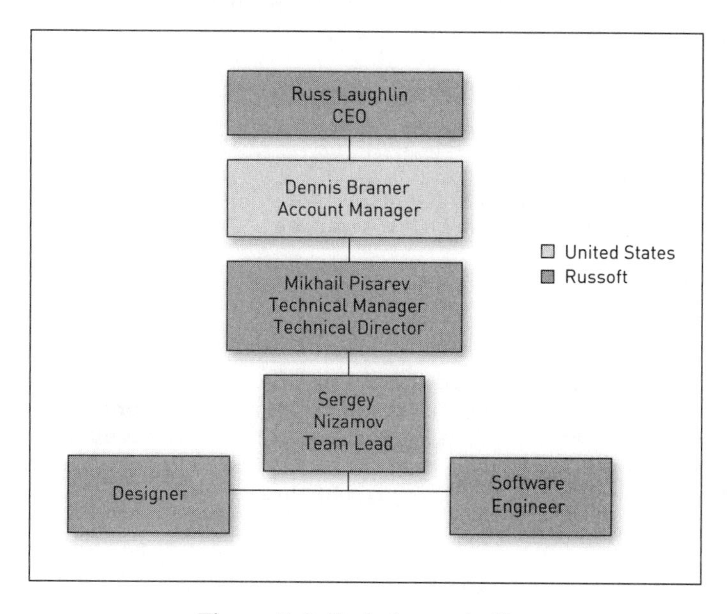

Figure 7–3: *Project organization*

Are We Getting Anywhere?

Upon his return to the United States the following Monday, Fisher updated both Bramer and his own department about his visit in Moscow. He asked Bramer to provide him with a formal count of the hours spent on the project thus far. Bramer recalled:

> Fisher asked me to get him the true count of the hours spent so far on the project. As a customer, he wanted to make sure enough hours were left for implementing the critical parts of the system. When the count from the Russia office came back at 130, Fisher was flabbergasted. He told me Sergey's original count (4 days before) of roughly 30 to 40 hours and mentioned that not much had changed in the GUI design to hike up the numbers that much. He was honestly upset and irritated. He didn't know whether Sergey had lied to him, was just inexperienced, or had thought this was the way that Russoft was used to doing business. The project was already behind schedule, and all I could do was apologize while trying to reassure him that I would get to the bottom of this first thing in the morning, when people in Russia were back in the office.

When Fisher returned from Russia, the semester had already started. He had left the day-to-day project interaction to Alex Rau, who kept him in the loop through his e-mail communication with Sergey Nizamov. Fisher was uncertain whether the ongoing communication issues that he and Rau were observing were caused by an issue they themselves had created, a cultural or language barrier, or a misinterpretation of the requirements communicated by Bramer to the Russians when the project originally started.

The following are typical e-mails exchanged between Alex and Sergey. They contain text that has not been edited for grammar, spelling, or other textual errors.

```
----- Original Message -----
From: Alex Rau
Sent: Tuesday, September 12, 2003, 11:17 AM
To: Nizamov, Sergey
Cc: Gene Fisher; Bramer, Dennis
Subject: Re: Madison :: Website sources

Sergey, Hi!

I know what you mean about IE with the extra bad tags issue.

Well, this is the idea that Gene had in mind, again almost along
the same line in terms of functionality as what Contribute does
from Macromedia at http://www.macromedia.com/software/contribute/.
All in all, I will need to be able to edit the pages in the future
using Dreamweaver and FrontPage, whether it be images or text.
```

```
There may have been some confusion in terms of the functionality of
this admin console and that's understandable.

We need to have the Search Engine functionality and Username and
Password w/ option to Register working. Can you host the SQL stuff
yourself so we can at least see it in action and then have a System
Admin guy take care of the installation and transferring of files
for maintenance?

Thanks for the hard work,

Alex

----- Original Message -----
From: Nizamov, Sergey
Sent: Wednesday, September 13, 2003, 5:22 AM
To: Rau, Alex
Cc: Gene Fisher; Bramer, Dennis
Subject: Re: Madison: Website sources

Alex, hello,

First, about the graphic design. I have already asked to Web-
designer to make some changes according with the new requiremens
and I'm expecting to get new version today evening or tomorrow
morning. I let you know when the site be updated.

About AdminTool: I know a little bit about Macromedia Contribute
product. This is the rather solid product. Unfortunatelly we did
not mention those functionalities before so we estimated AdminTool
as 40 hours' task.

Anyway, I have already asked to the programmer to compare currently
existing AdminTool with Contribute and deside what kind of changes
are possible to add to our tool to simplify them or to improve the
functionality. If it will be possible we implement it.

See you,

Sergey
```

At this point, it seemed to both Fisher and Rau that interacting with Sergey directly and having Bramer there to run interference in case things went off-course was a prudent way to make things work. Fisher, who did not like the fact that no official communication channels had been designated thus far in the project, let the inexperienced Rau get his feet wet firsthand with project management. Fisher knew that he could always call Russ Laughlin directly as a last resort.

In late October, with the project already two months past its estimated completion date (originally planned for August) with no end in sight, Fisher was notified that Bramer was leaving the project and Russoft. For various occupational and personal reasons, Bramer, who by now was friendly and on a first-name basis with Fisher, decided to move on with his life. Laughlin called from Moscow to reassure Fisher that he would be keeping a close eye on the project while Russoft were busy searching for a replacement in the United States. Fisher reflected:

> Losing Dennis was a big blow for us. He might not have been physically in Russia, but Sergey seemed to listen to him. He was a reassuring voice in this sea of madness. Whenever we thought things were over the edge, Dennis [Bramer] was able to let us relax and get things working again. I felt good that Russ [Laughlin] was actively looking for someone to take his place, because managing the project directly across continents seemed to be too much to handle. I hoped he would find someone just as capable and approachable.

Roughly a month later, when Fisher traveled to Russia for yet another teaching engagement, he finally met with Russ Laughlin and his newly appointed U.S. project manager, Mark Urlanski, at a local restaurant in Moscow. Mark Urlanski explained:

> I was just in Russia for a few days before Russ asked me to meet a client on a project I was going to handle. It was a relatively simple project involving a Web-based system for UW Madison. The project was not going as planned, and Russ, who was meeting the client in Moscow, wanted me there as support. Fisher, who had a list of things with him that needed addressing from the project management perspective, was calm and composed throughout our discussion. It appeared that most of his claims had somehow to do with the local person Sergey and his "unique" way of doing things. We listened very carefully, trying not to interject objections. Both Russ and I reassured Fisher that things were going to change effective immediately now that I was supervising the project and that I would more closely watch Sergey from this point forward.

Back in his office the following week, Fisher heard from Alex Rau that there was yet another snag in the project. This time the issue concerned the database implementation. While the requirement was to use an open source MySQL implementation, Sergey had decided to use Microsoft SQL Server, a different and costly database. The change might not have been a problem, but the stakeholders had not discussed it beforehand. Al Molsters, the department's system administrator, was out of the office for a couple of weeks to install servers at one of UW Madison's remote campuses, so Fisher could not immediately test the new database. The schedule would slip even more. Sergey had indicated in an e-mail that he thought Microsoft SQL Server was a better choice for them, but Fisher was not convinced. Fisher, who had to give a status report to his boss the next morning, was truly at a loss.

CASE PROBLEM

The following are the main problems and decisions to be made that involve risk management:

- How should this offshore development project be restructured to minimize future problems through risk management?
- What risk management practices and activities are needed to reduce future project risk?
- What should be done to mitigate the project risks associated with people, process, and technology?

Case Analysis

ANALYSIS ACTIVITY

In this section, we will try to analyze the case study using the PEAK decision model. We will focus on factors that influence the decisions to be made by the stakeholders in the case study.

Analysis Background

Let's look at the PEAK inputs to see how they can help us understand alternative solutions to the following key problem:

How should this offshore development effort be restructured to minimize future problems through risk management?

(P) Problem: This case study highlights the problem of conducting offshore development projects without systematic risk management. The solution should provide structured processes to promote effective communications, productive meetings, appropriate review and feedback, and ongoing issue identification and resolution with a remote development team (because the lack of these has contributed to the troubled state of the project).

(E) Experience: The skill sets for the project stakeholders are as follows:

For UW Madison:

- Good understanding of software engineering processes
- Extensive work with global projects
- Some expertise in risk management
- Some work expertise involving companies in Russia
- Extensive project management experience

For Russoft Technologies:

- Experience working with U.S.-based clients
- Experience in managing Web development projects

(A) Assumptions: The project stakeholder assumptions might include the following:

- The offshore development team recognizes the need to restructure the project to be more effective and is willing to cooperate.
- The key stakeholders on the project, both internal (within the department) and external (offshore), are interested in managing risks before they become problems.
- There are enough resources (budget, time, knowledge) to conduct process improvement.

(K) Knowledge: The knowledge base for the project stakeholders includes the following environment and facts:

- This is an offshore development project with stakeholders in the United States and Russia (environment).
- The project currently conducts no explicit risk management (fact).
- The project has multiple problems in the areas of planning and budgeting, communications, and scope and requirements (fact).
- The need to fix ongoing problems is immediate. There is no time for a "wait-and-see" approach (fact).

Solution: Alternative solutions to the problem might include some combination of the following:

- Apply Agile methodologies to structure a communication mechanism that allows stakeholders to acquire status and other project information regularly and expediently. The project management and staff need to be involved and knowledgeable.
- Create structured processes to achieve the project objectives through the performance of well-defined tasks to achieve milestones according to a clear and definitive schedule.
- Alter communication and control mechanisms to increase upper-level manager oversight and to decrease dependency on developer control of the project.
- Invest some process time and effort for both the U.S. and Russian stakeholders to formally identify project risks and to mitigate, track, and control those of high priority.

Requirement for the solution: Create a structured process that involves doing specific steps and taking specific actions at registered milestones with set timelines for software artifact delivery.

Assumed Risk: The following are the potential risks associated with the alternative solutions:

- Restructuring the project (essentially investing time in defining and executing different processes) might take longer than expected and result in further schedule slippage.
- The project stakeholders may resist changing to a more process-oriented approach.
- The project stakeholders may not like or distrust an approach that involves more management control. The result may be an "I don't care" mentality or attitude problems.

Analysis Questions

1. What risk management practices and activities would help minimize future project risk?
2. What should be done to mitigate project risks in the areas of people, process, and technology?

DISCUSSION

Since we are attempting to restructure a project in a way to minimize risk, the decision regarding what to do is dependent on evaluating the risk associated with alternative solutions. Whatever risk is assumed must still allow the project to succeed even if an assumed risk materializes. Naturally, any decision that negatively impacts the project requirements, schedule, or budget (which have already been compromised) is not a good choice. Fisher and his boss Johnson should look for solutions that would maximize their control over scope, time, and cost.

The solution needs to minimize the risk associated with communication and cross-cultural barriers because these are primary contributors to the problem. Handling the communication issue would be a viable mitigation strategy to reduce the likelihood that open issues fester into problems. Another approach might be to improve or to reduce the impact of the poor project management skills exhibited by the Russoft staff members assigned to the project.

With respect to cultural differences regarding work styles, the decision should focus on the amount of project control and oversight needed by the U.S. managers. Fisher should realize that giving Russoft unlimited flexibility in how it executes the project is a risk that he cannot afford. Fisher must also justify to his boss that he has the ability to control the project and to minimize the downside of working with Russian software developers. To do this, he must oversee and control the project deliverables, project execution processes, and communications with the developers.

CONCLUSIONS

Both Fisher and Laughlin face tough decisions that, in addition to influencing the daily implementation details, concern their ongoing relationship, reputation, and how each of their respective organizations is perceived. There is a tendency to ignore long-term implications when trying to finish a troubled project. Fisher and Laughlin should step back and carefully analyze their situation to avoid making a hasty decision without evaluating the options and risks.

Risk management is a way for decision makers to proactively handle project challenges. Although Fisher has not yet done this effectively, he is aware of the problems that his project has encountered and wants to minimize or solve them. Finding fault is easy for both Fisher and Laughlin, especially because of the distance and cultural issues. Future project risks might be greater if one of the key stakeholders takes a coercive stance with statements such as "Do it now because I said so." Fisher and Laughlin need to analyze the results and assumed risks of their previous project decisions before deciding how to go forward.

KEY IDEAS TO REMEMBER

This case study presents a typical project in which neither the developer nor the client explicitly practiced risk management. In general, the lack of risk management has led to a number of problems that could have been foreseen and avoided. We hope you will remember the following ideas after reading this case:

- Risk management needs to be planned and executed as part of the overall project plan. Decision makers often make decisions with limited information and under time constraints. Project managers should invest some of their time at the start of their projects to identify project risks and to mitigate those that might preclude project success.
- As projects become more complex, in terms of environment and domain, the need for explicit risk management increases. Complex projects usually involve multiple components, technical sophistication, and many decision makers. Project environment also contributes to project complexity, and even a small project with two to three project engineers may involve complexities associated with distance, culture, language, expertise, and so on. It is often easier to deal implicitly with project risks on a less complex project in which risk management practices are done on the back of an envelope. As project complexity grows, the complexity of the decisions made by project stakeholders also increases. Decisions for complex projects often involve more time, effort, and resources.
- Ignoring risk management, even for small-scale projects, can lead to significant problems. Decision makers use benefit-cost analysis to evaluate the value of performing risk management activities. From a business perspective, this may be a reasonable approach because it is often very difficult to precisely value the impact of various risks. Ignoring project risks may result in unexpected and significant project delays, poor product quality, and cost overruns.

CASE STUDY

Falcon Edutainment and the RiskSim Project

Directions

When reading this case study, focus on the risks associated with the miscommunications taking place during a short, time-constrained project. Identify issues associated with managing customer expectations and the risks they pose to the continuation of the project.

Case Summary

DESCRIPTION

Brain Wenzel is managing a short, six-month project for Falcon Edutainment. The project deals with converting a risk management simulation into a Web-based platform. When different opinions on "creative" choices arise between client and developer and the developer presses on with the project despite the lack of clear feedback from the client, both sides end up with having to manage the resulting "fallout."

CASE STUDY OBJECTIVES

After reading the case study, you will be able to do the following:

- Understand the risks and the decisions faced by developers working with little or vague feedback
- Understand the consequences of adding or changing requirements on project timelines and schedules, as well as the need for rework
- Review risks taken and decisions made on a small-scale project

SUBJECTS COVERED

Risk management, decision making, managing customer expectations, requirements management, and stakeholder communications

SETTING

The setting is a small project involving Web-based system development in the United States for a training/simulation application. The project is constrained by a small budget and a short time frame (approximately six months).

KEY CONCEPTS

- How to minimize project risks related to requirements, lack of client feedback, and constrained schedules
- The effects of decision making on project risks and on successful project management
- The downside of managing risks implicitly with no defined plan

The Case

SCENARIO

Brian Wenzel had plenty of time to think while driving to work this morning. He was stuck in traffic on one of the main highways heading into Boston in what seemed like an endless attempt to reorganize the travel patterns around the bustling metropolitan. It was early in the morning, and Brian was already having one of those throbbing headaches related to the e-mail he had gotten the day before from Lee Orman, the lead on the RiskSim project. Orman, a young graduate of Yale's School of Management, was the risk management practice director for ExecSoft and his principal client on the project. Wenzel knew he needed to manage the growing project risks while balancing scope, budget, schedule, and his customer's expectations. He didn't know where to begin.

RiskSim was one of the flagship teaching tools used by ExecSoft to train software professionals in risk management concepts. The company, a U.S.-based risk management training consultancy, had developed a board-based simulation to provide a lifelike environment of a software development project. The simulation was rather successful, and the company decided early in the year to turn it into a Web-based simulation. Though it was still under active development, the team at ExecSoft thought the simulation had matured enough to be able to move it to the online environment. To that extent, they had contracted with Falcon, a company that specialized in education centric software development. At Falcon, Wenzel, together with three other engineers, were put on the project. Figure 7-4 shows the ExecSoft and Falcon Edutainment organizational chart.

Wenzel recalled:

> ExecSoft was interested in having us help them webify their board-based simulation. It was a no-brainer because we've done these things multiple times in the past. After listening to what they were interested in doing, we explained how we did things and how we worked on eliciting requirements and doing the design, the project management work, and the actual development. The meeting was rather successful because it led to a short contract negotiation and a rather immediate work date. One thing that did strike me as odd was that ExecSoft put one of their new people to head the project. Don't get me wrong, Ms. Orman seemed very capable but not in the least experienced in anything that even resembled software development, education, or simulations. I feared having to spend too much time walking her through the ropes in explaining why we did certain things.

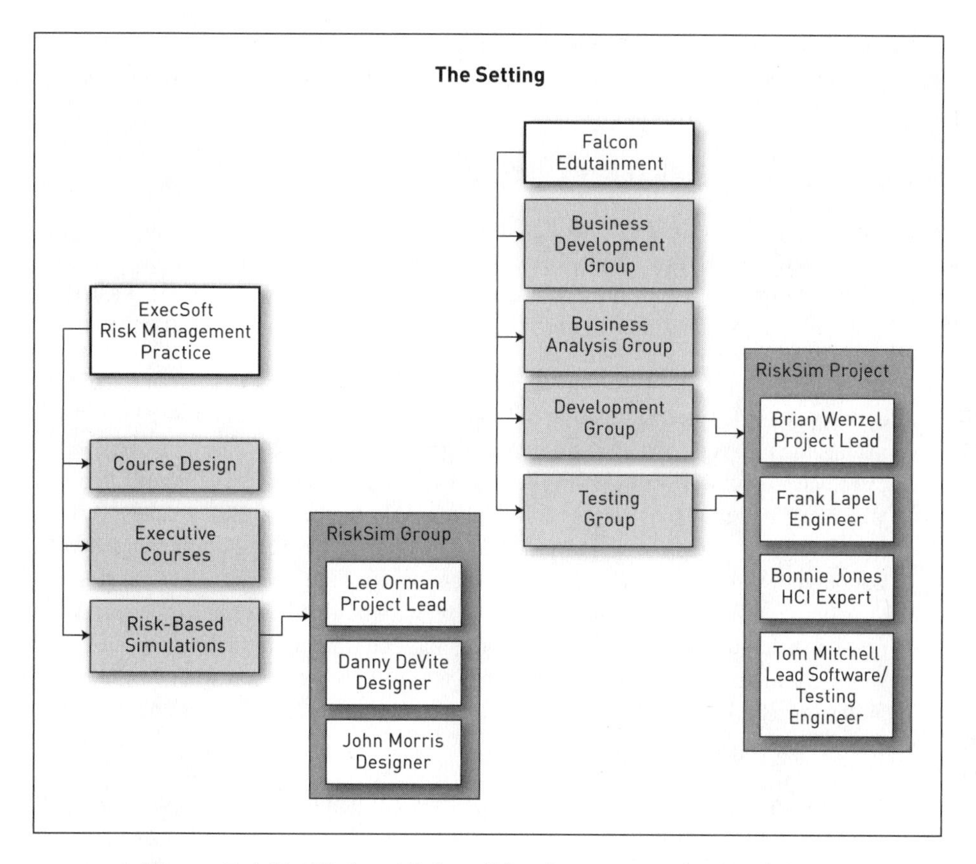

Figure 7–4: *ExecSoft and Falcon Edutainment organizational chart**

* Arrows represent a drilled-down view of people working within various business units.

Orman remembered:

> While searching for a company with a solid track record of developing educational focused simulations, we came across Falcon. One of our managers knew someone who was on their board of directors. They apparently were heavily involved in project work with universities, the U.S. Department of Education, and a number of large Fortune 500 companies who used their services for creating local in-house training simulations. Though I was still learning the ropes with respect to software development and simulations, the staff at Falcon seemed eager to help and get to know more about the project.

The work contracted between the two companies was for a fixed-fee, six-month-long contract for a working prototype. The timeline included a short requirements elicitation period, mostly to understand the existing simulation, its rules, assumptions, and mechanics, followed by three iterations of the actual prototype to refine the game's look and feel and to elicit feedback on other important characteristics such as ease of use and playability (see Figure 7-5).

RiskSim: Elicitation Phase

As soon as the project started in March, Wenzel met with Orman and one of the original simulation developers, Danny DeVite. DeVite, who was an expert in risk management, had a very clear idea of what he wanted to accomplish using the simulation. He wasn't sure, though, of how that would translate into the computer environment. Devite recalled:

> Two years earlier, a group of us involved in the risk management practice at ExecSoft developed a risk-based simulation to help practitioners understand how to use risk management in the context of a software development project. The simulation was extremely successful with glowing feedbacks on its realism, fun factor, and depth. We knew we wanted to port it to a computer to make it more robust, to make it easier to control, and to add elements we couldn't on a board. We were hoping that Falcon Edutainment could provide the guidance on how to do it. We were not experts in developing these kinds of systems. If we were, we wouldn't have needed Falcon. We needed their expertise to make it engaging and entertaining in the virtual sense. It was my understanding that we would be getting some advice on what works best under our constraints while keeping the rules of the simulation the same and the spirit of how it is played.

The Falcon team had spent the first few weeks getting a feel and a better understanding of how the simulation worked. They peered over design documents, user manuals, and two active off-site simulations conducted for two independent government organizations in Washington, D.C. Equipped with a solid understanding of how the simulation is played and having read what seemed like a cart full of documentation, Wenzel and two of his associates, Frank Lapel and Bonnie Jones (a human computer interaction specialist), set out to design a paper mock-up of how a GUI might look (see Figure 7-6).

The design seemed to impress Orman and her colleagues at ExecSoft yet appeared to create more problems than expected.

Charlotte, a software engineer at Falcon, recalled:

> We interacted with the simulation quite a bit to understand the rationale of how it was designed. We then created a design that conformed to the existing rules and mechanics of the game. From a design perspective, we wanted to achieve a balance between adapting the playability of the game to a setting where players would be drawn to playing it more than one time. This was not easy because the game on the board was rather simplistic and did not offer much interaction. We therefore used a different approach than the clients had asked for originally and went for a more interactive "office-like" environment rather than the simplistic Monopoly-style design.

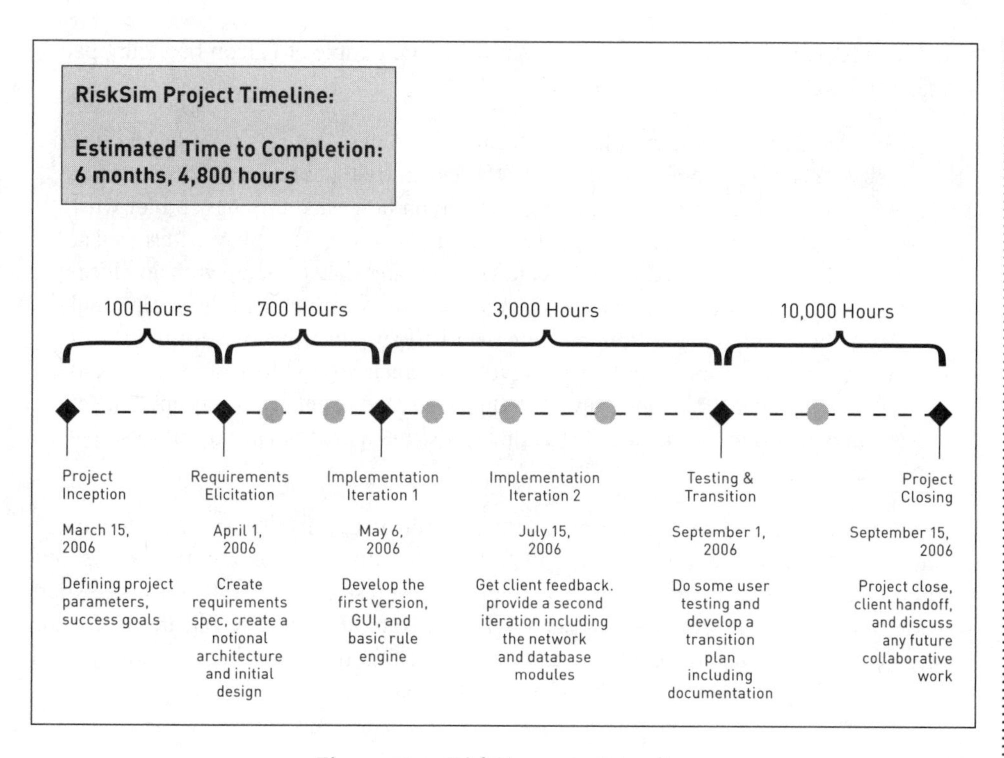

Figure 7–5: *RiskSim project timeline*

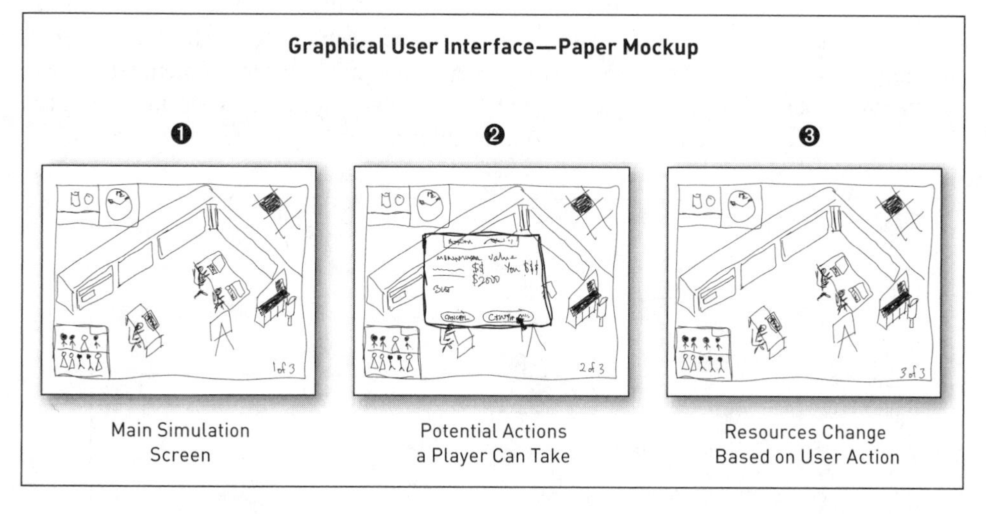

Figure 7–6: *Paper prototype of the GUI produced by Lapel and Jones*

Orman had a different take on things than what the people at Falcon had anticipated. Orman remembered:

> I was highly impressed with Falcon's technical abilities. Wenzel's team looked like they were taking it seriously the first few weeks in trying to understand what went into RiskSim. We did our best to educate them on how we did things and for what reasons. Then, when we finally got the mock-up, it was as if they haven't listened at all. RiskSim was designed using a board concept, and they came up with an office-like environment. Though the concept was certainly worthwhile, I distinctly recall DeVite saying in a closed team meeting he wasn't sure that this concept fit in with his ideas. I was the one who was going to have to tell Wenzel he had to go back to the drawing board. The poor guy . . . it almost seemed easier not to say anything at this point and simply wait for a better time to discuss more than just the mock-up—perhaps over the phone or in person.

Through this initial cut at the mock-up and the vague feedback that followed, it became clear to Wenzel that his clients were interested only in a replica of the exact simulation they had on the board. They seemed far less interested in having a creative expert provide them with an opinion on what would captivate an audience playing it. In line with that, Wenzel updated his project plan to reflect less time spent on "creativity" and more toward focusing the effort on replicating what existed.

Requirements Revisited

Wenzel decided to use a two-pronged approach for this project. As an experienced engineer, he wanted to utilize what he already had as initial requirements to build a notional architecture (see Figure 7-7). In parallel, he wanted to spend a little more time refining and verifying both the architecture and the requirements before moving into development. Sticking to his milestones, he was able to produce a draft of the initial requirements specification (SRS) that included a set of detailed use cases from the information he gathered from Orman.

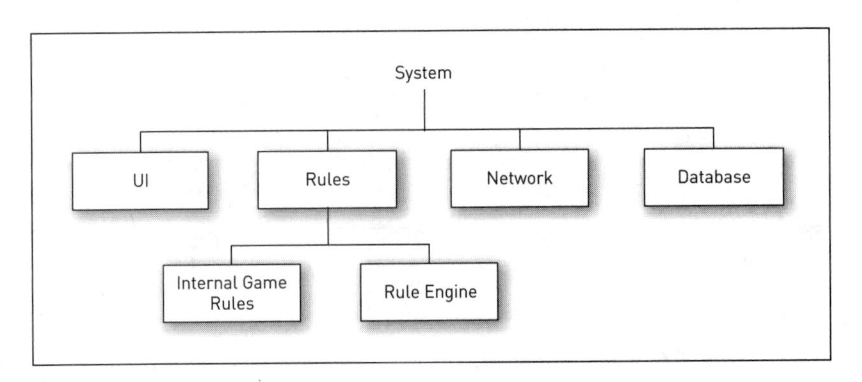

Figure 7–7: *Notional architecture*

Remembers Orman:

> When I got into the office on Monday, I had an e-mail waiting for me from Brian. It had a rather large document attached that included the RiskSim features we discussed put into a more technical language. I liked how the information was laid out in scenario-type format with a sequence of steps the player/user would go through to perform certain tasks. I remember printing it out and showing it to DeVite who said he would look at it later.

While DeVite and his colleagues were reviewing the requirements document and thinking of how to proceed, Wenzel instructed his team to press on with the GUI design work required before implementation. He did not want to waste time while waiting for more feedback from Orman. Lapel and Jones were strongly opposed to this move. It was their understanding that driving forward as fast as they could might lead to future rework for the team. If anything was to change, it was probably going to be the GUI. Any work done up to this point would most certainly go to waste. Lapel mentioned this to Wenzel over lunch the following day:

> Brian, I am not sure we are serving the best interest of our clients by pushing forward as fast as we can without validating our designs. The idea behind the GUI was to elicit requirements and refine them, not draw a line in the sand from which we can't go back. Do we even know whether they liked what we did?

Wenzel reacted:

> I don't need you to tell me how to run my projects! I have far more experience than you in doing this kind of thing. We are on a tight schedule, and we don't have the luxury of waiting until Orman and her gang gets to decide exactly what they want us to do. For all I know, they could change their minds regardless of what we show them.

Back at ExecSoft, DeVite and Orman discussed the requirements specification with one of the other RiskSim designers, John Morris. Morris was keen on integrating more features into the project based on recent feedbacks from two focus groups he had run through the simulation a month or so before. When Orman mentioned that adding more to the project currently was not in their original plans, Morris hinted that they could divide the project into two phases instead of one, where the impact on development would be minimal. DeVite remembered:

> John had an interesting idea. He wanted to incorporate some enhancements into the existing RiskSim effort. He was basing those enhancements on some user surveys from a recent run of the simulation with a group of 35 executives working at three different telecommunications companies. John shared our opinion that the computer version we were working on should have a design that followed our true-and-tried board concept but strongly encouraged us to talk to Falcon and see whether

> they could accommodate his enhancements. He asked whether we had finalized the requirements spec for the project. When I mentioned we had not, he suggested that we break the project into two phases, with only the first phase going through implementation but having the requirements captured for both.

Reluctantly, Orman communicated the request to Wenzel in an e-mail the following morning. She thought her colleague's approach might be a mistake but deferred to DeVite and Morris as the experts on what the simulation needed to make it a training success. In her e-mail to Wenzel, she mentioned they were interested in discussing additional requirements but specified these were only minor rule adjustments and not so much conceptual modifications. Orman had also discussed their desire to revisit the GUI concept with the office environment versus the playing board approach. She wasn't very specific on what she meant by that and finished her e-mail by saying she would also be available to discuss these requirements further on the phone once the RiskSim team at Falcon had time to review it.

CASE PROBLEM

The following are the main problems and decisions to be made that involve risk management:

- What project risks are associated with ExecSoft's request for change in the requirements?
- What risk management practices and activities should Falcon use to minimize and control future project risk?
- From a project management perspective, what key decisions should Orman consider to minimize the occurrence of similar issues on other projects?

Case Analysis

ANALYSIS ACTIVITY

Analysis Questions

1. What are the most important risks faced by Wenzel? What should he do to mitigate them?
2. What are some of the PEAK inputs that Wenzel needs to consider before evaluating and making a decision about alternative solutions to his problem?
3. How could have Wenzel avoided some of the problems faced on this project, specifically those that affect the way in which he managed his clients' expectations?

KEY IDEAS TO REMEMBER

The goal of this case study was to examine what could happen when project managers focus too much on their short-term project success without attempting to identify and mitigate risk conditions that might prevent long-term project success. Decision makers need to remember the following:

- Managing risks explicitly on software projects is very important. Identifying and mitigating project risk directly correlates to project success.
- Risk management is an activity that should be conducted throughout the project. Thinking about risk early in a project provides decision makers with more options and time to deal with potential future problems.
- Project success needs to be defined in a way that enables decision makers to understand what might preclude them from being successful (that is, risks). This threshold of success should be the criteria against which project actions are evaluated. Actions that directly contribute to project success should be performed, and those that detract from it should be avoided.

7.4 Summary

The chapter discussed the following activities for managing risk in the context of decision making for a software project:

- Defining a threshold of success
- Identifying risks
- Formulating risk statements
- Mitigating, tracking, and controlling risk
- Communicating about risk
- Trading off resources in making decisions about how to manage risk

The case studies focused on how poor or no risk management can lead to project problems. The first case, "SEWeb and Russoft Technologies," involved unexpected problems encountered while working with an offshore development team located in Russia. The second case, "Falcon Edutainment and the RiskSim Project," presented a project whose troubles stemmed from the client-developer interaction. The software project managers in both cases considered schedule and budget in making decisions, but they did not identify, evaluate, and mitigate the risks associated with their decisions.

Software project managers frequently do risk management in a haphazard way or simply ignore it. The case studies highlighted project risks that could have been identified and managed but were not. The resulting project problems are classical examples of project risk conditions that can be disastrous if they are not managed. Risk management is an integral part of evaluating and making project decisions.

Risk management is an ongoing event in the life of a software project and, when not done correctly or at all, can lead to disastrous results.

Chapter 8

Managing People Interactions

8.1 Chapter Objectives

After reading and thinking about the concepts and case studies presented in this chapter, you will be able to do the following:

- Understand factors that influence people interactions and how these factors could be influenced to make the interactions between software project stakeholders more successful
- Recognize that, because it is very difficult to change other people's behavior, you must adapt your own behavior in various situations to handle your people interactions more successfully
- Understand the value of clear and purposeful communication and the impact that communication has on successfully managing people interactions

8.2 Context

Interaction between people is a key component of software projects. The stakeholders in the case studies communicate, solve problems, and make decisions together; negotiate; and interact in other various ways throughout the lives of their software projects. Through these interactions, the project stakeholders engage in "mutual or reciprocal action or influence" to accomplish some objective together

(Dictionary.net). Stakeholder interactions help forge a rocky or smooth road for the progression of a project.

Observable factors influence people interactions. People can identify and possibly control these factors to conduct more successful interactions. Managing people interactions is therefore about understanding the nature of your interactions as well as analyzing and controlling, when feasible, factors that influence them. The chapter attempts to clarify what it means to manage people interactions and to highlight its importance to the success of software projects.

The following are activities involved in managing people interactions for software projects:

- Understanding different scenarios in which stakeholders interact
- Understanding factors that influence various project stakeholder interactions
- Deciding upon objectives for important stakeholder interactions
- Evaluating factors that potentially may influence important stakeholder interactions
- Deciding how to make feasible adjustments to factors that influence important stakeholder interactions, including one's own behavior
- Reflecting on the dynamics of stakeholder interactions and feeding this back into decisions regarding future interactions

Table 8-1 describes these activities and their target outcomes. Study the table, and think of any other activities that you may have performed to manage stakeholder interactions in the past.

Table 8–1: *Descriptions of Activities in Managing People (Stakeholder) Interactions*

Activity	*Description of Activity*
Understanding different scenarios in which project stakeholders interact	**Definition**: Recognizing that software project stakeholders interact in different scenarios such as communicating information, making decisions, negotiating, and so on, and bring different backgrounds and points of view to their interactions. **Target outcome**: Clear view of the nature of different stakeholder interactions that can occur in software projects.

Table 8–1: *Descriptions of Activities in Managing Stakeholder Interactions (Continued)*

Activity	*Description of Activity*
Understanding factors that influence various project stakeholder interactions	**Definition:** Recognizing factors that may influence the interactions between project stakeholders and identifying those that may be controllable and those that are not. **Target outcome:** Clear view of controllable and non-controllable influences on stakeholder interactions that can occur in software projects.
Deciding upon objectives for important stakeholder interactions	**Definition:** Determining how important stakeholder interactions contribute to the achievement of project objectives and then deciding upon the specific objectives for these interactions. **Target outcome:** Objectives for key stakeholder interactions are aligned with project objectives.
Evaluating factors that potentially may influence important stakeholder interactions	**Definition:** Analyzing factors that may influence stakeholder interactions that can critically impact a software project. **Target outcome:** Clear view of controllable and noncontrollable influences on key stakeholder interactions.
Deciding how to make feasible adjustments to factors that influence important stakeholder interactions, including one's own behavior	**Definition:** Once the factors have been evaluated, then using the information to influence stakeholder interactions to provide more win-win opportunities. **Target outcome:** Win-win approach to managing key stakeholder interactions.
Reflecting on the dynamics of stakeholder interactions and feeding this back into decisions regarding future interactions	**Definition:** Analyzing and evaluating past stakeholder interactions to increase the experience and knowledge inputs to your PEAK decisions in managing stakeholder interactions. **Target outcome:** Have a way to encapsulate what you have learned in one project to help manage stakeholder interactions on the next project.

People interactions are rich and diverse in their types and complexity. Table 8-2 describes interactions that software project stakeholders frequently encounter. You may think of others. We encourage you to reflect on these as you read this chapter.

The most common type of interaction is communications. You can imagine the many conversations in and outside the office, e-mails, face-to-face meetings, instant messages, letters, memos, plans, reports, specifications, telephone calls, and teleconferences, and so on, that occur for a project that involves many stakeholders or the development of a large and complex software system. Projects with low communication bandwidth involve few stakeholders, have few or minimally complex project deliverables, or probably are having problems. People need to communicate in order to work together toward shared objectives and goals. When they do not, they find it difficult to obtain the information that they need and to coordinate their work.

Table 8–2: *Typical Interactions Between Software Project Stakeholders*

Interaction	*Description of Interaction*
Communications	The transfer of ideas or information between people via some form of body language, oral communication, picture or other graphic art, sign language, written communication, and so on
Decision making	The process of deciding on a course of action based on a set of input data
Negotiation	Discussion between two or more people to reach some type of agreement (sometimes agree to disagree or agree to not pursue a joint venture, and so on)
Conflict management	Communication between people to resolve workplace issues and problems.
Leadership	Setting the vision or direction for a group of people and providing incentives for the people to make the vision a reality or to follow the direction.
Relationship management	Interacting in ways to preserve the relationship between project stakeholders and their organizations
Self management	How people present their positions and needs to others

The question is how project stakeholders can better manage their interactions with each other to achieve project objectives. To start, people need to realize that there are factors that influence their interactions. Table 8-3 describes common factors that influence the interactions between stakeholders of software projects. Explore the table, and think of any other factors that may have influenced your interactions with project stakeholders.

Table 8–3: *Factors That Influence People Interactions*

Factor	*Description of Factor*
Communication style	How information is transferred between people via different forms such as oral, written, body language, and so on, and characteristics such as direct/indirect, assertive/passive/aggressive, open/guarded, tone of voice, rate of speech, pitch, and so on.
Context situation	The background information and events that precede, lead to, or influence a particular interaction such as who is involved and what has happened; the reason for or nature of an interaction.
Culture, tradition, and mores	The set of learned behaviors that come from family and society on how to interact with people. For example, it is not socially acceptable in the United Kingdom to refer to a royal family member as "dude."
Goals, objectives, expectations, and motivation	The driving factors that currently influence the reasons for interaction.
Environment	The external influences that impact an interaction (such as a noisy room or global communications via teleconference).
Interaction size	The number of people involved in the interaction.
Personality traits	The personal characteristics of the people involved in the interaction.

Communication style is a highly influential factor for human interactions. Since most, if not all, people interactions involve communications, communication style plays a key role in influencing the situation for better or for worse. Communication style involves observable characteristics of speech such as the speed, loudness, amount of pausing, and so on. It also involves approaches to communication such as tendencies toward directness/indirectness or the level of assertiveness in how something is stated. Some people are natural communicators, while other people tend to listen. If you are interested in learning more about communication style, see works by Dr. Deborah Tannen, a sociolinguist at Georgetown University who has written extensively on language and its impact on people interactions (Tannen). Other interesting places to look for information about communication style are ASME, Jensen, and Pfleeger and Atlee (2006, 99–104). In particular, Pfleeger and Atlee discuss communication styles in the context of people who work on software engineering efforts.

The context of a situation impacts a particular interaction. Context concerns how or why an interaction occurs as well as the history of related events that precede an interaction. Interactions between stakeholders who are establishing the requirements for a software project are likely to be different from interactions between stakeholders who are trying to resolve a problem found in a software product that has been delivered. Interactions between stakeholders who have worked together or interacted in the past are likely to be different from those between stakeholders who are meeting for the first time.

Cultural differences can influence the interactions of people who are located in different countries or regions of the world. In some cultures, group discussions appear to be chaotic with multiple people talking at the same time; in other cultures, people tend to speak one after another. Stakeholders who are used to waiting until other people stop talking may wait forever, may never be able to interject their comments, and possibly may be offended if the other people don't stop. Dr. Geert Hofstede, who has extensively researched the impact of culture on international business and in the process developed a framework for assessing cultural impact, explains that if people go into other countries and make decisions based on how they operate in their own countries, they are likely to make bad decisions (Hofstede).

Likewise, environment has a significant influence on interactions between globally distributed stakeholders. The time and space differences preclude spontaneous interactions. Interactions between geographically separated stakeholders usually occur at planned times (often outside the normal working hours) or involve a time delay as when waiting for a response to an e-mail. During telephone calls and even teleconferences, the stakeholders frequently do not hear or see the voice or body language cues that can help them gauge the other people's reactions to what is being communicated or to the way in which the interaction is progressing. The absence of face-to-face communications complicates the interactions between people involved in global development projects. Environment and culture typically have a high influence on the interactions between globally distributed project stakeholders. See Chapter 10,

"Managing Global Development," for a discussion of factors that impact global software development projects.

Much has been written about motivation, an internal force that drives people to act and say what they do. The main idea to remember is that motivation is an internal force. People cannot really motivate others to do something. Each individual has objectives and goals, ways of reacting to external events, thoughts, and other internal motivating factors that influence what the person says or does. When people share common goals and objectives, they are more likely to cooperate or to work together more effectively in their interactions. See ChangingMinds.org for an online overview of theories about motivation.

The number of participants (interaction size) also influences an interaction. Decision making, in particular, becomes increasingly difficult as the number of joint decision makers increases. In general, group interactions are likely to proceed more smoothly if the group members have agreed upon a process for how they will interact to accomplish a common purpose.

Personality is a topic of study for psychologists and psychiatrists. We will not attempt to explain this unique characteristic of each individual but will refer to personality types and traits that are widely accepted. For comprehensive information on personality, see Carver and Scheier (2003), Capretz (2003), and Reinhold, who discusses practical business applications of the Myers-Briggs personality type model.

This would be a good time for you to recall a particular interaction that you recently had with one or more stakeholders on a project. Study the factors listed in Table 8-3, and reflect on which ones influenced your interaction. The following are some questions to help you reflect on your interaction:

- Were you aware at the time that something was influencing your interaction?
- Which factors from the table influenced your interaction? (Rate the impact of each factor as from low to high or possibly none.)
- What other factors other than those shown in the table influenced your interaction?

Now that you are aware of different types of interaction with factors that can influence them, you are ready to think about how to manage your interactions with other people for productive outcomes on your software projects. Although you may not have time in every situation to manage people interactions in a process-oriented way, there are benefits to doing so in those particular cases where it's important that successful interactions occur. Managing interactions may be important when you are trying to build or strengthen a relationship with a project stakeholder or when interactions involve short-term and or long-term goals.

To manage interactions successfully, you need to understand the objectives or reasons for a particular interaction as well as its nature. You can start by outlining, maybe in a written form, your own objectives or motivation for an upcoming interaction.

You need to think both about what you are trying to achieve as well as about what the other person is trying to achieve. Once you understand your own objectives and, to the best of your ability, the objectives of the people with whom you are going to interact, you can try to determine the factors that might affect the interaction. In Table 8-3, you will notice factors that might be within your control (for example, your communication style, your goals and motivation, or the environment to some degree) as well as those that might be outside your control (for example, the personality type of the person with whom you are interacting, the context, or possibly the location where you are meeting). You might use your influence to change the factors that are within your control to enable a better interaction to take place. For example, you might choose a convenient location and time of day to talk.

Although certain factors are controllable, each interaction involves aspects such as behavioral styles, personality types, and preferences that may not be controllable. As a stakeholder, you are able to control and adapt your own behavior to the dynamics of a given interaction but are not able to control or make others adapt to the situation, unless they so desire. Proper planning allows you to think ahead, to be prepared, and to adjust your behavior, as needed, in a focused and controlled way. It also helps you set realistic expectations for how to act in the event that things go outside the boundaries of your plan. Since people are different, you should not expect that they will behave in the way you think they should. A proper analysis of previous interactions with these people (if you had any) might reveal valuable information regarding their personality, preferences, behaviors, or communication style, all of which are key to understanding how to approach the interaction.

In their book *The Platinum Rule: Discover the Four Basic Business Personalities and How They Can Lead You to Success*, Dr. Tony Alessandra and Dr. Michael O'Connor use an interesting model to study personality styles. The model classifies people along two dimensions. The first dimension concerns directness or indirectness. It relates to whether people tend to be **direct** (expressive, fast moving, risk taking, and talkative) or **indirect** (reserved, risk averse, listening, and slower to decide). The second dimension has to do with a person's preference for being **open** (relationship and feeling oriented, warm, relaxed, and flexible) or **guarded** (planning and task oriented, formal, thinking, and fact based). The reason to use a model, whether the one suggested by Alessandra and O'Connor or by others, is to assess how people might react in various situations and to use that knowledge to plan people interactions. We also might need to alter or adapt our behaviors before, during, or after an interaction (Alessandra and O'Connor 1998).

Most important, we should understand that differences in personalities can often create conflict between individuals with respect to pace (**slower-paced** personalities that tend to be indirect versus **faster-paced** personalities that tend to be direct) and preference (**task-oriented** for those who tend to be guarded versus **people-oriented** for those who tend to be open). Our recognition that these differences can lead to potential conflict can help you flexibly manage your behavior in situations in which you know you are interacting with people who are different from you. Equipped with this knowledge, you can feel more secure in your ability to handle interactions and are less likely to be influenced by your emotions because you know there is a reason for the specific behaviors exhibited by the other people.

To help you use the information provided in Table 8-2 and Table 8-3, you can build a table that indicates the degree to which different factors are expected to influence a particular interaction. Table 8-4 correlates the influencing factors (on the top row) to the particular interaction (in the left column). In this example, three factors are shaded grayed to indicate that there is some expected influence (ranked from low to high or none) on the type of interaction referred to as *communications* that is to occur in the future. Naturally, the more you interact with the same person in the same context, the more you can build an experiential reference model or map of what you found to be influencing your interactions.

Now you'll examine the real-world scenario in which this table was used.

Upcoming Communications Scenario

Two members of a globally distributed team are meeting to discuss and ideally resolve an issue regarding the design of the interface for a software component that is being developed in France and will be integrated with other components in the United States. One of the stakeholders works at the company lab in the United States, and the other stakeholder works at the company lab in France. The company is headquartered in Germany. The U.S. project member, Bob Dawson, has never met Joe Ting, his counterpart in France. Bob has communicated frequently with other team members who work at the labs in France and has not encountered any problems in these interactions. He found the people at the labs in France to be open and direct in their conversations.

Table 8–4: *Factor Influence Analysis: Upcoming Communications*

Influencing Factors/Target Interaction	*Communication Styles*	*Context, Situation*	*Cultures, Tradition, and Mores*	*Goals, Objectives, and Motivation*	*Environment*	*Interaction Size*	*Personality Traits*
Communications	No influence (assumed)	Moderate influence	No influence (assumed)	High influence	Low influence	No influence (only two people)	Unknown (?)

On the day of the telephone meeting, Bob called Joe and greeted him with a hearty, "Hello, did you see the downhill ski race at Chamonix yesterday? Wasn't it awesome?"

Joe did not respond. There was silence on the line. Bob then continued the conversation and explained the issue that his team had with the current design of the software component interface. Joe did a lot of listening and said that he would report what Bob said to his team. Joe respectfully said that he would have to get back to Bob about the issue. Bob quickly realized that Joe's speech did not reflect a French accent (at least one that would sound like a French accent to Bob). Bob asked Joe whether he had lived very long in France and whether he had studied in Europe. Joe quietly said that he had come from China and had studied at a university in Munich, Germany. He had been working at the labs in France for about two years.

Reflecting on his interaction with Joe, Bob thought about his assumptions and about the differences in the communication style and pace between Joe and him and, for that matter, between Joe and the other members with whom Bob had talked from the labs in France. Bob had expected that Joe would be open and direct. He hadn't necessarily expected that they would reach an agreement that day, but he certainly had expected that Joe would express some ideas and opinions. Bob wondered what he should say or do next to get a resolution to the issue.

The shaded blocks in Table 8-4 show the factors that Bob considered before talking with Joe. How would he have shaded the table after talking with Joe? What does Bob still not know about the factors that might be influencing his interaction with Joe? How might Bob adjust his own behavior to resolve the issue while maintaining a good relationship with Joe and the other staff working at the lab in France?

Managing people interactions involves defining your objectives for important interactions, examining the various factors that might potentially influence them, and using that knowledge to plan your interactions. Once your interactions are over, you can reflect on your experiences and ideally improve your future interactions.

8.3 Case Studies

The two case studies in this chapter focus on aspects of managing people interactions at various levels within the organization. In the first case, "To Be or Not to Be: A Sense of Urgency at TestBridge," tough decisions have to be made with respect to the ability and willingness of specific players within the team to contribute as team members in light of an organization that is changing its focus and business direction. The second case, "A Friend or Foe at Hanover-Tech," focuses on the need to manage people interactions at the managerial level while balancing opposing constraints including financial, strategic, personal, and temporal. Decisions made in both cases appear to leave the stakeholders in difficult positions that have both short-term and long-term repercussions unless they are handled carefully. Read these cases to determine the steps taken to manage people interactions and the decisions and actions that led to the problems.

CASE STUDY

To Be or Not to Be: A Sense of Urgency at TestBridge

Directions

When reading this case study, focus on the various aspects involved in managing people interactions and what it would take to do that successfully. Try to identify the points in the case that either assist or undermine one's ability to positively manage people interactions.

Case Summary

DESCRIPTION

Berry Landis is managing a turnaround situation in a small software company in the United States. Landis is struggling to align his VP of engineering with his new business focus and is trying unsuccessfully to manage the interaction. Landis is at a loss to figure out how to proceed with his plan for organizational change and how to handle a strong-willed senior member of his team.

CASE STUDY OBJECTIVES

After reading the case study, you will be able to do the following:

- Understand the challenges faced when attempting to manage people interactions
- Understand the consequences of not explicitly managing people interactions on a project
- Identify various people interactions management activities and their positive or negative effect on project success

SUBJECTS COVERED

Managing people interactions, decision making, employee motivation, employee compensation, goal setting, communications, negotiations

SETTING

The setting is a small software company in the United States that must undergo changes in software product direction and company organization in order to retain market share and grow.

KEY CONCEPTS

- How to communicate with employees during difficult organizational change
- Some of the issues that need to be considered in order to have more successful people interactions
- Some of the effects of decision making on managing people interactions within organizations

The Case

SCENARIO

Barry Landis was facing a tough decision. In a half hour or so, he was going to meet with Bob Rowe, his VP of engineering, for a conversation he knew was not going to be easy. Barry had just returned from a two-week-long overseas trip to Hong Kong and Malaysia where he met with existing clients in an attempt to generate potentially new business. His time alone overseas had provided him with an opportunity to reflect on all that had happened in the past year with the company, on his interactions with Bob, and on what he cared most in chartering a course for the future (turning around TestBridge and getting some buy-in from his team). He had almost made up his mind but was going to see how the conversation developed before taking action in any single direction.

Background

TestBridge was a software development company established in 1996 and located in the United States. The company specialized in testing tools for safety-critical systems. The flagship product, Testerlogic, had been in the market for quite some time and was used by a variety of clients in the United States and abroad. Typical clients used Testerlogic in their quality assurance departments to automate various kinds of testing of their software applications and to enhance existing capabilities in the areas of unit, system, and performance testing. The system was developed by numerous developers over the years, was architected by Bob Rowe, and was constantly updated to make it compatible with ongoing upgrades in operating systems, with newer database versions, and with enhancements to the programming language in which it was implemented.

Unfortunately, over the past three years the company had witnessed a growing decline in product marketing and sales and shrinkage in extensions of client service-level agreements (SLAs), which in turn triggered a large reduction in support and technical personnel and the departure of mid- and senior-level management. Left at TestBridge were a few sales and marketing personnel, some technical folks who handled IT infrastructure, and Rowe as Testerlogic's primary care feeder.

It was obvious to the people currently at the company when Landis was hired, after a three-month search process, that other than refocusing their efforts on more sales and more market penetration, there would also have to be more "stuff to sell" in the context of what the software could do and whom it could serve. To that extent, Landis pressed Rowe to come up with recommendations on how he thought Testerlogic should be evolved.

The Real Deal Behind Testerlogic

Landis was a young software enthusiast in his mid-30s, with no formal training in software development, software engineering, or management. He was very outgoing and had a knack for getting things done, energizing people behind a vision, and driving them forward. He was quite outspoken and was one of those rare people for whom optimism ruled the day; things were never really impossible, and the word *no* only meant "Let's try it again and get it done."

Although Landis didn't have any of the formal qualifications to turn around TestBridge, he certainly had a strong sense of what to do, as well as plenty of experience in the software world from working in software development companies in various positions, including head of product development, head of sales, and marketing, and head of operations. He had a really strong intuition for how to drive things forward. He was also very passionate about what he did and would never take on something he didn't believe in from the get-go.

While being very strong willed, Landis recognized that to understand what people internally and externally thought about TestBridge and Testerlogic, he would have to listen more than talk, to ask pointed questions, and to sort out the details after he gathered all the facts.

He asked Rowe what he thought the system needed to look like in the future. Rowe said:

> I'm not a businessperson. You tell me what you think I should be coding, and I will. I am pretty good at that. In fact, I'm probably better at coding than anyone else you could find. Over the years, I've built a lot of functionality for this system that hardly anyone is using. It's a shame that the people who gave me these requirements are no longer with the company.

Landis dug a little further and asked Stan Neel, head of IT services, what he thought about Testerlogic. Neel said:

> The system is built in a very solid way on the back end. Our front end looks awful. Clients, as well as internal staff, have always complained that our user interface needs a face-lift. It looks like a 1996 implementation instead of a Web 2.0 application that people are using today. Unfortunately, I doubt whether Bob has the design or artistic skills to work on the UI. The reason that it looks as it does is because it uses the design Bob put in place more than ten years ago.

Other staff said:

> Today's clients are interested in things being integrated on a single console in a way that is simple and intuitive to use. Testerlogic uses inundated workflows where people click so many buttons to go from one screen to another that they take a week to go through our basic product training. This strains both the client's and our resources and doesn't necessarily give us a good name out there.

A New Sheriff in Town

In addition to changing the direction for Testerlogic, Landis faced two other challenges within his team. The first was profitability. He needed the staff to recognize that more business had to be generated in order for the company to survive and to keep jobs. The second and most important issue was accountability. He needed people to understand that they would have to work hard, get results, and answer for their actions. Landis remembered:

> I told people early on and very bluntly that whatever party they were in . . . well, that party was now over. If they wanted to get a different job, that was just fine with me. But if they stuck around and worked for me, they'd better be ready for a very different work ethic.

As part of his turnaround measures, Landis decided to focus on accountability by standardizing the employee compensation package and using a structure that promotes delivery rather than "seniority." Before the New Year, he wanted to establish a compensation system that included base pay, commission for sales, goal-driven bonuses, and profit sharing. His goal was to reduce base pay somewhat and, using the variable components commission and profit sharing, adjust total compensation to be equal or higher than before. With this system, people could get more than before but would have to work hard to make the company successful. More money for the company would translate into more money for employees, but the risk of not making more would be shared to some extent by all. For those with high salaries such as Bob Rowe, Landis intended to reduce base pay by a bigger margin. To get back to what he was making before, Rowe would have to put his heart and soul into "fixing" the system to merit a bonus big enough to cover the difference. As Landis put it:

> I wanted to get people's buy-in that this thing would work. I sat down with each one of them individually to explain that we needed to change for the company to survive and what they could do to help. I rationally showed them that compared to before, they could make a lot more money. For this to happen, they would now have to focus on helping the company make more money. It was surprising how easy it was to get most of the people to understand this idea.

With Rowe, and some of the others, it wasn't as simple as Landis had hoped. Things took longer than expected with some heated debates that didn't finish instantly. Landis recalled:

> Some of the people within my management team were very reluctant to accept the changes I proposed. They, from my perspective, were very comfortable living the way they had and didn't believe in this change. It was particularly difficult to persuade Rowe that this was a good thing for the company. He was not willing to take any personal risks. He said that he'd been working there for 13 years and had already sacrificed enough for this company by taking a de facto pay cut (no salary raises) in the past three years while the company was on the decline. Others simply wanted things that we couldn't give them: commission rates that were way out of proportion, bonuses that were not in sync with industry standards, or profit-sharing figures that were impossible to achieve.

Robert Rowe

Robert Hugh Rowe was in his mid- to late-fifties and was the VP of engineering at TestBridge where he worked almost since the company's formation in 1996. Part of the original team that joined the company in the beginning, he was also a minority shareholder and one of the original architects of its flagship Testerlogic product. He was an educated man with a PhD in computer science from Georgia Tech, and he had many years of experience working at different levels in various companies around the United States. From a technical perspective, he was very good, but as he clearly pointed out to others, he wasn't a businessperson and did not want to be. Landis remembered:

> We went out to lunch with a potential client on a wintry day in November. The lunch group included me, Rowe, our boss Mark, and these two gentleman from a company in New York called BellCourt. During the conversation, the BellCourt fellows had multiple ideas on things that they wanted to be added to the system. They had questions for Rowe about how you could get the system to do certain things and about other customers who we currently serviced that could use these features. Rowe answered them by saying that he was sorry but he was not the business guy. Pointing his finger at us, he said that if they wanted their questions answered, they'd have to talk to Mark or me. Boy, was I furious.

Before joining TestBridge, Rowe worked for a series of start-ups, none of which survived more than a couple of years. In a casual conversation with Landis, Rowe remarked, "It's interesting that none of the previous companies in which I worked failed because of me. In one of them, the product was simply immature. In another, we didn't get the market segmentation right. In yet in another, the CEO didn't know in what direction to take us, and in the last one, the competition was simply better than us."

Landis's first thought was that there seemed to be at least one common denominator across these companies, and it wasn't product oriented.

Rowe was very good at what he did but took forever to do it. He was a perfectionist and believed that a decision should stand the test of time. Hence, he made few decisions. He was married, had two girls who attended Ivy League colleges, and was happy to keep on doing what he was doing day in and day out without changing a thing. Rowe recalled:

> Landis didn't appreciate the amount of work that needed to get done when someone turned a piece of requirement into code. This was what I referred to as "neuron time." He expected things to happen instantly, or within a few days; and for me that wasn't possible. I wanted to make sure that whatever I gave him was well thought out and developed. I did not want to turn in something that looked half-baked.
>
> Landis also wanted me to take a base pay cut with the option that my total compensation could ultimately be higher if I met my goals. I had two girls in college, with tuition costs that went through the roof. As a VP of engineering, I'd never been treated like that, and I wasn't about to accept it. I knew what I was worth, and I wasn't afraid to admit it. I was the best programmer that Landis could have, and he knew it. I didn't need others to tell me what to do. I was the one to whom people came for advice when they needed technical help. People like me got paid the big bucks so that people like him wouldn't worry at night when something was crashing. It was my job to make sure the systems we built were top notch, and doing that took time and lots and lots of patience.

Goals, Goals, Goals . . .

When his initial approach didn't succeed, Landis decided to sit down with Rowe to define a set of quarterly goals that could be measured and tracked by both of them. The following is the complete list of goals that Landis outlined for Rowe to achieve during the first quarter. The goals Landis had in mind were technical as well as business oriented. Landis believed that Rowe needed to take some ownership of the business side of the house and to be more management focused rather than code focused.

Q1 Goals: Draft

Bob Rowe, Role: Vice President of Engineering

I. Leadership and Direction

a. Work with Barry to create a product plan for Testerlogic that would take into account:

i. Existing state

ii. Market requirements

1. Functionality

2. Interface

3. What "big picture" direction should we go for?
4. Map of the current testing market/landscape/competition

iii. Internal requirements—what does TestBridge need Testerlogic to have?

iv. What would it take to sell/license Testerlogic as a product?

v. Possible effects on revenue (direct or indirect)

vi. To understand the above requires, at least:

1. Conversations with customers/prospects about future requirements (including *Testerlogic* licensing)
2. Conversations with TestBridge staff about future support requirements (e.g., requirements for offerings other than existing functions)
3. Feedback from the customer session held in December

vii. Costs (based on technology, architecture, hosting)

Product Plan consists of "big picture" road map, contains first steps, and also indicates what additional information we would obtain. It addresses things such as major features (not details), look and feel, architecture, etc.

b. System updates work toward new user interface

i. Templates/layouts

c. Additional functionality to allow customers to customize testing scripts

d. Improve interface for script creation/development

e. Functionality for teamwork testing submissions

II. Migration

a. Complete internal infrastructure migration from existing hosting company to a new solution

III. Existing customer support and work

Landis recalled:

> If I had wanted someone to do simple development, I'd have just hired someone from India. I've had plenty of work done in the past in which we outsourced the development side of things to places where it could be done for less cost. I wanted Rowe to think more strategically. I wanted him to be in charge of design and scope. I wanted him to get a feel for what the market wanted. He was used to getting requirements handed to him by others. He needed to go out and talk to people to see what was needed. I didn't care that he might have been four times faster than whomever we could get to do the actual coding. The message I wanted to make clear was that management (of which he was a part) does . . . well, management.

Therefore, Landis sent his list to Rowe for review and asked for his input before the upcoming Q1 (the first quarter of the year is January through March) planning meeting. Landis used the quarterly planning meetings to coordinate and synchronize staff efforts for the following three months. Landis knew that in the next meeting some of the system enhancement issues were going to be discussed. He didn't want Rowe to be surprised. He was hoping that the two of them would have a chance to sit down quietly and to go over things once Rowe had some time to think. From Landis's perspective, he was giving Rowe a chance to take his time, to step up to the plate, and to show leadership. He knew Rowe might need extra time to get his bearings and offered to help if needed. He wasn't going to push him. He saw Rowe in the office sitting in front of his computer working on something over the next couple of weeks. If Rowe needed help, he knew where to find Landis.

Unfortunately, Rowe never showed up for the planning meeting. He mumbled something later in the week about working at a client site to fix some things and that he was sorry for missing the meeting.

One of the engineers recalled:

> It wasn't unusual for Bob to miss a planning meeting. He was often late or not in attendance. Whenever he did show up, he always seemed preoccupied with other things and had his laptop open. For the most part, Bob barely spoke a word and interjected something usually at the end of the meeting about some random thing that came up. I was not sure that Barry showed any emotion, but I knew he wasn't pleased.

It's Time for a Serious Sit Down

To get closure on the plan, Landis sent the following e-mail to Rowe:

```
----- Original Message -----
From: Barry Landis
Sent: Tuesday, December 4, 20--, 10:45 AM
To: Bob Rowe
Subject: Meeting to Discuss Q1 Goals

Bob,

Per my e-mail from last week, it would make sense to narrow down
what you think could be accomplished between now and April. I
suggest you use the document we created before with the draft
goals (attached) as a starting point. Let's see whether we can
review this and agree to a new plan sometime during the middle of
next week.

Barry
```

A week or so later, after one or two reminders, he finally got a response from Rowe. It read as follows:

```
----- Original Message -----
From: Bob Rowe
Sent: Thursday, December 13, 20--, 4:00 PM
To: Barry Landis
Subject: RE: Meeting to Discuss Q1 Goals

Barry,

I continue to work on the designs for two features: (a) the ability
for people to generate intricate testing scenarios between code
modules and (b) the ability to convert export test cases from one
testing platform to another. It is my hope that I can get started
on the implementation for at least part (a), since I can reuse a
fair amount of existing code.

Also, I have completed and deployed a change requested by one of
our clients that we will want for ourselves (deployed at the moment
only for the client's installation).

As far as changing the user interface, I continue to learn about
the Google toolkit -- what I have found so far is, assuming that
the design philosophy is consistent across different widgets, is
that I will be able to create a code library that renders UI [user
interface] objects that will also fit well within the Testerlogic
architectural philosophy. Depending upon (i) the need for me to
focus my attention on 'leadership', (ii) my time availability vis-
a-vis my other tasks, and (iii) the desire to move forward with a
new UI for Testerlogic, I might be able to start an implementation
of that code library.

Please note that a new UI for Testerlogic will involve much more
than a suitable code substrate for implementation. It will require
a new design of the basic UI philosophy, some graphics design, and
probably some new functionality to be designed and implemented,
some of which I know how to do and some of which I don't.

Hope this helps – please let me know of other questions.

Bob
```

Landis was very disappointed. He thought that he had clearly communicated his expectations, but Rowe was still focused more on the technical than on the business side of things. Didn't Rowe understand his communications? Was Rowe deliberately ignoring him? Didn't Rowe really have what it takes to act more managerially as Landis was hoping? Was he wasting his time with Rowe, and could this situation be changed? Working on Testerlogic was a key part of his strategy for long-term company survival.

Landis decided to invite Rowe to lunch where he hoped that they could comfortably talk over the issues and agree on a path to move forward. He got them a reservation at the Golden Dragon. This was Rowe's favorite Chinese restaurant that was close to their office location. As he walked over, Landis remembered to take with him the list of goals he had prepared for Q1, which he thought could serve as the basis for their discussion. When he walked into the restaurant, Rowe was already sitting in a corner waiting for him. He handed Landis a two-page document and asked him to review it. "What is this?" asked Landis. "This is a list of the features that I was hoping to work on for Testerlogic in the next few months," replied Rowe.

They ordered their lunch, but it was obvious that they were looking at the issue from two different perspectives. Landis started by explaining that the company was headed in a new and different direction. This direction was focused on understanding the customers better, looking for what the market wanted, and getting a better handle on what existed out there so that TestBridge could differentiate itself from others. He then shifted the conversation to more practical issues having to do with Rowe's inability to plan or execute accordingly. Landis recalled:

> I brought Bob over so that we could have a friendly chat. Clearly, this wasn't going to happen, or at least not in any easy way. We were a "little" way apart in our thinking, to be mild about it. I was going to have to push Bob for him to see how little was accomplished over the past six to eight months and how we needed to be much more goal oriented if we were to bridge our divide. Naturally, when I brought up the issue that had to do with his lack of planning and the lack of accountability, he was taken aback and became defensive.

Bob remembered he was hoping to finally show Barry that he was working hard to follow the direction he set for the company. He had been doing his best over the past few weeks to come up to speed on some of the relevant issues and to fulfill what he thought Barry wanted from him. He remembered the following:

> I brought with me my to-dos to show Barry. I felt that I was on top of things, having completed a lot of the items that others asked me to do over the past few months. Barry wanted a high-level plan and wasn't impressed with my list. I was trying my best, but the direction I was getting was probably insufficient to help me proceed. I was used to doing things in a different way. That seemed to work for the past ten years with all of my other bosses. Why should I need to change my approach when someone new comes around?

As the discussion heated up and accusations on both sides flew across the table, it was obvious they weren't communicating effectively. Rowe felt betrayed. Whatever he said did not seem to be what Landis was expecting. Landis, for his part, was convinced that Rowe was either not listening or playing games. He hadn't seen any real work from Rowe in the past few months other than empty promises and was adamant about him needing to change. After another round of heated shouting, Rowe got up and told Landis that if he was doing such a poor job as a VP of engineering, then maybe he was the wrong person for the job. He stormed out of the restaurant and left Landis with the bill.

Landis was puzzled. How could a seemingly simple discussion blow up in his face beyond any imaginable proportion? He left the restaurant with a very bad feeling. He felt frustrated that none of his efforts thus far yielded any real results. Because he was leaving for Asia the very next day, he didn't have much time to think this through. He certainly wasn't sure if he had dealt with the situation correctly.

CASE PROBLEM

The following are the main problems and decisions, related to managing people interactions, that the key stakeholders in the case study face:

- How could the interactions between Landis and Rowe have been managed in a more successful way?
- What should Landis do now to move TestBridge strategically forward with respect to enhancing the Testerlogic product line?
- What were the key factors that influenced the various interactions between Rowe and Landis, and what could they learn about them to improve their future interactions?
- What could Landis have done differently to gain a better outcome?

Case Analysis

ANALYSIS ACTIVITY

Analysis Background

Let's use the PEAK model to analyze and better understand the problems and decisions involving people interactions that Barry Landis faced. You are welcome to analyze Barry's problem of what to do next to improve the TestBridge business through enhancing the Testerlogic product line. Reading Chapter 6, "Managing Product," may help you better understand this problem.

(P) Problem: Barry Landis encountered several problems and decisions involving the management of people interactions. We will analyze the following two critical problems together since they are related:

- How could Barry realign employee attitudes, work, and performance to focus on business objectives?
- How can he better manage his interactions with Bob in order to influence Bob to focus more on business development through product management?

(E) Experience:

- Barry Landis has experience working in software development companies as head of product development, head of sales and marketing, and head of operations.
- Bob Rowe has many years of experience working at different levels in various companies around the United States. Rowe has worked for a series of start-ups, none of which survived more than a couple of years.
- Bob says that he is a technologist but not a businessperson.
- Bob may not have the design or artistic skills to improve the appearance and usability of the user interface for the Testerlogic product.

(A) Assumptions:

- As an outgoing, energetic, can-do person who does not readily accept that something he wants to do is not possible, Barry Landis assumes that he can get his staff to "buy in" to changing how they do their jobs.
- Barry seems to assume that he can get Bob Rowe to change his role in the company.
- Barry assumes that Bob has the knowledge and skills to do product management.
- Bob assumes that he can continue to do his job in the same way that he has been doing it with a new emphasis on features to enhance the Testerlogic product.

(K) Knowledge:

- Barry Landis has no formal training in software development, software engineering, or management.
- Bob Rowe has a doctorate in computer science from Georgia Tech.
- Barry knows that TestBridge needs more products and additional features for existing products in order to increase its sales and market share (to increase revenue). He learns by talking to staff that the Testerlogic product has an awkward interface that is unattractive and tedious to use.
- Barry thinks that one way to help turn around the company is to enhance the Testerlogic product.
- Barry thinks that he needs a VP of engineering who will focus more on product management and less on product development, especially implementation.

Solution: To influence his staff to tailor their performance to achieve business goals, Barry Landis decided to change the compensation structure. A portion of an employee's salary would be based on the individual's contribution to revenue (commission) and the overall company performance (profit sharing). In other words, employees would need to help the business achieve profits.

Barry decided to reduce the base-pay portion of compensation more for higher-paid people in management such as Bob Rowe. He also composed a list of goals that Barry should try to achieve for the next quarter. Barry thought that this list would help Bob to know how to focus his work more on product management as well as on the development of the Testerlogic business.

Assumed Risk: The risks associated with Barry Landis's decisions relate to his assumptions. With respect to the new compensation structure, there is an underlying assumption that there is a direct and easy way to measure employee performance with respect to company revenue in order to award commissions. This may be more easily done for marketing and sales staff than for engineering staff. Likewise, engineering staff may become discontent and less motivated when their efforts cannot be directly correlated to revenue for commission purposes. In addition, when poor performance by one employee group impacts company profits, other employee groups also experience lower profit-sharing rewards and may resent the underperforming employees. There is a risk that subjectivity and inequity in the system, as well as employees who think they have no control over business results, will influence employees to not respond as desired to the new compensation structure.

Another risk involves Barry's assumption that by interacting with people in a forceful and threatening way, he can get them to do what he wants. Some people will want to help the company's business but may not fully understand how to change what they do. Other people may resent his approach and look for ways to work around or avoid him. Likewise, some talented and key staff may leave the company. Some engineering staff may not readily accept a boss who has not done engineering and who tries to throw his weight around with statements about the "party being over." Engineers are typically problem solvers who like the challenge of product development and may not be likely to see what they do as a party. They may be more likely to accept change if the boss first tries to understand how they engineer products and works with them to find ways to be more time and cost efficient.

Barry also assumes that Bob Rowe has the knowledge, skills, and interest in doing product management. Bob has demonstrated in multiple ways that he is not interested in what he perceives to be business activities, such as talking with customers, generating new product specifications and plans, establishing product requirements for development projects, and estimating software development costs. Bob's proclivity to quickly assume responsibility for design and implementation certainly raises the question of whether he actually has the ability and confidence to manage a product line. Bob may not be able or willing to achieve the quarterly goals that Barry has given him.

Analysis Questions

1. What is the main problem that you think Barry Landis has in managing people interactions?
2. How does Barry's personality and communication styles as well as expectations influence the way in which he interacts with the staff in his company? In particular, how do these affect Barry's interactions with Bob Rowe?

3. What role does Bob Rowe think he has in the company? How does this role differ from what Barry expects that Bob should do?
4. Describe the ways in which Bob does not seem to do what Barry wants. If you think that Bob is doing some of what Barry wants, describe this as well.
5. What would you recommend that Barry do to resolve the difference between his expectations and Bob's expectations and actions? What needs to change?
6. If you were a software engineer at TestBridge, how would you respond to Barry's new policies and communication style?

DISCUSSION

In theory, it is reasonable to think that with the new compensation plan TestBridge employees will be motivated to work hard to make the business successful. In reality, this may not happen when one employee group has more control over the success of a business than another employee group. A compensation structure that includes commissions and profit sharing seems to be most effective when management has a measurable, understandable, reasonable, and equitable way to link employee performance to business results. Employees need to perceive or know how the work over which they have control does impact the business, that the impact of their work can be objectively measured with respect to revenue and profits, and that they will be fairly rewarded. You would need more information about how Barry Landis intends to implement his compensation structure before you could anticipate employee reaction to it. As the case study indicates, some employees are likely to resist change, while others embrace it.

There is a well-known quote from Shakespeare's play *The Tragedy of Hamlet: Prince of Denmark* in which Marcellus laments, "Something is rotten in the state of Denmark" (Shakespeare). Though he does not know the details, Marcellus perceives that there is something wrong at the court of the new king of Denmark (Hamlet's stepfather). Likewise, you may wonder whether something is not quite right with TestBridge's organizational structure. If Bob Rowe is the VP of engineering, why hasn't he been performing management tasks? Other related questions follow:

- What is the organizational structure of TestBridge? How many people work for the company?
- Are there engineering staff members other than Bob Rowe? If so, who are their bosses?
- Who organizes and manages software development projects?
- How are requirements established for software development projects? Who performs this function?
- Exactly what is Barry Landis's role in the company? What clout does he wield in the company, and why?

The case study purposely does not provide this information because it focuses on Barry Landis's expectations and his interactions with Bob Rowe. To fully analyze Barry's options within the organization for how to improve the business generated by the Testerlogic product, you could use this information. For instance, Bob Rowe may not be the best person to manage the Testerlogic product line. Bob may be better suited as a lead technologist or developer. Finally, you might ask why Bob Rowe has the title VP of engineering. Was he the first software developer for TestBridge and possibly one of the company founders? Considering Bob's history with TestBridge would also help you determine an appropriate role for him.

CONCLUSIONS

Barry Landis is motivated to increase TestBridge's revenue and profits, particularly through the evolution of the Testerlogic product line. He is enthusiastic, confident, and expedient, but his approach to interacting with staff is demanding and somewhat threatening. Barry expects his staff to change the way they do their jobs to maximize their contribution to achieving business goals. In particular, he expects Bob Rowe to transition from mostly product development to mostly product management with some product development. We might conclude that Barry's style of management appears to be "my way or the highway."

Employee reaction to Barry's demand for change, to be enforced through a new compensation structure, is mixed. Some people seem to understand what to do and are willing to try to change, and others do not necessarily buy in to the need for change. In particular, Bob Rowe does not agree with the reduction of his base pay and is not interested in changing the tasks that he performs. Bob does not seem able or willing to adjust his tasks and actions in a way that satisfies Barry's expectations with respect to the new quarterly goals that Barry outlined for Bob. Interactions between Barry and Bob are heated and hostile. Barry does not manage his interactions with Bob in a way that satisfies either Barry or Bob.

Somehow, Barry and Bob need to discuss their expectations in an objective and unemotional way. Barry might start by really listening to Bob and through dialogue determine whether Bob is the most appropriate person to manage the Testerlogic product. In turn, Bob should try to understand Barry's concerns about the Testerlogic business and be willing to consider whether he could, in fact, help with product management. Bob's somewhat flippant refusal to participate in activities relating to customers is certainly not helping matters. As you will see again in Chapter 9, "Managing Stakeholder Expectations," communications are key to managing people interactions and expectations.

KEY IDEAS TO REMEMBER

- Communications are an important component of managing people interactions.
- Personality and communication styles as well as expectations influence the interactions between people.
- When making decisions, it is important to consider the impact that these decisions will have on the management of people interactions.

CASE STUDY

A Friend or Foe at Hanover-Tech

Directions

When reading this case study, focus on the various aspects involved in managing people interactions and what it would take to do that successfully. Try to identify the points in the case study that either assist or undermine one's ability to manage people interactions in a positive way. Also observe how interactions impact short-term and long-term goals.

Case Summary

DESCRIPTION

Gloria Jones is the new president at Hanover-Tech, a medical imaging company located in Santa Monica, California. In the process of transitioning into her new role, her predecessor, Linda Pantelli, who was moving up to assume a role in the parent company, Hanover-Global, had offered to stay on as a part-time consultant and to support Gloria where need be on a part-time basis. Gloria is trying to manage the interactions with Linda in a way that is constructive, gets her what she needs when she needs it, and doesn't cost her too much. She is having problems identifying what and how to put it in a way that preserves relationships within and outside the company.

CASE STUDY OBJECTIVES

After reading the case study, you will be able to do the following:

- Understand the challenge of managing people interactions and stakeholder relationships simultaneously
- Understand the need to make decisions that require balancing opposing objectives while managing people interactions
- Identify various decisions that need to be made in the process of managing people interactions

SUBJECTS COVERED

Managing people interactions, decision making, managing stakeholder relationships, communications, negotiations, managing expectations

SETTING

The setting is a small software company, which is a subsidiary of a larger holding company, in Santa Monica, California. The company focuses on medical imaging technologies.

KEY CONCEPTS

- Managing people interactions is an ongoing process that needs to be planned and executed carefully.
- Managing stakeholder relationships requires balancing multiple objectives, some of which may be in conflict with one another.
- One must consider not only short-term and task-oriented objectives but also long-term and people-oriented objectives when managing people interactions.

The Case

SCENARIO

Gloria Jones was staring at her screen in disbelief. She had just gotten yet another e-mail from Linda that said she was busy and wasn't going to be able to review the agreement Jones gave her until the following Monday. Gloria didn't know what to do. She was new to her job. She thought Linda could help by giving her the necessary assistance as they've discussed and agreed to before, but it seemed that Linda was too preoccupied to make any of that happen. She got up from her chair, walked over to the window, and watched the boats out in the bay sailing into the sunset. She tried to think through all the things she had done to make the transition easier, amicable, and trusting. Pinpointing what to do was a tricky situation, and she didn't know where to begin. She left the window and went back to her desk. She tried to remember how it all started . . . .

Background

Three months before, as part of the reorganization at Hanover-Tech, Gloria Jones was promoted to the president's position, which was previously held by Linda Pantelli who had now moved up in the organization to be the senior VP for Hanover-Global (the parent holding company that owned Hanover-Tech and a few other subsidiaries). HTC, as insiders called it, was a software development company located in Santa Monica, California, that had been in business for more than 30 years. It was a market leader in medical imaging technologies and was very well connected with UCLA's and UCSF's schools of medicine.

Gloria was an industry veteran who was brought over a year ago with the purpose of running the company. She had spent most of her career with Siemens Medical and McKesson. She was looking for a change, a new adventure, and a new style of living out west, as compared to the dreary life she'd known back east with its harsh lonely winters and dark, cold nights.

In her 40s and probably in the best shape of her life, Gloria was a single woman with a childish nature who liked to live life to its fullest. She was very professional in what she did, an avid learner who always had a stack of books next to her bed, and an early riser. Gloria didn't believe in "wasting" time doing nothing and would keep her mind busy all the time trying to improve what was going on around her.

Linda, on the other hand, was a little older and a bit more experienced. She was a culinary expert who liked to travel (on company business preferably), eat well, and relax. Originally from New York City, Linda had a husband and three grown kids, who were now in college all over the United States. Linda was a hands-on workaholic with the attention span of a bumblebee (too short honestly to do too many things at once). She was a very amicable person who you could simply not like. She had friends everywhere in the organization and a quiet happy demeanor that made people like her. She made the people around her feel very comfortable and at ease, even when "bad news" had to be presented.

Not surprisingly, Linda and Gloria hit it off right from the get-go. They both believed in how things needed to get done and had no-nonsense attitudes. Over the next few weeks, the two of them got into a routine in which Linda taught Gloria what she needed while relinquishing more and more responsibility. Linda's coaching style met Gloria's expectations as it wasn't too "bossy" and gave a lot of freedom to experiment, reflect, and discuss. Gloria remembered:

> Working with Linda was very enjoyable. In the beginning she would let me "discover" things and then come back to ask questions, analyze, and think things through. Linda liked to role-play things with me. Every time we were faced with a tough decision, we used to sit down and talk things through where I would take one side and she would take the other. I found that to be very useful in avoiding costly mistakes when interacting and communicating with people in the organization.

As Pantelli was transitioning her duties over to Jones, they decided what role each of them would play once the transition was complete. Linda remarked:

> I knew I was going to be really busy with my new position at Global. I also wanted to make sure that Gloria got the support she needed. I offered to help as much as I could and even to stay part-time (maybe 10 to 15 percent for the first six month or even for a year) to help her. If I could help HTC, I was happy to do so, especially if I got paid for it and if it didn't take too much of my time.

Linda and Gloria both agreed that for the time being, at least until Gloria felt she had what she needed from a corporate knowledge perspective, Linda would be available to help her. Gloria put it succinctly:

> I was willing to pay to have Linda still be part of my team. She had valuable knowledge and a lot of connections within HTC that would help me get established. She knew how to do things, and learning things from her was going to make my life

> much easier. I was hoping to keep Linda's time to a minimum and figured that one half day a week would probably do the trick.

Things Aren't Working Quite Right . . .

Gloria brought with her a new spirit and energy that seemed to help move things around at HTC at a faster, more dynamic pace. As she was getting more and more into the thick of things, she had more questions than answers. She still hoped that Linda could teach her how to deal with challenging issues more quickly. She had many small issues to discuss and many more things to review than initially planned because business seemed to be picking up despite the market's downturn.

To help matters along and to make things a little more effective, Gloria chose to communicate with Linda mostly via e-mail, and when that didn't work, she left messages on Linda's voicemail. Whenever she would finally get a response, Gloria was pleased with its results. Linda knew her stuff, and her answers and critique tended to hit the mark regarding issues that needed to be handled and how to handle them. The real problem for Gloria was how to reduce the turnaround time between questions and answers from weeks to days or hours. She recalled:

> I wasn't getting responses from Linda at an adequate speed. Linda was a workaholic and an e-mail junkie. She couldn't go five minutes without checking her e-mail, whether we were in the car, in a meeting, or in a restaurant. Naturally, I assumed she was getting all of mine, but why she was ignoring them, I really couldn't say. In one case, I was working on a big contract and needed Linda's input and review. My request for help sat in her inbox for more than three weeks. After repeated e-mails, voicemails, and reassurances that Linda was handling it, I sent it off to the client, without Linda's review.

The relationship with Linda was very important to Gloria. Linda had friends in "high places," was very connected to the old management team (some of whom Gloria intended to replace), and was still sitting on the HTC board of directors where she was very much involved in the strategic direction of the company. Gloria was also very realistic about managing Linda's expectations with respect to getting paid and making sure that she wasn't throwing away company funds for a "service" she didn't really get (at least not in time) or that didn't have value. Gloria explained:

> I felt trapped. On the one hand, Linda expected to get paid for her work, probably more than I was hoping to pay her, not that we ever agreed on a sum. On the other hand, I was expecting to get something in return for that, something I didn't feel I was getting. I did not want to offend her, but I was feeling very frustrated at the quality of service (or speed) of things. It was all amicable, which perhaps made it even more frustrating. I knew that in the end someone's expectations were not going to be met, and I didn't want this to happen.

Gloria knew that if she brought the money issue into the open she might get push back from Linda. She remembered Linda saying before she left that she closed the loop about staying on as a "consultant" with Jim Oliver, the chairman of HTC's board. While Gloria was trying to get all of her "consultants" on the same page as far as standard daily rates, Linda's requested rate was a "little" too much and simply not feasible. More than the money, Gloria simply didn't know how to communicate with Linda in a constructive way. All she really wanted was either someone who would help when she needed it or no one at all. Gloria explained:

> It was not very consistent. There were times where I'd walk into the office, and there would be Linda sitting and waiting for me. She seemed genuinely interested in helping me deal with some very tricky issues involving human resources, finances, or strategy. Other times, I'd bang down the door while trying to get her to react, respond, or reply. The lack of consistency was making it very difficult for me to plan accordingly and respond to clients (some of whom had interacted with Linda for the past five years) in a business-like fashion.

Outside Help

A few weeks before the Memorial Day weekend, Gloria spent a week in the woods in a cabin with her family who was visiting from Tennessee. She caught her brother, Drew, after dinner one night for a chat. Drew was a management consultant who always seemed to have ideas on how to deal with situations that Gloria could only think about. He asked a number of questions and listened attentively to her story. After a few minutes of thinking, he told Gloria he thought that she had to change the interaction she had with Linda to make it more effective. She recalled:

> I told Drew the story about my interactions with Linda. He said that if I wanted to solve both of my problems, I should take a look at how to manage our interactions in a more effective way. He suggested I turn this into a project-based interaction where each "task" I had for Linda was like a mini-project, with timelines, scope, deliverables, and pay attached to it. That way, the rules would be clear up front; and if they weren't met, we wouldn't have issues regarding missed expectations. It was an interesting take on the problem, but I needed to sleep on it some more.

Gloria's problem had to do with how to approach Linda on the matter, even if she did use Drew's approach. She thought a few times of raising the issue but chickened out every time, feeling it might not be advisable. It wasn't as if Linda wasn't doing anything. She certainly did, and what she did was of high quality. It was just not as fast as Gloria had wanted it. Perhaps she should just say nothing and let sleeping dogs lie. What was the benefit for her by raising the issue? But then, could she really say nothing? What sort of message was she sending if she let it go on?

Gloria decided to approach Emily Patrosso, a close friend who used to work with her when she was a division head at Siemens. She trusted Emily and knew that, as a colleague, she might have good advice on how to deal with this. As it happened, Gloria had to be in Philadelphia for a conference, so she asked Emily out to dinner to catch up and discuss things.

Over a good dinner at Amada's, a Spanish favorite of the two of them, Gloria repeated the story and the advice she received from Drew. She explained her frustrations and her inability to walk up to Linda and lay things on the table. Emily recalled:

> Gloria was obviously frustrated. She had been facing this challenging issue for quite some time, and it was obvious she wanted to resolve it. Drew had given her some very strong advice, and having not implemented it yet, she told me she was not sure if she should. I liked Drew's approach, but I felt I could come up with a simple way to enhance it.

As desserts were served onto the table and as Gloria was scooping up a golden crusted, Philly-style cheesecake with blueberry/raspberry sauce, Emily said:

> I like Drew's plan for helping you deal with the situation. I'd like to suggest that you enhance it even more by taking away the need to manage each task independently as a project and grouping things together. You could, for example, have Linda accept tasks as an ongoing thing throughout the month, within 24 hours of submitting them to her. But then you can set a cap limit per month, say 60 or 70 percent on the amount of tasks that she need to get done to earn her pay. You might not get the work done at every point in time, but you'd certainly be managing the expectations.

Taking a Chance . . . or Not

As Gloria was trying to focus her thoughts, she knew tomorrow's board meeting would give her a chance to pull Linda aside and have a little heart-to-heart chat before or after the meeting. She went back to her computer to draft a message to Linda, but as she started typing, she paused for a minute to think specifically about what to say. It certainly wasn't easy, but she needed to get this resolved one way or another and to do it in a way that was amicable, didn't burn bridges, didn't upset anyone, and moved her agenda forward.

CASE PROBLEM

The following are the main problems and decisions to be made, in the context of managing people interactions, as faced by the key stakeholder in the case:

- What should Gloria do to be sure that she makes a decision that satisfies her short-term needs but doesn't hurt her long-term ones?
- What were some of the other options Gloria could use with Linda other than those suggested by her brother and her friend?
- How should Gloria handle her upcoming interaction with Linda to make it more effective and successful?

Case Analysis

ANALYSIS ACTIVITY

Analysis Questions

1. What is the problem that Gloria is having with Linda? Explain how the expectations of both stakeholders factor into this problem.
2. Describe in general how Gloria solves problems and makes decisions. In what way do you think her problem-solving/decision-making process/style contributes to her problem with Linda?
3. How are personality and communication styles affecting Gloria and Linda's interactions?
4. Now use the PEAK model to analyze Gloria's options for making a decision on how to resolve the problem that she is having with Linda.
5. What do you recommend that Gloria do next? Reference your analysis in question 4 to justify your recommendation.

8.4 Summary

This chapter focused on the following activities for managing people interactions in the context of decision making for a software project:

- Understanding different scenarios in which stakeholders interact
- Understanding factors that influence various project stakeholder interactions
- Deciding upon objectives for important stakeholder interactions
- Evaluating factors that potentially may influence important stakeholder interactions
- Deciding how to make feasible adjustments to factors that influence important stakeholder interactions, including one's own behavior
- Reflecting on the dynamics of stakeholder interactions and feeding this back into decisions regarding future interactions

The first case study, "To Be or Not to Be: A Sense of Urgency at TestBridge," focused on people interactions involving leadership and relationship management. The case showed how interactions between managers and staff can easily get out of control. The manager's decisions appeared to be good, but the solutions did not proceed as expected. The second case study, "A Friend or Foe at Hanover-Tech," looked at self-management, negotiation, and conflict management. Both case studies highlighted communication and decision making.

Managing people interactions is not easy. Analyzing factors that influence people interactions provides managers with a prism through which they can observe and better understand human nature and behavior. People are different, and treating everyone the same is not only futile but also potentially harmful. Studying people and their behavior, while recognizing their own strengths and limitations, can help managers understand their interactions with project stakeholders and decide what they need to do to improve them. The goal is to evaluate and make project decisions that embrace people as well as process and technology.

There is no silver bullet in managing people interactions for project success, but evaluating and making sound decisions about stakeholder interactions can lead to more successful project outcomes.

Chapter 9

Managing Stakeholder Expectations

9.1 Chapter Objectives

After reading and thinking about the concepts and case studies presented in this chapter, you will be able to do the following:

- Understand how managing stakeholders expectations is connected to the evaluation of project decisions and, conversely, how project decisions impact stakeholder expectations
- Understand the importance of communications, trust, and transparency in managing stakeholder expectations
- Understand how client, developer, and management expectations change over time and how the stakeholder's focus impacts the various activities that the stakeholder should perform over the course of the project in managing expectations

9.2 Context

Stakeholder is the latest overused and abused word in the software industry lexicon. The word can refer to everything from the end user to the code librarian in the project and has meaning based on the point of view of the person using the term. For developers, the stakeholder is the customer/user/manager entity. For the customer/user, the stakeholder might be the person who in turn buys the software from them. For the manager, the stakeholder is the customer/user/team/boss entity. Because of the many different types of stakeholders, managing stakeholder expectations on a project is a daunting task. You start by selecting a point a view. For the purpose of this chapter, the point of view will be that of the software project manager.

The project manager is primarily concerned about three main groups: the customer/user, the software development team, and the boss. Each of these stakeholders has a set of expectations. Some of their expectations overlap, and some are independent. Table 9-1 summarizes the key expectations for each of the three stakeholder groups for a software project. These expectations are not intended to be a complete set and therefore may seem to be self-centered, overly optimistic, and unrealistic. Throughout the rest of this chapter, we will discuss the project decisions that affect stakeholder expectations over the life of the software project. Conversely, we will also discuss ways to better analyze stakeholder expectations and their impact on project decisions.

Table 9–1: *Stakeholder Group Expectations for a Software Project*

Stakeholder Group	*Stakeholder Expectations*
Customer/user	The product will be available tomorrow or soon. The product will work out of the box. The product will solve all of my problems. The product will not cost more than what was budgeted.
Developers	The product is doable with the skills available. The scope changes, if any, will be reasonable. The work will be interesting. The team will get the resources it needs.
Management	The project will be completed on time. The project will cost less than expected. The customer will not call with any problems. The project manager will not ask for more resources.

You probably noticed that the expectations of the stakeholders described in Table 9-1 relate in some way to scope, time, quality, or cost (STQC). As discussed in Chapter 1, "Managing Decisions," these are the four dominant characteristics or dimensions of expectation that stakeholders have for a software project. Software project processes and decisions should focus on the production of deliverables that satisfy the STQC expectations of the various stakeholder groups, in particular those of the customer/user. To manage the expectations of software project stakeholders, the project manager must not only be able to understand what stakeholders expect of the product (project deliverables) and process (project execution) with respect to each of the STQC dimensions but must also be able to clarify and influence these expectations over the life of the project. Later, we will say more about how these expectations may change.

The stakeholder expectation management life cycle has three basic phases: setting, maintaining, and influencing expectations. The first phase ensures that the customer/user and developer/management stakeholders have the same understanding and focus for a project. Establishing a common understanding and project focus depends on effective communications. Communications that involve active listening and asking the right questions, as well as clear and unambiguous written representation of whatever was communicated help stakeholders maintain focus, clarity, and understanding. To manage stakeholder expectations for project success, software project managers need to think and make decisions about how they will communicate with different project stakeholders. Chapter 8, "Managing People Interactions," discusses ways in which software project stakeholders can evaluate and influence their interactions, such as communications, to make them more effective.

The software project manager stakeholder performs the following activities in managing stakeholder expectations:

- Communicating with the customer stakeholder
- Managing multiple dimensions of stakeholder expectation over time
- Managing product and process to satisfy stakeholder expectations
- Understanding different types of customers
- Managing stakeholder perception

Table 9-2 describes in more detail the primary activities in managing stakeholder expectations. Study the table, and think of other activities that you may have performed in managing stakeholder expectations in the past.

Table 9–2: *Descriptions of Activities in Managing Stakeholder Expectations*

Activity	*Description of Activity*
Communicating with the customer stakeholder	**Definition:** Effective communications with the customer stakeholder require an understanding of the following: • How to ask the right questions to elicit the desired information • How to listen to determine the customer's wants and concerns • How to present information to accomplish the objective for communication **Target outcome:** The project manager understands how effective communication contributes to setting, maintaining, and influencing customer expectations.
Managing multiple dimensions of stakeholder expectation over time	**Definition:** Managing multiple dimensions of stakeholder expectation requires an understanding of the expectations of the various stakeholders for the project with respect to the following dimensions: • Scope • Time • Quality • Cost **Target outcome:** The project manager understands how stakeholder expectations are related to each STQC dimension and how these expectations change over time.
Managing product and process to satisfy stakeholder expectations	**Definition:** Managing stakeholder expectations with respect to product and process requires an understanding of how to do the following regarding the project deliverables and project execution: • Set expectations • Monitor expectations • Influence expectations **Target outcome:** The project manager understands how to set expectations for the stakeholders with respect to both product and process, to monitor those expectations over the project, and to influence the expectations when they are not aligned with the project objectives.

Table 9–2: *Descriptions of Activities in Managing Stakeholder Expectations (Continued)*

Activity	*Description of Activity*
Understanding different types of customers	**Definition:** Managing stakeholder expectations requires an understanding of how to handle different types of customers such as the following: • *Loyal customers*: Completely satisfied and come back for more. The services/product exceeds or far exceeds the customer's expectations. • *Defecting customers*: Have had bad experiences with the software developer and will do *anything* to make their dissatisfaction public. Dissatisfied, neutral, and even satisfied customers can change to terrorists. • *Mercenaries*: Chase low prices, buy on impulse, and pursue fashion or change for the sake of change. Costly to acquire and retain. These customers don't stay around long enough for a profitable long-term relationship. • *Hostages*: These customers are forced to use a particular product or service (potentially because of monopolies). They will defect as soon as alternative products or services are available (Jones and Sasser 1995). **Target outcome:** The project manager understands different types of customers and will be able to identify the ones that are involved with the project. The manager will also be able to determine the value of these customers to the project and will know how best to influence the expectations of the specific types of customers.
Managing stakeholder perception	**Definition:** Managing perception requires an understanding of the following ideas: • Perception is reality. (The stakeholders' understanding of reality is based upon their perception of reality.) • Reality lies along the line between what stakeholders expect and what they perceive. If their perception does not match or exceed their expectations, they are likely not to be satisfied. **Target outcome:** The project manager understands the relationship between stakeholder perception and expectations as well as how to help the project be better perceived in the eyes of customers.

When managing customer expectations with respect to STQC, software developers set their own expectations about technology, process, and people. While establishing the requirements, developers interact with the customer/user stakeholder to determine want the customer wants. To decide whether they can achieve the customer's desired scope while satisfying cost and time constraints, developers are likely to think about the processes to be used on the project and about any technologies to be used to develop the product. Likewise, they focus on technology or process as they produce the project deliverables. The main point is that although the customer has STQC expectations about the project and project deliverables, the developer has expectations about the technology, process, and people needed to execute the project and produce the project deliverables.

In managing stakeholder expectations, the project manager and the development team make decisions about the composition of technology, process, and people that is needed to satisfy stakeholder expectations. Sometimes project decisions concern the relationship to be maintained with critical stakeholders such as the customer/user or upper-level management, and at other times project decisions involve the actual tasks that need to be done to produce project deliverables with respect to STQC. The focus or concern of project decisions also changes throughout the life of the project. Initially, project manager and development teams are interested in establishing strong relationships with their clients. That's when the focus is centered on relationships. As the project progresses, and especially on projects where time constraints become apparent, the focus changes to getting the tasks done as a mechanism for enhancing the client relationship.

Figure 9-1 models the relationship between the STQC expectations of the customer stakeholder, the technology/process/people expectations of the developer stakeholder, and related project decisions that correlate and help manage the various expectations of all sides. You need to understand that the actual customer expectations, developer expectations or focus, and decisions change over the life of a software project. Customers vary not only in the priority of their expectations with respect to STQC but also in the order in which they think about or focus on each dimension of expectation.

A typical order in which the focus of customer expectations changes is (1) scope, (2) cost, (3) time, and then (4) quality:

At first, requirements (scope) may be dominant: Customers may want to have everything they can think of at the start of the project. There is even a term called **desirement**, which highlights that at the beginning of the project the customer thinks about wants without considering cost (TheFreeDictionary by Farlex, Desirement). Customers can ask for anything until the project costs are understood and assigned to the requested features. When this happens, the dominant dimension of expectation changes to cost.

Cost impacts the budget: Customer stakeholders now consider what they will get for the money that they will spend. They begin to understand that there is a limit to the features that they can afford because they have a budget. The process of prioritization is now invoked, and decisions must be evaluated and made as to what is important. The decisions about cost are not about whether a feature costs more or less than expected but about whether it fits in the budget. After cost, the next dominant dimension of expectation is time (schedule).

The schedule is a factor after the price has been decided: The customer now wants to know how long it will take to get what they have decided that they want. The schedule will determine the necessary resources and the duration of the project. The schedule and project duration create a whole new set of expectations for a discussion that eventually leads to the final dimension of quality.

There is a saying that people will long forget the cheap price when they are left with poor quality: We always seem to know quality when we see it but sometimes have difficulty specifying and establishing quality in the product, especially software quality. Because it may not be understood until seen in the delivered product, quality is the most difficult and longest-lasting dimension of expectation. When describing services that we believe met or exceeded our expectations, we usually say, "Take a look at the job they did!" In other words, we express good service as a description of the resulting product's nice appearance. A nice paint job means good service. A piece of software that works flawlessly, or better yet, as described in the manual might be viewed as a miracle.

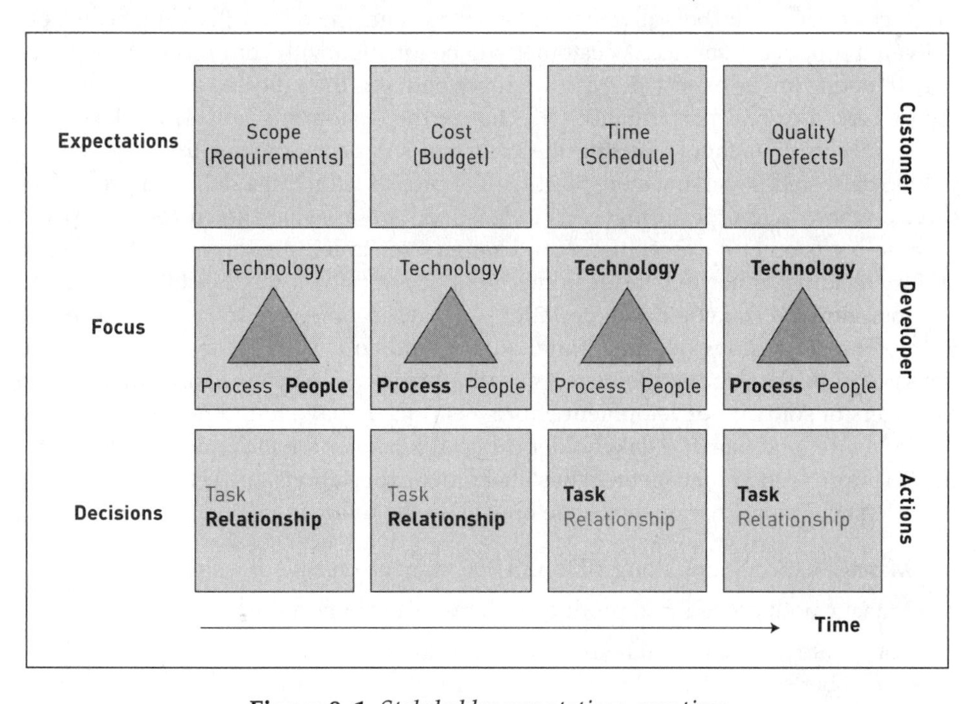

Figure 9–1: *Stakeholder expectations over time*

The following two examples about experiences at restaurants illustrate the historical effect of experience on expectation:

> **Case 1:** When you arrive at the restaurant, a waiter greets you at the door and leads you to a table. The waiter eagerly takes your orders and delivers the food promptly. The bill is presented in a timely fashion, and you leave. Two hours later you are sick to your stomach and must go to the hospital.
>
> **Case 2:** You arrive at a restaurant, and there is a sign that says to seat yourself. There is tape over the word *please*. Someone runs by your table and throws down two menus even though there are three people in your party. You finally grab the apron on a passing waiter who takes your order. Forty-five minutes later, the food arrives, but the smell alone is like one from heaven. You spend 40 minutes eating and enjoying every bite. You don't even notice that the bill is already on the table. You pay the bill and go home.

Which experience will generate the best expectations in the future? Which restaurant will you revisit? Expectations are both process and product based, and software developers and development managers must balance these two.

To be able to deliver a software product or service that will satisfy the customer/user stakeholder, a software project team needs to understand that customer satisfaction depends on two factors: the customer's expectations for the way in which the product or service to be delivered will perform and the actual performance of the delivered product or service. A customer will be satisfied with your product or service only if it performs as expected. Any difference between the expected performance and the perceived or real performance will change the customer's satisfaction level (not necessarily in your favor). Setting the customer's expectations for the product that will be delivered is the first step, but then the project team must deliver a product or service whose actual performance is at least as high as what the customer expects. Because a customer's expectations can change over time, it is important to monitor and try to adjust, if needed, the customer's expectations over the life of the project.

In summary, stakeholder expectations are based on some level of performance in the four dimensions of scope, time, quality, and cost. Stakeholders have expectations for both the product delivered and the process used to produce the product. Managers of software development efforts historically have found it difficult to help set, influence, and manage stakeholder expectations over the life of a project or product. To improve their management of stakeholder expectations, project managers need to understand and consciously decide how to do the following:

- Manage expectations along all four STQC dimensions
- Manage both process and product with respect to expectations
- Formulate questions that help them determine what stakeholders really want and remember that stakeholders may not be forthcoming or adept in clearly expressing what they want

- Consider stakeholder expectations when evaluating and making project decisions and understand that their project decisions impact stakeholder expectations

For readers who want to learn more about managing stakeholder expectations for software projects, we recommend the following references. McManus (2004) highlights the importance of understanding the stakeholder perspective in the context of software engineering projects. Giesen and Volker (2002) apply a marketing technique (based on utility functions) to analyze stakeholder preferences during requirements engineering. Damian (2007) presents lessons learned from practice about stakeholder needs in global requirements engineering. Roberts et al. (2009) advance scenario planning techniques through a parameterization and ordering of potential future contexts and stakeholder expectations to evaluate and make decisions about alternative system evolution strategies. Ruhe and Pfleeger (2007) discuss the challenge of making software development decisions in the context of conflicting objectives, restricting constraints, and stakeholder preferences.

9.3 Case Studies

The two case studies in this chapter focus on aspects of managing stakeholder expectations where the various stakeholders include customers, project team members, and management. In the first case, "TCP Enhancements at Gigaplex Systems," the software project encounters unexpected problems related to the customer expectations, the interaction between the team and its customer, as well as the internal team dynamics. The second case, "Tough Sell at Henkel Labs," presents a difficult situation in which stakeholder expectations need to be managed across a global organization involving people from different cultures residing in different countries who sometimes have opposing organizational and business objectives. Decisions made in both projects appear to have placed the stakeholders in positions that are not very favorable. Read these cases to determine the steps that were taken or not taken to manage stakeholder expectations as well as the decisions and actions that led to project problems.

CASE STUDY

TCP Enhancements at Gigaplex Systems

Directions

When reading this case study, focus on the need to manage stakeholder expectations at various levels in the organization, with peers, management, and subordinates. Try to identify the activities that assist or undermine one's ability to manage stakeholder expectations in a positive way.

Case Summary

DESCRIPTION

Stephanie White, one of CyCorp's program managers, is having a tough time explaining to herself and to her boss what the main problems are that have caused the Gigaplex project to get out of hand. Meeting stakeholder expectations and interacting with a diverse multinational team as well as a tough client has been difficult for everyone.

CASE STUDY OBJECTIVES

After reading the case study, you will be able to do the following:

- Understand the challenges of managing stakeholder expectations
- Understand the consequences of not performing stakeholder expectations management activities explicitly on a project
- Identify various stakeholder expectations management activities and their positive or negative effect on project success

SUBJECTS COVERED

Client/customer expectations, change in stakeholder expectations over time, managing stakeholder expectations, stakeholder expectations, team morale, team organization

SETTING

The setting is a networking project in the United States that has a short time frame (less than one year).

KEY CONCEPTS

- Managing stakeholder expectations is an ongoing process that needs to be done throughout the lifecycle of the project.
- Communication between all stakeholders is key to making sure that project objectives are met.
- Understanding stakeholder expectations with respect to scope, time, quality, and cost is mandatory.

TERMINOLOGY

Scrum: An iterative, incremental process for developing any product or managing any work. It produces a potentially shippable set of functionality at the end of every iteration (Advanced Development Methods).

TCP: Transmission Control Protocol (Cerf and Kahn 1974).

UDP: User Datagram Protocol (Postel 1980).

The Case

SCENARIO

It was late on Friday for Stephanie White, one of CyCorp's most accomplished program managers. She was looking forward to a relaxing weekend, where she could escape with her family on board their 42-foot yacht, Destiny, from their home port of Bellingham, Washington, to a pleasant weekend cruise in the San Juan islands. She knew, though, that, from a lot of different perspectives, this day was far from over. She was due to meet Blair Borman, her boss and the VP of engineering, in an hour or so to explain what was going on with one of her project teams. The meeting was to provide Borman with an update on the recent developments in the Gigaplex Project, a project everyone at CyCorp had hoped would provide happy customers, a good revenue source from follow-on projects, and enhanced visibility to the company and its services.

As she was getting ready for a meeting, which everyone knew would last longer than expected and involve a much heated discussion, she tried to recollect in her mind the events of the past few months that got them this far. Fresh in her mind were the details she heard from Amit Gupta, the Gigaplex team lead about issues the team was having with its client. She struggled in pinpointing the underlying cause for all of this and in determining how to resolve the situation. Borman would certainly want recommendations, and she had none.

Background

A few months before, a request came from Julian Chen, a former employee of CyCorp and now a software engineer at Gigaplex. Through a discussion over lunch with one of his former colleagues at CyCorp, Julian discussed the idea for a collaborative new project between CyCorp and Gigaplex. Amit Gupta, a team lead at CyCorp and the person to whom Julian spoke, asked for more information to present to management for review. It appeared that Gigaplex was having a hard time moving large volumes of data over the Internet using Transmission Control Protocol (TCP) in a way that provided both performance and reliability. To address the company's need, Gigaplex was looking to enhance the performance of existing communication protocols, other than TCP, while maintaining their reliability and to then embed them in an open source library used by Gigaplex internally for various file-transferring applications. Amit, from CyCorp, recalled:

> Julian had a lot of ideas, but it was clear that if we decided to collaborate on this project, he was going to leave it up to us to choose which protocol we should implement. From the short presentation he gave me, I thought we could end up with a project that would have a business impact and that would be technically challenging as well.

Although CyCorp was still growing as a company, its management was adamant about using a structured approach to project selection that included issues of scheduling, scope, client involvement, and expertise. Technical management had been trained in formal processes and software engineering best practices and was trying to get the software development teams to practice these concepts and understand their value for project success.

From various perspectives, the Gigaplex Project was very appealing. If successful, CyCorp could use Gigaplex as a good reference to get its name out there as a company that helped solve a major problem faced by one of the industry's giants. Despite that, some people at CyCorp couldn't help but wonder why a company the size and magnitude of Gigaplex would be courting a relatively small software development house such as CyCorp, which is located so far away in Seattle, on a project that was this important. Julian, from Gigaplex, recalled:

> At the time, Gigaplex was busy doing a lot of new product development. Company management usually pushed our internal needs for projects like these aside to take second chair to projects involving products that the market wanted. Gigaplex employees were each expected to help innovate company processes and protocols, which was how I got to think about solving our data transfer issues. Since I didn't have time to drop my other ongoing projects and because no one at the company minded that we look for outside assistance, I turned to CyCorp. From my experiences there, I've always remembered the CyCorp people for their hard work and technical expertise. I had my solution in mind but was not going to force it onto them. I was really looking for an interesting exchange of ideas as well as a deeper investigation of how to tackle this challenge, perhaps from a different perspective.

White, who was part of the decision-making group at CyCorp for evaluating the Gigaplex Project, along with Borman and a few others, seemed very interested in using this opportunity to help give CyCorp people a glimpse into a large company's work culture, processes, and product development. White remembered that another program manager stated in one of the discussions, "It would be nice to have the opportunity to do a great job on a real project for Gigaplex."

After a short evaluation process, CyCorp decided that the project should go forward without further delay. Borman, knowing the importance of the project, handed it off to White, who was then tasked with putting a team together to get started as soon as possible. White didn't have much time and was therefore forced to pick people who might not have worked together before. Borman asked her to keep him apprised of how things were going on a regular basis. It was important for Borman that this project be managed according to stakeholder expectations to enable future collaborations with Gigaplex. He also wasn't about to lose the opportunity to highlight the importance of his division in the eyes of the other C-level executives at CyCorp.

Knowing this, White decided to staff the team with five very qualified engineers, two of whom had worked with Julian in the past while he was an employee at CyCorp. Figure 9-2 illustrates the composition of the project team. Being pressured by both Borman and Julian to get things moving, White didn't have much time to assemble her team. Therefore, she chose a group of five team members who were very diverse in their personal styles, experience levels, and cultural backgrounds. She hoped that they would complement each other from a skills and qualifications perspective. The five included Amit Gupta, Patrick Adamson, James Famosa, Sathviha Jain, and Jin-Lee Han.

Gupta, who was a native of India, was tasked with the role of team lead and project manager. His background was in embedded systems, and he was experienced in large-scale implementation projects. He had experience in leading teams, and he was one of the people who had experience working with Julian in the past. He recalled:

> To me, Julian was a client who was both very passionate and also a real hands-on developer. Unlike conventional software development (which looks only at delivering a solution successfully), his approach was aggressive (trial and error including failures). Since he wanted to build something groundbreaking, most of his ideas regarding technology were the result of his aggressive approach.

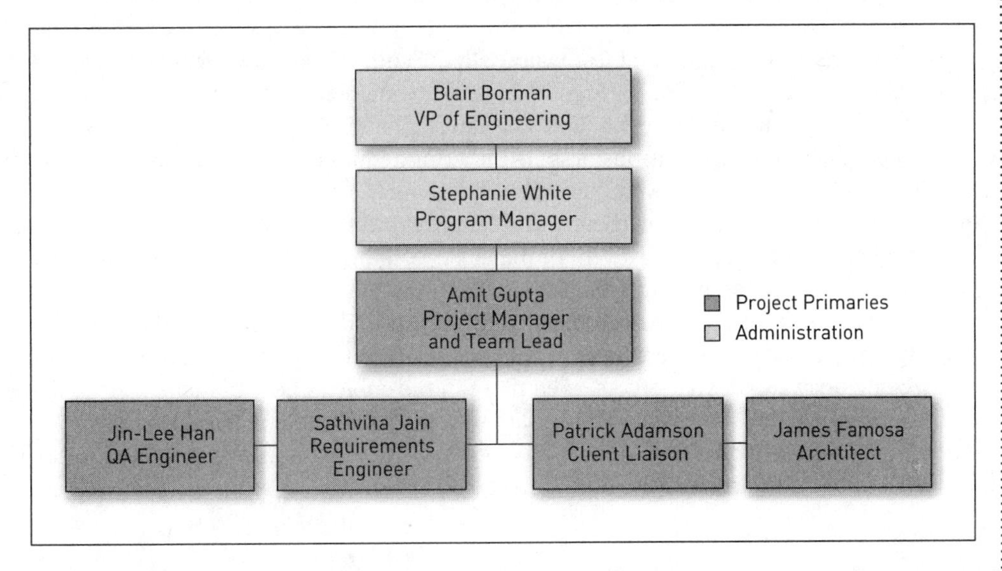

Figure 9–2: *Gigaplex Project team*

Patrick Adamson, the youngest guy on the team, was mostly quiet and shy but had an everlasting smile on his face any time someone asked him a question. Adamson used to work for Motorola on its telephony protocol stack and was familiar, at least at some level, with part of the issues Julian raised. James Famosa, another member of the team, was a native of Cuba who immigrated to the United States about nine years earlier and had spent the last five to six years working for a software company in Miami. He assumed the role of the software architect on the team. He was also the most experienced engineer on the team if one looked at it strictly from a perspective of the number of years of experience. The two others on the team were Sathviha Jain, another native of India who brought with her six years of experience working at Tata Consultancy Services (TCS), and Jin-Lee Han, a Korean who came to the United States to follow his wife who was doing her PhD at the University of Washington in marine biology.

Gigaplex Systems

Founded in 1998, Gigaplex Systems was an industry leader in content aggregation, content indexing, and search optimization. The company employed close to 4,000 engineers and business professionals (marketing, sales, and customer support) in offices all over the world with a large portion located in Silicon Valley. The company continuously looked for more ways to make content available to users anytime anywhere, at literally a tip of a finger. The company traditionally made its money from drawing users to its search pages, thereby creating a critical mass of viewers so that Gigaplex could generate revenue by selling advertising on its web pages. Other sources of revenue included paid subscriptions for provided services, which included access to its sophisticated search algorithms, search optimization for small businesses, and content organization/indexing.

The company's culture was very technical in nature with people hired directly from top computer science programs at Carnegie Mellon, Stanford, MIT, and Berkeley and paid well. Despite its large work force, the company did not maintain or enforce strict rules and regulations related to the process of software development. Projects were free to choose how to conduct their internal business in gathering requirements, choice of life cycle, planning and tracking, and even customer management. Since most of the company's projects were internal in nature, there was a certain project management know-how that was shared between people; however, for the most part, the free spirit of going where "no man has gone before" seemed to prevail.

One interesting aspect of the company's internal way of doing things was the emphasis on having projects be secretive in nature, with people in various parts of the company typically being unaware of what others, even those in the cubicles next to them, were really doing. This mysterious, hush-hush mentality was part of what drew people to Gigaplex, but it also made daily operations a little more complex because issues of communication, coordination, and transparency had become an overhead.

Wrapping Your Hands Around the Project

Gigaplex was using an open source library, called NetCom5, that supported peer-to-peer communication over a wide number of network configurations, including firewalls and Network Address Translations (NATs). To be able to go through firewalls, NetCom5 used a protocol based on User Datagram Protocol (UDP), which had a reliability mechanism—similar to TCP—embedded in the data section of the UDP messages. This protocol, dubbed Pseudo TCP, was faster than TCP but not as reliable. One of the project's objectives was to create an improved version, also based on UDP, which ideally would be faster than TCP for file transfers. The team decided to call this new protocol RUDP, where *R* stood for reliable. RUDP was not going to replace Pseudo TCP but was going to be part of NetCom5 library as another option.

A crucial part of the project was testing the reliability and performance of the new protocol. To accomplish this, the team needed to build a test suite that could automatically execute test cases using different parameters simulating different network conditions. One of the main objectives of the test suite was to evaluate the RUDP protocol based on its correctness (the protocol does what is expected, such as transfer a file) and its reliability (the protocol also works under adverse network conditions). In addition, the test suite was to measure the performance of the RUDP protocol by benchmarking it against Pseudo TCP and TCP (where appropriate). The client's goals were simple: to allow all Gigaplex applications using NetCom5 to transfer files using the implementation of the new protocol, thereby improving the performance and efficiency with respect to bandwidth of Gigaplex's file transfers within the organization.

As the project unfolded, Gupta set clear parameters for what his team needed to do. His main objectives were to implement the RUDP protocol, develop a test suite to test it thoroughly, and integrate it into the existing NetCom5 library. As the Netcom5 library was implemented in C++, the RUDP protocol had to be implemented using the same language. To make sure his team was able to achieve all of these objectives, he sat down with Julian (client) and Patrick Adamson, the "people person" on the team and the appointed client liaison, to define a set of responsibilities between them. Specifically, these responsibilities were the following:

Team Responsibilities

- Implement RUDP.
- Test the reliability and performance of RUDP.
- Merge RUDP into NetCom5.
- Keep the customer informed of the status of the project on a biweekly basis.

Client Responsibilities

- Keep team informed of any relevant project issues and their effect on the project.
- Be responsive to team's requests for meetings or additional information.
- Be willing to negotiate with team any changes to the project's requirements, based on the magnitude of the impact on the development effort.

Project Discoveries

To make effective use of his resources, Gupta split his team into two main task forces: the first included Patrick Adamson and James Famosa, and the second included Sathviha Jain and Jin-Lee Han. He tasked Adamson and Famosa with investigating existing networking protocols, including TCP and some of its variants (TCP Reno, Vegas, TCP Taho), Pseudo TCP, UDP, and the required RUDP. Gupta wanted to understand the differences and similarities in how issues of reliability, performance, and adaptability to existing network conditions impacted design choices in implementation. Getting a good handle on the various mechanisms the protocols employed, from loss detection to adjustable transmission rate, was part of the investigation. He then tasked the other part of his team with getting a clearer insight into the testing aspect of the project and the corresponding test suite. Although none of his team members (other than Adamson) had prior experience with networking protocols, it seemed that Famosa and Adamson spent quite some time digging into the mechanics involved with issues of reliability and performance. They compared the different protocols and even went to see Prof. Steven Row, who was one of the engineering professors at the University of Washington in Seattle whose research area was network protocols. Famosa remembered:

> We made a lot of progress in our understanding of TCP during the last few weeks, and we're now trying to understand FAST TCP, which is pretty much what Julian wants. Our goal, I think, should be understanding the protocol that Julian wants. The rest is easy. Prof. Row gave us a lot of reading materials. The situation is not simple. TCP was carefully designed, and that's one of the reasons why it has been so successful. Creating protocols that are faster and as reliable as TCP is not a trivial task and is probably the topic of some PhD thesis at Caltech and other top schools. This topic for me was fascinating since it dealt with improving the foundations of the Internet. There is some math and creativity involved, which makes it even more of a challenge.

While the team members were taking their time being thorough in understanding the issues and how to address them, their interaction with their client Julian, who was already becoming impatient at not seeing much progress in terms of actual deliverables, was not going as expected. Sathviha recalled:

> Julian was becoming impatient with us. He kept telling us that we should have been further along than we were and that coding a simple reliable UDP protocol was something he could do in his sleep. In fact, it seemed like he was testing us and not giving us the full picture for some reason we couldn't put our fingers on.

The team members tried to get the most out of their interactions with Julian by using two mechanisms. The first was by directing the conversation to focus on specific questions for which they needed answers and that were communicated in writing to Julian prior to the meeting. The second was by fielding some questions on Pseudo TCP and existing NetCom5 issues to Brian Sparrow, the person at Gigaplex who wrote the Pseudo TCP code and integrated it into the library.

The team members also struggled internally in wrapping their hands around the various problems and in moving forward cohesively at a more adequate pace. The team did not seem to gel, and the different personalities on the team made joint decision making a difficult task. The iterative nature of the process that the team was using (Scrum) required trust and agility, two qualities the team, at least at that point in time, did not really possess. To further complicate things, sometime close to the Christmas break, there was a specific incident that made the team members feel a little uncomfortable with their client and his approach to the whole project. Gupta remembered:

> It was a Friday afternoon, and we were having one of our regular client meetings. Julian was late (as usual), and we were discussing the items on the agenda when he walked in the door. We were going to start by addressing our list of questions, but Julian seemed irritated and claimed that we were wasting his time with questions that he had already answered. We knew Julian was hard to understand as it was, being a non-native English speaker with a heavy Taiwanese accent. Our problem had always been that his answers were vague and did not provide us with the specifics we needed to develop the solution. He could never really tell us what he meant in measurable terms, so we knew that meeting his expectations was going to be difficult. Julian kept pushing to have us commit to deliverables. He said that we were wasting time and that only by coding would we have enough insight into what we needed to do. When we claimed that our research has so far shown that creating a more reliable and faster TCP was probably unlikely, he claimed to have done this already a few months ago but said he couldn't give us the code because of company nondisclosure issues.

The team members left the meeting a little shaken up. They weren't sure what had just happened, but it certainly seemed that something was wrong. Was Julian really interested in this project? Was he just testing them to see what they could do? If he had already implemented the protocol, why not just incorporate it into NetCom5 and be done with it? They seemed to have been more questions than answers after that particular meeting than any one of them could answer.

Making Decisions

In the following weeks, Gupta directed his team to investigate whether creating a more reliable UDP was really as difficult as the experts had told them. Ongoing attempts to obtain Julian's code, which he claimed would solve the puzzle, yielded no positive results. Julian was willing to share with the team his design for the protocol that he suggested they follow. The team tried to emulate his design in their own implementation of the network protocol, which they dubbed JUDP, with *J* standing for Julian. The team was bothered because some of the basic business drivers for this project no longer made sense in light of the experiments they had run and the data they had collected.

Reviewing Julian's design, the team found that it was trying to improve on the Pseudo TCP algorithm in which there is network latency, typically because an out-of-order packet is received. Julian wanted to address that problem in a more fundamental way through the algorithm. His approach was to use a packet-based protocol, using acknowledgment types and a new property of window size adjustment based on packet round-trip time (RTT). The team couldn't figure out which specific scenario this would help, a question Julian wouldn't answer. Assuming there was something wrong with the existing Pseudo TCP algorithm that Brian Sparrow had already implemented and integrated into NetCom5, the team wondered whether there could be another existing TCP implementation that was already customized for this scenario, much like FAST TCP, which was for high-gigabit networks.

The team struggled to understand Gigaplex's business driver for having a new protocol integrated with NetCom5. Was it slightly improved file transfer? What was the intended benefit? It seemed that answering this question would certainly help the team members better focus their work, but yet again, this was another dead end.

Gupta shared his thoughts with White on how the project was going. He produced a tracking chart that his team was using on a weekly basis to capture team-based parameters (see Figure 9-3).

Gupta explained:

> Stephanie, we use this chart on a weekly basis to capture parameters we feel are important for team cohesion, productivity and process, and internal and external communications. As you can see, things have not gone too well aside from process maturity. It's starting to impact the team, and I'm not sure what to do. I was hoping you and I could explore this further and see how to get the project back on track.

Because her meeting with Borman was to be in a half hour, White did not have time to analyze the data, though the chart intrigued her. She was particularly interested in the specific metrics the team was using to quantify the team aspects being tracked. She told Gupta that they could explore this further after the weekend and that she needed some time to think about it and come up with ideas.

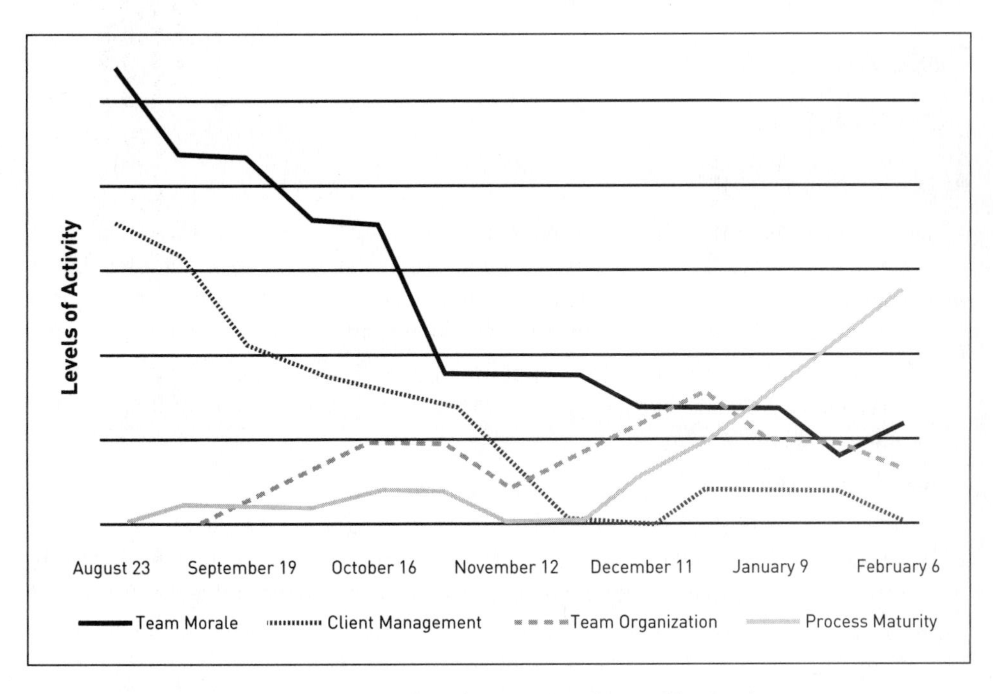

Figure 9–3: *Team-based parameters for tracking project*

CASE PROBLEM

Stephanie White, a program manager at CyCorp, has a software project team that currently is uncertain about what to do next to satisfy the client Julian from Gigaplex. The team members are frustrated in their efforts to satisfy Julian. The team's perception of its own morale, ability to manage the client, and organization is declining as the project goes forward in time. Wondering why they were tasked with implementing a protocol that supposedly has already been implemented by the client, the team members now question the original project objectives.

Stephanie must decide what to tell her boss Blair Borman, the VP of engineering, about the team's situation. She thinks that she will need to explain the underlying cause for this situation and to recommend a solution for how the team should proceed. She has not had time to reflect upon what Amit Gupta, the project manager, recently told her about the team's problems with the client and about the team's perception of its current status.

What should she say to her boss at the meeting, which is to be held soon?

Case Analysis

ANALYSIS ACTIVITY

Analysis Background

(P) Problem: Stephanie has the immediate problem of deciding what to tell her boss about the Gigaplex Project team's situation. Stephanie also thinks that she should determine the underlying cause for the team's current problems and that she should provide a recommendation for how the team should proceed.

(E) Experience: Stephanie is an accomplished program manager. Program managers usually manage a collection of projects whose objectives contribute to business and program-level objectives.

(A) Assumptions:

Stephanie's assumptions follow:

- There is an underlying reason for why the Gigaplex Project team is having problems with the client, though Stephanie has not yet determined this reason.
- At the next meeting, her boss will expect her to provide a recommendation for how the team should handle its problems.
- The diversity of skills, knowledge, experience, personality, and cultural styles among the Gigaplex Project team members would enable the team to be able to execute the project successfully. (She implicitly had assumed that this diversity would not prevent the team from working well together.)

The team's assumptions follow:

- There is a solution to the problem of implementing a communications protocol that can satisfy the requirements.
- The client would allow the team flexibility in determining the best solution.

(K) Knowledge: The following is an outline of what Stephanie knows about the CyCorp environment and project team as well as about the client Julian and the environment at his company Gigaplex. (You can assume that Gupta gave Stephanie this information, provided to you in the case study.)

- **Environment/fact:** The Gigaplex Project is important to CyCorp's upper-level management because of the opportunity that the project has to enhance the company's reputation, to promote future business with industry leader Gigaplex, and to develop the staff's awareness of how a large company operates.
- **Environment/fact:** Amit Gupta, the team lead and project manager, worked with the client Julian in the past and has experience in leading teams.
- **Environment/fact:** The CyCorp team members are diverse in their cultural backgrounds, experience levels, knowledge and skills, and personal styles.

- **Fact:** The team members are not working together effectively. They have problems making decisions as a team.
- **Fact:** The Gigaplex Project team thinks that the objective for the project is to implement a communication protocol that enables file transfers over the Internet that are faster while being just as reliable as those possible when using the TCP protocol. The implementation is to be based on the modification of an existing protocol such as UDP.
- **Fact:** In a meeting with the client Julian and the CyCorp client representative Patrick Adamson, Gupta clearly outlined the responsibilities for the team and for the client. The client is aware of and did not disagree with these responsibilities.
- **Fact:** The team has researched existing communication protocols, has implemented Julian's design for a communication protocol that is a modification of UDP, has tested the implementation, and has found issues regarding the ability of the implementation to satisfy the expected performance or reliability. Finding a solution to the protocol implementation problem has turned out to be very difficult.
- **Environment:** The Gigaplex company culture rewards technical innovation, but also fosters secrecy and information hiding among its staff. Gigaplex engineers are bright, well educated, and highly skilled.
- **Environment/fact:** The team has found it difficult to work with Julian.
  - The team has difficulty understanding what Julian says. Julian's first language is not English, and he has a heavy accent.
  - Julian has refused to answer some of the team's questions and has made comments that have demoralized the team.
  - Julian has pushed the team to go directly to code to determine the solution.
  - At the beginning of the project, Julian said that he would not push the team to follow his ideas for the solution but would welcome an exploration of solutions. He now insists that the solution involves an implementation of his own design, says that the solution is simple to code, and claims that he has already implemented his protocol.
- **Fact:** The team questions why it was tasked to build an implementation that was supposedly already done by the client. The team questions the client's reason for the project.

Solution: The case study ends with Stephanie not having time to analyze the underlying cause of the Gigaplex Project team's problems. She is not yet prepared to pose a solution to these problems. The analysis questions will challenge you to think about alternative solutions to the team's problems. The case study purposely does not discuss what Stephanie actually considered telling her boss at the upcoming meeting. This is left for you to analyze.

Assumed Risk: There are no assumed risks yet since Stephanie has not considered alternative solutions or decisions for her immediate problem or for the ongoing team situation.

Analysis Questions

1. After reading the case study and the analysis background information, what do you think is the primary problem that the Gigaplex Project team must solve? What other issues does the team need to resolve?

   For questions 2–6, specifically consider the problems related to managing the expectations of the Gigaplex client Julian.
2. What are the exact problems that the team is having in working with the client and in satisfying his expectations?
3. Describe what you think are the underlying reasons for the problems that the team is having in dealing with the client.
4. What characteristics of the client do you think contribute to the client management problems? In what way do these characteristics influence the interactions between the team and the client?
5. What characteristics of the team do you think contribute to the client management problems? In what way do these characteristics influence the interactions between the team and the client?
6. What alternative solutions do you have for how the team should proceed to better manage the expectations of the client? What risks, if any, are associated with these solutions?
7. What suggestions do you have for how the team can resolve internal issues so that the team members can work together more effectively? What risks, if any, are associated with these suggestions?
8. What alternative approaches does Stephanie have for reporting the Gigaplex Project team situation to her boss at the next meeting? What risks are associated with each approach?

DISCUSSION

The Gigaplex Project team has a problem in managing the expectations of the client Julian. More precisely, Julian has expressed his dissatisfaction that the team is not further along in implementing the solution. The client says that he thinks the solution is simple and that he knows this because he has already implemented it. The team does not know what to do next to find the solution or to satisfy Julian. If Julian has already implemented a solution to the problem, the team questions the purpose for the project. In addition, the team is having problems working together effectively and is demoralized, a topic left for your analysis.

As discussed in the chapter context, managing stakeholder expectations involves setting, monitoring, and influencing stakeholder expectations. In addition, stakeholders are not likely to be satisfied if their perceptions are less than their expectations. Julian may not be satisfied because his perception of what the project team has done is less in some way than what he expected the project team to do. You might start by trying to understand how Julian's expectations may have changed over the project. You may detect ways in which the project team could have been more effective in setting Julian's expectations at the beginning of the project as well as in monitoring and influencing them as the project progressed.

The project objective, as stated in Gupta's outline of responsibilities for the team, was to implement, test, and integrate a reliable communications protocol that would be based upon an existing protocol. At the beginning of the project, the team thought that it would have flexibility in determining the solution. Julian expressed a similar expectation when saying that he was not going to force his own ideas about the solution onto the team. The client and the team seemed to have similar expectations that the team would explore and develop its own solution.

So, what happened? Why did Julian push an implementation of his own design as the solution, and why did he do this if he had already implemented the solution? Julian was impatient when the team did not arrive more quickly at a solution in code. Julian seemed to have expectations about the process for how the team would determine the solution and about how quickly it would find the solution. We do not know whether Julian had these expectations at the beginning of the project.

When Julian saw the team struggle in finding a solution, his expectations regarding what the team should do probably changed. He may have welcomed the idea of exploring alternative solutions at the beginning of the project and then became unhappy when the exploration did not quickly yield an implemented solution. Julian now may be pushing an implementation of his own design because the team has not found another one that satisfies the requirements. He may think that by telling the team he has already implemented the solution, the team will work harder. On the other hand, Julian may want to compare the team's implementation of his design with his own implementation (if one exists) and for the stated reason of nondisclosure be unwilling to allow the team to use his implementation for this comparison.

How could the team have managed Julian's expectations in a better way? An issue from the beginning of the project has been the assumption, not fact, that a satisfactory solution could be found and implemented. There was a risk that Julian would be unsatisfied if a solution was not found in a timely manner. The team could have mitigated this risk by working with the client to specify and agree upon the process by which the team would determine whether a viable solution exists. Likewise, the team and client would have needed to agree upon measurable criteria for determining the viability of a solution. The main objective for this slightly different project would have been to determine the feasibility of a solution rather than to implement and integrate a solution, which could have been an add-on to the original project.

What should the team do now? One approach, in line with the team's responsibility to report status, is for the team to explain clearly, objectively, and unemotionally to Julian what the team has done, what the results show, and what the team recommends should be done next in the project. For instance, the team might recommend that it help Julian define and prioritize communication scenarios that would clarify the performance and reliability requirements. The team would use these scenarios to determine whether their current implementation satisfies these more specific requirements and possibly to compare their implementation to the implementation that Julian created. The objective would be to determine whether the current implementation will be acceptable, possibly with some modification. Alternatively, the team might recommend that in the absence of criteria to more conclusively test the current implementation, it would be best to end the project with the current results.

Likewise, the team could try to manage Julian's perception of what has been accomplished. The team did develop and test an implementation of RUDP that is based upon Julian's design, which is what Julian eventually said that the team should do. The team could explain why the implementation supports Julian's design. The team could then discuss what it knows about the pros and cons of the current implementation and ask Julian what he would like to do with this information. At this point, the team might offer one of the recommendations discussed previously.

It is clear that the team needs to communicate openly and objectively with Julian about its concerns. The team could explain how it has satisfied its responsibilities and ask Julian to satisfy his responsibility to provide them with requested information and to be willing to negotiate any changes to the project requirements that are needed in light of the time and effort required to accomplish them. Since the team is uncertain of Julian's expectations for the project, there is a risk that Julian will be unreceptive to the team's recommendation, but the team will not increase this risk by explaining what it accomplished in terms of its outlined responsibilities. If Julian is unwilling to listen to the team's concerns, to consider the facts, and to reasonably determine the direction in which the project should proceed, then the team probably has little hope of influencing Julian's perceptions or expectations. Closing the project may be the best solution in this case, regardless of the impact on Julian's view of CyCorp. Effective policies for working with clients are based on objectivity, honesty, transparency, and facts, especially when dealing with difficult or dissatisfied clients.

Since Stephanie does not thoroughly understand the team's problems, the best that she can reasonably do at this time is to brief her boss on what she knows about the team's situation and to recommend that she look into the situation in more detail and report back in the near future. Considering the corporate importance of the Gigaplex Project, Stephanie also might solicit her boss's advice on how he would like for her to proceed. The first approach introduces little risk since Stephanie does need more time to look into the problem. Asking for her boss's advice may be a double-edged sword. While Stephanie would convey her understanding of the client's importance, she also inadvertently might make her boss wonder whether she has the experience and confidence to manage a team that must deal with a difficult client. Stephanie could influence her boss's perception by first briefly and confidently explaining what she plans to do to learn more about the team's situation. She could say that because of the importance of the client she would like to know whether her boss has any particular directives regarding how she handles the situation.

CONCLUSIONS

In this case study, the client's expectations changed as the project progressed because the client did not see evidence of a software implementation as quickly as he expected. The change in the client's expectations concerned the process by which the client expected the product team to determine a viable solution. The team became aware of the client's expectations regarding its process when the client insisted that the team should solve the problem by constructing an implementation of his own design. This happened after the team had spent significant time studying existing communication protocols to determine their potential use in the solution. Later when the team had problems developing an implementation that would satisfy the requirements for performance and reliability, the client said that he had already implemented a solution based on his design that was simple to do. The team then questioned the client's purpose for the project.

From these facts, you can conclude that the team was not effective in managing the client's expectations. At the beginning of the project, the team did not address the risk associated with the assumption that a satisfactory software implementation based upon a modification of the UDP protocol was feasible. The team did not discuss this risk with the client and thereby missed the opportunity to set the client's expectation for how the project should proceed if the planned solution was found not to be feasible. The team also did not set the client's expectation for the process that it would use to explore alternative solutions and for the importance of studying existing communication protocols to determine their potential for use in the solution.

The client did not satisfy his responsibilities to provide requested information in a timely manner and to inform the team of project-related issues. Communications between the client and team were not transparent and complete. Trust between the client and the team decreased as the project progressed. The team questioned the client's motives for the project. The client's perception of the team's accomplishments may not match reality. The team still has the opportunity to correct the client's perception as well as to influence the client's expectations and satisfaction regarding the value of the project. The team will need to explain the facts in an objective and unemotional way to the client and to provide options that would require the client to make transparent exactly what he originally wanted to accomplish with the project and what he would like to do now. The state of the ongoing communications will likely help make or break this project.

KEY IDEAS TO REMEMBER

- Stakeholder expectations concern process as well as product.
- Communications, transparency, and trust are critical in managing stakeholder expectations.
- Stakeholder expectations can change as a project progresses.
- Managing perception is part of managing stakeholder expectations.

CASE STUDY

Tough Sell at Henkel Labs

Directions

When reading this case study, focus on the need to manage stakeholder expectations at various levels in the organization, such as with peers, management, or subordinates. Try to identify the activities that help or undermine one's ability to positively manage stakeholder expectations.

Case Summary

DESCRIPTION

Adam Stein, a manager at Henkel labs, which is a subsidiary of Henkel & Schöt, is trying to creatively collaborate with various project management offices within the company on multisite projects. In an attempt to generate more revenue for everyone involved, Adam sees opportunities in bidding for projects where one part of the company helps with development while other parts help with logistics, client or account management, and so on. Unfortunately, getting buy-in from the various stakeholders who are involved seems more challenging than it should be.

CASE STUDY OBJECTIVES

After reading the case study, you will be able to do the following:

- Understand the challenges faced when attempting to manage stakeholder expectations

- Understand the consequences of not explicitly managing stakeholder expectations on a project
- Identify various activities in managing stakeholder expectations and their positive or negative effect on project success

SUBJECTS COVERED

Stakeholder expectation management, decision-making, offshore development, project management, communications, and negotiations

SETTING

This case study takes place in the United States, Germany, Russia, South Korea, and Argentina. The company is a global software development company with overseas subsidiaries. The project has a short time frame (less than one year).

TERMINOLOGY

PMO: Project management office

The Case

SCENARIO

Adam Stein had already written and erased six different drafts of the same e-mail to his boss at Henkel regarding the situation. It was very late at night, and he needed to get it done before he left for the day. He wasn't exactly certain how to phrase the e-mail so that it wouldn't sound too negative while sending a clear signal that whatever was transpiring was simply not working.

Trying to wrap up what he thought was a simple cooperative agreement, between the various Henkel offices, had proven to be a major challenge for the past eight months. It was bad enough that they were geographically dispersed with Adam in the United States and his colleagues José Luis Martinez in Argentina and Hilde Vandenberg in Germany, but on top of that, things were moving at a snail's pace at best. The worst of it was that he, as a manager, couldn't pinpoint the problem, determine who was behind it, or figure out how to get it fixed. He had his thoughts, though. As he went back to look at his screen and review what he had drafted, Adam sat back on his chair and tried to recall how this whole thing started.

Background

Henkel Labs (HL), where Adam had risen to division head about 12 months ago, was a relatively small (about 75 employees) subsidiary of Henkel & Schöt (H&S). H&S was a much larger software development company (more than 3,000 engineers) headquartered in Munich (Germany) with offices in Buenos Aires (Argentina), Moscow (Russia), Seoul (South Korea), and San José (California), as shown in Figure 9-4. In addition to overseeing research and development projects involving embedded systems development for various vertical markets in which Henkel was active, Adam was responsible for identifying and bringing more business into his division by scouring the market for other projects that were strategically aligned with H&S' goals and initiatives. Adam's boss, Joachim Ruddoff, was a quiet guy who was very pleased to lend a helping hand whenever needed but left Adam to handle day-to-day decision making. Although their relationship was an amicable one, Adam had heard from others at the company that Ruddoff was expecting him to perform in driving the division forward one way or another.

Pulling Together for a Stronger Offering

About nine months before, when he was on a business trip to visit a client in Reno, Nevada, Adam got an interesting request for something he had never done before. While Henkel Labs was known for its development of custom-built embedded systems, the parent company, Henkel & Schöt, was engaged in other types of custom software development, some of which was sometimes quite different from that done by HL. This particular request, to convert a large financial system from an Oracle to an open source PostgreSQL database, involved systems that were unfamiliar to Adam. Not wanting to turn down the project until he fully investigated whether H&S could do it, he told the client he would get back to him regarding H&S' ability to support the project.

Back at his office, Adam wondered whether this was a good business opportunity. On the one hand, he and his staff primarily were soliciting embedded software projects even though these tough economic times made it difficult to survive. On the other hand, there may be significant opportunity to solicit and support other types of business with existing HL clients by partnering with the parent company Henkel & Schöt. Adam did not know, from an experience perspective, whether HL could partner successfully with H&S in joint projects. HL's role on such projects could be to provide some set of capabilities including, for example, project management, requirements elicitation, client liaison, and strategic account management. Adam decided, before jumping the gun, to touch base with Hilde Vandenberg, who was in charge of the project management office (PMO) at Henkel & Schöt's headquarters in Munich (Germany). Adam recalled:

> I was very excited at the opportunity to make things happen. I knew Hilde from before, when we both worked as junior engineers on development projects in the same H&S division in Germany. Despite her academic nature (Hilde worked for many years at the Fraunhofer Institute in Nürnberg), I knew she was going to listen. She had a good entrepreneurial mind on her shoulders and was knowledgeable about our business and financial needs.

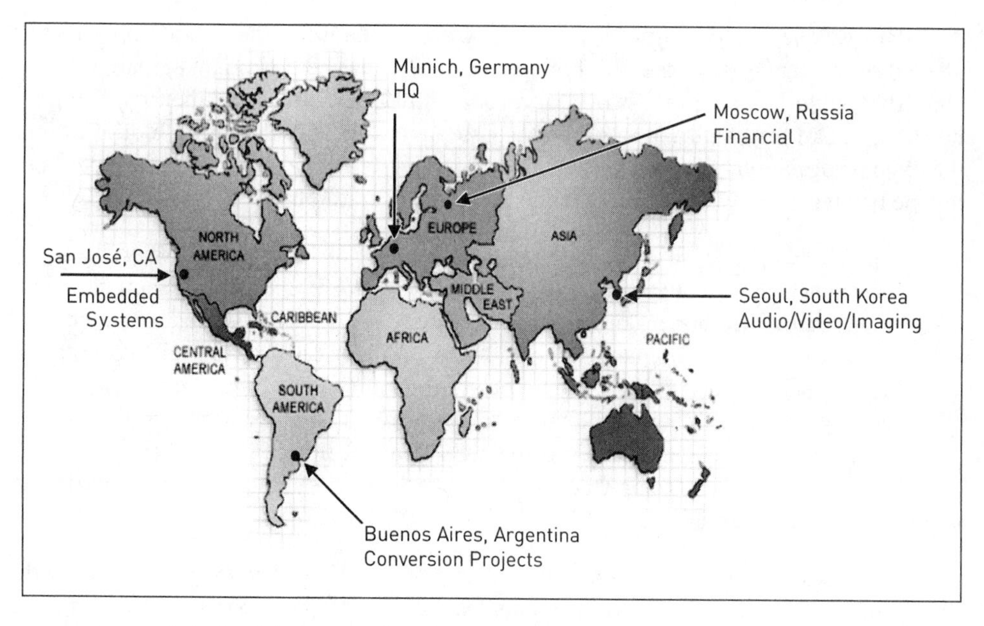

Figure 9–4: *Henkel & Schöt (H&S) worldwide deployment and areas of specialty*

In the coming weeks, Adam met with Hilde and her associate, Nicolas Stratti, a young chap from Milan who was very talkative and amiable with penetrating deep blue eyes. Hilde and Nicolas listened carefully to Adam's proposal and were very interested in pursuing it further, but they want to proceed slowly at first to make sure they weren't committing resources to things that weren't possible. Hilde recalled:

> Adam suggested a collaboration that on paper looked like a no-brainer. It seemed logical and made financial sense. Having our offices collaborate on projects in which some of the work might be done overseas while the client contact, account management, and even project oversight would be done locally, aligned with how things were done in today's fast-paced environment. Nonetheless, I wanted to make sure, before we went any further, that some of my other project managers in the PMO bought in to the idea.

Nicolas worked with Adam to create a memorandum of understanding between the companies that explained the project in terms of the resources, responsibilities, and financial arrangements and that could be circulated to the various H&S offices that might possibly be interested in participating. Hilde asked Adam to meet with her key project managers in Moscow, Seoul, and Buenos Aires in order to achieve consensus on the viability of this project from a current tasking/resource allocation perspective.

Adam was very encouraged at the turn of events. Drafting the memorandum progressed better than Adam expected. Both Hilde and Nicolas helped Adam prepare a document that could lay the groundwork for a very fruitful collaboration. Upon returning to his office in San José, south of San Francisco, Adam told his boss Joachim Ruddoff about the ongoing developments. While Joachim outwardly tried to be optimistic and encouraging, he had reservations about this collaboration. Joachim thought:

> This deal would be nice if we can get it. My knowledge of the different business units made me highly skeptical that anything would be decided, at least in the short term. Collaborative decision making across companies is not an easy task, and sometimes things can get stuck for months on end. As for Adam, he certainly was full of energy and a quick learner. His biggest drawback was that because of his optimistic nature, he would usually over promise things to clients and to management. Whether he could deliver on his promises was too soon to tell at this point, but I thought it was my responsibility to provide him some mentorship regarding the need to under promise and over deliver.

Adam worked on setting up a round of meetings, face-to-face wherever possible, with the various project managers at the locations that Hilde asked him to visit. If it was important to Hilde that they follow this process, he was going to stick to it and to prove to her, as well as everyone involved, that collaborative work across the company was not only possible but actually effective. He asked Nicolas's support in explaining to these managers what they were doing so that it wouldn't seem as if he was stepping on anyone's toes.

Meetings, Meetings . . .

Adam sat down to draft an e-mail to Alexander Nikiski and Soo-Young Han requesting a meeting. He looked it over a few times, adjusting words here and there, before clicking the Send button. He had learned the importance of doing this from a painful accident that happened to him with an agitated client who got an e-mail he shouldn't have seen. His e-mail read as follows:

```
Alexander/Soo-Young,

I am writing this note per a request from Hilde Vandenberg.

Henkel Labs, with its office in San José California, is interested
in establishing a formal relationship with groups within Henkel
& Schöt that will allow the company to represent and sell various
expertise and to engage (time permitting) project resources from
the various H&S offices worldwide to meet market needs/demand.

As part of my discussions with our parent company, Henkel & Schöt,
Hilde was hoping to get some feedback from you as her senior
```

```
project management officers regarding this proposition before
committing to an umbrella agreement.

I was hoping to talk about this further, using our video telecon-
ference system (unless you plan to be in the United States for
other company business, in which case a face-to-face meeting is
preferable). I know how busy you must be, but if you could spare
15 to 20 minutes of your time, I would greatly appreciate it.

Adam Stein, Henkel Labs

Head, Systems Development Division
```

As the days passed and while Adam waited for a meeting, he instructed two of his project managers to keep their eyes open and to see whether any of HL's existing clients were interested in other projects on which the parent company, H&S, could bid. Adam knew that meeting and getting consensus from Hilde's managers was going to take some time. He simply didn't want to wait and was hoping that, by the time they had internally gotten things organized, they would have solicited some new projects that could benefit everyone.

Within a month or so, Adam was able to arrange meetings with Alexander Nikiski from Moscow (who headed the Russian project management office) and with Soo-Young Han from Seoul (who headed the South Korean project management office), both of whom were on a business trip to a client in the United States. They seemed willing to listen and to explore opportunities for collaboration. With each of them separately, Adam discussed the business proposition, high-level goals, and how collaboration would work. Adam mentioned that he would cover any internal expenses while promoting their business. The two of them seemed very interested in understanding the financial model to support the collaboration. The model that he and Nicolas had developed, a month or so before in Munich, involved a standard split across H&S regardless of which unit was involved in a project and depending on the role taken by a unit. They seemed more at ease when hearing that no one was to be left out or treated unfairly.

José Luis Martinez

José Luis Martinez, head of the Argentinean project management office, was a bit different from his counterparts. Adam had worked with him a few times in the past and had a lot of respect for his thoroughness and perfectionist nature. The downsides to these traits, in Adam's opinion, were Martinez's rigidness, lack of ability to make quick decisions, and lack of desire to take any risk in the process.

Recognizing that negotiating with Martinez would be different, Adam decided that he would need to take a different approach. So, Adam put together an e-mail that he thought would clarify his case and would present an opportunity that José Luis would not be able to refuse. Adam's e-mail read as follows:

> Dear José Luis,
>
> I sat down with Hilde and Nicolas about two months ago to finalize what we think could be the terms for a Henkel Labs-Henkel&Schöt MOU to help HL solicit projects for the benefit of other global H&S offices (when they make sense financially to all sides). Hilde asked me to talk to some of the other H&S PMOs to get their perspective on what HL is offering as a value proposition. I've been doing this face to face with some of the folks.
>
> I wanted to get your feedback on a recent opportunity that we are considering. In recent HL discussions with its clients in Latin America (Mexico, Panama, and Colombia), the clients expressed their interest in conversion projects. HL has no expertise with these types of projects.
>
> The idea would be for us to work collaboratively by combining your expertise in conversion projects with our client management experience. We would conduct joint projects in the countries that I specified. When the HL-H&S agreement is signed, would working collaboratively on these specific projects be something that you might consider?
>
> Adam

A day or so later, Adam received a copy of an e-mail that Nicolas sent to José. The e-mail stated the following:

> From: Nicolas Stratti
> Sent: Wednesday, February 09, 20-- 12:26 PM
> To: José Luis Martinez
> Cc: Hilde Vandenberg; Adam Stein; Joachim Ruddoff
> Subject: Re: Henkel Labs - Henkel Schöt Project Agreement
>
> José Luis,
>
> Because any agreement will be between H&S and HL and because we need input from all of the project management offices that might potentially be involved, Hilde and I thought it wise to have Adam chat with other offices to assess interest and economics.
>
> We can't frame an agreement until we understand the scope and the various level of involvement that our various offices might have, and because this is not an Argentina-only deal, we need input from a broader group. Adam's discussions with other subsidiaries at this point should have been presented as only for information gathering.

```
As to South America, I do think Adam has jumped the gun (just a
bit), but I understand the need for him and HL to identify poten-
tial projects.

Once we have something (at the H&S level) that we think might work,
the plan is to present it to the senior PMOs and then to the entire
organization.

With that said, I suspect we are developing a straw-man that we
can discuss (right, Adam/Joachim?), and I see no reason that the
initial discussions on the straw-man term sheet can't be with you
and Hilde.

Shall I arrange a meeting for us on this topic?

—NS
```

There seemed to be some reluctance from Martinez to go forward that Adam couldn't explain. It might have something to do with Martinez's personality or decision-making style. It might also be an ego thing, or it might be a real issue involving resource limitation. From Adam's perspective, it was too early in the process and too difficult to tell. Nonetheless, Adam asked Hilde and Nicolas whether they wanted him to attend the meeting to clear the air and to contribute his thoughts on the matter.

As they were going back and forth in scheduling the meeting, Adam got a request for a video conference meeting with Martinez to go over things. Not wanting to refuse, Adam accepted but decided to bring along one of his most trusted project managers, Raúl Juan Ramirez, who was a native of Guadalajara (Mexico) and was intimately familiar with the types of projects that the Latin clients wanted but which HL could not support without H&S. Adam thought that having Raúl attend the meeting might be a great asset.

Adam's primary objective for the meeting was to bring up the topic of sharing resources in a common way across company subsidiaries for joint project delivery. At the meeting, Martinez expressed a general interest in the idea, though he said he'd have to get more specifics on what Adam had in mind before he could say yes or no to anything suggested. Martinez indicated that two of the most important things for him in project selection would be maintaining the quality of service and making sure that his resources weren't spent in a way that didn't make financial sense. Adam acknowledged both of these points and said that when various opportunities became available, he would forward information about them to Martinez.

To keep Nicolas and Hilde in the loop, Adam sent them a note that summarized his impression of the meeting with Martinez. Adam's note said the following:

```
Nicolas,

I met with José Luis regarding the HL/H&S deal. It was a pleasant
conversation. We discussed potential offerings that we are already
```

exploring in the system conversion project areas. It seemed that he was extremely receptive to it, which is why I plunged right in. I did not discuss numbers with him but wanted to let you know that he sees a lot of value from the relationship.

Martinez wanted to know what numbers we exchanged, and I told him to talk to you about them. He will talk to his people to get their thoughts on this as well.

Thx for the help,

Adam

In response, Adam received an e-mail that he didn't expect from Nicolas. The e-mail read as follows:

Adam,

I really wish you had waited to discuss this with him until the meeting we already have scheduled. Although I am pleased to hear that he is receptive, you've now put me in the position of having to share numbers with him, without having the benefit of adjusting those numbers based on the meetings you are having and have had. You've also created an expectation that I will be available to meet with him in the near term, which is unfortunate because I'm busy with other things for the next few weeks. Worst of all, by not sharing with José Luis the draft document, you've created a divide (perceptual at least) between the HL position and the current thinking of the H&S/PMO administration.

Waiting until our meeting on March 19 really wouldn't have cost HL anything in terms of time, but it will probably cost me some cycles and some heartburn. As St. Augustine wrote, "Patience is the companion of wisdom."

If we're going to work as a team on this project, then I need to know to whom on my team you are talking and when you will be talking to them.

I'm disappointed in this turn of events.

Nicolas

Adam read the e-mail carefully and didn't know whether he should respond. On the one hand, his relationship with Nicolas was something he wanted to preserve, but on the other hand, he didn't feel he had done anything wrong. He decided that it was better to say something rather than to ignore the e-mail altogether, and so he replied:

Nicolas,

José Luis wanted to meet and talk about the specifics of what we were doing (or planning to do) in Latin America, and I couldn't just simply refuse. Our discussion started with the generic principles and then unexpectedly moved to the type of terms we would offer. I danced around the issue but was adamant in saying that no terms had been reached, finalized, or agreed upon. I emphasized that everything was in the negotiation stage. José Luis made it clear that he wants to be an active participant in the negotiations (something that you guys will have to manage).

I assure you that I did not give him the impression (or set the expectation) that you will have time for him before our March 19 meeting. I don't even know for a fact that he will try to contact you before the meeting. He impressed on me the need for him to be involved throughout the process because he thinks that his office is the biggest asset that H&S has (you and I already discussed his feeling about this).

Over the years, I've found José Luis to work in a way by which he slowly, sometimes painstakingly, though eventually comes around to a certain position. You have to chip away at why it's good for everyone and convey to him the logic of it many times over. I did not communicate any numbers to him. I merely said that we are still in the process of discussing things.

I don't want to get into interorganizational politics, but I understand the underlying powers at play. My suggestion would be that if you want to hold everything close to the chest, you can dance around the issues (or avoid a meeting) and be more specific on March 19.

All I wanted to do was to give you a head's up so that you're not surprised if JL does try to approach you. I don't think you need to share any draft document with him if you don't think that will help. You can (if you like) give him the general guidelines. These are not likely to change much anyhow if we want to strike a deal between everyone. Anything astoundingly different will lead to us not being able to market time/expertise anyhow.

The last thing we want to do, IMHO, is to slap something on him as a take-it-or-leave-it package on March 19. He doesn't do well in those situations. If anything, letting him get used to the general guidelines/numbers and mull over them is not a bad thing. If he explodes...well then, we don't need a March 19 meeting anyway, but I really don't think that he will.

Try not to get a major heartburn just yet. All in all, I don't foresee a major fallout (but I might be wrong). Still working for

```
the same team, communicating, and updating. I am working on my ESP
skills so that I don't have to waste airtime talking <smile>.

Apologies,

Adam
```

The meeting, which took place a week or two later with Adam and Martinez on video and the others in their Munich office, was a good one, at least from some perspectives. The meeting did not go into any specifics regarding a financial arrangement that would make everyone happy. There seemed to be a clear unwillingness on the part of Hilde and Nicolas to bring up numbers and to make things concrete. Hilde only appeared to want to discuss principles and how, from an operational perspective, such an arrangement would work out. At the end of the meeting, it was decided that both Adam and Nicolas would create a term-sheet draft for review (after revisiting the older draft they already had in place) and circulate it to both Hilde and José Luis. Once they had some consensus on the terms, they would draft a more final legally binding agreement to be signed by the participants.

Are We There Yet?

While on a trip to Cambridge, Massachusetts, to meet a client a week or two later, Adam put the finishing touches on the draft agreement and sent it to Nicolas. Nicolas asked for some modifications to the document and specifically mentioned that the draft would be more appealing if Adam could add some revenue sharing projections even if the numbers were merely rough estimates. The idea was not to commit to anything but rather to understand the financial benefit that this type of commitment would have for all participants. When these modifications were made, Adam sent the document off to Nicolas, Hilde, and Martinez and hoped to get a quick turnaround with their review. When two weeks went by and no reviews were received, Adam sent a note to Nicolas to see what was happening. He got the following short e-mail from Nicolas:

```
Adam, José Luis had to cancel our meeting. We are rescheduling.
Hilde has been buried before leaving town to attend to some corpo-
rate business for all of next week. I've asked her to try to send
you a response prior to her departure. She is still working on her
e-mail even as I type this, so you may yet see something from her
before she departs.
```

A week or so later, Adam pinged Nicolas again to see whether progress had been made. He received another disappointing note:

```
Adam,

We had to cancel our meeting again, as JL had a visitor from IBM.
We're rescheduling.

Nicolas
```

In his disbelief that things were moving so slowly, Adam left a voicemail on Nicolas's answering machine at work to see whether they could move ahead without José Luis. Nicolas sent back the following e-mail.

```
Adam, Hilde has yet to review the document, due to her hectic
schedule. She is also counting on getting José Luis' buy-in. Trying
to bypass or short-circuit him might have some short-term benefit
but would be damaging in the long term. I will discuss the situa-
tion to see whether we can make some progress in my meeting with
Hilde later this week and see what she thinks....
```

Adam was frustrated. He thought that he had done everything right, talked to the right people in the right order, and still seemed to be getting nowhere. In a recent conversation with his boss at the office, Ruddoff offered to help by calling Hilde directly himself to find out what was really happening. Adam told him that he thought he had things under control. But did he???

CASE PROBLEM

- Should Adam be doing anything else to meet the various stakeholders' expectations?
- Should Adam call for upper-level intervention to move his venture forward for the good of the company?
- Is what Adam has seen so far in terms of interorganizational collaboration representative of what might happen in the future when a joint project is created?
- What should be the next move for Adam and for Hilde?

Case Analysis

ANALYSIS ACTIVITY

Analysis Questions

1. What problems does Adam think he has?
2. What problems do you think Adam actually has in managing stakeholder expectations in his work to establish collaborative projects across H&S?
3. Explain what you think are the expectations of each of the following stakeholders for collaborative projects (product) and for how the foundation for these projects is laid (process): Joachim Ruddoff, Adam Stein, Hilde Vandenberg, Nicolas Stratti, and José Luis Martinez.
4. How do you think differences in personal style (such as approach to decision making or problem solving) as well as differences in business needs and priorities might be influencing the stakeholder expectations and perceptions?

5. Use the PEAK model to identify and analyze alternative solutions/decisions for how Adam might better manage the expectations of the stakeholders for his venture. Be certain to factor in the expectations, perceptions, and personal styles of the stakeholders.
6. What would you decide to do next if you were Adam? Explain your rationale.
7. What would you decide to do next if you were Hilde? Explain your rationale.

9.3 Summary

This chapter focused on the following activities for managing stakeholder expectations in the context of decision making for software projects:

- Communicating with the customer stakeholder
- Managing multiple dimensions of stakeholder expectation over time
- Managing product and process to satisfy stakeholder expectations
- Understanding different types of customers
- Managing stakeholder perception

Decisions made by the stakeholders in both case studies placed them in unfavorable positions. In the first case, "TCP Enhancements at Gigaplex Systems," the software project encountered unexpected problems related to the customer's expectations as well as to the internal and external interactions with project stakeholders. The second case, "Tough Sell at Henkel Labs," portrays a difficult situation in which stakeholder expectations need to be managed across a global organization involving people from different cultures residing in different countries who sometimes have opposing organizational and business objectives.

Managing stakeholder expectations for a software project in a systematic way is challenging. Software project managers typically pay minimal attention to the impact of their project decisions on stakeholder expectations. All three phases of the stakeholder expectation management life cycle (setting, monitoring, and influencing expectations) are important. As with most interaction activities that are people oriented, managing stakeholder expectations depends on effective communications.

Effective communications enable software project managers to manage stakeholder expectations to achieve project success.

Chapter 10

Managing Global Development

10.1 Chapter Objectives

After reading and thinking about the concepts and case studies presented in this chapter, you will be able to do the following:

- Understand the impact of global software development on software project management
- Identify key issues and decisions involving the management of global development in the chapter case studies
- Use the chapter concepts to suggest feasible solutions to the problems faced by the case study stakeholders
- Recognize the importance of managing global software development

10.2 Context

Global software development typically refers to software collaboratively developed by one or more project groups whose groups members are located in different buildings, geographical areas, countries, or continents. The geographically dispersed group members may be working on the development of one or more interacting software systems and may consist of people from one or more organizations. Global development can go across companies as well as countries or cultural boundaries. The concepts **distributed software development** and **remote or virtual software development teams** also pertain to the collaborative development of software by people in different geographical locations, but they do not highlight the fact that the people may be globally separated. In the case of telecommuting, team members may be dispersed as they work in their homes but still be located in the same geographical area.

The demand for global software development continues to grow as companies search globally for economic benefits such as low-cost or specialized skilled labor; localities where the tax, regulatory, or other governmental policies are favorable to their businesses; better access to markets; and so on. Global software development frequently involves **outsourcing**, or contracting professionals from outside the company to perform software development. The outsourced people may work independently or be associated with another company. Outsourcing usually involves distributed software development. When deciding whether to outsource software development or maintenance, decision makers must weigh the costs with respect to the benefits.

For example, chief information officers frequently decide to outsource their computing infrastructures to reduce cost, to optimize service, to transform to new technologies, or to improve operational efficiency through the best use of resources (especially if the organization itself is global). Sometimes the cost savings do not outweigh the challenges posed by offshoring. CIOs must consider issues related to training, governance and compliance, politics, turnover, geographic and time zone differences, required skill sets, and custom code that needs support. Making decisions to outsource computing infrastructure to an offshore site requires you to consider many factors (Overby 2008).

Managing global software development has become a ubiquitous, inevitable, and challenging management issue for organizations that develop or maintain software. In particular, global software development makes project management more challenging. The geographical, time zone, and cultural differences of globally dispersed project stakeholders complicate communications and collaboration. The added complexity makes it difficult to handle the project management areas discussed in this book. Project activities that require high degrees of communication and coordination are most challenging. Front-end project activities such as eliciting requirements, architecting software systems, and negotiating and planning projects are difficult to accomplish when the software stakeholders are geographically separate and culturally different.

For a specific example in the area of managing plans, let's consider the development of task breakdowns and task assignments in the context of global software development. When developing a task breakdown, project managers need to consider task granularity as well as task cohesion and coupling. Smaller tasks increase the opportunity for tasks to be executed in parallel across distributed development sites but also increase coupling between related tasks. Maintaining the cohesive wholeness of smaller tasks being performed at different sites requires adequate communication and coordination, two factors that are complicated by distributed software development. Making decisions about task breakdowns and task assignments involves tradeoffs between the benefits of global software development and the added complexity of managing coordination of globally distributed tasks.

The management areas and activities discussed earlier in the book are the same for global software development projects, but additional factors influence the decisions that are made in these areas. To understand the complexity added by global development, you can look at some decisions in each management area that are more complex when the software project members are globally dispersed. For each management area, the project manager needs to consider how the global distribution of the team impacts the activities and decisions for that area. Table 10-1 outlines for each management area some example decisions that are impacted by global software development.

Table 10–1: *Impact of Global Software Development on Decisions by Management Area*

Management Area	*Examples of Decisions Influenced by Global Software Development*
Managing requirements	With respect to globally distributed project stakeholders: • Who should participate in the requirements activities? • When will they need to communicate, and how will they do this? • How could cultural differences impact the negotiation of requirements, and how should this be managed?
Managing estimation	How is communication and collaboration in a global software development environment being factored into the following estimates? • Time needed to accomplish the project tasks • Costs associated with the time/effort needed for communication and collaboration as well as with the purchase and operation of communication technologies • Amount of budget needed for travel between development sites to enable in-person meetings

Continued

Table 10–1: *Impact of Global Software Development on Decision Making by Management Area (Continued)*

Management Area	*Examples of Decisions Influenced by Global Software Development*
Managing plans	How can project plans for global software development promote the following objectives? Minimize the time needed to achieve the project objectives: • What task breakdown facilitates collaboration, shortens the critical path, and promotes working in parallel across development sites? • Which project tasks support meeting planning and participation to facilitate collaboration? Minimize the costs associated with a development project: • What task assignments best use staff skills while minimizing the cost of development across sites? • How can development technologies and resources be shared as much as possible across development sites?
Managing product	What controls are needed to ensure that software specifications are being satisfied across global development sites? • Functional and quality attribute requirements • Software interfaces specified in architecture or design
Managing process	How will the project manage the impact of global software development on process objectives such as the following? • Standardization of software processes with control of software process differences across development sites • Assurance that process execution achieves the target results • Staff education/training to enable process and product improvements

Table 10–1: *Impact of Global Software Development on Decision Making by Management Area (Continued)*

Management Area	*Examples of Decisions Influenced by Global Software Development*
Managing risk	What assumptions about communication, collaboration, coordination, and other issues related to global software development introduce risks associated with project decisions?
Managing people interactions and managing stakeholder expectations	How will the project manage factors, such as the following, that affect communication and collaboration in a global software development environment? • Calendar synchronization • Cultural differences • Dialogue without in-person contact* (distance separation) • Resource availability • Technology differences • Time separation • Trust

* In this chapter, *in-person* refers to communications in which one or more people are colocated in the same space so that they can see and talk with each other directly. This differs from being able to view video images of one another in real time as people in different geographical locations talk via teleconference.

As you probably noticed, many of the decisions in Table 10-1 are related to managing global communications, collaboration, and coordination. Best practices, such as the following, can facilitate effective communications and collaboration for global software development efforts:

- Establish trust across sites by being even more responsive to remote colleagues than to local ones.
- Set up liaisons at each site to facilitate cross-site communication practices.
- Establish etiquette for answering e-mail and voice mail messages in a timely way. Plan for travel early in the relationship between sites for people to meet and plan (Atkins et al. 2001).

Addressing the coordination problem that makes global software development challenging, Wagstrom and Herbsleb (2006) present an approach to systematically determine developers who need to coordinate their work and who therefore require more communication. This information can help project managers target and facilitate communications that are critical to project success.

In addition to nontechnical decisions related to communication and collaboration, project managers must make technical decisions such as the following that emerge in a global software development environment:

- What technologies will be used to facilitate voice and video communications (telecommunications) as well as collaborative work between geographically separated project members?
- What technologies will be used to store and share information across globally dispersed teams?
- When considering the use of commercial software components versus the development of custom components for a software solution, how does the opportunity to develop components globally factor into the decision?

Managers of global software development also need to pay particular attention to decisions about the software development and project management processes used across globally distributed sites. Global standardization of processes accompanied by localized process control helps ensure uniform productivity and quality across distributed development sites. Researchers have analyzed factors that enhance or hinder communication, coordination, and control for global software development with respect to geographical, temporal, and sociocultural differences (Ågerfalk and Fitzgerald 2006).

Two other research studies investigate the impact of process control on the success of global software development projects. Lee et al. (2006) discuss a survey of managers of global software development projects. They found that successful projects establish strategies for flexibly coping with challenges such as geographical and time separations early in the project along with agreements about processes that are be followed. Successful global software development projects exhibit both flexibility in coping with the challenges of software development and disciplined adherence to process agreements. Ramasubbu et al. (2008) empirically studied the effect of software process improvement initiatives on offshore software project productivity and quality. They found that investments in structured processes and the corresponding process-based learning activities can help improve offshore project performance.

Many authors have written about issues related to global software development and the management of globally distributed software development teams. See Carmel (1999), Carmel and Tjia (2005), Hussey and Hall (2007), Karolak (1998), and Sangwan et al. (2006) to acquire general background on global software development. For articles in the *Communications of the ACM* about global software development, globally distributed projects and organizations, and offshore outsourcing, reference Gupta (2009),

Desouza and Evaristo (2004), Lee et al. (2006), and Wagstrom and Herbsleb (2006), as well as other related articles in *Communications of the ACM* (2006). For a discussion of the effect of cultural, geographical, or time differences on decision making within organizations and projects, explore Bourgault et al. (2008), Brett (2001), Espinosa et al. (2007), Shore (2008), and Wang and Liu (2007). More specifically, Damian (2007) discusses stakeholder needs in global requirements engineering (GRE) and offers practical advice, based on industrial empirical studies, for managing the challenges associated with GRE.

As noted earlier, this chapter does not introduce new project management activities. Rather, it illustrates how project management activities and decisions discussed in prior chapters have additional challenges as well as potential opportunities when a software project involves global development. It shows how factors such as communication, culture, collaboration, and storage and sharing of information within a global development context are inputs to project decisions made with consideration of scope, time, quality, and cost.

10.3 Case Studies

The case studies in this chapter focus on project management issues that particularly affect global software development. The first case study, "Globally Distributed Team: FibreNet Project," highlights issues of communication, collaboration, and trust when project teams are globally distributed. The second case study, "Managing Global Software Development at FibOptia," looks at problems specific to global software development in managing process, product quality, and cost. Read these case studies to better understand the challenges of managing global software development.

CASE STUDY

Globally Distributed Team: FibreNet Project

Directions

When reading this case study, focus on the issues that impact the activities and decisions involved in managing a project team that is globally distributed. In particular, observe how communication, culture, and collaboration complicate the management of schedule, process, and cost in global software development.

Case Summary

DESCRIPTION

FibOptia is developing a network management system (FibreNet) to provide quality-of-service (QoS) features for voice, data, and video transmitted over fiber-optic networks. The development of the FibreNet software system is distributed across three software research and development (R&D) centers that the company selected because of their proximity to collaborating universities, to the needed software engineering expertise at competitive cost, or to markets for their products. The development of some parts of the software system is on schedule, while other parts of the system are behind schedule. Marc Delancy, the senior manager of software development for FibOptia, thinks that development at the project sites is being done in a vacuum rather than in synchronization with each other. In this case study, he determines why the project sites are not collaborating very well and decides how to try to improve the situation.

CASE STUDY OBJECTIVES

After reading the case study, you will be able to do the following:

- Better understand the following issues in managing global development:
    - Challenges of communication, collaboration, and coordination
    - Sharing information and making decisions across a globally distributed team
- Identify the impact of global development on the management of project decisions with respect to scope, time, quality, and cost.
- Explain the problems that occurred in the case scenario, the causes of the problems, some plausible solutions to the problems, and ways to eliminate the problems in the future or to reduce their impact. Relate these to the decisions faced by project stakeholders.

SUBJECTS COVERED

Communications between distributed project team members, cultural challenges in global software development, collaboration across a globally distributed project team, and storing and sharing information for global development projects

SETTING

The setting involves three software development centers of FibOptia, a company that builds management systems, applications, and services for fiber-optic communications. The centers are located in Hyderabad, India; Toulouse, France; and Montréal, Canada.

KEY CONCEPTS

- Managers must consider issues such as communication, culture, collaboration, and trust when making decisions for global software development projects.
- For effective collaboration, software project team members need to understand and follow best practices for communication and cooperation in a global development environment.
- Centralized project planning supported by localized management of project execution helps ensure successful achievement of project objectives across a globally distributed project team.

TERMINOLOGY

ARCEP: Autorité de Régulation des Communications Électroniques des Postes, an independent agency for regulating the telecommunication and postal services in France.

FTTH: Fiber to the home, also known as fiber to the building (FTTB).

Incremental software release: A model for releasing software as a series of versions that iteratively add more functionality or features. The development of each software version usually involves a cycle with phases such as requirements, analysis and design, implementation, and test. In this way, an incremental model is iterative. The terms **iterative** and **incremental** are often used synonymously. An iterative model does differ in that it emphasizes both refinement and augmentation of successive iterations, whereas an incremental model typically focuses only on augmentation of successive iterations. See Larman and Basili (2003) for further discussion of iterative and incremental software development.

IP: Internet protocol.

Iterative software development: A cyclical model in which a software system evolves over a series of development cycles where the system is iteratively refined and augmented. Each cycle includes phases for activities such as requirements, analysis and design, implementation, and test. The final product grows incrementally from iteration to iteration to become the final system. The phases within a cycle are frequently kept short by limiting the scope of the requirements so that an iteration is available sooner for user evaluation and feedback. See Larman and Basili (2003) for a discussion of the history of the formulation of the ideas of iterative and incremental development.

Open System Interconnection (OSI) Reference Model: A standard description or reference model for how messages should be transmitted between any two points in a telecommunication network. Its purpose is to guide product development so that products from different vendors are compatible. The reference model defines seven layers of functions that take place at each end of a communication. Although OSI is not always strictly followed in terms of keeping related functions together in a well-defined layer, many if not most products involved in telecommunication make an attempt to describe themselves in relation to the OSI model. It is also valuable as a single reference view of communication that furnishes everyone a common ground for education and discussion (SearchNetworking.com, OSI).

Packet-switched: The type of network in which relatively small units of data called **packets** are routed through a network based on the destination address contained within each packet. Breaking communication down into packets allows the same data path to be shared among many users in the network. This type of communication between sender and receiver is known as **connectionless** (rather than dedicated). Most traffic over the Internet uses packet switching. The Internet is basically a connectionless network (SearchNetworking.com, Packet-switched).

V Model of software development: A software development approach that focuses on the verification and validation (V&V) of a software system at each stage in the software development process. Two objectives to be accomplished by following a V Model are to discover defects in a software system as early as possible and to assess whether the system is usable in an operational situation (Graphical Development Process Assistant).

VoIP: The transmission of voice over packet-switched IP networks (National Institute of Standards and Technology 2005).

The Case

SCENARIO

Marc is an experienced manager who has led multiple teams in the development and delivery of software products on time and within budget. Marc has led virtual teams but is new to global software development. He faces challenges that he did not have when managing teams located at one site or within the same geographical area. He thinks that he has recently been troubleshooting problems rather than managing decisions to minimize problems in the project execution.

As the senior manager for the FibreNet Project, Marc Delancy is responsible for delivering a new product to manage transmissions over fiber-optic networks. The FibreNet product will enable Internet service providers (ISPs) to provide voice over the Internet (VoIP), data, and video transmissions over fiber-optic networks with differing types and levels of quality of service (QoS). To achieve a product delivery that is on time, within budget, and according to specification, Marc must ensure that project resources are used purposefully and carefully throughout the project. He oversees not only the use of physical resources but also the investment of human effort, time, and capital.

From prior experience, Marc knows that project stakeholders are the most important resource for the successful development of the first version of the FibreNet Manager product. Since the product is to be launched within metropolitan communities in France, the direct stakeholders are the French telecommunication companies and ISPs, the business and marketing planners for FibOptia, and the product development team. Ultimately, the French consumer of telecommunications services will benefit from the availability of higher levels of QoS, which is also a mission of Autorité de Régulation des Communications Électroniques et des Postes or ARCEP (the agency for regulating telecommunications and postal services in France). Through regulation, ARCEP seeks to ensure that French consumers have access to affordable telecommunication services comparable or better than those available in other technologically advanced nations, especially to services emerging within the European Union (ARCEP).

Marc was one of several FibOptia managers who influenced the vice president of engineering's decision to locate the company's development sites in strategic but geographically dispersed places to, over time, achieve substantial reductions in development cost and time. Marc had specifically argued that the software engineering expertise available in Hyderabad is strong, versatile, and low-cost compared to the same expertise in Western Europe. As an adjunct faculty, Marc has taught software engineering courses at the local university and has been impressed with the talent and dedication of students who come from undergraduate schools in Hyderabad. Marc had also explained that development potentially could be done around the clock because of the time differences between globally distributed sites.

Another motivating factor for a distributed team approach is that the source of core technology for FibOptia products is not located near the target market of France and Western Europe. A critical component of FibOptia's products is the underlying network hardware needed to manage QoS via the reservation of fiber bandwidth, packet scheduling, and routing. Other important intellectual property are algorithms to manage QoS in software at the application and lower communication levels in the Open Systems Interconnection (OSI) Reference Model. The company currently funds the needed investigation and laboratory testing at academic and other research institutions in Montréal. Many of the employees at the FibOptia R&D site in Montréal have completed their academic studies at one or more of these institutions. In the heart of the target market, the Toulouse center focuses on QoS policy formulation (driven by business incentives and governmental regulations), on customer studies, and on developing user interfaces for FibOptia products.

Déjà-Vu

Marc is hearing the same comments from his project managers repeatedly. From Marc's perspective, each site seems to be working in a vacuum. The tasks involving collaboration between the sites are behind schedule, while those that can be done solely within the local sites are on schedule.

The time is 10 p.m., and Marc turns off his laptop. He leans back in the chair at his office and thinks about what he heard this week at his teleconference with Robert Johnson (Montréal), Henri Baroque (Toulouse), and Janet Kumar (Hyderabad). Figure 10-1 shows an organizational chart of the FibreNet software project management.

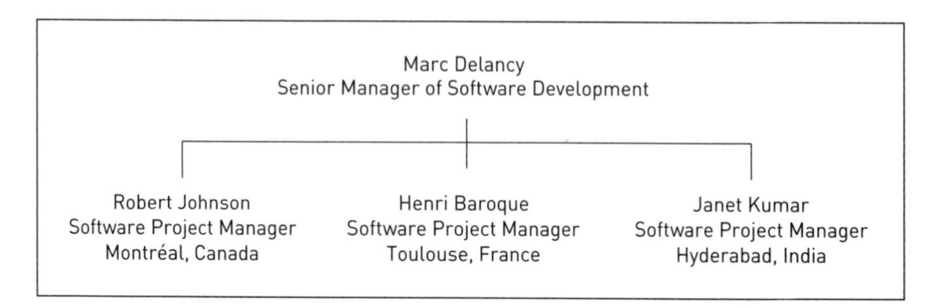

Figure 10–1: *FibreNet software project management*

Marc recalls a humorous but strangely insightful movie titled *Groundhog Day* that he watched on a flight to the United States. In the movie, a disgruntled weatherman relives a particular day in time over and over again. The weatherman decides to use what he learns from one instance of the day to the next instance to his advantage. Ultimately, the character in the story realizes that despite his attempts to improve the situation that repeatedly unfolds, he is doomed to spend the rest of his life in the same place, doing the same things, and seeing the same people every day until he changes the way he looks at life (IMDb.com, *Groundhog Day*).

Marc suddenly sits straight up in his chair as he realizes that his project managers have been indirectly telling him that global communications and collaboration across the three development sites are not happening. Marc recalls the conversation between the three project managers at the last weekly teleconference. He realizes that there is a recurring pattern to what is being said and how it is being said. Since the three managers and Marc use teleconferencing software that supports face-to-face communications via Web cameras on their desks, Marc remembers the expressions on the managers' faces even though there were occasional lags in the refresh of the video streams from the different sites.

At the Last Teleconference

Henri smiled and said, "Good news. The design of the architecture for the Network Manager's user interface layer is still on schedule. We have iteratively prototyped the user-oriented screens and gotten feedback from the customer test group. We specifically included people who oversee and test the network services provided to consumers. These systems administrators are happy with the planned functionality as well as the ease by which they will be able to monitor network performance at the network (packet) and application levels."

"This is good news," Marc commented. "Has your group been involved in the development of the interface to the business software layer design? I understand that the Network Manager will consist of a three-layer architecture with a middle layer that contains the QoS policy components."

Figure 10-2 shows the Network Manager software architecture. This diagram provides only a sample of the functionality to be performed by each layer of the software system. The arrows show the layers that communicate with each other and the directions of the communications. Henri frowned and emphatically replied, "Hyderabad has released no documents describing the architecture for the business layer, or at least no documentation is available in the shared repository." It seemed that Henri wanted to say more, but he hesitated.

Marc then asked Janet how the design of the architecture for the business layer software is progressing.

Janet explained clearly and succinctly, "We have determined basic components of the architecture for the business layer but cannot complete the design until we receive the specification of requirements for the QoS policies as well as descriptions of the QoS algorithms to be used in managing QoS based upon these policies. We are waiting on Toulouse and Montréal for these specifications."

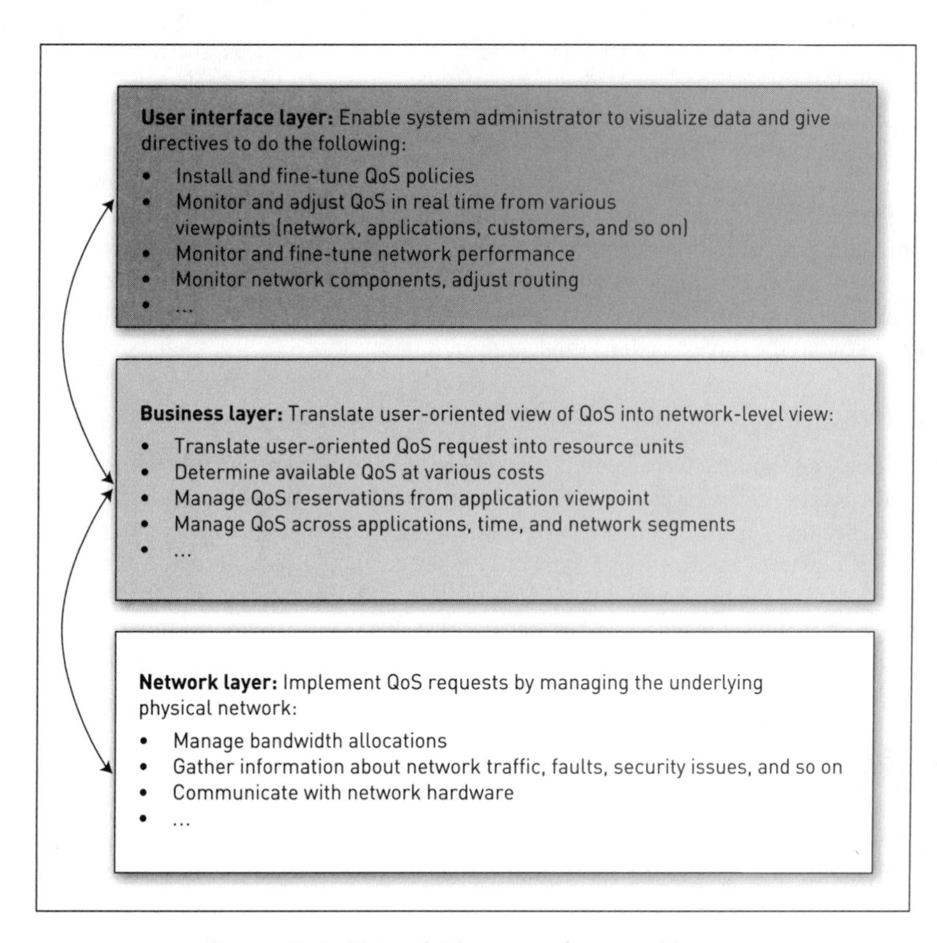

Figure 10–2: *Network Manager software architecture*

When Marc again asked whether there have been joint discussions regarding the interface to the business layer, Henri stared and said that his team has been busy working with potential customers on the user interface. Janet sighed and said nothing.

Robert had a blank look on his face as Henri and Janet were talking. It was obvious that he was not in the loop regarding the interface between the user and business layers. He did seem to come alive when Janet mentioned her group's need for information about the algorithms for managing QoS. Robert explained, "The QoS algorithms are complete. The reviewers verified that the mathematical models are correct, and our engineers simulated the application of the algorithms in the lab. We have started the patent process and will release the algorithms when this process is further along."

Marc then asked, "How about the design of the interface to the network layer of the Network Manager? Is your group talking with Janet's group?"

Robert replied, "We are working on the interface, but the design is evolving. We are not ready to release it."

Marc now realizes that other than these weekly teleconferences, the three managers probably have minimal communication with each other. The three sites are obviously not collaborating on the design of the interfaces to the different layers of the Network Manager. Marc also noticed, as best that he could tell, that all three of the managers looked tired at the last teleconference. Pulling up a global clock in his Web browser, Marc quickly sees that at the start of the meeting the times in the different locations were 8 a.m. in Montréal, 2 p.m. in Toulouse, and 5:30 p.m. in Hyderabad. The times roughly correspond to the start and end of the working day as well as the time directly after lunch for the participants. This may be why everyone seemed sluggish. Marc wonders how the time differences between the three locations is affecting communications.

In-Person Meetings with the Project Managers

Marc does not think he has acquired "the whole picture" from his weekly teleconferences with the local software project managers. When planning his travel budget for the project, he had decided on traveling to the Hyderabad and Montréal sites every three months. Over the eighteen-month project, he would take six trips to each of these sites. The first three months of the project have passed. Considering the current state of communications between the software managers, Marc decides that this is the time to communicate in person and in private with the project managers at each site. He wants the project managers to feel comfortable in talking candidly.

In a French Café

Marc had observed that Henri seems more relaxed and talkative on Friday afternoons. He invites Henri to join him at a local café for coffee around 3 p.m. to discuss the project.

"Bonjour, Henri. Ca va cet après-midi?" Marc inquires if Henri is doing well this afternoon when he meets him at the café.

"Mais, oui. C'est vendredi." Henri laughingly replies that of course he is, because it is Friday.

"Henri, at our last meeting, I think you wanted to say more about the interactions between the project groups at Toulouse and Hyderabad. Would you share your thoughts with me now that we are alone?" Marc asks quietly while looking inquisitively at Henri.

Henri knowingly replies, "Certainly. Your observation is correct. I do have more to say, but I did not want to embarrass Janet in our meeting. She is very thoughtful and careful about what she says in our meetings. I think she may be hesitant to say what she is thinking.

"My group has tried to talk with Hyderabad about the interface to the business layer software. Sometimes, we have a difficult time communicating in English on our teleconferences. We do not always understand what each other is saying," Henry explains.

"Another issue is that the engineers at Hyderabad are not assertive in the discussions that we have had. They do not seem to be comfortable in collaborating with us in real time on the design. They seem cautious about proposing their own ideas and usually respond to our proposals by saying that they will need to think about what we said."

Henri continues, "We are not trying to dominate the discussions, but they do not seem to contribute openly. They do try to understand clearly the details of our proposals. We also do not know why they are reluctant to release their current design of the business layer architecture even though we have explained that we understand that the design is still evolving. We realize that the design may need further refinement as the QoS policy requirements become more clear."

Marc explains, "Yes, the final design will not be complete until we make decisions about these requirements, but we do have a specification of representative types of services and service levels. The specifics of these may change depending on how telecommunication companies and ISPs share access to the fiber. As you probably read in the news, ARCEP has decided that telecommunication companies must share access to fiber that they install to the home [FTTH]. Of course, nothing has been decided yet regarding individual ownership of fiber that would be managed using a communal approach such as is done with condominium resources" (Baritault 2009; T-REGS 2008).

He continues by asking, "Have there been discussions about the overall architecture for the business layer?"

Henri replies, "No, we are stuck. We cannot seem to motivate Hyderabad to share a draft of the architecture. But this is not much different from the way Montréal approaches collaboration. Our colleagues there have circulated no preliminary information regarding the QoS service management framework other than their original white paper. We have not been so worried about this, though, since our software does not directly interface with the network management layer software.

On to India

After his meeting with Henri, Marc travels to India to talk with the Hyderabad team members. The team members are very interested in what Marc has to say about the development of the QoS policies and user interface layer in Toulouse. They are also eager to show him the design for the architecture of the business layer that they have been drafting.

Apparently, Janet had reassured the team that Marc would be interested in hearing the technical details of their work. They are reluctant to comment on the collaboration with Toulouse and Montréal. Marc observes that information tends to flow down hierarchically within this team. He next meets in private with Janet.

Marc thanks Janet for having her team members share their technical work with him and says that he can see that they are making good progress. After a few comments about how the team seems to respect and appreciate her leadership, Marc says, "Since your group is working on the middle layer of the Network Manager, you have double duty in determining the interfaces to your layer. This requires more communication with your group. How would you describe the communications with other development sites?"

Janet pauses and then asks, "Do you want my frank assessment or a more diplomatic description?"

"I want to know what is working and not working. Tell me as you see it," Marc reassures her.

"OK. Communications with Toulouse are sporadic and strained. One week, I receive several calls from Toulouse with lots of pressure for us to release the current design of the business layer architecture to the shared repository; then the next week, I receive no responses to my e-mails or calls regarding the state of the business policy requirements," Janet explains.

"Your team has made good progress on drafting an architecture for the business layer. The team clearly explained the architecture to me. Based on the agreed-upon requirements for QoS management, I think the design is sound thus far but would benefit by having it reviewed by engineers working on the user interface and network interface layers. Do you think that this might be a good time to release the draft documents?" asks Marc.

Janet responds enthusiastically but cautions, "Yes, I have encouraged my team to start the external review process, but the team members are reluctant to have others see 'half-baked' designs. They know that the designs may change as the requirements become clearer. They also sense that their designs would be under the microscope and that the value of their participation in the project is being judged."

Marc then asks, "Why does the team call this an 'external review'? After all, we are one project team even if we are geographically separated."

"My team members feel as though they are outsiders. So, I am glad to hear you say that we are one project team. May I share your words with them?" Janet asks.

"Please do, and tell your team members that I will attend their next discussion with Toulouse," Marc thoughtfully replies. "In fact, I will be looking for their design drafts in the repository."

"By the way, how is collaboration with Montréal?" Marc inquires.

Janet more quickly replies, "Communications there are subdued and formal. When I inquired about the QoS algorithm development, Robert said that the algorithms cannot be released until the patent process is further along. We certainly understand and appreciate the value of intellectual property, but we are working for the same company. I think we signed nondisclosure forms at the beginning of our employment. I do not understand why there should be a problem with sharing the information within the company in order to accelerate product development."

"Are there regularly scheduled meetings between your site and other sites to discuss open issues and to make design decisions?" Marc probes.

Janet answers, "No. I tried to establish weekly teleconferences between the people working on the interfaces to the business layer and to the network layer, but many of the meetings were canceled because of low attendance from the Toulouse and Montréal sites. At the meetings that we had, the Toulouse and Montréal people normally explained what they decided and asked whether we had any questions. There was little to no dialogue."

Last Visit, Canada

After his meeting with Janet, Marc has some ideas about why his team is having problems with communications and collaboration. He hypothesizes that there are issues involving trust among the different sites. Hyderabad is in the middle because the software being developed there must interface with software being developed at both Toulouse and Montréal.

When Marc talks with the project members in Montréal, he commends them on their QoS research and on the innovative results that they have achieved. Marc notes that he is aware that many midnight hours have been spent getting this research into a form that can be commercialized. He explains the need to move quickly in getting the technology into the market place. He asks the team members to be catalysts in getting the interface to the network layer of the Network Manager designed. He also requests that they collaborate with the project members at other development sites who are designing the interface to the business layer.

Back in Robert's office, Marc directly asks why the Montréal team members are reluctant to release the specifications for the QoS algorithms.

Robert reports, "We want to provide Hyderabad with the specifications but are concerned that the team there will make design decisions that will need to be redone since the description of the algorithms is not yet complete."

Marc queries Robert regarding any concerns that his group may have about sharing information regarding intellectual property that is to be patented.

Robert emphatically states, "That is not the problem. We do not know what Hyderabad will do with the information. We have not had time to complete the documentation of the QoS algorithms or the instructions on how to incorporate these algorithms into the design of QoS policy management schemes."

Marc then states that there are several excellent mathematicians on the team who are located in Hyderabad. He suggests that Robert involve these people in the review of the algorithms and preparation of instructions on their use. Marc says that this would help jump-start any learning needed to incorporate the algorithms into the design of the business layer software.

Then Robert says, "It is clear that the business decisions based on governmental policies will not be firm in time to meet the scheduled product release. So, why not fix a set that will work now? Why is Toulouse waiting for the ultimate solution? Couldn't the India team design a business layer that can be evolved?"

Marc enthusiastically replied, "That is an excellent suggestion. Would you like to pitch this idea to Henri and Janet?" Marc smiles to himself. Apparently Robert was listening to Henri and Janet more closely than he originally thought.

Robert expands upon this idea, "The V Model shows that the software design is dependent on the software system requirements. The model appears to imply that specification and analysis of the software system requirements must be complete before starting the software system architecture."

Robert continues, "Diagrams of the V Model present ideas that apply in general to particular phases of software development, but they do not illustrate how the ideas can still apply when phases are overlapped. Following the V Model for software development does not preclude decomposition of the system requirements and architecture blocks. We can work on aspects of the architecture that are related to system requirements that are stable. Decomposition along with decoupling of project tasks may allow more parallelism in task scheduling."

"Yes, I have been wondering whether the tasks in the project's critical path might be further decomposed and decoupled to reduce the path length," Marc agrees. Then he adds, "On another note, I hear that the hardware manufacturing unit has held up the release of the hardware-software interface and drivers. What have you heard about this?"

"Yes they have, but this interface has not stopped our work on the architecture for the network software layer," Robert confirms.

Reflections

On his flight back to Toulouse, Marc thinks about what he has heard from the three project managers. He identifies factors that he thinks may have influenced his team's problems with communication, collaboration, and coordination. Marc records these factors in his engineering notebook and adds some notes. Next, Marc formulates questions that he needs to answer in order to better understand each factor's influence. Table 10-2 shows Marc's notes and questions for each factor. Marc suspects that the influence of each factor would differ if individual team members, rather than groups of team members, were dispersed.

Table 10–2: *Marc's Notes on Factors Influencing His Team's Communication, Collaboration, and Coordination*

Factor (Marc's Notes)	*Questions*
Trust (very influential)	How well do the team members trust that their colleagues can and will complete their project deliverables according to the quality specifications? How does the grouping of team members into distinct clusters affect the trust shown across the whole team? How else does trust impact collaboration across the team?

Table 10–2: *Marc's Notes on Factors Influencing His Team's Communication, Collaboration, and Coordination (Continued)*

Factor (Marc's Notes)	*Questions*
Cultural differences (influential)	How do the development sites differ in the following aspects that affect collaboration and coordination? • Styles of communication • Approaches to collective problem solving • Approaches to making group decisions • Communications with people at different levels of responsibility within the team and across the various locations
Time separation (influential)	How does the difference in time zones affect the ability of the team members to communicate? In what ways does the difference in time zones support productivity through opportunities for the team to work around the clock?
Communication protocols (not established)	What guidelines are established for communicating across globally distributed teams? What practical help do the guidelines provide for resolving problems that involve issues such as courteous language and timely communication?
Planning for collaboration (probably not adequate)	How well does the task breakdown and schedule do the following: • Promote working in parallel and around the clock? • Clarify the tasks and information that will need to be coordinated within given time frames? What understanding do the project members (and project managers) have about the way in which they need to collaborate to develop and deliver project deliverables on time and within budget? What plans do the project managers have for ensuring the necessary communication and collaboration?

Marc recalls the issues that were discussed among the project managers and technical leads early in the project. They had spent most of the time discussing the software system requirements and architecture. In conjunction with marketing, they had agreed upon an iterative and incremental development strategy in which the product would evolve as successive releases. The releases would build upon each other through refinement based upon user feedback and the addition of features. The development of each release would follow the typical progression of requirements, architecture and design, implementation, and test. The hardware product development managers pushed for the verification of the QoS algorithms using simulation rather than hardware prototyping. They said that the additional value provided by verification using hardware prototypes did not warrant the additional cost of building the prototypes or the increase in the time to market.

Marc reflects that they had spent little time discussing issues related specifically to the management of global software development. They had made the following decisions regarding communications across the distributed team.

Prior decisions regarding communications:

- Communications would be in English.
- The communication technologies would be Internet-based: e-mail, video conferencing, VoIP, and instant messaging.
- A central repository for sharing documents, code, and other software artifacts would be located at the Montréal site. The repository would support configuration control.
- The project managers would have Web cameras on their desks and use headsets. Each site would have a meeting room equipped with videoconferencing equipment for group discussions with the other sites.

Marc now realizes that they had not discussed nontechnical issues that affect communication and collaboration such as trust, cultural differences, time separation, and protocols for how to communicate and work together in a globally distributed environment. Everyone seemed to assume that the project task breakdown and schedule would be the primary plan for collaboration across the three sites and that the project managers would provide any other help with coordination that was needed. This assumption did not take into account other key factors that influence global communications and collaboration.

The next section in the case describes Marc's own analysis of the problems that he must solve. The section also describes Marc's rationale for the decisions that he makes to try to resolve these problems.

CASE PROBLEM

Marc knows that he must determine ways to improve the communications and collaboration across the globally distributed FibreNet Project. He thinks that tasks that require high degrees of collaboration, such as the specification of software interfaces for the layers in the Network Manager, are potential stumbling blocks in the schedule when there are breakdowns in communication and coordination. He realizes that special efforts are needed to ensure the appropriate levels of collaboration on these types of tasks.

Tasks in the critical path that are not on schedule because people do not have the information needed to work on them are alerts that there may be problems with communication or collaboration. For instance, the tasks requiring decisions about business policies dependent on government regulations and hardware interfaces are behind schedule.

Some of these tasks could be more independent than shown by the current task breakdown and schedule, thus enabling them to be done in parallel or even in different releases. For instance, the requirements based upon government policies for now could be based on what is currently known, or product features based on these requirements could be incorporated into a later product release. The critical path probably should not contain tasks related to undecided government regulations.

In addition, Marc now knows that some of the team members do not communicate well in English. A change in the language for communicating across the team is not feasible because few of the team members located in Hyderabad speak French, but each site could select team members with the best English language skills to help interpret what is being said during joint meetings across the development sites. He is concerned that the team members at each site feel isolated. He thinks that, because of lack of knowledge, they do not trust what their colleagues at other sites are likely to do or not do with incomplete specifications. How can he guide the teams at different sites to work together more effectively?

First, Marc decides that he wants to talk with the project managers together about the problems that the project team is having with communications and collaboration. Should he spend more of his travel budget for Janet and Robert to come to Toulouse for an in-person meeting, or should he try to have the discussion via teleconference? From his recent experience in visiting each development site, Marc thinks that communications would be more open and that he would be able to lead the discussion more easily if they were to meet in person. In addition, Marc would like the project managers to formulate and adopt project policies for collaboration across development sites. He wants the project managers to enforce weekly meetings between the sites whose software interfaces with each other and expects that by meeting in person they will develop a better understanding of why the team members at each site have been having difficulty in doing this.

If the project managers come to Toulouse, Marc will hold a brainstorming session that includes people from marketing as well as some key customers to discuss the idea of "fixing" the business policies to be incorporated in the first release of the FibreNet product. If he can negotiate an agreement by the project stakeholders to reduce the product scope for this release, then he could work with the project managers while they are together to adjust the task breakdown and schedule to reduce the length of the critical path. Another option would be to postpone the support for policy-based QoS management to a future release of the software.

Based upon what the project stakeholders decide, Marc would like the project managers to analyze the task breakdown and schedule to find ways to get the project back on schedule without a substantial increase in cost. Reducing the scope by postponing the QoS policy management would certainly make this easier because the new hardware would not be needed until the next release of the product. Marc knows from experience that an initial in-person session is critical to these types of negotiations.

Marc decides to bring Robert and Janet to Toulouse for four days. In the meantime, he schedules a meeting between the project stakeholders in the area. Marc is convinced that central planning with local follow-up will help solve the problem that his team is having with communications and collaboration.

In his preparation for the project manager meeting, Marc again ponders the issue of trust. He thinks that there are no immediate solutions to the problems related to trust. Marc rationalizes that trust is established over time as team members work together to accomplish project objectives. Marc decides that a first step would be to get the team members at different development sites to work together to successfully accomplish project tasks. Another step would be to find opportunities to further collaboration so that the team members get to know their colleagues at other development sites. He decides to discuss the trust issue at the meeting and to suggest that the project managers find ways for team members across the development sites to have more interactions in which they get to know each other.

RESULTS

The meetings in Toulouse were successful. The project managers and Marc had an open discussion of communication and coordination issues and were able to pinpoint factors that need to be controlled to facilitate cross-site collaboration. Later, each of the project managers discussed within their groups the importance of working closely with their colleagues at the other development sites. They explained that collaboration depends on the flow of information in both directions between the collaborators. The development sites moved forward with weekly meetings and co-designed the interfaces for the business and network layers. Robert talked with Janet about involving team members across their sites in the collaborative review of design specifications. Improvements in the detection of defects encouraged the two sites to continue this approach for component implementation as well as for the design of test plans.

The customers argued for the incorporation of a few core business policies that could be implemented using existing hardware. The first release was one month behind schedule but still on budget because of the reduction in scope related to the business policies. Communications between Toulouse and Hyderabad are still somewhat strained, but the two sites were able to complete the interface to the business layer on time with respect to a revised schedule.

Case Analysis

ANALYSIS ACTIVITY

Analysis Background

Let's use the PEAK model to analyze the problems related to communication, collaboration, coordination, and trust between the development sites because these are the ones that are particularly challenging for global software development projects. Project managers are likely to identify and understand these problems but may find it difficult to implement their solutions. You are welcome to analyze the problem of project tasks that depend upon information that is incomplete and likely to change.

(P) Problem: The FibreNet Project has encountered the following problems:

- Poor communication, collaboration, and coordination between the geographically distributed development sites has resulted in the delay of tasks involving collaboration on the design of interfaces to the business and network layers of the Network Manager system.
- Because of lack of knowledge about each other, the development sites do not trust what team members at other sites are able and likely to do. This has resulted in the reluctance to share and discuss design specifications that are not complete across the development sites. Each site is working in isolation with minimal collaboration with each other.
- Tasks dependent on decisions regarding business policies related to changing government regulations and hardware interfaces are behind schedule.

(E) Experience: From experience, Marc realizes that there needs to be a standard set of protocols for communication and collaboration that are applied across the development sites. He also knows that putting them into practice requires reinforcement by project leaders local to each site. If a particular means of communication is used most frequently, then these communication channels become critical to the successful completion of project deliverables. For instance, if two development sites coordinate primarily through weekly teleconferences, then it is imperative that these meetings result in the resolution of the critical issues. The meeting planners and moderators must keep the discussions focused on issues and decisions needed to satisfy the project objectives.

(A) Assumptions: Marc assumes that the project managers are able to provide the leadership needed to stimulate communication and collaboration between the development sites. He expects that they will lead the way in promoting collaboration on the designs of the interfaces to the business and network layers of the Network Manager software, once he has talked with them together about the issues related to managing coordination across globally distributed development sites. The options that Marc considers to solve the communication and collaboration problems are all based on his premise that the project managers will work with him to implement the solution to the problem. He also assumes that through in-person discussions the project managers are more likely to develop a camaraderie that will motivate them to work together in solving the communication, collaboration, and trust problems.

(K) Knowledge: From the comments of the project managers during the weekly status meetings and during his talks with them in person, Marc understands that the team members know very little about their colleagues at the other sites. They do not know what the other sites are likely to do with incomplete requirements or design specifications and are therefore reluctant to release specifications until they are complete. They also do not feel comfortable working with the other development sites to develop the specifications because they do not know how the people at the other sites will interpret the information that they contribute during these meetings. In particular, team members in Hyderabad feel as though their value to the project is being judged. They are cautious about contributing ideas during meetings with the other sites. Some of the sites also have difficulty understanding the English spoken by project members at another site.

Solution: Marc decides between an in-person meeting with the project managers in Toulouse and a teleconference. An in-person meeting would be more expensive but would enable Marc to more easily engage the project managers in open discussion of the communication and collaboration problem. Marc wants to impress upon the project managers the need for them to institute planned and timely meetings between the development sites whose project tasks must be accomplished through collaboration. While in Toulouse, the project managers also could help Marc negotiate a reduction in scope of the business policies to be supported in this release of the software and could work together in revising the schedule if the project stakeholders agree to some form of reduction in scope.

Assumed Risk: Marc presumes that the project managers are able and will provide the leadership needed locally to institute the improvements in communication, collaboration, and coordination. He expects the project managers to lead weekly meetings between their development sites to collaborate on project tasks. Marc can monitor the results of these meetings through his own conversations with the project managers, but there is a risk that the project managers may find that working to improve communication, collaboration, and coordination between their groups may take more time and energy than they have available.

Marc also assumes that after the in-person meeting, the project managers will be motivated to work together in promoting collaboration across their development sites. It is possible that the in-person meeting will not inspire the project managers to collaborate in solving the problem. How well the project managers work together in the future may depend more upon incentives that Marc provides as they go forward.

With an in-person meeting, the project managers will be away from their groups for about a week. Depending on the dynamics within each group and the current issues requiring input from the project manager, the absence of a project manager may negatively impact the progress that a group can make while the project manager is away.

Analysis Questions

1. Which factors that Marc listed in the case are affecting the communication, collaboration, and coordination between the global development sites? Describe the impact of each relevant factor.
2. What other factors do you think could be affecting the communication, collaboration, and coordination between the global development sites? Describe how these factors might be contributing to the problem.
3. What experiences have you had in which trust negatively or positively impacted the collaboration among team members? If you were one of the project managers, what would you decide to do to help minimize or resolve the trust issue?
4. What other solutions to the problems involving communication, collaboration, coordination, and trust would you have considered? Use the PEAK model to analyze and explain the value as well as the risks associated with each of your alternatives.

DISCUSSION

Being new to global software development, Marc was not aware that communications, collaboration, and coordination often interfere with the successful achievement of objectives by globally distributed project teams. In the project planning phase, he thought about the means of communication across geographical distances; however, he did not consider the impact that factors such as trust, cultural differences, and geographical and time separation could have on communication, collaboration, and coordination across his globally distributed team. He has learned through firsthand experience that understanding and controlling how these factors affect communication can help project managers minimize the tendency for globally distributed groups to work in isolation rather than to collaborate and coordinate their work.

Marc has decided that the solution to the problem centers on the leadership that the project managers will provide to their teams regarding communication protocols and the need for collaborative and coordinated work across the development sites. Establishing an organizational culture of open communications and collaborative thinking usually starts from the top. Marc's idea that the project managers will have to lead this effort at the development sites is reasonable since Marc cannot provide the necessary hands-on guidance at three geographically dispersed sites.

One might also expect that training may be needed in addition to leadership to help the team members understand the factors that affect communication and how to apply protocols that the project leaders or organization define for communications and collaborations. Lastly, there is the practical reality that the project managers may not have the time and energy required for effective leadership in this area. Marc should discuss these issues with the project managers at their meeting in Toulouse. The project managers should determine realistically what they can and cannot do and ask for help with training and planning for meetings across the development sites if they think that they need this.

CONCLUSIONS

Communication, collaboration, and coordination are essential elements of global software development. Factors such as trust, cultural differences, time separation, communication protocols, and planning are likely to influence communication, collaboration, and coordination more than the selected technology for communication. Project planners must make decisions about how much to spend on communication technology and travel between development sites. They should make decisions at the beginning of the project about the types and amount of communication, collaboration, and coordination that will be needed to complete the specific project deliverables. Establishing protocols for communication are useful but may require training and guidance to put them into practice.

KEY IDEAS TO REMEMBER

- Problems involving communication, collaboration, coordination, and trust are common to global software development.
- Decisions about how to communicate, collaborate, and coordinate in a global software development environment are equally, if not more, important than decisions about communication technologies.
- Planning for global software development projects should include the establishment of protocols for how to communicate, collaborate, and coordinate.

CASE STUDY

Managing Global Software Development at FibOptia

Directions

When reading this case study, focus on the intricacies of managing process and product across global software development projects. Though not necessary, you may want to read "Globally Distributed Teams: FibreNet Project" first to establish more background for this case.

Case Summary

DESCRIPTION

FibOptia is developing the second version of a network management system (FibreNet II) to provide quality-of-service (QoS) for fiber-optic communications. The development of the system software continues to be globally distributed across development centers in Canada, France, and India. Lakshmi Singh, a new senior manager of software development for FibOptia, talks extensively with Marc Delancy, the senior software manager for the first version of the FibreNet product. Marc explains the challenges that he faced in managing globally distributed software development. Lakshmi now faces decisions about how to handle communication, collaboration, and coordination for the new project and about how to standardize the development and management processes used across the team. She is also deciding whether to engage a consultant to assist her team in achieving processes that are defined, established, and subject to improvement over time, a characteristic of an organization that has achieved a Capability Maturity Model Integration Level 3 (CMMI Product Team 2002). Lakshmi's goal is for the project to serve as a test bed for improving the management of global software development at FibOptia.

CASE STUDY OBJECTIVES

After reading the case study, you will be able to do the following:

- Better understand the following issues in managing global development:
  - Managing communication, collaboration, and coordination across a distributed team
  - Managing process and product in a global development environment
  - What it means to improve the management of global software development
- Examine how global development impacts the management of project decisions with respect to scope, time, quality, and cost.
- Explain the problems that occurred in the case scenario, the causes of the problems, some plausible solutions to the problems, and ways to eliminate the problems in the future or to reduce their impact. Relate these to the decisions faced by project stakeholders.

SUBJECTS COVERED

Communication and collaboration in global software development and managing product and process in a global development environment

SETTING

The setting involves three software research and development centers of FibOptia, a company that develops network systems, applications, and services for fiber-optic communications. The centers are located in Hyderabad, India; Toulouse, France; and Montréal, Canada.

KEY CONCEPTS

- Collaboration in a global software development environment requires particular attention to communication and culture.
- Stationing representatives from remote sites with local team members promotes effective communication, cultural integration, collaboration, and coordination between globally distributed project sites.
- Managing process and product across globally distributed projects requires definitions of standard software processes and product quality requirements to be applied at all software development sites. Local control of process execution and product quality is critical.

TERMINOLOGY

Agile software development processes: A group of software development methodologies that are based on similar principles. Agile methodologies generally promote a project management process that encourages frequent inspection and adaptation; a leadership philosophy that encourages teamwork, self-organization, and accountability; a set of engineering best practices that allow for rapid delivery of high-quality software; and a business approach that aligns development with customer needs and company goals. Beck et al. (2001) describes the mission of agile software development. Fowler (2006) gives an overview of issues involving the use of agile software techniques.

Rational Unified Process (RUP): A software engineering process delivered through a Web-enabled, searchable knowledge base. The process enhances team productivity and delivers software best practices via guidelines, templates, and tool mentors for all critical software life-cycle activities. The knowledge base allows development teams to gain the full benefits of the industry-standard Unified Modeling Language (UML) (Rational 2001).

V Model of software development: A software development approach that focuses on the verification and validation (V&V) of a software system at each stage in the software development process. Two objectives to be accomplished by following a V Model is to discover defects in a software system as early as possible and to assess whether the system is usable in an operational situation (Graphical Development Process Assistant).

The Case

SCENARIO

The vice president of engineering has asked Marc Delancy, the senior software manager for the first release of the FibreNet product, to lead the planning team for the ongoing evolution of the FibreNet product. The mission of this team is to develop a strategy for the development of a FibreNet product line. One of the team's deliverables will be a release plan for FibreNet II and FibreNet III. The vice president selected Marc to head this team because of the leadership that Marc demonstrated in negotiating the change in the scope of the first release of FibreNet to better align with changing governmental regulations and market conditions.

The senior software manager for the development of FibreNet II will be Lakshmi Singh. Lakshmi has managed several global software development projects at other companies. She worked in the past on several projects with Janet Kumar, who is currently the project manager for the development of FibreNet software in Hyderabad. Lakshmi and Robert Johnson, the software project manager for the part of the FibreNet team located in Montréal, were classmates in graduate school. Lakshmi met Marc last year at a telecommunications conference and talked with him extensively about FibOptia and the FibreNet product. When they later connected via a professional networking site on the Web, they were pleasantly surprised to find that they both had worked with Janet and Robert. After being asked to head up the product planning team, Marc recommended that Lakshmi be considered for his former position of senior software manager.

Lakshmi traveled to Toulouse to talk with Marc. The purpose of their meeting was twofold:

- To identify and resolve issues related to the smooth transition from one senior manager to another
- To transfer information about the development of FibreNet I that will help Lakshmi to succeed in managing the development of FibreNet II.

Management Transition Meeting

"Welcome to Toulouse!" Marc greeted Lakshmi in his office at FibOptia-Toulouse. "How was your flight?" Marc asked.

"Not bad. The service is still good for international flights," Lakshmi replied. "I am glad that you suggested meeting on the day after my arrival. I was able to rest when I arrived and then walk around Toulouse to adjust to the time difference."

"How often did you travel to Montréal and Hyderabad for the FibreNet Project?" Lakshmi asked.

"At first, I planned to visit both sites about every three months," Marc replied. "But when I found that the development sites were having problems with communications and with the coordination of their work, I started to visit each site once a month until I could see that collaboration was improving. Another purpose of the monthly visits was to boost the team morale at each site," Marc explained.

"Ah, yes. I too have seen that communication and collaboration can be difficult for software development teams," Lakshmi commiserated. "You must have found some ways to get around these problems. Your team delivered a product that is doing well in the market. What magical wand did you wave to solve these problems?"

"Nothing magical, I assure you. Here is a list of my decisions that I think helped to solve the problems," Marc replied and then handed Lakshmi the list.

"After each decision, I listed the results of implementing the decision," Marc explained. See Table 10-3.

Table 10–3: *Marc's List of Decisions and Results*

Decision/ Result (D/R)	*Description of Decision or Result*
D	*To conduct an in-person meeting, rather than a teleconference, between the software project managers (from the different development sites) to work on ways to solve problems*
R	Project managers talked openly and got to know each better.
R	Project managers became aware of what the team members at the different sites were thinking about their interactions with team members from other sites.
R	After reviewing the project schedule together, the project managers better understood how the communication problems were negatively impacting the ability of the team to accomplish tasks that required collaboration.
R	Project managers could see that I was serious about changing the collaboration environment and that I would commit time and budget to provide training or whatever was needed to get the different sites to work together more effectively.
D	*To require the project managers to establish weekly meetings between development sites that needed to collaborate on project tasks and to report the status of tasks requiring collaboration.*
R	Project managers held these meetings and reported the status of the collaboration efforts at the weekly project manager meeting with me.

Table 10–3: *Marc's List of Decisions and Results (Continued)*

Decision/ Result (D/R)	*Description of Decision or Result*
R	All of the project managers delegated the planning of these meetings to team leads but participated in most of the meetings.
R	The weekly meetings between sites stimulated other regular meetings between team members across sites who needed to work together on the details of specific tasks.
D	*To require project managers to make certain that people from different development sites who were working on related project deliverables were involved in reviewing each other's deliverables.*
R	The project managers explained the need for integrated review teams and asked for volunteers to serve on these teams. They made it clear that contributing in a meaningful way to the review of the software artifacts being developed by other sites was mandatory for promotion.
R	When the cross-site reviews improved the team's ability to detect defects, more people became interested in participating. Some people are still reluctant to participate.

"It looks as though you made a lot of progress in a short time," observed Lakshmi.

"Communication, collaboration, and coordination across the development sites had to improve, or we would not have been able to finish the product in time to satisfy the window of market opportunity. Entrepreneurs say that necessity breeds opportunity. In our case, I would say that necessity forced action," Marc replied.

"Possibly, we can think of collaboration as an opportunity for increased innovation. What do you think that we need to improve in order to produce FibreNet II on time, within budget, and with the desired quality? In fact, what do we need to do better to develop a successful FibreNet product line?" Lakshmi asked.

"That is an insightful question," Marc replied. He thought a moment and then said, "Let me give this some thought, and I will provide you later with more detail. But for now, how about if we discuss some areas that I have already considered?" Marc then pulled out his engineering notebook.

"This sounds good. I welcome your suggestions." Lakshmi agreed.

"Effective communication and coordination across globally distributed teams requires local leadership, at least until the team develops its own culture of collaboration. The project managers have talked with their groups and have used the project tasks to motivate planned collaborations. But to establish an effective global development organization that can roll out product innovations in a timely way, we need some process improvements and changes in our development culture," Marc explained.

"Trust is an ongoing issue. The team members at each site still do not know each other very well. The Hyderabad team members continue to listen but not speak much during their cross-site meetings," Marc said.

"This may be because of differences in how authority is handled at the various development sites. The Hyderabad team members may think that their responsibility is to gather information and convey this information to their project leads or manager. They may not think that they have the authority to present their own ideas before having these ideas approved by their supervisors. Possibly the software engineers in Toulouse or Montréal feel more empowered to propose ideas without having to have them approved first," Lakshmi explained.

"In other words, cultural differences with respect to dialogue and decision making may be affecting the way in which the team members across sites collaborate," Marc summarized.

"Exactly," Lakshmi confirmed. "In this particular case, the issue is probably not one of trust. It seems as though our team could use some training to understand cultural differences that affect their ability to dialogue and solve problems in a global work environment." Marc smiled when Lakshmi said "our team."

After observing a few of the cross-site meetings, I thought that "mixing up" the team would help promote understanding of how team members at other sites work and assist with communication during the group meetings. For example, we could bring some people from India to Canada and France, and so forth. Of course, housing people away from their homes for the duration of a project can be expensive," Marc commented.

"Maybe we could place a liaison for each site at every other site. In other words, each development site would host one visitor from each other site or a total of two for the duration of the project," Lakshmi reflected.

"At a minimum, there could be exchanges between Hyderabad and Montréal as well as Hyderabad and Toulouse since the Hyderabad team members need to work on tasks that require high degrees of communication with both sites. This plan would involve four rather than six temporary relocations of staff," Marc replied.

"What software development processes are being used at each site?" Lakshmi asked.

"At the beginning of the FibreNet Project, we decided to follow a process involving incremental release of the product with iterative development for those parts of the software that we could obtain feedback from users. All of the sites have used the V Model to guide test planning, development, and execution. Different interpretations of this model across the sites did cause some coordination problems," Marc replied.

"How did the interpretations differ, and what problems did this cause?" Lakshmi inquired.

"Hyderabad engineers thought that they should not have the design specification for the business layer software reviewed by the other sites until it was complete. Also, they were reluctant to work collaboratively on the interfaces to their software because there were decisions to be made regarding the required QoS service policies. The Montréal engineers working on the QoS algorithms were also reluctant to release the algorithms without full documentation because they were concerned that the software engineers working on the business layer software might not know how to interpret the algorithms. There seemed to be a general concern all around that partially complete project deliverables should not be reviewed, released, or even discussed across the development sites until they were complete, including the documentation," Marc explained.

"How does this reluctance to share partially complete information relate to differing interpretations of the V Model?" Lakshmi inquired.

"In the case of Hyderabad, the software engineers interpreted the blocks in the diagram literally. When the model showed that the software system requirements are done before the software architectural design, they interpreted this to mean that all the requirements were to be specified and released before the architectural design could be reviewed outside the local group. In Montréal, the concern was simply that releasing the QoS algorithms before they were fully documented might lead to misinterpretation. In both situations, the team members did not see the value of reviewing those parts of a specification that are complete and of discussing the parts that are still evolving," Marc replied.

"Are any of the development sites using the Rational Unified Process or Agile techniques?" Lakshmi asked.

"Yes, the user interface group in Toulouse has applied both of these techniques. These software engineers work directly with customers on the design of the user interface. They have found that use cases are helpful tools for describing requirements in a way that can be discussed with customers. They are comfortable with creating mock-ups of user interfaces that can be quickly modified in response to customer feedback," Marc explained.

"How familiar are the team members at each site with the processes being used at the other sites?" Lakshmi probed.

"Other than the processes that were outlined in the project plans, such as iterative development and incremental release, no processes have been documented for use across the software development sites," replied Marc.

"I am interested in helping FibOptia standardize and fine-tune the software product development and project management processes that it uses at the different development sites. FibOptia has made significant investments of capital to establish the three research and development sites, and I think global software development is here to stay. Therefore, we need to understand how to manage global software development effectively. Considering the speed at which new technologies emerge, effective management of global product development may differentiate us from other companies that develop telecommunications products and services," Lakshmi commented.

"You might start by identifying and documenting the processes that were used to develop the first release of the FibreNet product and then continue with the FibreNet II project," Marc suggested.

"That is exactly what I was thinking. That engineering notebook of yours will come in handy," Lakshmi agreed.

"You may want to think about whether process formalization is a good idea for FibOptia at this stage in its organizational development. The people involved in managing product development at each site have not yet standardized the processes that they use for product development. Standardization across sites will be even more challenging," Marc cautioned.

"That is a good point. As you said, we could start with the identification and documentation of the processes being used at each site. Engineers and managers need to know what their colleagues are doing both locally and globally," Lakshmi replied.

"This could require significant time of the people who participate in the investigation. I found that planning and making collaboration happen required effort and therefore time. People are more likely to commit their time if the effort appears as tasks in the project schedule or as other organizationally recognized tasks for which they can receive credit. My advice is that you get buy-in for the process investigation from the vice president of engineering as well as budget to pay for the time that people spend on this," Marc advised.

"Are you interested in submitting a proposal for this investigation with me? We could jointly propose this to the vice president of engineering to get some funds to pay for help that we would need from FibOptia staff and possibly some external consulting," Lakshmi queried.

"Yes, I am interested in helping to get this effort off the ground; but with my new role as the lead for the FibreNet product-line strategy, I may not be able to commit much time to the investigation. From my experience with the first release of FibreNet, I know that you will be very busy getting the next release out the door. You will need to decide how much time that you think you could commit to this investigation. I recommend that you start small first. Possibly begin with one site such as Hyderabad where you will probably spend most your time, with one process area such as software development, and with only a few project managers and team leads. After managing the software development for a successful product release, you will have more leverage with upper-level management. By then, you will know people who may be willing to help with the investigation," Marc suggested and then added, "Also, I should have my team organized and the development of the strategy for developing the FibreNet product line well underway. I would probably be able to provide more help at that time. I am going to be traveling frequently between Toulouse and Montréal during the next six months."

"During my interview with the vice president of engineering, he stated his expectation that the senior manager for software development will lead the way in standardizing the software processes being used across the development sites. He said that you had enlightened upper-level management about the need to pay attention to communication, collaboration, and coordination issues across the development sites. The upper-level management is now interested in knowing how well we coordinate the way in which we do development across the sites. I think that I am expected to shed some light on this issue while being responsible for the development of the software for FibreNet II," Lakshmi explained.

"I see . . . ," Marc slowly replied.

No more was said about the process investigation issue. Marc and Lakshmi formulated a plan by which Marc would introduce Lakshmi at each of the development sites. They scheduled a regular meeting between the two of them to work on issues related to the requirements for FibreNet II. Marc reassured Lakshmi that he would help smooth the transition to a new senior software manager. Before Lakshmi flew back to India, Marc invited Lakshmi to dinner. Her comment about the vice president's expectations had weighed on his mind, and he wanted to reassure her that he would provide whatever help that he could.

Over dinner, Marc told Lakshmi that he would be glad to talk with her about the decisions that she would need to make to handle this issue as well as those that she would need to make in planning for the next release of FibreNet. He explained that he found that it sometimes helped to have another manager's viewpoint when evaluating decisions.

Reflection on Decisions to Be Made

Back in her new office at the FibOptia site in Hyderabad, Lakshmi reflected on what she had learned from Marc in Toulouse. She will soon be working with other project stakeholders on the schedule and budget for the development of software for the FibreNet II product. To effectively manage this global software effort, she will need to make some decisions to resolve issues that she knows exist.

One ongoing issue has been to improve the communications, collaboration, and coordination across the globally distributed development sites. Trust still seems to be an influential factor. What can Lakshmi do to help resolve or alleviate the impact of this issue for the development of the FibreNet II software? How will her choices affect the budget and schedule?

She brainstormed some ways to help improve communications, collaboration, and coordination across the development sites:

- Exchange project members between sites for the project duration. For example, relocate one project member from Montréal and one from Toulouse to India to help the Hyderabad team members work with the remote sites. Likewise, two team members from India could be relocated to Montréal and Toulouse, respectively. How many relocations would be most effective? Should there be at least one team member from each remote site at each local site (six relocations), or would some other arrangement be most effective from communications/collaboration and budget points of view?

- Eliminate any references to separate teams. The title for the group of staff who work on the FibreNet product could be the FibreNet Group or FibreNet Project for the current release. The names of the staff working in a particular location could be FibreNet Project, Hyderabad; FibreNet Project, Montréal; and FibreNet Project, Toulouse. What would need to be done to institutionalize this formally (upper-level management agreement, letterheads, and so on) as well as informally (in conversation)? What are the associated costs?
- Require project managers to incorporate team members who specify requirements, architecture, and design to participate in the review of acceptance, system, and component test plans and writers of test plans to participate in the review of specifications for requirements, architecture, and component design. How would this decision affect the task breakdown, schedule, and budget?

Which of these solutions, if any, should she select? Are there other ways to resolve this issue? Lakshmi pondered these questions and realized that she may need more information to answer them. Her mind drifted to the issue of the vice president of engineering's expectation that she help standardize the software processes being used across the development sites. What did he expect her to do? What could she realistically do while managing the development of the software for FibreNet II. She faces multiple decisions that need to be made soon.

CASE PROBLEM

Lakshmi Singh will be the new senior software manager for the FibreNet II product development. She recognizes that communications, collaboration, and coordination are not working as well as they need across the globally distributed development sites to ensure the development of products on time, within budget, and with the required levels of quality. There is an ongoing issue of trust among the team members at different development sites. The vice president of engineering has assigned Lakshmi the responsibility for leading the standardization of software processes used across the different development sites. He expects that she will do this while managing the software development for FibreNet II.

Case Analysis

ANALYSIS ACTIVITY

Analysis Questions

1. Use the PEAK model to evaluate each of the ways that Lakshmi has considered in order to help improve communications, collaboration, and coordination across the global development sites.

   For each way that Lakshmi has considered, do the following:

- Describe any information that you think is missing to be able to fully evaluate it using the PEAK model.
- List any of assumptions that you think Lakshmi has about its usefulness.
- What are the risks, if any, associated with each approach?
- Decide whether you would apply it for the FibreNet II Project. Use your application of the PEAK model to explain your rationale for each decision.

For questions 2 and 3, suppose that Lakshmi decides to relocate team members as liaisons to assist with communication and collaboration at remote sites.

2. Which arrangement of relocations would you consider and why? (For example, each site would host precisely one team member from each of the other sites.) Discuss the pros/cons of each arrangement in terms of trade-offs involving schedule, budget, product quality, and any other issues that you think are important.
3. Which arrangement would you ultimately select?
   - Explain the rationale for your decision.
   - Discuss other information that you would like to have had (but did not) before making this decision.
   - List any assumptions associated with your decision.
   - Describe any risks associated with your decision.
4. Discuss any other ways that you think might help to improve communication, collaboration, and coordination across the global development sites.
5. If you were in Lakshmi's position, how would you handle the vice president's statement that he expects Lakshmi to lead the standardization of software processes across the development sites?
   - Formulate your ideas in terms of problem statements with alternative solutions.
   - Use the PEAK model to evaluate each alternative solution.
6. Describe any other problems or decisions specifically related to global software development, rather than to software development in general, that you think Lakshmi will face in the FibreNet II Project.

10.4 Summary

Global software development is a ubiquitous and critical element of the global computer, software, and information technology industries. Managers worldwide face decisions that are more complex because of the impact that global software development has on communication, collaboration, and coordination across globally distributed project teams. Factors such as cultural differences, geographical and time separation, trust, and the limits of communication technologies affect the ability of a global project team to conduct the dialogue needed to achieve project objectives in a collaborative way. Failure to plan for communication, collaboration, and coordination at the beginning of a project and then to follow the agreed-upon protocols for how these should be accomplished frequently results in projects in which team members who are geographically separated have problems working and making decisions together on project tasks.

The case studies in this chapter focused on project management issues and decisions that affect global software development. The first case study, "Globally Distributed Team: FibreNet Project," highlighted issues of communication, collaboration, and trust for a globally distributed team. More specifically, the case study revealed challenges associated with sharing information and making software decisions in a global development environment. The second case study, "Managing Global Software Development at FibOptia," focused on problems and decisions regarding how to manage process, product quality, and cost in a global software development environment. The senior software manager in this case also needed to decide how to establish trust among a globally distributed team.

Managing global software development starts with an evaluation of decisions regarding how to handle communication, collaboration, and coordination within a global environment.

References

Advanced Development Methods, Inc. What is scrum? www.controlchaos.com/about/ (accessed May 31, 2009).

Ågerfalk, P. J. and B. Fitzgerald. 2006. Flexible and distributed software processes: Old petunias in new bowls. *Communications of the ACM* 49(10): 26–34.

Albrecht, A. J. 1979. Measuring application development productivity. *Proceedings of the Joint SHARE, GUIDE, and IBM Application Development Symposium*, pp. 83–92, Oct. 14–17, Monterey, CA.

Alessandra, Tony and Michael J. O'Connor. 1998. *The platinum rule: Discover the four basic business personalities and how they can lead you to success*. New York: Hachette Book Group-Grand Central Publishing.

ARCEP: L'Autorité de Régulation des Communications Régulation des Communications Électroniques et des Postes. www.arcep.fr/ (accessed May 22, 2009). Use Google to translate the page.

Aronoff, Stan. 1989. *Geographic information systems: A management perspective*. Ottawa, Canada: WDL Publications.

ASME. What's your communication style? www.asme.org/Jobs/Manage/Whats_Communication_Style.cfm (accessed June 2, 2009).

Atkins, D., M. Handel, J. Herbsleb, A. Mockus, D. Perry, and G. Wills. 2001. Global software development: The Bell Labs collaboratory. *Proceedings of the 23rd IEEE International Conference on Software Engineering*, p. 0681b, May 12–19, Toronto, Canada. www.cs.uoregon.edu/~datkins/papers/icse-collab.pdf (accessed May 22, 2009).

Barbacci, M., M.H. Klein, T.A. Longstaff, and C.B. Weinstock. 1995. *Quality attributes*. Technical Report CMU/SEI-95-TR-021. Pittsburgh, PA: Software Engineering Institute, Carnegie Mellon University.

Baritault, Alain. 2009. Stimulating FTTH investments in France. *MuniWireless*, April 9. www.muniwireless.com/2009/04/09/stimulating-ftth-investments-in-france/ (accessed May 22, 2009).

Bar-On, D. and S. Tyszberowicz. 2007. Derived requirements generation: The DRAS methodology. *Proceedings of the IEEE International Conference on Software-Science, Technology, and Engineering*, pp. 116–126, Oct. 30–31, Herzlia, Israel.

Barry, E., C. Kemerer, and S. Slaughter. 2006. Environmental volatility, development decisions, and software volatility: A longitudinal analysis. *Management Science* 52(3): 448–464.

Bass, L., M. Klein, and G. Moreno. 2001. *Applicability of general scenarios to the architecture tradeoff analysis method*. Technical Report CMU/SEI-2001-TR-014. Pittsburgh, PA: Software Engineering Institute, Carnegie Mellon University.

Beck, Kent. 1999. *Extreme programming explained: Embrace change*. Boston: Addison-Wesley.

Beck, Kent, et al. 2001. Manifesto for agile software development. http://agilemanifesto.org/ (accessed May 22, 2009).

Bennatan, E.M. 2000. *On time within budget: Software project management practices and techniques*, 3rd ed. Hoboken, NJ: John Wiley & Sons.

Boehm, Barry W., Chris Abts, A. Winsor Brown, Sunita Chulani, Bradford K. Clark, Ellis Horowitz, Ray Madachy, Donald J. Reifer, and Bert Steece. 2000. *Software cost estimation with Cococmo II*. Upper Saddle River, NJ: Prentice Hall.

Borck, James R. 2006. The long road to RFID interoperability: The Gen2 standard means vendors and consumers finally have a common platform. *InfoWorld*, April 13. www.infoworld.com/t/platforms/long-road-rfid-interoperability-821 (accessed May 22, 2009).

Borland Software Corporation. 2006. *Effective requirements definition and management: Improves systems and communication*. Borland White Paper. www.borland.com/resources/en/pdf/solutions/rdm_whitepaper.pdf (accessed May 22, 2009).

Bourgault, M., N. Drouin, and E. Hamil. 2008. Decision making within distributed project teams: An exploration of formalization and autonomy as determinants of success. *Project Management Journal* (Special PMI Research Conference Ed.) 39(S1): S97-S100.

Brett, Jeanne M. 2001. *Negotiating globally: How to negotiate deals, resolve disputes, and make decisions across cultural boundaries*. San Francisco: Jossey-Bass.

British National Science Center (BNSC). 2008. Second Galileo satellite launched successfully, Ref. No. 03/08. www.bnsc.gov.uk/7235.aspx (accessed June 3, 2009).

Brooks, Frederick P. 1995. *The mythical man-month: Essays on software engineering*, anniversary ed. Reading, MA: Addison-Wesley.

BusinessDictionary.com. Definition of product management. www.businessdictionary.com/definition/product-management.html (accessed May 22, 2009).

Cao, L. and B. Ramesh. 2008. Agile requirements engineering practices: An empirical study. *IEEE Software* 25(1): 60–67.

Capretz, L. F. 2003. Personality types in software engineering. *International Journal of Human-Computer Studies* 58(2): 207–214.

Carmel, Erran. 1999. *Global software teams: Collaborating across borders and time zones.* Upper Saddle River, NJ: Prentice Hall.

Carmel, Erran and Paul Tjia. 2005. *Offshoring information technology: Sourcing and outsourcing to a global workforce.* Cambridge, UK: Cambridge University Press.

Carver, Charles S. and Michael F. Scheier. 2003. *Perspectives on personality*, 5th ed. Boston: Allyn & Bacon.

Carver, J.C., N. Naqappan, and A. Page. 2008. The impact of educational background on the effectiveness of requirements inspections: An empirical study. *IEEE Transactions on Software Engineering* 34(6): 800–812.

CBS Studios Inc. *Star Trek Voyager*. www.startrek.com/startrek/view/series/VOY/character/1112409.html (accessed May 22, 2009).

Cerf, V. G. and R.E. Kahn. 1974. A protocol for packet network intercommunication. *IEEE Transactions on Communications* 22(5): 637–648.

Ceschi, M., A. Sillitti, G. Succi, and S. De Panfilis. 2005. Project management in plan-based and agile companies. *IEEE Software* 22(3): 21–27.

ChangingMinds.org. Motivation theories. http://changingminds.org/explanations/theories/a_motivation.htm (accessed June 1, 2009).

Chapman, Chris and Stephen Ward. 2002. *Managing project risk and uncertainty: A constructively simple approach to decision making*. Hoboken, NJ: John Wiley & Sons.

Cleland, David and Lewis Ireland. 2007. *Project manager's handbook: Applying best practices across global industries*. New York: McGraw-Hill Professional.

Clements, Paul and Linda Northrop. 2002. *Software product lines: Practices and patterns.* Boston: Addison-Wesley.

CMMI Product Team. 2002. *Capability Maturity Model® Integration (CMMI℠), version 1.1.* Technical Report CMU/SEI-2002-TR-011. Pittsburgh, PA: Software Engineering Institute, Carnegie Mellon University.

Cohn, Mike. 2004. *User stories applied: For agile software development*. Boston: Addison-Wesley.

Ibid. 2006. *Agile estimating and planning*. Upper Saddle River, NJ: Prentice Hall.

Commander, Simon. 2005. *The software industry in emerging markets*. Cheltenham, UK: Edward Elgar Publishing.

Communications of the ACM 49(10), Oct. 2006. http://cacm.acm.org/magazines (accessed May 22, 2009).

Cox, K., J.G. Hall, and L. Rapanotti. 2005. A roadmap of problem frames research. *Information and Software Technology*, Special Issue on Problem Frames, eds. K. Cox and J. Hall, 47(14): 891–902.

Crosby, P.B. 1995. *Quality is still free: Making quality certain in uncertain times*, 2nd rev. ed. New York: McGraw-Hill.

Damian, D. 2007. Stakeholders in global requirements engineering: Lessons learned from practice. *IEEE Software* 24(2): 21–27.

Damian, D. and J. Chisan. 2006. An empirical study of the complex relationship between requirements engineering processes and other processes that lead to payoffs in productivity, quality, and risk management. *IEEE Transactions on Software Engineering* 32(7): 433–453.

Deleris, L.A., S. Bagchi, S. Kapoor, K. Katircioglu, R. Lam, and S. Buckley. 2007. Simulation of adaptive project management analytics. *Proceedings of the 39th Conference on Winter Simulation: 40 years! The best is yet to come*, pp. 2234–2240, Dec. 9–12, Washington, D.C.

DeMarco, Tom. 1982. *Controlling software projects: Management, measurement, and estimates*. Upper Saddle River, NJ: Prentice Hall.

Desouza, K.C. and J.R. Evaristo. 2004. Managing knowledge in distributed projects. *Communications of the ACM* 47(4): 87–91.

Dictionary.net. Definition of interaction. www.dictionary.net/interaction (accessed June 3, 2009).

Dillon, R.L. and C.H. Tinsley. 2008. How near-misses influence decision making under risk: A missed opportunity for learning. *Management Science* 54(8): 1425–1440.

Ebert, C. and J. De Man. 2005. Requirements uncertainty: Influencing factors and concrete improvements. *Proceedings of the 27th International Conference on Software Engineering*, pp. 553–560, St. Louis, MO.

Ebert, C. and A. Hickey. 2008. Requirements engineering—industry needs. *Proceedings of the 16th IEEE International Conference on Requirements Engineering*, p. 298, Sept. 8–12, Catalunya, Spain.

El-Azazy, Saad. *Seismic bridge design improvements through research implementation.* Sacramento, CA: California Department of Transportation (Caltrans). www.dot.ca.gov/hq/esc/earthquake_engineering/stap/Bridge_Design_Improvements_.pdf (accessed May 22, 2009).

Espinosa, J.A., S.A. Slaughter, R.E. Kraut, and J.D. Herbsleb. 2007. Familiarity, complexity, and team performance in geographically distributed software development. *Organization Science* 18(4): 613–630.

Finkenzeller, Klaus. 2003. *RFID handbook: Fundamentals and applications in contactless smart cards and identification*, 2nd ed. Hoboken, NJ: John Wiley & Sons.

Fowler, Martin. 2006. Using an agile software process with offshore development. www.martinfowler.com/articles/agileOffshore.html (accessed May 22, 2009).

Garfinkel, Simon and Beth Rosenberg. 2006. *RFID: Applications, security, and privacy.* Boston: Addison-Wesley.

Giesen, J. and A. Volker. 2002. Requirements interdependencies and stakeholders preferences. *Proceedings of the IEEE Joint Conference on Requirements Engineering*, pp. 206–209, Sept. 9–13.

Gluch, D. 1994. *A construct for describing software development risks.* Technical Report CMU/SEI-94-TR-014 Pittsburgh, PA: Software Engineering Institute, Carnegie Mellon University.

Goldratt, Eliyahu M. and Jeff Cox. 1992. *The goal: A process of ongoing improvement*, 2nd rev. ed. Great Barrington, MA: North River Press.

Graphical Development Process Assistant (GDPA Online). V Model of development. www.informatik.uni-bremen.de/gdpa/def/def_v/V_MODEL.htm (accessed May 22, 2009).

Gupta, Amar. 2009. Deriving mutual benefits from offshore outsourcing. *Communications of the ACM* 52(6): 122–126.

Gutierrez, E., O. Sandstrom, J. Janhager, and S. Ritzen. 2008. Innovation and decision making: Understanding selection and prioritization of development projects. *Proceedings of the 4th IEEE International Conference on Management of Innovation and Technology*, pp. 333–338, Sept. 21–24, Bangkok.

Hofstede, Geert. Cultural dimensions. www.geert-hofstede.com/ (accessed June 2, 2009).

Hull, Elizabeth, Kenneth Jackson, and Jeremy Dick. 2005. *Requirements engineering*, 2nd ed. London: Springer.

Humphrey, Watts S. 1989. *Managing the software process*. Reading, MA: Addison-Wesley.

Ibid. 2000. *Introduction to the Team Software Process*^{SM}. Boston: Addison-Wesley.

Hussey, James M. and Steven E. Hall. 2007. *Managing global development risk*. Boca Raton, FL: Auerbach Publications.

IBM Systems Journal: Model-Driven Software Development, 45(3), 2006. www.research.ibm.com/journal/sj45-3.html (accessed June 17, 2009).

IEEE Std. 1058-1998. *IEEE standard for software project management plans*.

IEEE Std. 830-1998. *IEEE recommended practice for software requirements specification*.

IEEE Std.1061-1998. *IEEE standard for a software quality metrics methodology – description*.

IMDb.com. *Groundhog Day*. www.imdb.com/title/tt0107048/ (accessed May 22, 2009).

Ibid. Memorable quotes for *Blazing Saddles*. www.imdb.com/title/tt0071230/quotes (accessed May 22, 2009).

Ibid. Memorable quotes for *Casablanca*. www.imdb.com/title/tt0034583/quotes (accessed May 22, 2009).

ISO/IEC Std. 9126-1:2001. *Software engineering—product quality—part 1: quality model*.

Jackson, Michael. 2001. *Problem frames: Analyzing and structuring software development problems*. Boston: Addison-Wesley.

Ibid. 2005. Problem frames and software engineering. *Information and Software Technology*, Special Issue on Problem Frames, eds. K. Cox and J. Hall, 47(14): 903–912.

Jackson, M. and D. Jackson. 2006. Separating concerns in requirements analysis: An example. *Springer Lecture Notes in Computer Science (LNCS)*, Special Issue on the *Proceedings of the Workshop on the Rigorous Engineering of Fault-Tolerant Systems (REFT) 2005*, eds. M. Butler, C. Jones, A. Romanovsky, and E. Troubitsyna, 4157: 210–225.

Jacobson, Ivar. 1992. *Object-oriented software engineering: A use case driven approach*. Reading, MA: Addison-Wesley.

Jensen, David G. Communication styles. http://searchmastersinternational.com/web/us/smi/en/pages/careers_career_dev_commun_styles.html (accessed June 2, 2009).

Johnson, Jim. 2006. *My life is a failure: 100 things you should know to be a better project leader*. Boston: The Standish Group.

Jones, T.O. and W.E. Sasser, Jr. 1995. Why satisfied customers defect. *Harvard Business Review*, Nov.–Dec.

Karolak, Dale W. 1998. *Global software development: Managing virtual teams and environments*. Hoboken, NJ: John Wiley & Sons.

Klein, Mark, Thomas Roya, Thomas Ralya, Bill Pollak, Ray Obenza, and Michael González Harbour. 1993. *A practitioners' handbook for real-time analysis: Guide to rate monotonic analysis for real-time systems*. Boston: Kluwer Academic Publishers.

Krishnan, V. and K. Ulrich. 2001. Product development decisions: A review of the literature. *Management Sciences* 47(1): 1–21.

Kulak, Daryl and Eamonn Guiney. 2004. *Use cases: Requirements in context*, 2nd ed. Boston: Addison-Wesley.

Larman, C. and V.R. Basili. 2003. Iterative and incremental development: A brief history. *Computer* 36(6): 47–56.

Lee, G., W. Delone, and J. A. Espinosa. 2006. Ambidextrous coping strategies in globally distributed software development projects. *Communications of the ACM* 49(10): 35–46.

Leopold, George. 2000. U.S. ends degrading of GPS signals. *EE Times*, May 1. www.eetimes.com/story/OEG20000501S0065 (accessed May 22, 2009).

Lomer, Malcolm. 2007. Designing for a dual Galileo-based GPS system. *EE Times*, June 25. www.eetimes.com/showArticle.jhtml;jsessionid=0SC5IC2UFLXG2QSNDLRCKH0CJUNN2JVN?articleID=199905165 (accessed May 22, 2009).

Mangione, Carmine. 2003. Software project failure: The reasons, the costs. *CIO Update*, Jan. 3. www.cioupdate.com/reports/article.php/1563701/Software-Project-Failure-The-Reasons-The-Costs.htm (accessed June 3, 2009).

McConnell, Steve. 1997. *Software project survival guide: How to be sure your first important project isn't your last*. Redmond, WA: Microsoft Press.

Ibid. 2006. *Software estimation: Demystifying the black art*. Redmond, WA: Microsoft Press.

McManus, J. 2004. A stakeholder perspective within software engineering projects. *Proceedings of the IEEE International Engineering Management Conference,* 2:880-884, Oct. 18–21, Singapore.

McManus, John and Trevor Wood-Harper. 2008. A study in project failure. www.bcs.org/server.php?show=ConWebDoc.19584 (accessed June 3, 2009).

Messerschmitt, D.G. 2004. Marketplace issues in software planning and design. *IEEE Software* 21(3): 62–70.

Microsoft Corporation. 2007. Enabling "people-ready processes" through business process management. www.microsoft.com/downloads/details.aspx?displaylang=en&FamilyID=b047729c-4e94-40b1-ac55-ab728ba69921 (accessed May 22, 2009).

Mojtahedi, S.M.H., S.M. Mousavi, and A. Makoui. 2008. Risk identification and analysis concurrently: Group decision making approach. *Proceedings of the 4th IEEE International Conference on Management of Innovation and Technology,* pp. 299–304, Sept. 21–24, Bangkok.

Muñoz-Avila, H. and M.T. Cox. 2008. Case-based plan adaptation: An analysis and review. *IEEE Intelligent Systems* 23(4): 1541–1672.

National Institute of Standards and Technology (NIST). 2005. *Security considerations for voice over IP systems,* Special Publication 800–58. http://csrc.nist.gov/publications/nistpubs/800-58/SP800-58-final.pdf (accessed May 22, 2009).

National Park Service (US Dept. of the Interior). Glossary of common GPS terms. www.nps.gov/gis/gps/glossary.htm (accessed May 22, 2009).

Object Management Group (OMG). UML® resource page. www.uml.org/ (accessed June 17, 2009).

OGC (The U.K. Office of Government Commerce). PRINCE2. www.ogc.gov.uk/methods_prince_2__overview.asp (accessed May 22, 2009).

Overby, Stephanie. 2008. Remote controlled. *CIO,* April 1.

PDMA: Product Development and Management Association. 2006. The PDMA glossary for new product development. www.pdma.org/npd_glossary.cfm (accessed May 22, 2009).

Pfleeger, Shari L. and Atlee, Joanne M. 2006. *Software engineering theory and practice,* 3rd ed. Upper Saddle River, N.J.: Prentice Hall.

Pikkarainen, M., J. Haikara, O. Salo, P. Abrahamsson, and J. Still. 2008. The impact of agile practices on communication in software development. *Empirical Software Engineering* 13(3): 303–337.

Pollack-Johnson, B. and M. J. Liberatore. 2006. Incorporating quality considerations into project time/cost tradeoff analysis and decision making. *IEEE Transactions on Engineering Management* 53(4): 534–542.

Postel, J. 1980. *IETF RFC 768: User Datagram Protocol.* www.rfc-archive.org/getrfc.php?rfc=768 (accessed May 31, 2009).

Pressman, Roger S. 2004. *Software engineering: A practitioner's approach*, 6th ed. New York: McGraw-Hill Science/Engineering/Math.

Princeton University. WordNet search—3.0. http://wordnetweb.princeton.edu/perl/webwn?s=estimate (accessed May 22, 2009).

Proceedings of the IEEE International Conference on RFID. http://ieeexplore.ieee.org/xpl/conhome.jsp?punumber=1001363 (accessed May 22, 2009).

Raja, U.A. 2009. Empirical studies of requirements validation techniques. *Proceedings of the 2nd International Conference on Computer, Control and Communications*, pp. 1–9, Feb. 17–28, Karachi, Pakistan.

Ramasubbu, N., S. Mithas, M.S. Krishan, and C. Kemerer. 2008. Work dispersion, process-based learning, and offshore software development performance. *MIS Quarterly* 32(2): 437–458.

Rational. 2001. *Rational Unified Process: Best practices for software development teams.* Rational Software White Paper TP026B, Rev. Nov. 1. www.ibm.com/developerworks/rational/library/content/03July/1000/1251/1251_bestpractices_TP026B.pdf (accessed May 22, 2009).

Reinhold, R. *Articles on MBTI® applications & personality types: Practical business applications of the MBTI Myers-Briggs personality type model.* www.personalitypathways.com/article/applications.html (accessed June 3, 2009).

RFID Journal. Glossary of RFID terms. www.rfidjournal.com/article/glossary/3 (accessed May 22, 2009).

Roberts, C.J., M.G. Richards, A.M. Ross, D.H. Rhodes, and D.E. Hastings. 2009. Scenario planning in dynamic multi-attribute tradespace exploration. *Proceedings of the 3rd Annual IEEE Systems Conference*, pp. 366–371, Mar. 23–26, Vancouver, B.C.

Rönkkö, K., Y. Dittrich, and D. Randall. 2005. When plans do not work out: How plans are used in software development projects. *Computer Supported Cooperative Work* 14(5): 433–468.

Rovira, Alex and Fernandos Trias de Bes. 2004. Winners make their own good luck. *BusinessWeek*, July 26. www.businessweek.com/smallbiz/content/jul2004/sb20040726_7503_sb022.htm (accessed May 22, 2009).

Royce, W.W. 1970. Managing the development of large software systems. *Proceedings of IEEE WESCON*, pp. 1–9, Aug., Monterey, CA.

Ibid. 1987. Managing the development of large software systems: Concepts and techniques. *Proceedings of the 9th International Conference on Software Engineering*, pp. 328–338, March 30–April 2, Monterey, CA.

Ruhe, G. and S.L. Pfleeger. 2007. Software engineering decision support. *Proceedings of the 40th Annual Hawaii International Conference on Software Systems*, p. 282, Jan. 3–6, Waikoloa, HI.

Ruhe, G. and M. Saliu. 2005. The art and science of software release planning. *IEEE Software* 22(6): 47–53.

Sangwan, Raghvinder, Matthew Bass, Neel Mullick, and Daniel J. Paulish. 2006. *Global software development handbook*. Boca Raton, FL: Auerbach Publications.

Schmidt, J.B., M.M. Montoya-Weiss, and A.P. Massey. 2001. New product development decision-making effectiveness: Comparing individuals, face-to-face teams, and virtual teams. *Decision Sciences* 32(4): 575–600.

Schneider, Geri and Jason P. Winters. 2001. *Applying use cases: A practical guide*, 2nd ed. Boston: Addison-Wesley.

SearchMobileComputing.com. Definitions: GPS (global positioning system). http://searchmobilecomputing.techtarget.com/sDefinition/0,,sid40_gci213986,00.html (accessed May 22, 2009).

SearchNetworking.com. Definitions: GNSS (global navigation satellite system). http://searchnetworking.techtarget.com/sDefinition/0,,sid7_gci827051,00.html (accessed May 22, 2009).

Ibid. Definitions: OSI reference model. http://searchnetworking.techtarget.com/sDefinition/0,,sid7_gci212725,00.html (accessed May 22, 2009).

Ibid. Definitions: packet-switched. http://searchnetworking.techtarget.com/sDefinition/0,,sid7_gci212737,00.html (accessed May 22, 2009).

Shakespeare, William. *The tragedy of Hamlet: Prince of Denmark*, Act 1, Scene 4. Original electronic source is *Complete Moby Shakespeare*. http://shakespeare.mit.edu/hamlet/hamlet.1.4.html (accessed May 28, 2009).

Shore, B. 2008. Systematic biases and culture in project failures. *Project Management Journal* 39(4): 5–16.

Software Engineering Institute. Software product lines. www.sei.cmu.edu/productlines/framework.html (accessed June 23, 2009).

Stellman, Andrew and Jennifer Greene. 2005. *Applied software project management.* Sebastopol, CA: O'Reilly.

Taimour, Al Neimat. 2005. *Why IT projects fail.* The Project Perfect White Paper Collection. www.projectperfect.com.au/info_it_projects_fail.php (accessed June 3, 2009).

Takeuchi, H. and I. Nonaka. 1986. The new new product development game. *Harvard Business Review*, Jan.1.

Tannen, Deborah. https://www9.georgetown.edu/faculty/tannend/ (accessed June 2, 2009).

TheFreeDictionary by Farlex. Definition of desirement. http://encyclopedia2.thefreedictionary.com/desirement (accessed May 22, 2009).

Ibid. Definition of plan. www.thefreedictionary.com/plan (accessed May 22, 2009).

Ibid. Definition of project. www.thefreedictionary.com/project (accessed May 22, 2009).

Thurston, Jeff. 2002. *Galileo, GLONASS, and NAVSTAR: A report on GPS for GIS people.* www.integralgis.com/pdf/GALILEO.pdf (accessed May 22, 2009).

T-REGS. 2008. France: FTTH law adopted and new ARCEP decisions, new access obligations. www.t-regs.com/content/view/395/1/ (accessed May 22, 2009).

Ullah, M.I. and G. Ruhe. 2006. Towards comprehensive release planning for software product lines. *International Workshop on Software Product Management*, pp. 51–56, Sept., Minneapolis, MN.

U.S. Department of Defense. 2007. DoD permanently discontinues procurement of global positioning system selective availability. News Release No. 1126–07, Sept. 18. www.defenselink.mil/releases/release.aspx?releaseid=11335 (accessed May 22, 2009).

U.S. Department of the Navy. EVM glossary. http://acquisition.navy.mil/acquisition_one_source/cevm/evm_glossary (accessed May 22, 2009).

Verine, Lev and Michael Trumper. 2007. *Project decisions: The art and science.* Vienna, VA: Management Concepts.

Verner, J.M. 2008. Quality software development: What do we need to improve in the software development process? *Proceedings of the 6th International Workshop on Software Quality*, pp. 1–2, Leipzig, Germany.

Wagstrom, P. and J. Herbsleb. 2006. Dependency forecasting in the distributed agile organization. *Communications of the ACM* 49(10): 55–56.

Wang, L. and L. Liu. 2007. Cultural barriers to the use of Western project management in Chinese enterprises: Some empirical evidence from Yunnan Province. *Project Management Journal* 38(3): 61–73.

Wang, Y., S.A. McIlraith, Y. Yu, and J. Mylopoulos. 2007. An automated approach to monitoring and diagnosing requirements. *Proceedings of the 22nd IEEE/ACM International Conference on Automated Software Engineering*, pp. 293–302, Atlanta, GA.

Warkentin, M., R.S. Moore, E. Bekkering, and A.C. Johnston. 2009. Analysis of systems development project risks: An integrative framework. *ACM SIGMIS Database* 40(2): 8–27.

Wideman, Max. Max's: Wideman comparative glossary of project management terms v3.1. www.maxwideman.com/pmglossary/PMG_E02.htm (accessed May 20, 2009).

Wiegers, Karl E. 2003. *Software requirements*, 2nd ed. Redmond, WA: Microsoft Press.

Ibid. 2006. *More about software requirements: Thorny issues and practical advice*. Redmond, WA: Microsoft Press.

Williams, R.C., G.J. Pandelios, and S.G. Behrens. 1999. *Software Risk Evaluation (SRE) method description (version 2.0)*. Technical Report CMU/SEI-99-TR-029 Pittsburgh, PA: Software Engineering Institute, Carnegie Mellon University.

Xu, K. and H. Muñoz-Avila. 2008. CaBMA: A case-based reasoning system for capturing, refining, and reusing project plans. *Knowledge and Information Systems* 15(2): 215–232.

Index

B

C

N

O

P

More Resources for Successful Software Project Management

ISBN-13: 978-0-201-83595-3

The Mythical Man-Month

Few books on software project management have been as influential and timeless as *The Mythical Man-Month*. With a blend of software engineering facts and thought-provoking opinions, Fred Brooks offers insight for anyone managing complex projects.

Agile Project Management

Renowned agile pioneer Jim Highsmith thoroughly updates his classic guide to APM, extending and refining it to support even the largest projects and organizations.

ISBN-13: 978-0-321-65839-5

ISBN-13: 978-0-321-50275-9

The Software Project Manager's Bridge to Agility

Two long-time certified Project Management Professionals (PMP®s) and Scrum trainers—Michele Sliger and Stacia Broderick—show experienced project managers how to successfully transition to agile by refocusing on facilitation and collaboration.

Catastrophe Disentanglement

Author E. M. Bennatan describes a 10-step process to identify severely troubled projects and avoid costly failure. Whenever projects are in trouble—whether you are a senior manager, project manager, team member, or software customer—this book could save your career.

ISBN-13: 978-0-321-33662-0

For more information and to read sample material, please visit informit.com.

Titles are also available at safari.informit.com.